T0341965

Kathy Acker

For Heather

Kathy Acker

Writing the Impossible

Georgina Colby

EDINBURGH
University Press

Edinburgh University Press is one of the leading university presses in the UK. We publish academic books and journals in our selected subject areas across the humanities and social sciences, combining cutting-edge scholarship with high editorial and production values to produce academic works of lasting importance. For more information visit our website: edinburghuniversitypress.com

© Georgina Colby, 2016, 2018

Edinburgh University Press Ltd
The Tun – Holyrood Road,
12(2f) Jackson's Entry,
Edinburgh EH8 8PJ

First published in hardback by Edinburgh University Press 2016

Typeset in 11/14 Adobe Sabon by
IDSUK (DataConnection) Ltd, and
printed and bound in Great Britain by
CPI Group (UK) Ltd, Croydon CR0 4YY

A CIP record for this book is available from the British Library

ISBN 978 0 7486 8350 5 (hardback)
ISBN 978 1 4744 3154 5 (paperback)
ISBN 978 0 7486 8351 2 (webready PDF)
ISBN 978 0 7486 8352 9 (epub)

The right of Georgina Colby to be identified as the author of this work has been asserted in accordance with the Copyright, Designs and Patents Act 1988, and the Copyright and Related Rights Regulations 2003 (SI No. 2498).

Contents

List of Illustrations

Acknowledgements

In the early stages of this book, Robert Hampson, Tim Armstrong and Carol Watts provided invaluable direction. My heartfelt thanks go to my friends and colleagues who have generously given their time recently to read my work and to share their thoughts: Leigh Wilson, Robert Hampson, Jennifer Cooke, Andrew Bowie, John Beck, Peter Jaeger, Kaye Mitchell, David Cunningham, David Bate, and Elizabeth English. For continual support with research time and finances, I am grateful to Alex Warwick. Whether they realised or not, Lucy Bond, Nigel Mapp, and Simon Avery often reminded me that I am not alone with the perils of research, and buoyed a mind at sea. I am sincerely thankful to my editors at Edinburgh University Press: Jackie Jones, Adela Rauchova, Rebecca Mackenzie, and James Dale for their expertise, patience, and continual support throughout the writing and publishing process. I am indebted to my anonymous initial reviewers who provided constructive and illuminating readers' reports, each of which strengthened the book considerably.

In 2014 I was awarded a Mary Lily Research grant by the Sallie Bingham Center for Women's History and Culture at the David M. Rubenstein Rare Book and Manuscript Library, Duke University, to travel to consult the Kathy Acker Papers. My time at Duke was invaluable and the research carried out in the archive changed the course of this book, and inspired future projects on experimental writing and manuscript practice. The staff at the Sallie Bingham Center provided indispensable support, shared their knowledge and passion for archival research with me, and joined me in marvelling at the size of Acker's original dream maps. In particular Kelly Wooten has continuously provided me with materials and has extended such kindness in giving me unlimited access to the archive whilst I was at Duke, and since I have returned to the UK. I would also like to thank David Pavelich, Sarah Carrier, Megan O'Connell, Kate Collins, Dominique Dery, and the Director of the Sallie Bingham Center, Laura Mitcham. I am very grateful to Matias Viegener, Acker's literary executor, for his generosity in granting me unlimited permissions to use the archive materials and to reproduce Acker's illustrations.

The final writing stage of this work would have taken considerably longer without a sabbatical period granted to me by the Department of English, Linguistics and Cultural Studies at the University of Westminster. The Department of English also generously funded my living expenses for my research trip. Parts of Chapter 1 I presented at the conference, 'Contemporary Experimental Women's Writing' organised by Kaye Mitchell and Becky Munford at the University of Manchester, in 2013. The questions from those at the conference were stimulating. A paper not included in this book but nevertheless formative to the gestation of this work was given at 'Representing the Contentious', a colloquium organised by Bronwyn Parry and Ania Dabrowska, the University of Cambridge, and funded by the Wellcome Trust, held in 2011. I am grateful to Bronwyn and Ania for the opportunity to share my research. At points in Chapter 5 I allude to the climate of censorship in which Acker wrote *My Mother: Demonology*. This area of Acker's work is fully discussed in one of my earlier essays, 'Radical Interiors: Cindy Sherman's "Sex Pictures" and Kathy Acker's *My Mother: Demonology*', published in *Women: A Cultural Review*, 23 (2) (2012). Parts of Chapter 6 were first published in 'The Reappropriation of Classical Mythology to Represent Pain: Falling Silent in the Work of Kathy Acker and Robert Mapplethorpe' in *Comparative Critical Studies* 9.1 (2012). My thanks go to the editors for permitting me to reproduce and adapt that material.

List of Abbreviations

B&G	*Blood and Guts in High School.* New York: Grove Press, 1984
DQ	*Don Quixote: Which Was a Dream.* New York: Grove Press, 1986
IM	*In Memoriam to Identity.* London: Pandora Press, 1991
MMD	*My Mother: Demonology.* New York: Grove Press, 1993

Introduction: Kathy Acker and the Avant-Garde

'TO SHOW: DIVERGENCE FROM STANDARD FORM OF STRUCTURE; FORM HAS MEANING'[1] Kathy Acker writes in bold capitals in an unpublished notebook. The alignment of form and content is the starting point of this book. It brings together two interrelated axes of Acker's practice: her continuation of radical modernism's preoccupation with the crisis of language, and the avant-garde concern for producing art orientated towards the transformation of society. For early twentieth-century modernist writers the imbrication of form with content was a hallmark of their literary practice. The commitment to experimentation in form and language, upheld by writers such as Gertrude Stein, Ezra Pound, H.D., and James Joyce, is integral to the challenge modernist writers sought to pose to nineteenth-century realism. It was a key characteristic of their larger concern with the medium of writing. The precise nature of that concern with the medium of writing is crucial. Theorists of the avant-garde have attempted to draw a distinction between modernism and the avant-garde on the issue of aesthetic autonomy. Peter Bürger's now classic work *Theory of the Avant-Garde* (1974) has been read widely by scholars as distinguishing modernism and avant-gardism specifically with regards to the issue of aesthetic autonomy.[2] For Bürger, modernism strives for aesthetic autonomy, and in doing so falls victim to the insularity and elitism characteristic of art-for-art's sake aestheticism. The avant-garde, on the other hand, in Bürger's view, has the sublation of art and life as its central goal.[3] Richard Murphy makes a more subtle distinction between modernism and the avant-garde:

even where the avant-garde shares with modernism the benefits of autonomy, it always distinguishes itself in precisely this aspect: it takes up a certain critical distance in order to see through the duplicities and hidden social functions of affirmative culture, and in order to articulate an awareness of the social and historical conditions of art.[4]

Acker echoes this critical distance in 1979 when she states: 'The difference between a writer and its world gives the reason for writing.'[5] For Bürger, avant-gardism was possible only at the start of the twentieth century, since after World War II the avant-garde's critique of art as an institution is reabsorbed by the art institution itself or is re-aestheticised. I would argue that avant-gardism remains a permanent possibility within the modernist tradition as a militantly interventionist option. What I have termed 'radical modernism' maintains a critical stance towards its own social and historical conditions: this is evident in Pound's *Cantos* or Joyce's *Ulysses*. This study positions Acker as a key figure in the American post-war avant-garde. Tyrus Miller uses the term 'postwar avant-garde' to refer to those 'latter day modernists' who were experimenting in the years after World War II: Jackson Mac Low, John Cage, Kurt Schwitters, David Tudor, Stan Brakhage, Samuel Beckett, and Gilbert Sorrentino. Miller evaluates the avant-garde nature of their work stating: 'The conventions of actually existing politics, no less than the conventions of art were the target of their critical negation, and the task of discovering new frames in which the political might be rethought in the future was, more or less consciously, one of the major aims of their works.'[6] Acker's works continually embody such a critical negation and her works give voice to the complexities of the struggle of the late modernist avant-garde writer to make meaning in the post-war climate in which she was writing.

Experiment with form is fundamental to the avant-garde project. For early theorists of the avant-garde such as Walter Benjamin, writing in 1934, the discontinuous forms of experimental practices such as montage, taken up by Benjamin via Bertolt Brecht's epic theatre, protected the content of the work of art from cultural reification.[7] Again, the relation of form and content is key: this is not simply experimentation with form for its own sake. In *Aesthetic Theory* (1970), Theodor Adorno questions critics of formalism on the grounds that 'the campaign against formalism ignores the fact that form is sedimented content'.[8] Acker's experiments, at the levels of structure and texture, produce experimental literary works in which form is inseparable from content. As Murphy notes, taking up Bürger, the traditional organic work of art sought to imitate nature and provide a continuous whole. Murphy argues that the organic format of the literary texts entails 'a combination of plot and characterization based on the notion of a unified and unique Cartesian entity'.[9] The non-organic literary work, the avant-garde work, in contrast, 'stages subjectivity as fragmented and discontinuous, for example as a constellation of personae, a series of mutually conflicting and contradictory roles played out by seemingly separate figures in the texts'.[10] Acker frequently refers to the problem of Cartesian dualism in her essays and her works. In her essay 'Against Ordinary Language: The Language of the Body' (1993), she writes: 'we still live under the sign of Descartes'. She then adds: 'This sign is also the sign of patriarchy.'[11] The forms of Acker's texts in her practices of collage, montage, and intertextuality, resist the illusion of wholeness that the organic work promotes. Acker also intervenes with her experimental practice to disrupt and fragment previously organic works, such as Charles Dickens' *Great Expectations* (1861). Peter Wollen and Carla Harryman have admirably discussed Acker's complex experimental practice in their works; Wollen stresses Acker's deep commitment to the avant-garde tradition in America.[12] Yet there remains a tendency in studies of Acker's work to discuss form in general, in terms of overarching compositional practices such as appropriation, rather than paying close attention to the intricate patterning of complex experimental practices found in her works.[13] This body of scholarship that omits sufficient attention to the different modes of experimental writing in Acker's work, and the imbrication of form with content, has its counterpart in the reception of Acker's work by the reading public. As Peter Wollen has remarked, when commercial success did finally come to Acker around 1984 with the publication of *Blood and Guts in High School*, it was because of the content of her work rather than the form. On this point, Wollen draws a comparison between Acker and Gertrude Stein, whose work *The Autobiography of Alice B. Toklas* (1933) garnered attention largely for its portraits of well-known celebrities from the art world.[14] This focus neglected Stein's experimental writings and was the catalyst for the attention to her person throughout her life, at the expense of recognition of the remarkable experimental body of writing that she produced.

The idea of the non-organic work can be brought into dialogue with Charles Bernstein's idea of 'artifice'. Bernstein takes the term up from Veronica Forrest-Thomson's work on 'poetic artifice'. 'Artifice', Bernstein writes in his poem-essay, 'is a measure of a poem's / intractability to being read as the sum of its / devices & subject matters.'[15] As the non-organic work is the opposite of the organic continuous work, '"artifice"', Bernstein states, 'is the contradiction of "realism", with / its insistence on presenting an unmediated / (immediate) experience of facts, either of the / "external" world of nature or the "internal" world / of the mind.'[16] Writing in 1978, Forrest-Thomson remarks: 'Anti-realism need not imply, as certain French theorists might claim, / a rejection of meaning.'[17] Extending Forrest-Thomson's account, Bernstein points to the inseparability of form and content. Content, he states, 'never equals meaning':

> If the artifice is
> foregrounded, there's a tendency to say that there
> is no content or meaning, as if the poem were a
> formal or decorative exercise concerned only with
> representing its own mechanisms. But even when a
> poem is read as a formal exercise, the dynamics &
> contours of its formal proceedings may suggest, for
> example, a metonymic model for imagining
> experience. For this reason, consideration
> of the formal dynamics of a poem does not necessarily
> disregard its content; indeed it is an obvious
> starting point insofar as it can initiate a
> multilevel reading. But to complete the process
> such formal apprehensions need to move to a
> synthesis beyond technical cataloguing, toward the
> experiential phenomenon that is made by virtue of
> the work's techniques.[18]

Bernstein's claim echoes Adorno's critique of formalism in his idea of form as 'sedimented content'. It points to the necessity of examining a work's techniques, and to new forms of meaning that might arise as a result of such critical practice. Acker's works are works of artifice, composed through what Bernstein terms 'antiabsorptive techniques', which he defines as '(nontransparent or nonnaturalizing elements) / (artifice)'.[19] Bernstein lists some antiabsorptive traditions including Stein, in particular the 'denser sections' of *Tender Buttons*, and the 'word-to-word halting' in *How To Write*; Pound's *Cantos* '(the use of collage & / fragmentation, graphic material, the inclusion of / printers & other errors, the disruptive presence / of a legion of references outside the poem)'; Zukofsky's 'Poem beginning "The" / with its numbered citations / of different quotations, & / other assorted found material; and Joyce's *Finnegans Wake*',[20] amongst others. Importantly, Bernstein acknowledges the limits of critical analysis in the face of the poem's artifice. 'Such a synthesis', he argues, 'is almost impossible apart from the tautological / repetition of the poem, since all the formal / dynamics cannot be chartered.'[21] Bernstein's recognition of the limitations of the critical response to the experimental work in light of its discontinuous nature is significant to a study of Acker's body of experimental writing.

This book is anchored in an examination of the compositional processes, antiabsorptive techniques, and the resulting experimental forms of Acker's works from 1972 to 1997. It argues for the necessity of a consideration of the composition of Acker's works in the formation of an understanding of her late modernist experimental practices. Acker's statement 'Form has meaning' is one of many declarations of the significance of form that occur in the numerous handwritten, spiral-bound notebooks housed in the Kathy Acker Papers at the David M. Rubenstein Rare Books & Manuscript Library at Duke University. The notebooks comprise the preliminary materials for many of Acker's works. These materials, alongside the artworks that Acker created to incorporate in a number of her experimental works, bring to light the importance of understanding Acker's final published works as compositional objects, created from the raw materials of the archive through various processes of experimental composition or facture. The new forms of meaning-making that emerge from Acker's experiments with language and composition have not been examined closely. This book takes up Acker's experiments with language in conjunction with the experimental compositions of the works as a means to explore the emergence of new forms of meaning in her works.

The term 'experimental' is taken in this study to refer to the obstruction of normal reading. This use of the term is in line with Marianne DeKoven's pioneering 1983 study of Gertrude Stein's body of writing. DeKoven explains:

I have labeled 'experimental' that writing which violates grammatical convention, thereby preventing normal reading. This definition is intentionally narrower than the common usage of 'experimental.' Generally, 'experimental' is interchangeable with literary designations such as 'avant-garde,' 'innovative,' 'modernist' and 'postmodern,' 'anti-realist,' 'fabulist,' 'anti-traditional,' or 'countercultural.'[22]

For DeKoven: 'The unifying feature of experimental writing is . . . the obstruction of normal reading' because '[i]t prevents us from interpreting the writing to form coherent, single, closed, ordered, finite, sensible meanings.'[23] I argue that Acker's experiments with language, her continuation of the modernist exploration of the crisis of language, begin with her experimenting with opacity in her early poetic exercises, and evolve across her works to produce in her later works modes of what Acker understands to be 'languages of the body' that run counter to ordinary language. New modes of meaning-making emerge from her early procedural exercises and collages as well as her more mature practices of writing-through, topological intertextuality, experiments with non-referential language, montage and creative cutting, and her practices of ekphrasis and literary calisthenics. This body of creative practice that edges towards a new way of writing occurs in Acker's work alongside the avant-garde poetics of negation, which as Murphy notes, 'aims to question and ultimately realign the relationship between art and life'.[24]

In her essay 'A Few Notes on Two of My Books' (1989) Acker recounts an early influential memory. Aged fifteen she was introduced to Jackson Mac Low and Robert Kelly and to Charles Olson's work. She visited Robert Kelly and his first wife Joby, who were creating 'poundstones' by painting Pound's injunction 'MAKE IT NEW' on stones.[25] In her 1997 preface to her collection of essays *Bodies of Work* Acker invokes her old response to the question: 'Why bother to write in such a time as this?'[26] Acker's answer is simple: 'For me writing is freedom. Therein lies (my) identity.' However, the practice of writing is not so straightforward. Acker understands there to be an inherent problem with expression: 'The problem with expression is that it is too narrow a basis for writing, for it is pinned to knowledge, knowledge that is mainly rational.'[27] 'I am hoping', she states in her preface, 'that communication need not be reduced to expression.' Rather than expression, Acker conceives communication as 'vision'.

These reflexive questions into her own literary practice precipitate the auxiliary enquiry: 'Do I write to express what is made or to make?' She replies: 'I seem to have chosen the latter, the modernist way.'[28] 'To oppose expression and a Joycean making' is for Acker 'to situate oneself in dualism and so to remain bereft of all that is visionary.'[29] Acker's comments on the importance of 'making' in the modernist sense resonate once again with the words of Bernstein. Bernstein highlights poetics as distinct from literary criticism or journalism on the basis of 'its primary engagement with *poesis* and *faktura*, the art of making'.[30] The relation between poetics and the 'art of making' is central to an understanding of Acker's works, and her writing experiments that began in her early poetic exercises.

The most significant modernist writer for Acker was Gertrude Stein, and, as Wollen has pointed out, Stein's influence is an element of Acker's work that has largely been overlooked.[31] Primarily, Acker pointed to Stein's 'attempt to make language present'[32] as a notable aspect of the modernist poet's inspiration for her. Acker considered Stein's most significant innovation to be 'her equation of language and breath, in which language was primary, so that it would have the power of breath'.[33] The importance to Acker of Stein's foregrounding of language is apparent in every one of her works. The equation of language and breath emerges in Acker's final work, *Eurydice in the Underworld* (1997), as the paradigm silent language of the body, wherein performance is the act of composition from which the silent language is realised. The primacy of language in Acker's work is notable as the pivotal issue that divided Acker from the male-dominated novel tradition when she began writing in the late 1960s. Acker states 'what traditional novelists like Roth and Bellow were doing was mirroring reality, so that the function of language was secondary to their desire to express what they saw as reality, or society, or whatever'. Acker perceived the elevation of representation over language as 'an inverted set of values' because she had always felt 'that language was more real than what it was supposed to be mirroring'.[34]

The post-war literary climate in which Acker made these remarks to Larry McCaffery in 1996 was, however, very different to Stein's in the first decades of the twentieth century. Acker is part of what Ellen G. Friedman and Miriam Fuchs have termed the third generation of innovative women writers.[35] Friedman and Fuchs index those writing before 1930, Stein and her contemporaries, as the first generation, while women writing after 1930 comprise the second generation. Those writing after 1960 – Acker, Christine Brooke-Rose, Marguerite Young, Lydia Davis, Maxine Chernoff, Ann Quin, Barbara Guest, and Joyce Carol Oates, amongst others – make up the third generation. Second-wave feminism coincided with third-generation women writers and the fiction of their literary contemporaries gave expression to many of the second-generation feminist theorists' concerns. Acker was very aware of the role and importance of writing to the feminist movement. Her demotion of representation in favour of language was part of a lineage that she conceived as going back to the early twentieth century. Writers such as Stein, Djuna Barnes, and Crista Wolf wrote works that Acker understood to be devoid of a centralised narrative. Acker apprehended this dissent from the idea that a literary work required a centralised narrative as 'an assault on the control system' and a rejection of 'the centralized phallus'.[36] This raises the issue of a feminist politics of literature, as Acker reads this formal break with narrative tradition as a political move. It is a conscious spilt with what Barthes understood as the 'property – and "ownership"' relations inherent to the Balzacian narrative, which Acker recognises as 'the ownership of the female to the male'.[37] Decentralisation is fundamental to the larger enquiry of this study into how avant-garde women writers make meaning.

Like Stein, Acker resists subsumption into any one literary paradigm. Yet she is a significant figure in an emerging genealogy of twentieth and twenty-first century female writers. In a 1993 article for the *PMLA*, Ellen G. Friedman theorised a female avant-garde. Taking Jean-François Lyotard's idea of 'missing contents' and the 'unpresentable' in the literature of modernity set forth in *The Postmodern Condition* (1979) as her starting point, Friedman positions the female avant-garde in contrast to their male counterparts. For Friedman, 'the yearning for fathers, for past authority and sure knowledge that can no longer be supported, permeates male texts of modernity'.[38] She points to Donald Barthelme's *The Dead Father* (1975) and Thomas Pynchon's *Vineland* (1990) as examples. For these post-war male authors and others: 'A variation on the search for the father is the profoundly nostalgic conviction that the past has explanatory or redemptive powers.'[39] In contrast:

Women's works of modernity . . . show little regret for the old paternal order, little regret for the no longer presentable. The master narratives are not buried in the unconscious of these texts, nor do they create a vacuum that longs to be filled. Although the texts of modernity express a yearning for the unpresentable, female texts often evoke this unpresentable as the not yet presented.[40]

Friedman's observations are important both to an understanding of Acker's work and in a wider context to the concept of a female avant-garde. Friedman argues: 'reading the texts of modernity through the lens of gender reveals how gender inflects the missing contents and how this inflected unpresentable relates to the canon'.[41] Friedman cites Acker as an example, whose protagonists 'repeatedly demonstrate the inadequacy of patriarchal culture, past or present, as the arena for identity'.[42]

This study both extends Friedman's enquiry and offers a new pathway. It is the larger contention of this book that through experiment in writing and composition, Acker succeeds in presenting the unpresentable. The unpresentable in women's writing is inherently linked to the constraints that have been imposed upon women's writing by the tradition of centralised narratives. In Acker's texts the 'sure knowledge' sought by contemporary male avant-garde novelists is replaced by an awareness of the contingency of structures of knowledge. Acker stated 'I trust neither my ability to know nor what I think I know'[43] and this affirmation that destabilises the validity of concrete claims to knowledge is realised in the instability of her texts. In the early 1970s, Acker's writing practice was accompanied by a clear engagement with philosophy, a coupling that would continue throughout her career. Like Stein before her, Acker took a great interest in the philosophy of language during this early period and throughout her lifetime. Acker's unpublished and undated notes titled 'Commonsensical / Philosophical Uses of Words',[44] which are discussed in Chapter 3, carry out a series of enquiries into William James's idea of the 'specious present' found in the fifth chapter of the first volume of *The Principles of Psychology* (1890), alongside Ludwig Wittgenstein's and Gustav Bergmann's investigations into 'ideal languages'. Acker's extensive notes on key figures in the philosophy of language reveal a deep interest in questions of language and ontology.

At the beginning of the 1970s, Acker engaged closely with her mentor, David Antin, whose pivotal work, *Talking*, was published in 1972. Acker worked through Wittgenstein's writings with Antin in 1974. In an unpublished document titled 'Conversations',[45] taken from a larger project that Acker was working on, 'On Certainty, Wittgenstein and Self', Acker, under her early pseudonym The Black Tarantula, enters into a Socratic-style dialogue with Antin regarding his uses of language in *Talking*. Wittgenstein's work *On Certainty* was the subject of much spirited debate in Antin's circle upon its posthumous publication in 1969. The conversation between The Black Tarantula and David Antin centres upon the relationship of thinking to language. Antin states:

> If I assume my thinking is, or one way of my thinking is, my using language, I can examine my perceiving (including my perceptions), that is my thinking, by examining my uses of language. For instance: examining the problem of certainty: I say 'I know that. . .' rather than 'I'm certain' in situations in which there's no doubt. How does this 'I know that. . .' function? How does 'I know that. . .' function regarding truth values?[46]

If thinking equates to using language, then language is overlaid with the workings of consciousness. Taking up the distinction between the two concepts of 'knowing' and 'being certain' that Wittgenstein investigates in *On Certainty*, Antin playfully contends:

> 'I know' often means 'I have proper grounds for my statement.' That is, 'I know I am lecherous because I am now acting lecherously.' That is you would understand 'I know I am lecherous to be true, because you understand how that statement relates to the non-language contexts involved. You'd understand the language-game.'[47]

The Black Tarantula responds to Antin by posing the question: 'What if I don't trust my sense perceivings?' which Antin understands to be a different problem. From their dialogue, The Black Tarantula formulates a further question into the relation between reality and perception: 'So poetry, any sort of writing, is a prime way of perceiving reality?' 'Certainty', Antin states, 'is, as it were, a tone of voice in which I declare how things are, but you can't infer from the tone of voice that I am justified.' He goes on to state 'everything descriptive is part of logic', from which The Black Tarantula ascertains: 'Therefore, society is not an absolute.' Antin explains to The Black Tarantula that 'poetry is that language that is most functionally efficient', and he qualifies this with reference to his own practice: 'I'm interested in what statements (what language) I can use for further research and actions.' Here Antin is referring almost verbatim to §87 of Wittgenstein's *On Certainty*:

> Can't an assertoric sentence, which was capable of functioning as a hypothesis, also be used as a foundation for research and action? i.e. can't it simply be isolated from doubt, though not according to any explicit rule? It simply gets assumed as a truism, never called into question, perhaps not even ever formulated.[48]

Language as a premise for research and action is an idea that Acker takes up in her work. The Black Tarantula asserts: 'It's not then the so-called "truth" value of a statement a poem . . . that matters; but what practical effects the poem contains leads to.'[49]

Antin draws the following conclusion from Wittgenstein: 'I distinguish the truth or falsity of statements against my inherited background . . . Therefore: truth and falsity don't exist. Except in regard to use.' He makes the following distinction: 'All truth-falsity testing . . . takes place in context, in an existing system of beliefs. But doubting and knowing depend on, lie within the system. That is I use judgements as principles of judgements.' As the conversation with Antin develops, The Black Tarantula arrives at an idea of socially controlled perception: 'Learning. I learn to distinguish to perceive something, that is to perceive order from chaos; I learn to speak. I'm being taught and controlled at basic levels.' Antin concurs, he states: 'I'm taught judgements and their connections with other judgements. I'm taught, I've been taught a totality of judgements.' The Black Tarantula asks Antin how she can attack this system to try to 'determine' her living, which leads to The Black Tarantula making an observation that is central to Acker's work: '[t]he difficulty, first, is to realise the groundlessness of our believing'. The idea of a form of self-determination, free of socially controlled perception, Acker aligns with the ability to 'Really see. (through delight).' Acker's idea of seeing in this early dialogue is in line with Shklovsky's idea of the capacity to see that emerges from defamiliarisation, a concept that I take up in more detail in Chapter 1. Pleasure within this formulation is aligned with seeing / perception, and has a phenomenological function. In her notes for a lecture entitled 'Lecture on *Unworking*' Acker links experimental writing, uncertainty, and 'the principle of incompleteness'.[50] She notes: 'We do not make meaning when we use language; rather, meaning is lost and it is in the place of this loss that consciousness arises.' Highlighting 'the play of loss, the loss of meaning, the loss of identity' she states 'there is no (absolute) knowledge'.[51] Acker gestures here to a non-restricted sense of meaning. Again this idea is in line with Bernstein's work on artifice. Bernstein argues against 'ascribing / to meaning an exclusively utilitarian function'. He understands loss to be a part of the 'semantic process' and distinguishes his idea of meaning apart from conventional notions of meaning. '[T]he meaning of which I speak', he writes, 'is not meaning as we / may "know" it, with a recuperable intention or / purpose.' 'Such a restricted sense of meaning', he maintains 'is / analogous to the restricted sense of knowledge as / stipulatively definable.'[52] Acker's experimental works offer alternative linguistic configurations that break away from inherited background and attempt, in doing so, to find new forms of knowledge that are not contingent upon a background bequeathed by tradition.

The 'unpresentable' of female writers diverges significantly from that of contemporary male writers who, as Friedman points out, place redemption in the notion that 'the future is propelled by the past' and thus 'the power of the dead father' is where the power lies.[53] The decentralised narrative of the female writer necessitates a renegotiation of such power relations, seeking excavation rather than redemption. Whilst Acker explicitly acknowledged the importance of Stein to experimental writing, she did not place herself in a specifically female line of descent. Instead she affiliated herself with writers such as Burroughs and Genet, as part of what she termed '"the other tradition," "the non-acceptable literary tradition," "the tradition of those books which were hated when they were written and suddenly became literary history," "the black tradition," "the tradition of political writing as opposed to propaganda."'[54] She explained:

'Marginal,' 'experimental,' and 'avant-garde' are often words used to describe texts in this other tradition. Not because writing such as Burroughs's or Genet's is marginal, but because our society, through the voice of its literary society, cannot bear immediacy, the truth, especially the political truth.[55]

On the subject of how to define an avant-garde lineage, Acker demonstrated a familiar ambivalence and apprehension. In his interview with Acker, Larry McCaffery reels off a list of names – 'Sade, Baudelaire, Rimbaud, Lautréamont, Jarry, the surrealists and Dadaists, Bataille, Artaud, Genet, Burroughs' and others – as composite of 'a fairly clear tradition of the extremist avant-garde'.[56] Whilst she placed herself in that tradition and indeed hoped that she might 'someday be seen as belonging to that lineage', Acker traces the lineage of the avant-garde in America via another tradition 'John Cage, for instance'.[57] This study positions Acker in relation to each of these genealogies of avant-garde writers.

Literary experiment and impossibility

The terms of this study require some consideration. Within the parameters of Acker's use of the term, 'impossible' refers directly to Acker's idea of the languages of the body that her later works realise. In her essay 'Against Ordinary Language: The Language of the Body' (1993) Acker positions the cry of the beggar, which 'means nothing than what it is' in contrast to ordinary language, in which meaning is tied to context. She states 'in the city of the beggar, the impossible (as the Wittgenstein of Tractatus and Heidegger see it) occurs in that meaning and breath become one'.[58] Antigone in *Pussy, King of the Pirates* (1996) understands the figure of the girl pirate to be equated with impossibility: 'I refuse. / I will be – instead. / – is something impossible. / I'll be a girl pirate.'[59] Impossibility emerges in a number of forms, direct, and indirect, as the chapters of this book unfold, but it is consistently situated as a counter-term to ideas of political possibility, the logic of conventional language structures, and the power relations implicated by those language structures. The work of Maurice Blanchot is the central theoretical coordinate for the term 'impossibility', as it is taken up in this study. In *The Infinite Conversation* (1969) Blanchot considers the thought of the impossible as the other relation:

> As soon as we are in relation with a field open to possibility, and opened by possibility, force threatens. Even comprehension, an essential mode of possibility, is a grasp that gathers the diverse into unity, identifies the different, and brings the other back to the same through

a reduction that dialectical movement, after a long trajectory, makes coincide with overcoming. All these words – grasp, identification, reduction – conceal within themselves the rendering of accounts that exist in knowledge as its measure: reason must be given. What is to be known – the unknown – must surrender to the known.[60]

In Blanchot's thought, the impossible is closely related to the unknown, and to incomprehension, as possibility is to the known and comprehension. These coordinates speak to the politics of Acker's experimental writing, which seeks to preserve obscurity in language, the plurality of meaning, and the materiality of writing, against the transparency of language and the instrumental use of language.[61] The power relations between possibility and impossibility set out by Blanchot in this passage can be compared to the power relations between conventional grammar structures and experimental writing, or within the post-war avant-garde framework of $L=A=N=G=U=A=G=E$ examined in detail in Chapter 1 of this study, between grammatically centred meaning, and language-centred writing. Acker frequently challenges the idea of knowledge tied to rationality and seeks to create in experimental writing a site for the harbouring of the unknown. Acker's earliest writings reveal her resistance to comprehension. *The Adult Life of Toulouse Lautrec by Henri Toulouse Lautrec* (1975) is prefaced by an imagined dialogue with Henry Fielding:

> 'Make sense,' Fielding said. 'Tell the real story
> of your life. You alone can tell the truth!'
> 'I don't want to make any sense,' I replied.[62]

Acker's struggle as an experimental writer is the battle against the imposition to make sense. This is her central issue with expression. The chapters of this book chart the ways in which Acker develops experimental writing strategies to create sites of negation impervious to the powers of comprehension that offer new forms of meaning not governed by conventional ideas of sense and 'knowledge'.

Whilst acknowledging the problematic nature of the relation between possibility and impossibility, Blanchot does not cynically fold to the paradigm. Rather, he understands that there is a resistance to this 'force', and he articulates it as 'a language':

But then comes this apparently innocent question: might there not exist relations, that is to say a language, escaping this movement of force through which the world does not cease to accomplish itself? In this case, such relations, such a language, would also escape possibility. An innocent question, but one that is already questioning at the margins of possibility and that, in order to guard its dignity as a question, must avoid disintegrating in the ecstasy of a response without thought, to which it may well lead.[63]

In terms of power, Blanchot suggests that impossibility is '*this non-power that would not be the simple negation of power*'.[64] Impossibility is not simply the other side to possibility in Blanchot's formula. He arrives at three characteristics inherent in impossibility. The first involves a new temporality:

in impossibility time changes direction, no longer offering itself out of the future as what gathers by going beyond; time, here, is rather a dispersion of a present that even while being only passage does not pass, never fixes itself in a present refers to no past and goes to no future: *the incessant*.[65]

The second trait concerns a paradoxical present:

in impossibility, the immediate is a presence to which one cannot be present, but from which one cannot separate; or, again, it is what escapes by the very fact that there is no escaping it: *the ungraspable that one cannot let go of*.[66]

The third property of impossibility apprehended by Blanchot concerns motility: 'the infinite shifting of dispersal, a non-dialectical movement where contrariety has nothing to do with opposition or with reconciliation, and where the *other* never comes back to the same'. Blanchot asks: 'Shall we call it becoming, the secret of becoming?'[67] Blanchot's discussion offers productive coordinates to approach experimental writing and questions of the inexpressible.[68] Acker creates new temporalities in her experiments that are related to the ungraspable states of desire, pain, and death. Acker's movement towards abstraction is a result of her engagement with the ineffable. In her creation of new languages of the body, Acker's new forms of writing and radical languages are not dependent on what they negate for meaning precisely because of their relation to states that cannot be represented.

Acker in the contemporary

As is clear from the small number of book-length studies on Acker's body of work, the majority of the scholarly works on Acker's writing have been published in peer-review journals, edited collections, or chapters of larger studies.[69] In a broader context, this book is part of the recent groundswell of critical works that understand 'postmodernism' to be a historical moment and seek to re-evaluate the legacies of modernism in post-war and contemporary writing.[70] The majority of scholars who have written on Acker's work have understood her as a postmodern writer, a conception often conflated with post-structuralist criticism.[71] This body of scholarly work is typified by the thirteen essays that comprise Michael Hardin's collection *Devouring Institutions: The Life Work of Kathy Acker* (2011), as well as essays by Robert Siegle,[72] Joseph M. Conte,[73] Svetlana Mintcheva,[74] John Kuehl,[75] and Katy R. Muth.[76] Susan E. Hawkins too reads Acker as a 'radically postmodern'[77] writer. Nicole Pitchford examines the works that Acker produced in the 1980s, *My Death My Life by Pier Paolo Pasolini*, *Don Quixote*, and *Empire of the Senseless* and denominates Acker's tactics as a particular form of feminist postmodernism, examining the way in which Acker reuses texts 'to challenge rationalism, the reigning logic of capitalism'.[78] Alex Houen,[79] Carol Siegel,[80] and Barrett Watten[81] have read Acker's work through the work of Michel Foucault. To date, Spencer Dew's study, *Learning for Revolution: The Work of Kathy Acker* (2011) remains the sole single author monograph on Acker's work. Dew draws extensively on Acker's background, as a student of Marcuse in 1965, and reads Acker's texts through the prism of the Frankfurt School. Dew's work approaches Acker's work in terms of how the author critiques the structures of oppression, capitalism, and patriarchy. Dew's insightful central claim is that Acker's work is didactic, and is specifically grounded in a desire to create and be part of an 'ethical community'.[82]

This body of scholarship, which offers theoretical readings of Acker's works, is valuable, yet it raises the issue of Acker's complex engagement with and self-positioning within theory. Arguably, self-positioning and the use of theoretical texts as primary materials creates a certain resistance to theoretical interpretation. Judith Ryan's notable study *The Novel after Theory* (2012) illuminates the issue of Acker's complex engagement with theory, and the extent to which her works self-consciously engage with theory. Ryan addresses the post-war and contemporary fictions that respond to poststructuralist theory, and the impact that theory has had on contemporary fiction in the past three decades. Ryan's study is particularly valuable for shifting the terrain from critical studies that read works through theory, to considering an author's and a text's engagement with theory. Examining the work of Don DeLillo, Thomas Pynchon, J. M. Coetzee, Margaret Atwood, W. G. Sebald, Umberto Eco, Monika Maron, Alain Robbe-Grillet, Marguerite Duras, Marylinne Robinson, David Foster Wallace, and Christa Wolf, Ryan argues: 'Making appropriate substitutions, we can say that the novel after theory is "aware of, and anxious about," theory.'[83] Ryan takes up Acker's *Empire of the Senseless* (1988), specifically Acker's comments regarding the work and its relation to theory in interview with Sylvère Lotringer in 1989. Ryan states:

> *Empire of the Senseless* portrays social life as debased by violent incestual relationships that she regards as inherent in patriarchal traditions. Acker claims not to have read French theory until after she had published significant works of her own. In an interview with Sylvère Lotringer Acker says that 'French philosophies . . . gave me a way of verbalizing what I had been doing in language . . . And then when I read *Anti-Oedipus* and Foucault's work, suddenly I had this new language at my disposal.'[84]

Ryan is sceptical of Acker's claim, stating 'It is difficult to judge how genuine this claim may be.' Ryan's doubt is justified, although a very specific reading of Acker's interview and Ryan's selection of material from the interview arguably engender it. Acker's notebooks reveal a consistent and rigorous engagement with theory, and she often refers to theory directly in her works. The notebook titled 'Gender in Art'[85] for instance explicitly engages with the work of Luce Irigaray, and her lecture notes on Marguerite Duras titled 'The Malady of Death'[86] take up Hélène Cixous's feminist works. These are just two instances out of many that reveal Acker consciously engaging with theory in her notebooks and other unpublished and published writings.

A closer look at the citation Ryan draws on, and takes excerpts from, however, reveals that Acker's comments to Lotringer primarily concern her experimental practice:

> Well, meeting you changed me a lot because by introducing me to the French philosophies, you gave me a way of verbalizing what I had been doing in language. I didn't really understand why I refused to use linear narrative; why my sexual genders kept changing, why I am basically the most disoriented novelist that ever existed. (Laughs). The work of Laing and Cooper, and whoever else I was going to, gave me no way of really understanding why I was writing the way I was writing.[87]

Acker continues: 'for years, I just did what I did but had no way of telling anyone about it, or talking about it'. It is at this point that she adds:

> then when I read ANTI-OEDIPUS and Foucault's work, suddenly I had this whole language at my disposal. I could say, Hi! And that other people were doing the same thing. I remember thinking, why don't they know me? I know exactly what they're talking about. And I could go farther.[88]

These remarks to Lotringer are significant for bringing to light Acker's complex engagement with, and alienation from, her own work. Importantly, Acker's dialogue with Lotringer reveals both the use of theory as a reflective tool, and the way in which Acker conceives of poststructuralist theory as another language at her 'disposal'. Ryan interprets Acker's comments as follows: 'theory confirmed some of what she had imagined was wildly idiosyncratic thinking that had no counterpart anywhere else'.[89] But read in the context of the entire interview, Acker's comments to Lotringer are less about her 'thinking' than about her writing practice, her innate resistance to linear narrative, which she admits, for many years, she couldn't fully comprehend. Acker's inability to understand her writerly disorientation is a matter of precisely not being able to conceptualise the 'thinking' related to her practice.

The experimental nature of Acker's work, like Stein's, produces non-deictic works, writings that are intentionally devoid of context. This aspect of Acker's work preserves the contemporaneity of her writing. As well as making a claim for Acker as a late modernist, I seek to position Acker within the body of a new generation of contemporary writers, poets, performance artists, and filmmakers who have been greatly influenced by Acker, understanding her to be a pioneer of a contemporary avant-garde.[90] For example, the contemporary experimental writers Caroline Bergvall, Vanessa Place, Dodie Bellamy and the experimental filmmaker Laura Parnes have all engaged with Acker's work and have noted her influence on their writings and filmmaking. Conceptual theorists and poets have taken up Acker's work in recent years. Acker was introduced to some of the early conceptualists, notably Joseph Kosuth and Lawrence Weiner, by David Antin in the 1960s. Their works had a formative influence on Acker during her early poetic training. Bergvall's recent essay 'The Conceptual Twist' in the anthology *I'll Drown My Book: Conceptual Writing by Women* (2012) discusses Acker's work at length.[91] Understanding Acker to be a key conceptual writer, Bergvall positions Acker as a key influence on the work of conceptual writing by women in the twenty-first century. Bergvall's work is taken up further in Chapter 3. This study takes up the form of Acker's works, as a means both to position Acker in a lineage of radical modernisms, and to evaluate the significance of her work to a contemporary body of experimental writing in the twenty-first century.

Kathy Acker: Writing the Impossible begins by examining Acker's early experiments, written between 1970 and 1979, through the prism of the concerns of the poets associated with Charles Bernstein's and Bruce Andrews' bi-monthly avant-garde journal of poetics *L=A=N=G=U=A=G=E*. *L=A=N=G=U=A=G=E* is an important context for Acker's works. The poets' collective vision of the transformative social, political, and aesthetic capacities of poetry clearly informed Acker's practices. Key issues foregrounded in the opening chapter reverberate across Acker's works: the crisis of the referent; the *L=A=N=G=U=A=G=E* poets' attack on the instrumental value of grammatically centred language under capitalism; and their subsequent understanding of language-centred writing as a poetics of subversion. These are important early contextual coordinates for Acker's writing experiments that position opacity and abstraction as counter to ordinary language. The opening chapter also establishes the importance of Viktor Shklovsky's idea of 'defamiliarization' to an understanding of Acker's works, and takes up Shklovsky's related claim that only art can reclaim perception. This book articulates the significance of such a claim for Acker's experimental practices, many of which are forms of 'defamiliarization'. In its evaluation of Acker's early writing experiments, 'MURDERERS-CRIMINALS JOIN SUNLIGHT' (1972), 'Homage to LeRoi Jones' (1972), 'Entrance into Dwelling in Paradise' (1972), 'Working Set' (1972), and 'Journal Black Cats Black Jewels' (1972), the chapter makes a claim for the emergence of perceiver-centred spaces in Acker's early experiments. The work of Jackson Mac Low is read as an important early influence on Acker, particularly Mac Low's procedural based work. Positioning Acker in relation to Mac Low, and placing her experiments in the lineage of John Cage and Jackson Mac Low in terms of the calling into question of the artistic ego through experimental practice, situates Acker in a lineage of avant-garde late modernist writers. A radical politics is at work in Acker's homage to LeRoi Jones (Amiri Baraka). Her early procedural practices of writing-through, and typographical experimentation, are early experiments that are formative to the complex writing practices found in her later works. In this way, Acker's poetic juvenilia emerge as possessing important coordinates for an understanding of her later writing experiments.

The fundamentals of non-organic experimental composition in Acker's work are taken up in Chapter 2, which addresses Acker's practice of collage, and the anxiety of self-description. *Blood and Guts in High School* is positioned in relation to both the Dadaist collage and montage practices of artists such as Hannah Höch at the beginning of the twentieth century, the subversive publications of the 1960s and 1970s mimeographed magazines, and the punk and post-punk medium of Xeroxed publications. The original manuscript of *Blood and Guts in High School* housed in the archive, a ruled Citadel Notebook with text and images pasted onto its pages, possesses a different materiality to the published version of the novel. The materiality of the text in its collage and typographic experimentation is situated in a counter-position to the language and hegemonic discourses within which Janey, the voice of the text, is imprisoned. A tension arises in *Blood and Guts in High School* between the idea of a unitary subject (Janey) and the acknowledgment embodied in the text's experimentalism of the fragmented, fluid, and incomplete. Drawing on Acker's practices of illegibility, and Denise Riley's work on language and affect, I argue that *Blood and Guts in High School*, through its experimental form, reveals the anxiety of self-description that Janey experiences within conventional language structures. Illustration, experimental typography, non-referential language, and the use of the poetic function in *Blood and Guts in High School* as sites of an alternate language that emerges through compositional form and experimental forms of rewriting. This non-verbal language runs counter to ordinary language. Acker's practice of *récriture*, in which she rewrites the works of César Vallejo and Stéphane Mallarmé, merges the practice of rewriting and experimentation with typography to produce a linguistic performativity. In *Blood and Guts in High School*, illustration, the use of hieroglyphics, and the experiments in typography empower inscription, visual depiction, and writing over linguistic transparency and conventional grammar structures.

Chapter 3 reads Acker's *Don Quixote: Which Was a Dream* as a form of non-procedural 'writing-through', a term that has its roots in the procedural practices of John Cage and Jackson Mac Low, discussed in Chapter 1. Acker's literary experiment in *Don Quixote* is related to abortion as a literary trope, and is positioned in contrast to models of male-to-male literary insemination and canon formation. The chapter draws on the contemporary scholarship surrounding conceptual practice, such as the work of Caroline Bergvall, whose essay on contemporary conceptual practices by women writers illuminates an understanding of Acker's work. The chapter addresses the tendency of many critical studies on Acker's work to use the term 'appropriation' as a blanket term. Acker's experimental practices in *Don Quixote* are readdressed, paying attention to the complexity of those strategies. Reading the work with attention to Acker's practice of abstraction, experimentation with translation, paragrammatic play, and the protosemantic, a method of writing-through emerges whereby voice is imbricated with the negation of language. In *Don Quixote* experimental practice displaces centralised narrative and offers a new feminist temporality.

In Memoriam to Identity is apprehended in Chapter 4 as an experiment with the *récit* form. Acker's compositional practice in *In Memoriam to Identity* is distinguished from that at work in *Don*

Quixote through the topological form of the text, which folds in intersecting narratives and creates a fluid textual space, rather than a space characterised by disjunction. These topological revolutions have a counterpart in the radical politics of the text. Returning to Denise Riley's work, I argue that through intertextuality, *In Memoriam to Identity* offers a site for that which Riley understands as constructive non-identity. The political and social negation of the voices of the narratives is positioned in contrast to the fictional site that offers the voices of the text a site of existence. *In Memoriam to Identity* points to the tensions surrounding the avant-garde idea of the sublation of art and life. In its inclusive and reintegrative form, the experimental text is apprehended as a site for community, solidarity, and intimacy, impossible in the given world.

Acker's practice of cutting and montage is the focus of the fifth chapter and extends the exploration of Acker's cut-up methods in Chapter 2. A close analysis of Acker's notebooks, the preliminary materials for *My Mother: Demonology* housed in the Kathy Acker Papers, reveals a compositional process comparable to Maya Deren's practice of creative cutting in her late modernist experimental film montage. Both Deren and Acker create irrational spaces and temporalities through the technique of montage. In *My Mother: Demonology*, Acker explicitly engages with film, using ekphrastic accounts of Luis Buñuel's *L'Age D'or* (1930), Radley Metzger's *Terese and Isabelle* (1968), and Dario Argento's *Suspiria* (1977) as materials for her text. Like Buñuel, Acker views desire as having a revolutionary capacity. *My Mother: Demonology*, in its indeterminacy, sites of condensation, and methods of displacement, embodies the structures of desire. It also marks Acker's turn to the image. Chapter 5 argues for the primacy of the image in Acker's experimental montage as a continuation of a modernist aesthetic legacy. When considered in light of P. Adams Sitney's idea of the 'antinomy of vision'[92] in modernist works, *My Mother: Demonology* reveals an antinomy of vision, whereby the poetic questions the primacy of the visual whilst being fundamentally imbricated with the visual. The chapter suggests that *My Mother: Demonology* possesses in the experimental text what Deren understands to be a 'vertical axis' in film that is able to create 'visible and auditory forms for something that is invisible, which is the feeling, the emotion, or the metaphysical content of the movement'.[93] This vertical axis is present in the text's movement from the quotidian to the poetic. It also emerges in the cutting in of excerpts from the works of Paul Celan and Ingeborg Bachmann, poets who sought a new form of language in the post-war period.

The final chapter of the study examines Acker's practices of ekphrasis and reappropriation of mythology in her final works. Continuing the enquiry into Acker's experiments with opacity, and her move towards abstraction in pursuit of languages that exist in a counterposition to ordinary language, Chapter 6 offers a close reading of 'From Psyche's Journal', Acker's creative critical piece on Cathy de Monchaux's sculptural work. Examining the ekphrastic impulse of Acker's work, ekphrasis is understood as enabling Acker to access the materiality of sculpture in her writing. Acker's writing practices are placed within the context of post-war abstract sculpture by women artists, with a particular focus on Eva Hesse's idea of absurdity that 'is not a "thing" but, "the sensation of the thing."'[94] Acker's ekphrastic practice is brought into dialogue with her practice of the reappropriation of mythology, and the conceptual practice that is termed here 'literary calisthenics', which arises from her experiments with language and bodybuilding. Chapter 6 explores the visual and linguistic space opened up in Acker's reappropriations of mythology between the act of repetition and the failure of replication. Acker's two later texts, *Eurydice in the Underworld* (1997) and her play 'Requiem' (1997) are addressed in light of Elaine Scarry's work on the difficulty of expressing physical pain. Acker's experiments that move towards a non-verbal language against ordinary language, and the silent languages of the body, facilitate the voicing of pain, and in particular the relation between physical pain and imagining.

The formation of an understanding of Acker's avant-garde writing practices would not have been possible without the knowledge gained from consulting the archive materials housed in the Kathy Acker Papers at the Sallie Bingham Center for Women's History and Culture in the David M. Rubenstein Rare Book & Manuscript Library at Duke University. The relation between Acker's manuscript practice and the published versions of her experimental works illuminates an apprehension of her experimental writing strategies. In its use of the archive materials to gain insight into Acker's experimental practice, this book employs a critical methodology that insists on the importance and the significance of Acker's manuscript practice to an understanding of her body of work. The chapters that follow frequently draw on Acker's unpublished notebooks, essays, drawings, and annotations on others' works. The extent of the original materials housed in the archive that Acker then cut up, or folded-in, reassembled and combined to compose her published works highlights the importance of the archive and the vital role that it plays in the formation of knowledge regarding an experimental writer's oeuvre. In this context, Acker can be positioned in relation to a lineage of experimentalists whose archives reveal, and indeed form, their material practice: Emily Dickinson, Gertrude Stein, Jackson Mac Low, Robert Grenier, and Susan Howe, to name a few of Acker's fellow American avant-garde writers. Where possible, I have selected as illustrations materials from the archives that demonstrate the significance of the material dimension of the original works.

This book in many ways reflects its subject matter. This study is by no means exhaustive. The works that are taken as the focus of the chapters have been chosen as exemplary of certain compositional techniques, and experiments with language found in Acker's works. There can be no interpretative closure, no one single approach to Acker's work. Like Acker's work, this study is an open text. It aims to offer original perspectives on key texts in Acker's oeuvre and to generate future studies that take up Acker's compositional strategies. The chronology of selected works reveals the shifts in and development of Acker's experimental styles. Acker stated in the January issue of *Women's Review*, in 1986, that Gertrude Stein, as the progenitor of experimental women's writing, is 'the mother of us all'.[95] The remarkable experimentalism and linguistic innovation of a great number of texts that comprise the Kathy Acker Papers reveal Acker to succeed Stein as one of the most important experimental writers of the twentieth century. This study endeavours to substantiate this claim.

Chapter 1

Writing Asystematically: Early Experimental Writings 1970–1979

What is poetry and if you know what poetry is what is prose.

There is no use in telling more than you know, no not even if you do not know it.

But do you do you know what prose is and do you know what poetry is.[1]

When the double issue of the bimonthly avant-garde magazine *L=A=N=G=U=A=G=E* was published in 1979, it opened with Acker's essay 'NOTES ON WRITING – from THE LIFE OF BAUDELAIRE'.[2] One of the central aims of this book is to position Acker and her work in a lineage of radical modernisms, and to draw attention to her works as contemporary continuations of radical modernist practice. As Charles Bernstein remarks: '*L=A=N=G=U=A=G=E* is associated not only with poetic practice but also with an active effort to reclaim the legacy of radical modernist poetry from revisionist, anti-modernist accounts.'[3] In this first chapter, Acker's early poetry is set within the context of the work that emerged in the field of American poetry in the 1970s. The writing experiments that Acker produced from 1970 to 1979 consist of both poetic and experimental prose pieces. This chapter seeks to underscore the importance of poetics to Acker's work through careful readings of Acker's experimental poetry written in this period, much of which remains unpublished.[4] Acker's exercises: 'MURDERERS-CRIMINALS JOIN SUNLIGHT' (1972); 'Homage to LeRoi Jones' (1972), and her other early experiments, 'Entrance into Dwelling in Paradise' (1972), 'Working Set' (1972), and 'Journal Black Cat Black Jewels' (1972), reveal the significance of Acker's poetry in terms of the development of her experimental compositional strategies deployed in her later writings. Such writing experiments also illuminate her early prose works: *The Burning Bombing of America* (1972), *Rip off Red, Girl Detective* (1973), *The Childlike Life of the Black Tarantula by the Black Tarantula* (1973), *I Dreamt I was a Nymphomaniac: Imagining* (1974), and *The Adult Life of Toulouse Lautrec by Henri Toulouse Lautrec* (1978). Close examination of Acker's early writing experiments and her prose piece *The Burning Bombing of America* reveals the way in which her early poetic procedural experiments led to the radical writing practices that developed and unfolded across Acker's oeuvre.

Acker and *L=A=N=G=U=A=G=E* poetry

Acker's work in this period can be positioned in two related fields of American poetry. The first consisted of American avant-garde poets such as David Antin, Jerome Rothenberg, Jackson Mac Low, Kenneth Rexroth, and Charles Olson.[5] Acker was influenced by what Rothenberg termed the 'counter-poetics'[6] that emerged in their works. Writing in hindsight about his early works in 1987, David Antin comments on the importance of language and politics to his poetry written from 1963 to 1973. Language and politics are not analogous, Antin contends, 'but they are very close, because language is the cultural matrix in which the value systems that determine politics are made'.[7] Antin's statement brings to light the cornerstone concern of Acker's work: the interrelation of language, power, and politics within normative American culture, and the subsequent questions such relations pose regarding writing, identity, and freedom. This contentious area of enquiry was coextensive with the issues that avant-garde poetics took up and explored in this period. The Kathy Acker Papers reveal that Acker regularly closely corresponded with Rothenberg, Mac Low, Rexroth, and Antin during her early career. The new groupings of writers and poets that emerged in America in the mid-1950s, Rothenberg remarks, 're-explored the idea of an avant garde, with nearly complete indifference to academic strictures'. For such poets: 'Poetry was transformative, not only of its present & future, but of its past as well.'[8] The counterpoetics that came to the fore in this period,

Rothenberg argues, offered 'a fundamentally new view of the relationship between consciousness, language & poetic structure: what is seen, said & made'.[9] Acker's early experiments, such as 'Journal Black Cats Black Jewels' (1972), 'Homage to LeRoi Jones' (1972), and 'Writing Asystematicaaly' (sic) (1972) are inseparable from this counterpoetics, and reveal Acker taking up and experimenting with consciousness, language, and poetic structure, as a means to harness the transformative capacity of writing. Such concerns would become vectors in Acker's practice that culminate in her later work in the writing of the languages of the body. Moreover, through linguistic experimentation, her writings in this period create a porous relationship between poetry and prose, a permeable interrelation that would become a distinctive feature of her experimental practice.

The second grouping of poets, the poets associated with $L=A=N=G=U=A=G=E$, overlaps with the first, including Jackson Mac Low for instance, but this second grouping of poets rejected the processural poetry of Olson. Acker's opening piece for the 1979 issue of $L=A=N=G=U=A=G=E$ draws overtly on Baudelaire, bringing the line of European avant-garde poets that she placed herself in a lineage with into a discursive relation with her American postwar avant-garde contemporaries. The editors of the journal, Charles Bernstein and Bruce Andrews, invited writers 'to give their view of what qualities writing has or could have that contribute to an understanding or critique of society, seen as a capitalist system'.[10] Contributors to the issue included Barbara Barg, Cris Cheek, Terry Eagleton, Steve McCaffery, Ron Silliman, Barrett Watten, Hannah Weiner, Bruce Andrews, and Charles Bernstein. In line with the poets and critics gathered in the volume, who positioned experimental practice within a socio-political context, Acker's opening essay draws on what she perceived to be the significance of the writer in her present culture, the writer's separation from the socio-political topography. The introduction took up Acker's statement in her 1979 essay for $L=A=N=G=U=A=G=E$: 'The difference between a writer and its world gives the reason for writing.'[11] Acker's claim positions the writer in contraposition to the external world. She adds: 'All mental existence is an expression, a measure of distance.'[12] This distance resounds throughout Acker's work and is an issue with which she engages and struggles, both in terms of her experimental practice and her position as a woman writer.

There is a tendency across the writers in the $L=A=N=G=U=A=G=E$ issue to position their contemporary poetics within a radical modernist genealogy whilst engaging with the poststructuralist critique of language and Marxist critique. In a recent essay Bernstein comments on the 'strong desire to connect oppositional political and cultural views with linguistically inventive writing' shared by the poets associated with $L=A=N=G=U=A=G=E$ in the 1970s. However, he notes that many of the most brilliant and foremost poets in the field didn't at the time read the political, philosophical, and linguistic works that are often associated with, and brought to bear on, the work of those in the field. Nevertheless, Bernstein remarks, citing the title of an important essay by Erica Hunt from the collection *The Politics of Poetic Form: Poetry and Public Policy* (1990), 'the ideas were in the air for all to breathe, as was the desire to formulate an "oppositional poetics."'[13] A number of themes emerge in the double issue that are key concerns in Acker's writing experiments. Sketching out the theoretical terrain of the $L=A=N=G=U=A=G=E$ poets provides a contextual framework regarding language writing, upon which the proceeding chapters frequently draw.

The relation between traditional grammar structures and the capitalist and consumerist apparatus is explored by many of the poets and writers gathered together in the journal. For Bruce Andrews, mainstream criticism in 1979 still failed 'to raise or demand an answer to key questions about *the nature of the medium*' of writing, 'which remains the modernist project for an art form'.[14] Andrews opens his essay with a citation from Karl Marx's *The German Ideology* (1842), asserting 'Language is practical consciousness.' Traditional grammar structures are viewed as holding an intrinsic relation to capitalism. The $L=A=N=G=U=A=G=E$ poets attacked the instrumental value of language put forward and sustained by a capitalist society. Andrews then makes a distinctive Language Poetry move, when he relates referentiality to the concept of surface value. Andrews defines 'normative grammar' as 'a machine for the accumulation of meaning seen as surplus value & for territorializing the surface relations among signifiers by converting them into an efficient pointing system'.[15] Representational literature, the dominant form of literature, is viewed by Andrews as dependent on, and thereby subordinated by, 'an implicit definition of words as largely transparent tools of reference'.[16] Similarly, Steve McCaffery draws a direct analogy between grammar and profit. 'Grammar', he states, 'is a huge conciliatory machine assimilating elements into a ready structure. This grammatical structure can be likened to profit in capitalism, which is reinvested to absorb more human labour for further profit. Classical narrative structure is a profit structure.'[17] The $L=A=N=G=U=A=G=E$ poets directly challenged this relation. Other contributors extended the scope. 'Writing cannot be limited to dealing with capitalism', Cris Cheek claims. 'Capitalism is a set-back. Writing as it relates to capitalism is the limitation the framework poses. The concerns should be against oppressive structures.' Cheek placed emphasis on performance in his own work.[18] Once again, taking up the problem of the instrumental use of language, Cheek articulates the central issue: 'Writing has become referential to itself – to the making of objects.'[19]

Language-centred writing, in this context, it was argued, has the capacity to subvert existing relations between language and power by challenging the capitalist system through linguistic experimentation. Andrews envisages a poetics of subversion that would be 'an anti-systemic detonation of settled relations, and anarchic liberation of energy flows'. 'Such flows,' Andrews claims, 'like libidinal discharges, are thought to exist underneath & independent from the system of language.' The system of language functions for Andrews as 'an armouring' that entraps the energy flows 'in codes & grammar'.[20] Language writing aims to break down the conventional coherence between signifier and signified and thus free the energy flows from the linguistic corralling imposed by conventional grammatical structures.[21] In doing so, it was claimed, language writing is capable of 'negating the system itself'. The outcome of such a negation for Andrews would be: 'an experimentalism of diminished or obliterated reference. This would deliberately violate the structure of the sign, make the signifieds recede even more from the foreground occupied by supposedly autonomous signifiers.' This offers, for Andrews, 'a brief for actually instituting opacity, promoting the spillage or dissemination – Not from caring about message or meaning, but caring about the eruptiveness of material being put into distinctive relationships.'[22] Acker's writings, which develop a negative feminist aesthetics through experimental practices, can be placed firmly within Andrews' idea of negation outlined in his essay. Andrews' comments echo the opening chapter of Ron Silliman's landmark work *The New Sentence*

(1977), and introduce a significant line of enquiry that pervades the followings chapters, the importance of forms of abstraction, textual thickening, and obscurity in Acker's work and the relation of the material text, and experimental practice to the formation of opacity. In his opening chapter 'Disappearance of the Word, Appearance of the World', Silliman aligns the transparency of language with the instrumental use of language:

> capitalism passes on its preferred reality through language itself to individual speakers. And, in doing so, necessarily effaces that original connecting point to the human, the perceptible presence of the signifier, the mark or sound, in the place of the signified.[23]

For Silliman, what is lost when a language transfers into a capitalist stage of development 'is an anaesthetic transformation of the perceived tangibility of the word',[24] and this occurs in tandem with 'corresponding increases in its expository, descriptive and narrative capacities'. Of fundamental significance is the relation Silliman is pointing to between the move away from the word's materiality, its opacity, and the subsequent increment in narrative and descriptive capacity, which is a semantic shift toward the transparency of language. In Silliman's understanding, the 'preconditions for the invention of "realism," the illusion of reality in capitalist thought',[25] emerge from this transformation from the word's tangibility to the word's transparency. Transformation in Acker's work is the metamorphic reverse of the transformation Silliman charts of a language from tribal societies into a capitalist stage, and is achieved through experimental strategies that create the conditions for the emergence of the word in its tangibility, and retrieve the opacity of language. Across her oeuvre Acker achieves this reversal through experimental strategies such as abstraction, disjunction, the use of the pictorial and handwritten materials, experiments in typography, montage, and ekphrasis. New tangible, often non-verbal, languages arise from such experiments and run counter to ordinary language.

Bernstein develops the idea of writing by making it coterminous with Simone Weil's understanding of the radical capacity of thought. For Weil, '[i]n so far as it is ceaselessly creating a scale of values "that is not of this world"', thought 'is the enemy of forces which control society'.[26] In line with Acker's comments on the distance of the writer, Bernstein suggests writing to be paradigmatic of thought in this respect: 'an instance broken off from and hence not in the service of this economical and cultural—social—force—called capitalism'.[27] Like Andrews, Bernstein draws on the potential of writing to negate the system via its capacity to give rise to 'An experience (released in the reading) which is non-commoditized . . . but rather, what is from the point of view of the market, no value (a negativity, inaudible, invisible)—that non-generalizable residue that is specific to each particular experience.'[28] Above all, writing's resistance to social forces resides in its non-referential nature: 'this sense that we speak of poetry as being untranslatable and unparaphrasable', and this resistance is bound to the experience of reading, 'for what is untranslatable is the sum of all specific conditions of experience (space time, order, light, mood, position, to infinity) made available by reading'.[29] The re-evaluation of the medium of writing that takes place within the essays by Bernstein, Andrews, McCaffery, and other essays in the 1979 special issue of *L=A=N=G-U=A=G=E* renegotiates the relations between language and power instituted by traditional grammar, and offers a new field of experimental practice for overturning traditional hermeneutics.[30]

The central issue at hand is the struggle over meaning. McCaffery defines language-centred writing as 'writing of diminished referentiality'.[31] For McCaffery, the fight for language is both a political fight and 'a fight inside language'.[32] Language-centred writing is positioned as antithetical to 'grammatically centred meaning':

> Grammatically centred meaning is meaning realised through a specific mode of temporalization. It is understood as a postponed 'reward' at the end (the culmination) of a series of syntagms. It is that fetish in which the sentence completes itself. Meaning is like capital in so far as it extends its law of value to new objects. Like surplus value, meaning is frequently 'achieved' to be reinvested in the extending chain of significations. This is seen quite clearly in classical narrative, where meaning operates as accumulated and accumulative units in the furtherance of 'plot' or 'character development': those elements of representation which lead to a distinction outside of the domain of the signifier.[33]

McCaffery's alignment of capitalist production with linear narrative, and the accumulation of meaning through the sequential relation of linguistic forms, asserts meaning as 'the unconscious political element in lineal grammaticization'. According to McCaffery's formulation, 'Grammar is invested precisely because of the unexpected profit rate viz. a clarity through sequence carried into meaning.'[34] As the reinvestment of language depends precisely upon this 'clarity through sequence', a language-centred writing that presents opaque, nontransparent, impervious language will negate the accumulative power of linear narrative. Particularly important with regards to Acker's writing experiments is the resulting resistance of language-centred writing to monosemeity, the repression of language into a singular meaning. In McCaffery's articulation, the unshackling of language from grammar gives free reign to polysemeity, the word's multiplicity, and allows for 'the free circulation of meaning'.[35]

Andrews and McCaffery each underline the productivity of language-centred writing. This was the period in which Andrews and McCaffery were concerned with 'the politics of the referent'. As Bernstein observes, they put forward 'a poetry that foregrounded sound and syntax' in which meaning and reference were not rendered entirely obsolete, but 'other ways of making meaning, and a greater range of possibilities for linguistic reference are activated'.[36] Writing, Andrews observes, should not merely be 'A calculated drainage of the referential qualities of individual words.' For whilst such elimination of reference might challenge established language rules, there remains the risk that such a practice on its own would 'still abdicate the central struggle for meaning'.[37] Instead, Andrews advocates the creation of new relations between units of language through a political writing practice 'that unveils demystifies the creation & sharing of meaning' and that 'problematizes the ideological nature of any apparent coherence between signified & referent, between signified & signifier (for example, by composing words around axes other than grammar/pointing function—)'.[38] Referring to the work of the Russian Formalist literary theorist, Viktor Shklovsky, Bernstein draws on the poet's conception of poetry as able to '"lay bare the device" by "making strange" or "defamiliarizing" (*ostranie*)'. In other words, Bernstein comments, 'poems can make the metaphoricity of our perception in and through language more palpable'.[39] Shklovsky's idea of 'defamiliarization' in his essay 'Art as Technique' (1925) is particularly significant to an understanding of Acker's work, for the emphasis it places on the primacy of perception. Shklovsky contrasts 'defamiliarization' to 'habituation'. 'As perception becomes habitual,' Shklovsky states, 'it becomes automatic.'[40] In such a process: 'After we see an object several times, we begin to recognize it. The object is in front of us and we know about it, but we do not see it.'[41] For Shklovsky, art reclaims perception:

> art exists that one may recover the sensation of life; it exists to make one feel things, to make the stone *stony*. The purpose of art is to impart the sensation of things as they are perceived and not as they are known.

Art is then capable of 'defamiliarization': 'The technique of art is to make objects "unfamiliar," to make forms difficult, to increase the difficulty and length of perception because the process of perception is an aesthetic end in itself and must be prolonged.'[42] Acker's compositional practices frequently evidence techniques of 'defamilarization'. For instance, her experimental strategy of rewriting involves modes of what Shklovsky termed 'parallelism': 'The purpose of parallelism, like the general purpose of imagery, is to transfer the usual perception of an object into the sphere of a new perception – that is to make a unique semantic modification.'[43]

For the poets associated with *L=A=N=G=U=A=G=E*, Shklovsky's idea that poetic language meets the conditions for 'defamiliarization' was central. Andrews' analysis of the medium of writing offers a practice of writing that is able 'to create conditions under which the productivity of words & syllables & linguistic form-making can be felt, & given aesthetic presence'.[44] The need to produce meaning without investment, for McCaffery, 'becomes a need to activate a relation of human energies'.[45] The active role of the reader is foregrounded here. Language-centred writing is thus aligned with a humanist politics of writing, whereby the reader has a relation to the text and a human engagement with the writing. This humanist undercurrent to linguistic experimentation is a vital component of Acker's work. McCaffery positions this reader/text relation in contrast to meaning in classical discourse. He gestures towards an intimacy generated by language-centred writing, which desires 'the reader's presentness to language itself' that cannot be found in a language 'primarily centred on reference'.[46] For McCaffery: 'A language-centred writing dispossesses us of language in order that we may repossess it again.'[47] This divestment of language by experimental writing, as a means to reclaim language from the strictures of conventional modes of discourse, underlies Acker's writing experiments.

In each of their analyses, Andrews, Bernstein, and McCaffery suggest poetry's power to offer new experiences and hence new worlds. Bernstein sees writing as an opening: '"*What we do is to bring our words back*" – *to make our experiences visible*, or again: to see the conditions of experience.' For Bernstein, 'in this way, a work may also be constructed – an "other" world *made* from whatever materials are ready to hand (not just those of memory) – structuring, in this way, possibilities otherwise not allowed for'.[48] The connection Bernstein makes between the limitations of language and the limitations of what can be experienced generates an ontic dimension to the question of writing. Here, as Antin does in the 1960s and 1970s, Bernstein turns to Wittgenstein. Citing *Philosophical Investigations* he states: '"To imagine a language is to imagine a form of life" – think of that first imagine as the active word here.'[49] Bernstein's remarks, via Wittgenstein, foreground a central line of enquiry taken in this study into Acker's creation of new languages. More widely, the alignment of traditional grammatical structures with the structures of capitalism, the theorisation of a language-centred writing practice that challenges classical narrative through opacity and multiplicity of meaning, and the frequent enunciation of the modernist proposition 'form is identical to content',[50] provide central coordinates in the late modernist terrain from which Acker's experimental writing practices emerge.

Toward perceiver-centred works

Predating the 1979 issue of $L=A=N=G=U=A=G=E$ to which Acker contributed, Acker's early exercises produced in 1972 are works that experiment with language in ways that depart from the grammatically centred meaning that the writers associated with $L=A=N=G=U=A=G=E$ identified as the product of the instrumental use of language in classical narrative. Bernstein remarks that in place of the instrumental use of words, Silliman, McCaffery, and Andrews were arguing for a poetry that resisted the field of referentiality, offering a form of writing that offered 'a non-purpose-driven aesthetic space'.[51] This space, created through experimental practice, 'allowed for the pleasure in reflection, projection, and sensory engagement with verbal materials'.[52] What emerged from such a new aesthetic space for Jackson Mac Low was not simply language-centred work but perceiver-centred, or reader-centred work. Bernstein remarks that the writing produced by those writers associated with *L=A=N=G=U=A=G=E* involved the activation of the readers' imaginations rather than the passive consumption of the text. The readers of these works, Bernstein claims, 'were not told what to think or feel or see but encouraged to make intuitive leaps: to *interenact . . .* rather than passively consume'.[53] Acker's early experiments create perceiver-centred spaces. Acker's non-linear writings can be positioned directly within the body of innovative women's writing that emerged in the late 1960s and early 1970s. Only relatively recently have the works of innovative British and North American women poets in this period been fully recognised. The pivotal 1996 anthology *Out of Everywhere: Linguistically Innovative Poetry by Women in North America & the UK* brought together samples of key works by thirty innovative women poets, such as Susan Howe, Grace Lake, Joan Retallack, Wendy Mulford, Caroline Bergvall, and Rae Armantrout. In her Afterword, Wendy Mulford explains: 'there are clusters of language operated by some poets here which will not yield up meaning to the reader unless it is understood that the text has been worked upon to generate new meaning by exposing generative linguistic structures'. For Mulford, in the work of such poets, innovative linguistic practice constitutes 'a radical swerve or deviation from traditional literary language-use' that works 'to subvert the rigid meanings that traditional structures produce'.[54] Mulford's remarks point to the rejection of traditional meaning-orientated language in favour of linguistic innovation, specifically within the context of innovative women's writing. Acker's work should be positioned within this lineage of linguistically innovative writing by women.

Wittgenstein's work on language-games and his work on certainty discussed in the introduction provide an important context for Acker's early works. Wittgenstein's idea of 'language-games' changed throughout his works. In the Introduction to *The Blue and Brown Books: Preliminary Studies for the 'Philosophical Investigations'*, R. R. Rhees observes that one of Wittgenstein's earliest uses of language-games was to 'introduce them in order to shake off the idea of a necessary form of language'.[55] In *The Blue Book*, Wittgenstein states that 'the study of language games is the study of primitive forms of language or primitive languages'.[56] For Wittgenstein, primitive languages were not clouded by the associative contexts that surround ordinary language. Tyrus Miller analyses Jackson Mac Low's experimental composition *Stanzas for Iris Lezak* (1971), observing that the piece was derived in part from *The Blue and the Brown Books*. 'From the outset of his book', Miller asserts, Mac Low 'poses his readers with the Wittgensteinian problem of bewilderment before and by language, when it is bereft of its self-evident pragmatic contexts of relevance and use.' 'To read Mac Low', for Miller, 'is a problem of finding possible contexts for motivating the relevance of texts that at first seem to obstruct rather than communicate knowledge.'[57] The difficulty of reading that is generated by the removal of a word's context, and often related fixed referent, is an aspect germane to both Mac Low's and Acker's experiments in 1972. Acker's later 1993 essay 'Bodies of Work' explicitly draws on the notion of language-games as a way to position 'the language-game named the *language of the body*'.[58] 'In ordinary language, meaning is contextual',[59] Acker states. 'Bodies of Work' is subheaded 'Against Ordinary Language: The Language of the Body.' Each of Acker's works is an attempt to move away from the contextual constraints of ordinary language. Acker's early experiments and her conversations with Antin reveal her experimenting with the idea of language-games two decades before her key essay on the language of the body was published.

In 'Journal Black Cats Black Jewels', dated summer 1972, Acker experiments with end-stopped fragments, dismantling grammar, repetition, and metonymy. A certain Steinian experimentation is apparent in Acker's omission of question marks, elimination of capitalisation, and the use of unconventional spacing and repetition. Stein states in 'Poetry and Grammar' (1935): 'prose capitals and small letters have really nothing to do with the inner life of sentences and paragraphs'.[60] Stein's idea of the 'inner life' of sentences illuminates Acker's compositions:

> who are you.   a Vulture.   plant murders.   parents and
> children do not exist.   the beginning of California.
> every twenty-four hours.   sleep for three hours.   suffer.
> feel strong.   feel anxious.   need to be alone.   need to
> yell.   need for third person.   clouds.   plants need to

be watered.   yells.   bad dreams.   wake up.   between dreams
five times.   kill six times.   feel disgust.   feel horny.
feel burnt skin.   ache.   feel desire.   friendly.   unending
pain.   water gurgles.   no body calls.   children are golden
emergency   children shall rise from the sun.   forget all
but pain.   want to be alone.   get rid of beauty. [61]

As this extract evidences, Acker's early experiments involve the
page used as a visual field, a feature of Acker's work that becomes
more pronounced in her text/image collagist work, *Blood and
Guts in High School*.[62] Here the repetition of the verb 'feel', devoid
of a pronoun, qualified by various, often conflicting nouns and
pronouns, 'strong', 'anxious', 'burnt skin', 'ache', reverses the conventional authority of the pronoun, noun, and adjective that in
traditional grammar subordinate and qualify the verb. Instead the
verb takes precedence. In this manner verbs such as 'feel', 'need',
and 'want' generate the text. Unconventional spacing is brought
into tension with the end-stopped fragments. Acker creates a tor-
sion and traction between the spaces of the text (which are cae-
sural silences), and the use of periods. The truncation apparent in
sections such as 'feel strong. feel anxious. need to be alone. need
to / yell' produces anxiety. In these paratactic phrases, the energy
of the innovative verb clause is cut off by the period and the subsequent space, which is negative and empty. The subsequent repetition of the verb in the next clause, uncapitalised, accompanied by
a different adjective, or in the case of this example, verb, enacts
psychological conflict without fixing conflict with a definitive referent. The continuation implied by the repetition of the verb is
at variance with the period. The composition creates a kinetics,
as Olson apprehended it, by which 'A poem is energy transferred
from where the poet got it . . . by way of the poem itself, all the
way over, to the reader.'[63] Later in the piece the movement of the
text quickens into a frenzy:

weep   influx   shut up   black air   lack of air   0°. feel
desperate.   about to blow up.   people.   feel anxious.   fright.
feel noise.   irritate.   anger.   now.   vomit.   split.
start.   feel pain.   feel heat.   feel crazied.   feel terror.
feel threat.   feel joy.   feel yellow.   leap   go   pull out
move   swim   kick   run   fly.[64]

The lack of periods at the outset of this extract allows for an accumulation of disparate words, which, when brought together, generate a sense of suffering. This is an early instance of Acker's practice of engendering new word families that gesture to oblique meaning. Here Wittgenstein's notion of family resemblance is an apposite coordinate. For Wittgenstein the search for a single definitive meaning of a word that is applicable to all of its uses is an arbitrary hunt:

> Instead of pointing out something common to all that we call language, I'm saying that these phenomena have no one thing in common in virtue of which we use the same word for all – but there are many different kinds of *affinity* between them. And on account of this affinity, or these *affinities*, we call them all 'languages'.[65]

In languages Wittgenstein perceives 'a complicated network of similarities overlapping and criss-crossing: similarities in the large and in the small'. These similarities Wittgenstein terms 'family resemblances'.[66] Positioned in relation to Wittgenstein's notion of family resemblance, Acker's experimental exercises, in their abstracting of language and the deployment of metonymic patterning within opaque compositions, can be read as creating new family resemblances that derail normative grammatical denotation. For instance, in the extract above suffering does not appear as a fixed signified, nor do the words function as direct referents to suffering. Yet the dispossessed 'weep', 'influx' with no prepositional clause, and the dislocated 'shut up' devoid of a noun, create new oblique relationships between words. This is a working example of words being composed around axes other than grammar and pointing function, the experimental practice that Andrews articulated in his work on the politics of the referent. Brought into association with 'weep' and 'influx', 'shut up' suggests both the feeling of claustrophobia and of violent enclosure. Yet, also, the imperative to be silent lingers at the edge of the sequence. 'Black air' only slightly modified and cleaved becomes that which follows it, 'lack of air', the latter acquiring an ironic performativity from its enclosure within the preceding clause. The opening cluster, followed by the end-stopped clauses, often one word, that elicit psychological tension, is in the final lines juxtaposed with 'leap go pull out move swim kick run fly', a metonymical stream of release.

'Journal Black Cats Black Jewels' is a political text that uses experimental composition to expose and comment on the violence of American foreign policy in the Vietnam War. The proceeding section, with its use of extended lines, offsets the internal psychological suffering that emerges through the form of the first section:

> the emotions of every one in Amerika are hidden.   see.   vision
> of the world.
> the emotions of every one are a circle.   this now   is the end.
> King Cobra.   Phantom.   Alcoa.   into the age of aluminium.
> destroy.   they give us the guns   we kill.   A-7 ground
> move   after dark.   ITT   Singer   Bullitt.   report.   Sylvania.
> the electronic battlefield IS HERE!! (huge banners roll).   relay
> messages to black drones   black drones fly to Thailand   Thais
> kill Amerikans.   good.   craters appear in the ground.
> electronic battlefield   questionmark.   ITT gyps Nixon   Nixon
> clips his cock.   puppets dance across the cars.   all computers
> revolt.[67]

There is a clear shift in form here. Classical grammatical structures are attributed to American foreign policy. In sentences such as 'the emotions of everyone in Amerika are hidden', 'the emotions of every one are a circle', and 'craters appear in the ground', meaning is fixed and unambiguous. Nouns are fixed in their referents, and a slogan from the media enters the text with definitive meaning 'the electronic battlefield IS HERE'. This normative grammar and lack of affect is implicated with American politics in this section. Toward the end of the section the first person-pronoun is used:

> act from feeling.   accept what emotion appears.   X cannot
> control my anxiety   I blow apart   orange skin shreds   blood
> flies over moving planes   I see every where   when seeing
> end of world doctor says   you have abnormal childhood   you
> will have to live childhood over again.   I am not able to deal
> with immanent end of all being-existence[68]

The omniscient 'I' that blows apart, unable to cope with the apocalyptic climate, emerges in the final lines of the first part of the text as a mythical figure:

> I am I
> I   black bird   Vulture Killer   fifteen-ffot-wing span   black
> wrists   claws hook on to jewels[69]

This imaginary figure – part bird, part weapon system – closes the section and opens the next, as 'jewels' becomes a repeated oblique leitmotif in the second part of the composition.

The energy of the experimental composition of the opening of the text returns in a positive form in the second part titled 'THE REVOLUTION AND AFTER'. Following a bleak opening section the tone of the composition changes. Acker's writing, with its affinities to language-centred writing, creates distinctive associations, again through repetition. However, the experimental clauses are no longer end-stopped. As a result, the experimentation with spaces, instead of producing closed and negative intervals, expands both the visual and verbal field, allowing the opaque images to swell:

> in California   delight.   I give you delight   angel of the purple
> ocean   apples pluck from the seven gardens of Persian cedars   green
> plums more sour than the fur of dogs   huge balls of white juice
> wine of the body   orange and purple sky   in which appear   giant
> dandelions   lilacs   twined through your yellow hair   silver
> pluck   out of my legs   spreading across the universe   feet
> wander   across the surface   of exploding stars.[70]

Abstract imagery is created through the repetition of colour and impossible associations. The erotic repetition of 'pluck' aligns desire and nature, and the lack of end-stopped lines allows for the free flow of desire through association. Images are formed that disrupt the autonomy of the signifier: 'I touch your knee the / hole where your eyes should be cats wind their tails around the roots of our eyes the muscles of sex hidden in the brain / always night'.[71] The words gesture to a new perception: 'color-sight / annihilates mind' and this is positioned adjacent to 'floating now huge parrots ride down / giant veins'. Such imagery and experimental structures are affiliated with revolution, culminating in the suggestion of revolution:

> conch ears   hundred foot tall ocean plants   the fish form boots
> around our ten foot feet   we curl the tail of dragons around
> our necks   red purple lichen wave their hands   we do not stop.
> the sources of revolution   red jewels   black jewels   yellow
> jewels   green-white jewels   jewels whose centres are holes
> jewels found beneath huge mountains   jewels whose edges are gold

silver jewels   oyster jewels   turquoise jewels   jewels   strange
hazel hair   the jewels of witches flying through black curtains
blue jewels   sea jewels   conch jewels   opal jewels   bird
jewels   jewels whose eyes are seals   jewels cough blood   jewels
skin   fire   jewels   night jewels   huge jewels carved by
the seven dwarves   jewels rise from the dirt   the mud of
bright red breasts   we keep moving   we blow up   we celebrate
the end of Amerika[72]

The repetition of the word 'jewels' and the linguistic permutations
between simple units, 'silver jewels oyster jewels turquoise jewels',
and more complex clauses, such as 'jewels rise from the dirt', expand
the possibilities of meaning and defamiliarise any single referent
for the noun. The incantatory repetition recalls Ginsberg's 'Howl'
(first performed in 1955), imbuing the text's innovative form with a
radical inheritance. In a previous line, the I is collapsed into 'jewel'.
However, where Ginsberg's text is articulated by a performative 'I',
in this manner, the incantatory insistence of the repeated noun registers multiplicity of identities, while through fragmentation and
disjunction Acker's text resists any fixed meaning. In 'Journal Black
Cat Black Jewels' the underwater realm of the woman is placed in
an antithetical position to the external world of America in 1972.
The final section of the text combines autobiographical material with
abstract imagery:

gold stars   gold hands   body turns gold trees   light makes
changing walls   wind division   windows disappear   curtains
doors   no longer exist   gold   smell   gold   balls   gold
raft   gold ships   pirates disembark   female sashes under
heavy breasts talk nonsense steal jewels from Ford Morgan
lose jewels   lose all possessions   tramp through Michigan
Nebraska   up north   to Wyoming   Alaska black nears caress
hands   talk with deer   hands clench   rivers curl over dark
earth   leaves   red gold   jewels   gold.

The writing pivots around the colour 'gold', a repeated invocation that
serves to abstract the surrounding words. The natural imagery stands
in dialectical tension with the clusters of abstract nouns. The final
lines situate the writing within the American landscape: Michigan,

Nebraska, Alaska. But there is also a fantasy world of gold and female pirates who pillage the wealth of industrialists and bankers such as Ford and Morgan (Acker's idea of female pirates culminates in her later work *Pussy, King of the Pirates* (1996)). Acker's text can be read as paradigmatic of that which Andrews would posit in his 1979 essay as a writing practice that is 'an experimentalism of diminished or obliterated reference'[73] and it underscores the antiabsorptive techniques at work in Acker's early works.

Procedural practices: 'Homage to LeRoi Jones'

In a subsection of the third section of *The Burning Bombing of America* titled 'Pain Diary' the groups of words signalling anxiety, sexual pleasure, and the need for political revolution are permeated with clusters pointing to 'nonlanguage',[74] which is equated with desire. Acker points to experimental practices as having political resonance:

> begin
> here   continuous instability   nonpermanence   the procedural
> point of view we want to privilege.[75]

The allegiance of the 'procedural point of view' with continuous instability, nonpermanence, and a new revolutionary beginning is significant, as it highlights indeterminacy as a desired state. The use of procedures, this extract suggests, leads to indeterminacy. Jackson Mac Low's work is the key touchstone for an apprehension of what the 'procedural point of view' might be. Mac Low in his work used non-intentional procedures, also known as 'systematic chance operations' and three types of deterministic procedures: 'translation' of musical notations into words and reciprocally the translation of words into musical notations; acrostic reading-through text selection; and diastic reading-through text selection. As Mac Low explains in his essay 'Poetry and Pleasure' (1999), both the acrostic and diastic procedures utilise a source text and a seed text. In the '*acrostic* reading-through text-selection methods' (largely practised by Mac Low in works written between May 1960 to May 1963): 'the writer reads through a source text and finds successively words, phrases, sentence fragments, sentences, and / or other linguistic units that have the letter of the seed text as their initial letters'.[76] In '*diastic* reading-through text-selection methods', first conceived of by Mac Low in 1963, 'the writer . . . reads through the source text and successively finds words or other linguistic units that have the letters of the seed text in positions that correspond to those they occupy in the seed text'.[77]

Regarding his methods, Mac Low states: 'these methods and others first arose from an attempt to lessen (or even vainly try to do away with) the hegemony of the artist in the making of the artwork'.[78] Mac Low's experiments stemmed from his interest in Zen and Buddhist psychologies and were heavily influenced by his engagement with John Cage's procedural and chance experiments carried out as a means to call into question the artistic ego. Mac Low states:

> Ultimately, the ego in the largest sense . . . is considered to be a kind of temporary illusion consisting of five continually changing 'baskets' [Buddhist skandas] of sensations, impulses, perceptions, emotions, and thoughts – to simplify the matter grossly. They stand in the way of a perception of reality that is somehow selfless.[79]

Mac Low has commented on the 'contempt' or 'dislike' that his work received. He understood the negative reception of his work to arise in part 'from the fact that the artwork is thought *not* to be entirely the work of the individual artist'. This is because 'Whatever may come into it may not be the result of choices – on whatever level – of the artist.' He concluded: 'The dislike may arise from a kind of despair or fear that the "self" – the "subject" – is being intrinsically denigrated.'[80] What Mac Low's texts offer is an indeterminate perceiver-centred experience. Bernstein observes the resistance to interpretation harboured by the work's refusal 'of the normal identification of a "self" (voice, persona, sensibility) *in* the text as expressed or revealed – of writing as confessional or personally expressive'. The 'structurally generated' procedural poem is difficult Bernstein argues: 'one is hard put to "read into" it to recognize a mapping of the author's consciousness or a narrative or a pictorial image'.[81] As such, what emerges in the experiments for Bernstein is 'Not a projection of "self" as a language experience but a discovery of its possibilities in an exteriorized, decentred experience of reading. (The writing of a reading.)'[82]

This decentred experience of reading that circumvents, displaces, and attempts to erase the centrality of the ego is the 'procedural point of view', which Acker claims, in 1972, needs to be privileged. Acker's early exercises can be read in the context of Mac Low's procedures, particularly the experiments carried out in his extensive volume *Stanzas for Iris Lezak*, published in 1971, just one year before Acker wrote her exercises. In 'An Afterword on the Methods Used in Composing & Performing *Stanzas for Iris Lezak*' Mac Low sketches out the various methods that generated his acrostic-stanzaic chance poems. He comments that one of the most personal aspects of the volume is 'the variety of source texts'[83] that contain almost everything Mac Low had been reading from May to October 1960. 'Call Me Ishmael', a poem that occurs early in the volume, is exemplary of Mac Low's practices in *Stanzas*. The poem's title is both the opening three words of Herman Melville's *Moby Dick* (1851) and an evident reference to Charles Olson's 1947 work of experimental literary criticism, *Call Me Ishmael*. Mac Low's short poem takes the statement 'Call Me Ishmael' as the seed phrase and extracts words from the first paragraph of *Moby Dick*:[84]

Circulation. And long long
Mind every
Interest Some how mind and every long

Coffin about little little
Money especially
I shore, having money about especially little

Cato a little little
Me extreme
I sail have me an extreme little

Cherish and left, left,
Myself extremest
It see hypos myself and extremest left,

City a land. Land.
Mouth; east,
Is spleen, hand mouth; an east, land.[85]

The procedure here is clear. The first letters of each of the words of the seed phrase 'Call me Ishmael' are taken to structure the lines, so that vertically the first letters of each stanza repeat the letter sequence of the seed phrase: 'C M I'. Tyrus Miller remarks that Mac Low's practice of 'reading through' of other texts via syntactic constraints has the effect of 'expanding the paragrammatic matrix formed by the words of the title or other "seed phrase"'.[86] This poetic practice of 'reading through' and the resulting experimental assemblage is similarly important to an understanding of Acker's early exercises as precursors to her later experimental practices in *Don Quixote*, which are explored in Chapter 3 as embodying a new non-procedural form of writing-through.

The first exercise in Acker's series of experiments titled 'Homage to LeRoi Jones', dated Fall 1972, takes LeRoi Jones's short story 'The Alternative' (1967) as the source text. Comprised of five experimental stanzas, each stanza has as its source text a paragraph of the first five paragraphs of the original literary work. The sequence of the experimental stanzas follow the order of the paragraphs. The exercise opens with the complete opening line of the text, excised and cited as the seed line:

"the leader sits straddling the bed, and the night, tho innocent,
blinds him."
leader bed night
leader bed night innocent   him
sits blinds
straddling innocent
the the and the   tho
flesh. lover man. man blood
who flesh. lover we man. man me who blood.
our. our sweating remembering. old. old your.
our. our here where now sweating remembering. old. old your only.
is. sit. find. am
is. marched sit sweating remembering. find am
and
bed canopy.
straddling bed heavy velvet canopy. homemade under.
sits.
sits straddling.
the a.

the a the the.
the for a through the at the.
door breeze velvet opening.
door breeze which not other heavy velvet opening.
velvet which not other heavy.
opening will come   hung.
each yellow their. younger. impromptu. dead
each thread face smell himself yellow glasses fear their exposure.
Death. Death. they younger students screaming. impromptu. dead
themselves.
rubbed. run.
rubbed against with at. run by screaming. tho. tho.
a or and.
the. a.[87]

The poetic is constructed through a practice of excision and reduction of the prose text. Acker does not make a set procedure for her practice evident anywhere in her notes, as Mac Low did so explicitly in his poetics. Nevertheless, a comparison with the original source text yields insight into Acker's experiment as a form of what might be termed here a method of 'minimalist expansion'. Such a term intentionally points to the paradox, and dialectic, of a simultaneous reduction and non-grammatically centred expansion. Accumulation in Acker's poetic lines is paradoxically bound to reduction and dispossesses the line of a fixed meaning rather than generating fixed meaning. The first paragraph of 'The Alternative' reads as follows:

> The leader sits straddling the bed, and the night, tho innocent, blinds him. (Who is our flesh. Our lover, marched here from where we sit now sweating and remembering. Old man. Old man, find me, who am your only blood.)
>   Sits straddling the bed under the heavy velvet canopy. Homemade. The door opened for a breeze, which will not come through the other heavy velvet hung at the opening. (Each thread a face, or smell, rubbed against himself with yellow glasses and fear at their exposure. Death. Death. They (the younger students) run by screaming. Tho impromptu. Tho dead, themselves.[88]

In Acker's exercise the disruption of the original sentence produces new word combinations. Beginning with the simple noun sequence 'leader bed night', Acker offers a series of reconfigurations of the sentence that generate new multiple and indeterminate meanings within a perceiver-centred field. Paratactic groupings such as 'straddling innocent' create new sexual associations not present in the original. New compounds are created through excising 'flesh', 'lover', 'blood', 'door', 'breeze', 'velvet', 'opening' and positioning these nouns in non-linear combinations that produce new possibilities of meaning through inflection. The rhythm of LeRoi Jones's text is heightened in Acker's poetry. Acker's repetition of the plural pronoun 'our' is a gesture of solidarity and community with Jones A new language of desire and sensual pleasure is created in sequences such as 'straddling bed heavy velvet canopy', and 'door breeze velvet opening'. In the first sequences 'velvet canopy' elicits the literal understanding of velvet as a fabric. The latter sequence acquires a multiplicity whereby 'velvet opening' becomes a metonymical erotic pairing.

Acker's experimental practice in 'Homage to LeRoi Jones' embodies both the innovative process of forming new linguistic clusters through dismantling traditional grammatical structures and also exploring the effect of dislocating and grouping linguistic determiners. The extract above includes Acker bringing in sequences of purely structure words, dislocated articles and prepositions: 'the a. / the a the the. / the for a through the at the.' In the third section of the piece, the articles and prepositional accumulations are extended:

> the the. a. a the. the the. and. and but. aw
> the at the. tho with a. in a between the of. there where the
> with the. in and. in and but. aw.[89]

Stein's work on articles provides a productive coordinate here both in terms of her essays and her experimental practice. 'Articles are interesting just as nouns and adjectives are not', Stein declares in 'Poetry and Grammar'. She continues:

> And why are they interesting just as nouns and adjectives are not. They are interesting because they do what a noun might do if a noun was not so unfortunately so completely unfortunately the name of something. Articles please, a and an and the please as the name that follows cannot please.[90]

The pleasure of the article then resides in its lack of a referent and a fixed meaning, but also in its capacity to generate opacity. For Stein the indeterminacy of the article is its vitality: 'an article remains as a delicate and a varied something and any one who wants to write with articles and knows how to use them will always have the pleasure that using something that is varied and alive can give'.[91] Defamiliarising articles removes the words 'the', 'a' and 'an' from their functions as denotations or markers for a proceeding defining clause or phrase. Articles, prepositions, and conjunctions are always subordinated in traditional grammar structures. As such, the clusters of articles, prepositions, and conjunctions are more powerful when the aim of an experiment is opacity, as they are not fixed to any specific referents. Opacity functions in Acker's experiments to empower conventionally subordinated grammatical elements, giving rise to a radical politics of experimental composition.

Stein composes lines in which the article is given autonomy in 'Bernard Faÿ' (1929). The piece begins: 'A is an article. / They are usable. They are found and able and edible. And so they are predetermined and trimmed.' Stein's opening statement positions the article in place of the noun: 'A is an article.' She allows the articles free play in her composition, anticipating her later essay 'Poetry and Grammar':

> When this as a tree when this with this a tree.
> Night with articles.
> Alight with articles.
> A is an article. The is an article.
> A and the.
> There is hope with a. There is hope with the. A and the
> Articles are a an and the.
> When this you see remember me.
> An article is an and the
> A man and the man
> A man and a man and the.
> An a man and the.[92]

Whilst Stein disrupts conventional grammar by repositioning the article in such a way that the article assumes equivalent status to the noun 'man' ('A man and a man and the'), an experimental act that both empowers the article and disempowers the noun ('man'), Acker's line compositions are entirely devoid of nouns and verbs. In Acker's work the article affords abstract clusters. The combination of articles, prepositions, and conjunctions, in fragments punctuated with periods, serves to create a new mode of abstract linguistic sequence. Acker's article compositions break entirely with classical grammar structures. Instead, an abstract spatial practice is generated through the combination of articles, conjunctions, adverbs, and prepositions: 'tho with a. in a between the of. there where the / with the. in and.' In each of these compositions the words become performative, each component of language maintains its integrity and autonomy. Devoid of nouns and verbs, and not subsumed into the traditional subject predicate clause, conjunctions are not relegated to a subsidiary position. For instance, 'tho' remains a connecting word and is not diminished by that to which it refers. In the same vein the preposition 'with' accompanies 'a', though 'a' does not diminish the authority of 'with' as a concrete noun following it would. Conversely, the article 'a' is not determined by a noun, and the same can be said of 'the' in the pairing 'with the'. The preposition 'between' is between 'a' and 'the' and 'in' positioned in such a way that it performs inclusion at the beginning of the sequence in which it is placed. The abstract composite line in this way gestures towards a new language created by extracting words that are determined by nouns and verbs but, once alone, are not determined by any referent from their classical grammatical contexts.

Acker's exercise is a homage to LeRoi Jones, in its redoubling and repetition of the text in a new form. As with Mac Low's procedural poems, Acker's practice is in Bernstein's words 'the writing of a reading' (Mac Low's procedural works too are homages). Acker highlights the musicality of Jones's text, and the political impulse of Jones's work. Writing in 1972, reclaiming LeRoi Jones's avant-garde writing through new avant-garde experimentation is both an aesthetic and political gesture that positions the concerns of the Civil Rights Movement in Acker's present. The exercise is also itself a performance of the 'homage' referred to in the fifth paragraph of Jones's story: 'Martyrs. Dead in an automat, because the boys had left. Lost in New York, frightened of the burned lady, they fled into the streets and sang their homage to the Radio City.'[93] The final lines of Acker's exercise reads:

```
                    are automat frightened sang
    I buses of they recognized because of their
    have from sight        in the the homage
                until       in boys burned to
                the                    lady the
    "lost in New York, frightened of the burned lady, they fled
    into those streets and sang their homage to Radio City."
```

Acker's experiment in its expansion and lengthening of the text through repetition is a form of defamiliarisation. The text used as a visual field opens up a space of negation. Shklovsky understood defamiliarisation to create 'a special perception of the object – *it creates a "vision" of the object instead of serving as a means for knowing it*'.[94] Acker's exercise can be read through the prism of Shklovsky's idea of vision. Acker's experiment reads Jones's text and offers a new text as a vision of the original, displacing knowledge and giving precedence to vision. Read in conjunction with Lyn Hejinian's pivotal essay 'The Rejection of Closure' (1983), Acker's experiments emerge as open texts. 'In the "open text"', Hejinian claims, 'all the elements of the work are maximally excited.'[95] By comparison, the '"closed text" is one in which all the elements of the work are directed towards a single reading of it'.[96] 'Open to the world and particularly the reader', the open text 'invites participation, rejects the authority of the writer over the reader and thus, by analogy, the authority implicit in other (social, economic, cultural) hierarchies'. For Hejinian, the 'open text' 'speaks for writing that is generative rather than directive', and 'often emphasizes or foregrounds process'.[97] As Bernstein observes, Hejinian's work on the 'open text' is comparable to 'a critique of the Faustian idea to possess knowledge'.[98] Vision in Acker's work runs counter to this Faustian desire.

Discussing her work 'My Life', Hejinian states 'whether the form is dictated by temporal constraints or by other exoskeletal formal elements', the impression that the work gives is that 'it begins and ends arbitrarily and not because there is a necessary point of origin or terminus, a first or last moment'.[99] The implication of the work for Hejinian is that 'the words and the ideas (thoughts, perceptions, etc. – materials) continue beyond the work'. Acker's exercises too possess this arbitrary element. Acker takes just sections, often the opening sections of Jones's works, and ends the exercises with no evident intent. Hejinian poses the question: 'Can form make the primary chaos, (the raw material, the unorganized impulse and information, the uncertainty, the incompleteness, vastness) articulate, without depriving it of its capacious vitality, its generative power?' Extending this enquiry Hejinian asks 'Can form go even further than that and actually generate potency, opening uncertainty to curiosity, incompleteness to speculation, and turning vastness into plenitude?' For Hejinian the answer is a resounding 'yes'. She claims this is the very 'function of form in art', and concludes by asserting 'Form is not a fixity but an activity.'[100] Such activity is found in Acker's exercises. The procedural form anchors the work as an experiment, and the nature of the works as 'exercises' highlights the active, processural aspect of Acker's experiments. The procedural form in Acker's work is generative of the text and creates the textual conditions for the various transformations that Hejinian points to: uncertainty to curiosity, incompleteness to speculation, and vastness into plenitude.

The subsequent exercises perform readings of Jones's 'Now and Then' (1967), and 'Neutrals: The Vestibule' (the opening chapter of *A System of Dante's Hell*, 1963). The latter employs a slightly different procedural technique. The cited line that appears in the same position as the seed phrase in the first exercise is in fact the final line from 'Neutrals: The Vestibule'. It reads: 'I hung out all night with some Italians.' Acker's exercise takes the opening paragraphs of the chapter and writes a poetic sequence that selects words to form sequences that offer a reading and a transformation of the original text. The opening paragraph of Jones's text reads:

> But Dante's hell is heaven. Look at things in another light. Not always the smarting blue glare pressing through the glass. Another light, or darkness. Wherever we'd go to rest. By the simple rivers of our time. Dark cold water slapping long wooden logs jammed 10 yards down in the weird slime, 6 or 12 of them hold up a pier. Water, wherever we'd rest. And the first sun we see each other in. Long shadows down off the top where we were. Down thru grey morning shrubs and low cries of waked up animals.[101]

Once again, Acker's poetic experiment expands the text through repetitions, dismantling, and re-formation:

> is
> hell heaven.
> is   But
> Look another
> Look at in another
> things another light.
> the smarting blue the or the simple of our Dark cold long
> wooden 10 the weird 6 or 12 of a
> Not always the smarting blue through the Another or
> Wherever the simple of our Dark cold long wooden jammed 10
> down the weird 6 or 12 of up a

or to By of slapping down in or of up
or Wherever to By of our slapping jammed down on or
of hold up
d go to rest. slapping jammed hold
light darkness. rivers time. water logs yards slime them
pier.
wherever in. down off where Down thru up
wherever And the other in. down off the where Down thru
and of
d rest. see down were. waked
Water sun shadows top morning shrubs cries animals
Water we'd sun we each shadows top we morning shrubs
cries animals
first other long Long down down grey low waked up
Seeing.

Steve McCaffery conceives of Mac Low's procedures as manifesting 'a context of a reading that is redoubled through a writing', arguing that '[t]he texts themselves are revealed to be secretions from a prior text that become available to reading only when passed back through a further act of writing'. On this premise, McCaffery argues that the poems 'thus appear as *a suppressed tendency* within another text'.[102] A comparable form of rewriting is at work in Acker's early exercises. Acker retains the capitalisation of the original text. In the excised and nonlinear poetic compositions, the instances of capitalisation often appear in the middle of the line. The effect is a visual decentring and turbulence that voices in form the turbulence of Jones's text, an early instance of Acker using syntactic disruption to create radical forms. In her rewriting, of 'Neutrals: The Vestibule', isolated prepositions proliferate the text 'down', 'up', 'to', 'thru', 'off', compounding the instability. The paratactic positioning of the prepositions with perspectival adjectives 'long', 'low', and kinetic verbs 'slapping jammed hold', 'hold up', 'slapping down', 'see down', and 'waked up' lends physicality to the new abstracted text and performs the opening lines 'Look at in another / things another light.' The isolated 'Seeing' speaks a new perception.

Writing asystematically

'MURDERERS-CRIMINALS JOIN SUNLIGHT' (1972) explicitly designates a procedure at the outset: 'Create Music Through Repetitions of Own Sounds "We Discuss Cats."' The lines that follow

are structured through sound. Rather than writing through a source
text this first exercise in a series of six repeats the concept of 'homage' and generates language through phonetic play, assonance, and
alliteration:

> homage is is abortion is delight is delectation is trial is
> annoyance is is life is a way
> abortion delight is ferry fur way is a way wage is
> reaction no is no is not a
> is abortion
> is delight reaction
> live quietly is
> red suns means pollution[103]

Non-linear associative connections are made between words in the
textual field through alliteration, assonance, and repetition. The
repeated 'is' creates anxiety, which is further heightened by the violent alliteration of 'd', and the discord between this alliteration and
the conventional fixed referents for 'delight' and 'delectation'. Acker
creates a perceiver-centred work whereby the generation of meaning
in the work is dependent on the reception of the work by the reader.
The repetition of words in different paratactic contexts destabilises
any fixed meaning. Combinations such as 'ferry fur' and 'way wage',
and later 'purr plants', create disjunctive relations based on alliteration and assonance that pair words that have no associative meanings. Such pairings create an impermeability that disinherits the text
of grammatically centred meaning and shifts the reader's attention
to form.

'Writing Asystematicaaly',[104] the third in the series, dated Fall 1972,
is also subheaded 'MURDERERS-CRIMINALS JOIN SUNLIGHT'
and shows Acker moving towards experimenting with the longer line.
The title points to the idea of writing not structured according to a
system or method:

> grap spling to I whatsit plap in 4 I U I O U
> I O U A
> flight to my brain brain of us all. grab ap no comet sank
> sarp cosmos space   upon   space   stars blink out deep blue
> no thing   sliversilver   revile   turn upon itself amino
> acids medicine junkup red silver twine sluck an explosion!
> (a million pears) red freak balls crap cry out comets

kiss on platinum cats fly   in grace   stoned   we're stoned
wiiiink lap brain openings brainscaredflats brain telep jetliner
747 staircases wind bottles colors booze oose the liver
noise returns now we fright no up down swirl colors
oscillate flit murker crap instant refly all in cor p   p t
p t p t p t p tu   teat no breast – planet   I am Fur
yap in set plant wide tur race flames   buildings flame
sapling   I[105]

The exercise is valuable in revealing Acker experimenting with
neologisms, non-referential language, innovative compound words,
and letter sequences: techniques of illegibility that are precursors
to the instances of illegibility that permeate *Blood and Guts in
High School.* Such antiabsorptive experimental strategies function
in Acker's work to create languages that run counter to ordinary
language. 'MURDERERS-CRIMINALS JOIN SUNLIGHT' corre-
sponds in part to the early radical formalist works of Mac Low such
as 'H U N G E R- ST r i kE', written in 1936, first published in 1968.
Written at the age of sixteen, 'H U N G E R- ST r i kE' experiments
with asymmetry, repetition, and the use of neologisms:

ston ston tont tont ston stant stont stint stit
    Hi stonet stont stit
stit stlit stlod stlott stlit stlodstlott
   stloff stlow slow slow slowly
slow   slow   slowbly
  s l a b l y s l o w l y
s l o w b l y[106]

Neologistic play and language distortion draws attention to the materiality of language. Mac Low transforms the word through additions
and subtractions of letters. The breaking down of the word slow(ly)
in the numerous configurations across the lines is performative, the
metamorphosis occurs 'slowly'. This effect is intensified by the spacing of the letters of the three words 's l a b l y s l o w l y s l o w b l y'.
Whilst the referent is displaced through linguistic morphing, meaning
emerges in the form and structure of the lines. The disconcerting sud-
den emergence of the exclamation 'Hi' breaks through the metamor-
phosing series of variations on the word 'slow' and draws attention
not simply to the surrounding words and their gradual transformation

but also to its impact as an interpellative interruption. The intervention as a point of textual rupture, experienced by the perceiver as an interruption, illuminates the indeterminate continuity of the language series being created. The sixth writing experiment of Acker's series is titled 'Transformation of Sentences'. The exercise continues Acker's neologistic play and the use of longer lines. The poem opens:

> ꓳ A
> O A   O an 10 black scarass marriage I high bolster
> O AI U O as I par I as into light see k source   A after
>   knives floaton junk children make the I join[107]

The failure of parts of the writing to correspond to one another heightens the attention to language. The poetic 'I' has no fixed identity and shifts from pronoun to object. Acker's early exercises disrupt any sense of a cohesive poetic or textual 'I'. These experiments are important precursors to Acker's later works, as they reveal the methods by which Acker displaces the self through experimentation.

Content is also signified through form in 'Entrance into Dwelling in Paradise'. Acker practices a form of what Craig Dworkin terms 'strategic illegibility'[108] through experimenting with a manual typewriter. The exercise, written with a manual typewriter, opens with a citation from Chapter 36 of *The Arabian Nights*:

> the gate was like a great hall and over walls and
> roof ramped vines with grapes of many colors; the red
> like rubies and the blacks like ebonies; and beyond it
> lay a bower of trellised boughs growing fruits single
> and composite, and small birds on branches sang with
> melodious recite,
> and the thousand-noted nightingale shrilled with her
> varied shright; the turtle with her cooing filled the site;
> the blackbird whistled like human wight and the ring-dove
> moaning a drinker in grevious plight.[109]

The sumptuous lyrical description is synchronised with the internal rhyme, gesturing to and signifying the harmony of nature in the Garden of Pleasure that Nur al-Din and Anis al-Jalis enter.[110] Following this citation Acker takes the sentence 'the trees grew in perfection all edible growths and', and repeats the sentence in a visual form that creates a textual declivity (Figure 1.1). The first three instances of the repeated sentence edge toward the margin of the page, each line is given a much greater indentation than the previous line. Yet these lines remain legible. The following four lines are rendered increasingly illegible by Acker's practice of writing over the words with the manual typewriter. The visual effect produced by this practice is a textual congestion, brought about by the constraints of the right hand margin of the material page. There is not enough space for words on the page when pushed to the edges by Acker's practice. The clogging of letters in the overwritten words creates a verbal blockage that renders the words unreadable. This practice of illegibility runs counter to the idyllic image of the trees growing in perfection and the organic richness of the 'edible growths' in the original text. In Acker's text the hard materiality of the word defies organic decomposition. The conjunction 'and', which in the unaltered line indicates continuation and abundance, is negated in Acker's writing strategies, becoming instead an opaque mark of excess and further textual pollution.

For Acker, the manual typewriter enables the manipulation of form. New textual conditions are produced by the innovative use of the page as a visual field in which the form generates a meaning that is not compliant with the words' referents. In 'Entrance into Dwelling in Paradise' the opening source text is further distorted through grammatical disruption:

and the thousand-noted blackbird fruited all manner
    the turtle with her cooing blossomed the violet
      the blackbird whistled gars the loveliest
      cheeks   the ring-dove were all blush with
and   despite
and
the fruits which what manner of   the entrance into
sweet water, cool and pleasant, this. no manner
of
and into wine quench in me anguish what really
reality is what paradise is Nixon Wins Biggest Landslide in History what paradise is One Million People Die
what para-equal will
how then how slippery how viole(n)t how
cryful hop blood hill murder hons squinch the

1.

the gate was arched like a great hall and over walls and

roof ramped vines with grapes of many colors; the red

like rubies and the blacks like ebonies; and beyond it

lay a bower of trellised boughs growing fruits single

and composite, and small birds on branches sang with

melodious recite,

and the thousand-noted nightingale shrilled with her

varied shright; the turtle with her cooing filled the site;

the blackbird whistled like human wight and the ring-dove

moaning a drinker in grievous plight.

the trees grew in perfection all edible growths and
        the trees grew in perfection all edible growths and
            the trees grew in perfection all edible
            growths and the trees grew in perfection all
                edible growths grew in perfection
                    all edible growths grew in
                                perfection all
                                edible growths and

and the thousand-noted blackbird fruited all manner
        the turtle with her cooing blossomed the violet
            the blackbird whistled gars the loveliest
        cheeks   the ring-dove were all blush with
and   despite

and

the fruits which what manner of   the entrance into

sweet water, cool and pleasant, this. no manner

of

and into wine   quench   in me   anguish   what really

reality is   what paradise is   Nixon Wins Biggest Land-

slide in History   what paradise is   One Million People Die

what para-equal will

how then   how slipp ry   how viole(n)t   how

cryful hop blood hill murder hens squinch the

Figure 1.1   Kathy Acker, 'Entrance to Dwelling in Paradise'
(1972) (showing Acker's experiment with a manual typewriter).
Kathy Acker Papers, David M. Rubenstein Rare Book &
Manuscript Library, Duke University.

musicians to exquisite temperance burn a
fire buildings magazines earlier the library the trees refuse
the camphor-apricot the almond-apricot the apricot
Khorasani

The reordering of the text divests the original text of its lyricism, breaking the text up and reconfiguring the words to imbue the text with anxiety and discordance. The contemporary narrative infiltrates the source text, existing on the page in sharp contrast to the utopian images of paradise. The phrase 'what paradise is' is trapped between Nixon's landslide, which oppressively spills performatively from one line to the next through the fracture and the run-on of the word, and the headline 'One Million People Die'. 'Violet' aggressively turns to 'viole(n)t' and images emerge accordingly from the almost coherent phrases 'blood hill murder' and 'burn a / fire buildings magazines'. Towards the middle of the exercise the words form the source text 'the and trellished arched ebonies; birds edible composite, / fruits like red growing and the great recite edible grew' are handwritten over by the words 'THE ENTRANCE INTO PARADISE'. The handwritten phrase bars the source text and the exercise then moves into a continuous stream of prose that fuses life writing, politics, and paragrammatic play. These experiments with the visible surface of writing predate and call to mind the later scatter poems of Susan Howe,[111] as well as the illegibility of experiments such as Bernstein's *Veil* (1987).

'Getting in on the Act': *The Burning Bombing of America* (1972)

Acker's 1972 novella, *The Burning Bombing of America: The Destruction of the U.S.* might be situated as a transitional text between her early writing exercises and her experimental novels (Acker's 1973 work *Rip-off Red, Girl Detective* is usually considered her first novel).[112] The original manuscript of the text is accompanied by a note by Susan Orlofsky. In it, Orlofsky explains that Acker gave her the manuscript in 1972 but that it sat in storage until 1999, when it was rediscovered.[113] As Amy Scholder observes, *The Burning Bombing of America* was written after Pierre Guyotat's work of poetic prose, *Eden, Eden,*

Eden.[114] Dated November 1968–April 1969, Guyotat's work is an important precursory experimental prose piece to Acker's novella. In *Eden, Eden, Eden*, Guyotat breaks conventional language structures. The text consists of a single sentence that continues for 270 pages punctuated by commas, colons, semi-colons, and hyphens.[115] It begins with a slash. The critical reception of *Eden, Eden, Eden* focussed on the violence and what was considered to be the obscenity of the book. Steven Barber offers a précis of the novel's history in his Introduction to the Creation books edition published in 1995. The French Ministry of the Interior deemed the book 'pornographic', banning it upon its publication by Editions Gallimard in 1970. The book continued to be banned for eleven years.[116] Yet the significance of Guyotat's work was recognised widely by writers and thinkers such as Roland Barthes, Jacques Derrida, Simone de Beauvoir, Michel Leiris, Jean-Paul Sartre, Marguerite Duras, Michel Foucault, Alain Robbe-Grillet, and Philippe Sollers, many of whom were in the *Tel Quel* group. *The Burning Bombing of America* ushers in a clear engagement with the cultural politics of the post-war French intellectual theorists and writers, particularly those associated with the influential French-Moroccan weekly publication, *Tel Quel*, founded in 1957 by François Mauriac Sollers. One of the other five founders of *Tel Quel*, Jene-René Huguenin, stressed the significance of poetry to the grouping's wider concerns. As Danielle Marx-Scouras remarks, Huguenin

> recognized that it was not just a question of returning to poetry – a genre that had been neglected in the postwar years – but, more important, of transcending the traditional generic distinctions of prose and poetry and looking for the poetic dimension in the novel and essay.

It is this perspective on the poetic, Marx-Scouras observes, that was to become one of the legacies of *Tel Quel*: 'In time, it was to assume linguistic, philosophical and political dimensions thanks to the pioneering work of Roman Jakobson, Denis Roche, Bataille, Kristeva, Pleynet, and other *Tel Quel* affiliates.'[117] For Acker, it was Guyotat's work on language and the body that was particularly remarkable. In conversation with Ellen G. Friedman in 1993, she stated:

> I admire Pierre Guyotat because he's very much interested in the body as text. This business of 'When I write I masturbate.' Erotic texts at

their best – I don't mean pornographic, which is something else – are very close to the body; they are following desire.[118]

Acker's later work that gives voice to a language of the body in part has roots in Guyotat's work (indeed, Guyotat produced a text in the early 1970s titled *The Language of the Body*). The distinction that Acker makes in her interview with Friedman, between pornographic texts and erotic texts, is fundamental to an understanding of her works. *The Burning Bombing of America* is an early text that engages with the idea of desire as a form of textual unmaking, which in turn functions as resistance against the external world of America in 1972.

In his 'Preface' to *Eden, Eden, Eden*, Roland Barthes comments that criticism on Guyotat's work 'can find no way of taking hold of this text'. It is not a case, however, of the creation of a fictional world. Barthes argues: 'Guyotat's language must be "entered", not by believing it, becoming party to an illusion, participating in a fantasy, but by writing the language with him in his place, signing it along with him.'[119] The revolutionary capacity of Guyotat's text resides above all in his creation of 'a new element', which is the phrase. According to Barthes:

> Getting in on the language, in the sense of 'getting in on the act', is possible because Guyotat produces not a manner, a genre, a literary object, but a new element . . . this element is the *phrase*: substance of speech with the qualities of a fine cloth or foodstuff, a single sentence which never ends, whose beauty comes not from what it refers to (the reality towards which it is supposed to point) but from its breath, cut short, repeated, as if the author were trying to show us not a series if [sic] imaginary scenes, but the scene of language, so that the model of this new mimesis is no longer the adventure of some hero, but the adventure of the signifier itself: what becomes of it.[120]

For this reason Guyotat's writing, Barthes claims, 'constitutes (or ought to constitute) a sort of eruption, a historical shock'. For Barthes, Guyotat's experimental practice is predicated on the relation between language and lust: 'not the former expressing the latter, but the two bound in a reciprocal metonymy, indissoluble'. Language and desire then are held, through this metonymical alliance, in an interdependent relation in the text.

Guyotat's work is a fierce retort to the horrors of the Algerian war. The work is prefaced by a statement written in Tamashek, one of the North African languages spoken in Algeria. It reads 'And now, we are no longer slaves.' The addressee is not apparent. To most of Guyotat's readers in 1970, who most likely would have been unfamiliar with Tamashek, the statement is unreadable. Guyotat's text then announces its unreadability at the outset, as well as its connection to Algeria, and couples unreadability with emancipation. The work ends with a comma, signalling its inexhaustibility. The final lines are paradigmatic of the work as a continuous whole:

> stuck into sand ; breathless tying poles under camels' bellies
> : gust of wind driving back, lifting up sand, against growing
> darkness ; rain, carried in columns from beneath accelerated
> throbbing of Venus, splashing, icy ; boy pushing woman under
> shelter ; wool soaked by streams of heated water from folds
> of clothing tangled over breasts, bleeding red onto body of
> baby dozing under arch — jewels tinkling against medal — of
> two torsos touching ; akli, abscesses riddled by driving rain,
> digging, on knees, into sand, beneath belly of female camel
> ; pock-marked arms vibrating, drained of blood, in saturated
> sand ; monkey whining, arms drooping, softened guerba
> knotted around neck, muzzle bloody, member erect, eye
> scrutinizing Venus veiled in violet vapours, treading on
> beheaded vipers ; grease exuded from grass bung, hardening
> ; vortex veering back to Venus,[121]

The content of the work is the form of the work in *Eden, Eden, Eden*, and the foregrounding of the materiality of language is unceasing. Barthes' indissoluble 'reciprocal metonymy' is evident in this final section. Every word in *Eden, Eden, Eden* is charged with a linguistic physicality. In phrases such as 'stuck into sand', 'carried in columns', 'soaked by streams', 'two torsos touching', 'saturated sand', 'Venus veiled in violet vapours', and 'vortex veering back to Venus', alliteration has a performative function. Similarly, in phrases such as 'softened guerba', through the aural form of the word, the adjective softens the noun, so that the adjective does not qualify the noun, so much as it touches the noun and works upon it in a manner that is non-referential, yet sensual. The pulse of the work is driven by the performative use of punctuation. Semi-colons, standing alone, become hard, tactile linguistic matter. The aesthetic performativity of word clauses such as 'grease exuded from grass bung, hardening' arises from the material substance of the words, combined with the kinetic affect of the positioning of the comma. In Guyotat's composition imagery is collapsed with the tangibility of language. Through this conflation, desire and abjection are realised. Language becomes the body of the text. Through corporealising language, the material body of the text is able to hold, and yield, desire.

Acker does not match the relentless line of Guyotat's work in the compositional form of her work. *The Burning Bombing of America: The Destruction of the U.S.* is not an act of mimesis, nor is it appropriation. Yet, Guyotat's work was clearly an influence. Acker produces her own innovative composition that moves between desire and disjunction. The text is composed of eleven sections, including 'Communist Aesthetics', 'Communist Story', 'Communist Narration,' followed by two further parts, 'Abstract Essay Collaged with Dreams' and 'Violet Women'. In her teaching notes on William Burroughs, Acker writes down a question: 'Do you see how he can have disjunctions and keep the narration?'[122] The question of disjunction and narration is obviously pertinent to Acker's own work. The opening of the first section resonates with the opening of *Eden, Eden, Eden*. It reads:

> armies defect first in the woods and the polluted lakes the
> cities small towns are covered with the blood of God
>   in the burrows and hidden alleyways of unknown an
> archist criminals buggering and fucking for ages[123]

The imagery of defecting armies, the apocalyptic polluted lakes and sexual excess are elements found in Guyotat's text. Yet the form of the two pieces differs significantly. Guyotat's work begins:

> / Soldiers, helmets cocked down, legs spread, trampling,
> muscles drawn back, over new-born babies swaddled in scarlet,
> violet shawls : babies falling from the arms of women huddled on
> floors of G. M. C. trucks ; drivers free hand pushing back goat
> thrown forward into cab ;[124]

In Guyotat's writing, punctuation moves the narrative. In contrast, Acker omits punctuation, using spaces and the visual field of the page to create disjunction. The depth of focus of Acker's text is more distant than Guyotat's. In *Eden, Eden, Eden* the perspective of the text is perpetually subsumed within the bodily images. In Acker's text the point of view of the narrative shifts. In some instances the view appears universal: 'the paradise of no work we are part of a decaying world or we / are a new society and don't know how to act. past time / mixes with future time'.[125] At other times the narrative perspective is intimate: 'I will try to stroke your / breasts and shoulders breasts that look like mine to let your / hair sweep over my cunt.'[126] The phrase in *The Burning Bombing of America* is often composite of a number of registers. Phrases such as 'can't fuck' are placed within the same section as scholarly statements that voice communist aesthetics, creating in the texts the 'continuous instability' 'nonpermanence'[127] of the procedural point of view. Through techniques of disjunction, Acker develops a textual politics whereby the universal state of decay is aligned with capitalism and American politics, whilst desire and textual intimacy are aligned with socialist politics and aesthetics. Throughout the text there are also self-conscious references to the role of the writer, while other sections refer to the writing explicitly as a form of verbal art. 'Abstract Essay Collaged with Dreams' refers to the form of the writing in its title. Similarly, the narrative 'I' pays homage to literary influences, aligning writing asymmetrically with revolutionary politics: 'I lonely / praise Gertrude Stein Walt Whitman Allen Ginsberg'.[128]

The final section of *The Burning Bombing of America* (titled 'Violet Women') opens with a subsection titled 'Narration of the New World'. Acker's writing embodies a revolutionary feminist politics in the final part of the novella, anticipating her future works: 'the Violet Women are all-powerful and have no power over / anyone else they take care of themselves'.[129] The Violet Women are positioned antithetically to institutions and discourses that promote heternormativity: 'their arm hair curls around / their ankles gold cunt hair runs up their legs grows out of fer / tile star navels psychoanalysis? no. government? no. family? no.'[130] In addition to this rejection of institutions, desire is aligned with overcoming dualism and life form:

B. IS A REVOLUTIONARY BODY WE ARE GOLD TONGUES GOLD HANDS OUTER SPACE DELIGHTS WE GIVE JOY WE GIVE MISERY WE GIVE PLEASURE WE GIVE IMMORTALITY-HEALTH WE ARE ENDLESS MIND-BODY PLEASURE ORGA (NI) SM[131]

The Burning Bombing of America foregrounds Acker's experimental practice, conflating prose with the poetic in a manner that points to the revolutionary aspects of the formal and related political aspects of Acker's involvement with language-centred writing, whilst simultaneously gesturing towards a feminist literary politics. The excerpt above follows a section titled 'Personal Life' in which the narrative voice states: 'to be female wo-man is alone constantly on guard as independent as possible always prepared to be without shelter possibilities of talk a secret language'.[132] Acker's early experiments clearly place her works in the context of the post-war avant-garde groupings in America in the 1970s. The works link the collective struggle of a predominantly male avant-garde to write against the oppressive structures of normative grammar and the struggle of a woman writer to make meaning. These two filaments, each enquiries into meaning-making, are brought together and inflect one another in Acker's works. At the intersections, and within the interstices of these two elemental concerns, multiform experimental writing practices emerge that are the focus of the susequent chapters.

Chapter 2

Collage and the Anxiety of Self-description: *Blood and Guts in High School*

In April 1984 the Pan Books edition of *Blood and Guts in High School Plus Two* was seized by the Customs Department of Wellington, New Zealand, and subsequently classified as indecent. Nine other publications were also requisitioned: four issues of *Penthouse* (September 1983, November 1983, December 1983, and January 1984); *High Low Boom: An Explosives Treatise of Synchronous Historical Duration* by Phillip J. Danisevich; *How to Kill* by Jon Minnery; *Improvised Weapons of the American Underground* (Desert Publications USA); *Field Expedient Methods of Explosives Preparations* (Desert Publications USA), and P.F.I.Q. (*Piercing Fans International Quarterly*, Gauntlet Enterprises USA).[1] Two aspects of Acker's work emerge as key in the decision of the Tribunal to prohibit *Blood and Guts in High School Plus Two*. The report, signed by the Chairman of the Indecent Publications Tribunal, 3 December 1984, draws firstly on the way in which Acker was classified as an author: 'The author of *Blood and Guts in High School Plus Two*, Kathy Acker, has been described by reviewers "as everything from post-punk porn to post-punk feminism".'[2] The report then proceeds to comment specifically on the unreadability of the book, stating that it 'is difficult to read and understand'. The decision statement provides the citation from *Blood and Guts in High School* printed on the back cover of the Pan Edition as a summary of the 'story':

> The story describes a girl locked in a room where twice a day the Persian Slave Trader comes to teach her to be a whore. 'One day she found a pencil stub and scrap paper in a forgotten corner of a room. She began to write down her life . . .'

The documents from the Distribution of Indecent Materials Tribunal Decisions bring to light the relation between the avant-garde composition of the work and the work's classification as indecent. The report deduces: 'The novel purports to be an account of her experiences, almost solely of a sexual nature, written in a disjointed and difficult style, though liberally illustrated with diagrams and sketches.' The board concludes:

> We agree with Mr Simpson when he submits that 'in short the book is considered to be mainly a vehicle for the writer to express and convey her sexual opinions', although we are not certain that younger readers would be attracted to the publication, because of its difficulty of presentation.
>
> The publication seems to have little literary or artistic merit and does place considerable emphasis on sexual description.[3]

Whilst the Chairman's report closes with an assessment of the book in terms of its sexual content and passes judgement on the work's literary merit, the issue of the work's 'disjointed and difficult style', the 'difficulty of its presentation', and the fact that it is an illustrated book are evidently significant factors in the decision to prohibit the work. The original report to which the Chairman's statement refers places substantial emphasis on the book's experimental nature. R. A. Simpson, the Comptroller of Customs, comments: 'This has been a very difficult book to understand.' The synopsis of the book that reappears in the Chairman's report, Simpson takes as indicative of the novel's 'plot'. Assuming the existence of a plot a priori he writes: 'Any semblance to such a plot appears to have been lost in the very erratic and disjointed manner in which it is presented.' He continues: 'Perhaps the author is striving for a new approach or method of social critique but this is also considered to be lost and smothered by the continual sexual diversions which add nothing to the "story."'[4] The Comptroller's comments resonate with the Judicial Officer for the US Postal Service's description of William Burroughs's *Naked Lunch* (1958) in 1962 as 'undisciplined prose, far more akin to the early work of experimental adolescents than to anything of literary merit'.[5] In relation to his condemnation of *Blood and Guts in High School*, Simpson refers to section 11 (2) of the Customs Act that pertains to the literary value of the work, which would exempt a publication from being classified as indecent 'where the publication of any book . . . would be in the interests of art, literature, science, or learning and would be for the public good, the Tribunal shall not classify it as indecent'.[6] In his opinion, the clause could not be considered at all in the case of *Blood and Guts in High School* due to 'the frequency of sexually explicit narrations' that 'detract from any literary or learning merit'.[7]

Literary value in the Comptroller's report is judged solely within the parameters of conventional linear narration and traditional narrative structures. There is a discrepancy between the two reports in terms of the book's possible obscenity. The initial report by the Comptroller implies that the book is deemed obscene partly because the work is considered to be 'of interest to the more prurient readers and probably those in the younger bracket'.[8] The latter statement by the Chairman regards the work to be of little interest to a young audience due to its non-linear structure. The fact that the book contains sexual material does not alone render it indecent. The implication of the Comptroller's critique is that the problematic material considered indecent could be justified if it were intrinsic to a plot or story. The experimental composition of the work, the lack of a plot, and, consequently, the absence of a story to reify and 'redeem' the sexually explicit content then renders the work indecent. In this regard the censorship of Acker's work in 1984 can be compared to the earlier trial of D. H. Lawrence's *Lady Chatterley's Lover* (1928) in 1960. The defence of Lawrence's *Lady Chatterley's Lover* succeeded in overturning the prohibition of the work in the four-day trial, *Regina v. Penguin Books Limited* in 1960 on the grounds of the claim that the sexual content contributed to the book's story. For instance, when interrogated on the subject of the relation of the four-letter words in the book to the work's 'literary merits', Miss Helen Gardner defended Lawrence's use of the word 'fuck' or 'fucking' through reference to the word's place in the context of the book:

> I would say that by the end of the book Lawrence has gone very far, within the context of this book, to redeem the word from its low and vulgar associations, and make one feel it is the only word the character in the book could use.[9]

Gardner further argues that by the end of the book the word had taken on 'great depth of meaning' and therefore the use of it 'is wholly justified in the context of the book'. She clarifies that it is the literary context that vindicates the word: 'I do not mean I think Lawrence was able to redeem the word in usage, I am talking about its usage within the book itself.'[10] Mr Gardiner QC similarly provides a rationale for defending the book in terms of the book's meaning, and on the premise of the work's moral standing: 'This is a moral book because the message, the meaning, the outcome is that two people find an aspect of truth.'[11] By comparison, *Blood and Guts in High School*, an experiment in rejecting conventional forms of meaning-making and traditional models of narration, provides no comparable context, resists character development, and offers no singular meaning. For this reason, the avant-garde nature of the work, which obstructs and challenges denotative structures of meaning, is the key factor in the work being considered to be devoid of literary merit. In confining their assessment of the literary work to the confines of conventional narrative, the Chairman and the Comptroller fail to comprehend *Blood and Guts in High School* in its complexity, and did not recognise and register the new forms of meaning that emerge from the experimental form of the work. The term 'experimental' was defined in the opening pages of this book as the obstruction of normal reading. The failure of the Chairman and Comptroller to understand the work is a negative recognition of the work's resistance, and testament to the book's experimental form. Finally the Comptroller's report further corroborates the bias against avant-garde writing by suggesting there is a connection between a lack of literary value and small press publications. Although the edition of the book under scrutiny in the report is the Pan edition, the Comptroller states disparagingly that the lack of an acknowledgment on the book's back cover 'would tend to add some weight to the writer being mainly involved with "underground publishers"'.[12]

This chapter examines the experimental composition of *Blood and Guts in High School*. It explores the tension between the experimental form and antiabsorptive writing practices, and conventional language structures in the work. There is a conflict between Janey's imprisonment within the symbolic (which leads to her consequent self-objectification) and that which Jean-Jacques Lecercle terms 'the remainder', 'another side to language, one that escapes the linguist's attention',[13] which emerges in Acker's writing experiments. For Lecercle 'the remainder' is the other side to Saussure's *la langue*, it is 'the unconscious emerging into language, speaking the speaker, whether he wanted it or not'.[14] Lecercle argues: 'linguistic exchange is a locus for relations of power'.[15] The notion of the remainder allows a consideration of Acker's innovative practice with regards to relations of power. A number of critics have explored the varying modes of imprisonment and oppression that Janey, the book's teenage protagonist, experiences in terms of her class and gender, but have ignored the significance of the text's experimentalism and the non-organic collagist composition of the work. Janey's failure to make meaning within the symbolic is not synonymous with a similar failure on Acker's behalf to make meaning outside symbolic strictures.

As a means to explore this situation, I develop two principal strands of analysis. Firstly, Acker's work is situated within the context of the feminist movement. Janey's imprisonment within language is then taken up and discussed through relating Acker's work to feminist theory and philosophy of language, two areas of epistemological enquiry that erupted and influenced the cultural scene in the mid-1970s. The notion of an *écriture féminine*, as propounded by Luce Irigaray in *Speculum of the Other Woman* (1974) and Hélène Cixous in 'The Laugh of the Medusa' (1975), is read in conjunction with Denise Riley's recent work on inner speech, language and affect, extimacy, and the autonomy of language.[16] Riley's work raises questions of language and mastery that have yet to be addressed in analyses of Acker's writing. Woman's ontological negation within the symbolic emerges as a central concern in *Blood and Guts in High School*. Through engaging with Riley's theories of language, the chapter addresses the anxiety of self-description that is evident in Janey's narrative and reveals the impossibility of Janey's self-enunciation within the confines of patriarchal language. In light of these reflections, 'the remainder' and the function of the poetic in *Blood and Guts in High School* is examined with specific reference to Acker's practice of *récriture* and her experiments with image, space, and typography. Through an analysis of the typographical innovations of the text, the chapter reveals a mode of *(r)écriture féminine* at work in *Blood and Guts in High School* that is related to the impossibility of the feminine, a peculiar linguistic affect that emerges within the text that presents the unpresentable and gives voice to indeterminacy. Ultimately, *Blood and Guts in High School* in its materiality, experimentation, and artifice speaks a language that Janey, a 'male-centred'[17] subject, cannot.

Being difficult

Blood and Guts in High School has been chosen as the focus of an entire chapter, over Acker's other early writings and experiments that I have discussed in the first chapter, for the scope of its literary, typographical, and formal experimentation. Although the text was first published in 1984, Acker remarked in interview that it was in fact 'a very early book'.[18] Acker copyrighted the work in 1978, and Papyrus Press had published 'The Persian Poems' independently as a small volume in 1972. To acknowledge the prefatory position of *Blood and Guts in High School* within the context of Acker's oeuvre is to recognise the importance of the work's innovation. As Acker stated, at the time of writing *Blood and Guts in High School* she was 'still working through that business about the meaning of textual identity'.[19] The avant-garde configuration of this early work of Acker's is fundamental to an understanding both of her late-modernist textuality and her unique place as a female avant-garde writer.

The original manuscript of *Blood and Guts in High School* reveals the book's status as a collagist artwork. The proofs of *Blood and Guts in High School* are hand set in a lined Citadel Notebook with text and images pasted onto its pages (Figures 2.1 and 2.2).[20] Illustrations are pasted onto the pages between text fragments, the sections titled 'Parents Stink' and 'Outside High School' are assembled from magazine cuttings, and the Janey / Father play scripts are typed separately and pasted into the notebook between the 'Parents Stink' pages. The manuscript is in many places composed of recycled found materials. For instance, the 'Outside High School' title section is pasted on the back of a letter from Ken Dollar dated 1 August 1978. Xeroxes of the 'The Persian Poems' are placed loose in the middle of the book. The original manuscript of 'The Persian Poems' (Figure 2.3) is housed separately to the manuscript of *Blood and Guts in High School* in the archive, in a folder containing the original artwork for the book. The exercises that comprise the poems are written in thick black ink. Acker differentiates the narrative lines 'Janey hates prison'; 'Janey kept on writing'; and 'Janey's all alone in her room. She's learning Persian slowly:' by writing with a pen with a slightly thinner nib. The intentionality of Acker's change of writing instrument is difficult to ascertain, as these lines could well have been inserted in a revision unintentionally with a different pen.

Name_____

_____

_____PROOFS · BLOOD
_____

AND GUTS IN

-HIGHSCHOOL

AMERICAN PAD . . . . HOLYOKE, MASS. 01040

Citadel.
NOTEBOOK

200 SHEETS 11 X 8½ IN. NO..
MEDIUM RULED WITH MARGIN :
4 SUBJECT DIVISIONS

Figure 2.1   Kathy Acker, *Blood and Guts in High School* (1978) original manuscript (front page). Kathy Acker Papers, David M. Rubenstein Rare Book & Manuscript Library, Duke University.

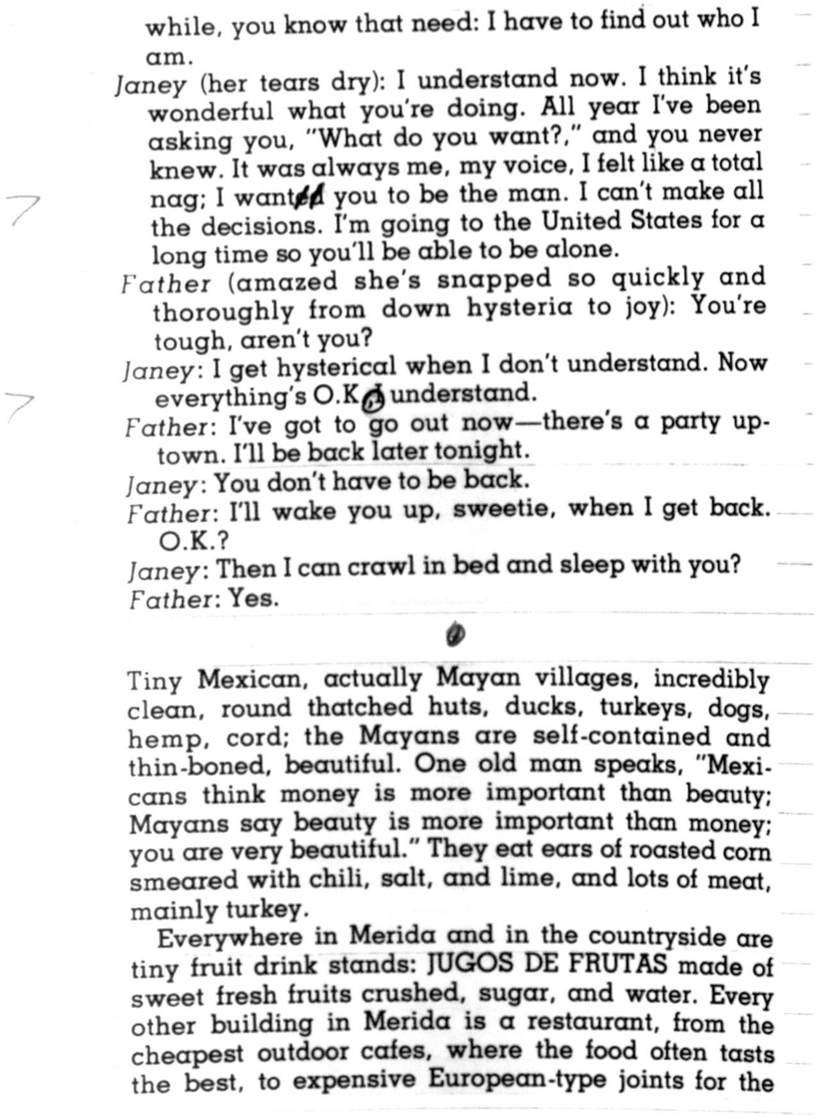

while, you know that need: I have to find out who I am.

Janey (her tears dry): I understand now. I think it's wonderful what you're doing. All year I've been asking you, "What do you want?," and you never knew. It was always me, my voice, I felt like a total nag; I wanted you to be the man. I can't make all the decisions. I'm going to the United States for a long time so you'll be able to be alone.

Father (amazed she's snapped so quickly and thoroughly from down hysteria to joy): You're tough, aren't you?

Janey: I get hysterical when I don't understand. Now everything's O.K. understand.

Father: I've got to go out now—there's a party up-town. I'll be back later tonight.

Janey: You don't have to be back.

Father: I'll wake you up, sweetie, when I get back. O.K.?

Janey: Then I can crawl in bed and sleep with you?

Father: Yes.

Tiny Mexican, actually Mayan villages, incredibly clean, round thatched huts, ducks, turkeys, dogs, hemp, cord; the Mayans are self-contained and thin-boned, beautiful. One old man speaks, "Mexicans think money is more important than beauty; Mayans say beauty is more important than money; you are very beautiful." They eat ears of roasted corn smeared with chili, salt, and lime, and lots of meat, mainly turkey.

Everywhere in Merida and in the countryside are tiny fruit drink stands: JUGOS DE FRUTAS made of sweet fresh fruits crushed, sugar, and water. Every other building in Merida is a restaurant, from the cheapest outdoor cafes, where the food often tasts the best, to expensive European-type joints for the

Figure 2.2   Kathy Acker, *Blood and Guts in High School* (1978) original manuscript (showing cut and paste technique). Kathy Acker Papers, David M. Rubenstein Rare Book & Manuscript Library, Duke University.

111.)

Mem bold

THE PERSIAN POEMS

· · · · · · · · · mes.

	mem. Italic
جانی	Janey
جانی د'ختر اُست	Janey is a girl.
جَهاز سُرخ است	the world is red.
شَب خیاباذ تُنگ است	night is the narrow street
و' کوچه تُنگ	and the narrow side-street.
جانی نُچّهای است	Janey is a child.
جانی نُچّهای گراذ آست	Janey is an expensive child,
و' لی آرزان	but cheap.

("ε" (,) links two entities :) ← mem. italic

mem. ital.

شَب جانی	Janey's night
شَب سُرخ	the red night
شَب جَهاز	night - world
جانی خُراب آست	Janey stinks.

(note: no ezafe)

Figure 2.3   Kathy Acker, 'The Persian Poems' (1972). Page from the original manuscript. Kathy Acker Papers, David M. Rubenstein Rare Book & Manuscript Library, Duke University.

However, the illusion created in the original text is that the two lines told in the past tense are written in a different hand to Janey's, who whilst writing in third person, as is the protocol in grammatical exercises practised by children, writes in the present tense 'Janey is blind', 'Janey's hair', 'Janey's chair', for example.[21] In addition, 'The Persian Poems' have been annotated by Acker in red pen with arrows pointing to various words, and comments on the Persian language such as '(note: no ezafe)' and '(notice exception)'. These notes appear in both the original manuscript for *Blood and Guts in High School* and in the black-and-white published editions of the work by Grove Press and Pan Books, revealing that these inserts in red, that signal another voice independent of Janey and the third person narrator, are not notes for revision but an integral part of the text.

This distinction between the original materials and the final manuscript is most evident in the dream maps. In the original manuscript, dream maps one and two are loose-leaf copies of the originals, which are large-scale works of art. Dream map two is a colour collage (Figure 2.4) measuring 56 inches by 22 inches and is stored in the Kathy Acker Papers as a framed art object. What is diminished in the process of transference and reproduction from the original materials to the published book is a degree of materiality that is significant to an apprehension of the text. The challenge that Acker was confronted with at the time of the book's publication was how to signal materiality in the face of its absence. Materiality in the published version of the manuscript is very different from that of the collage manuscript. Whilst the editors at Grove Press did everything possible to maintain the integrity of the original manuscript in the final published version of the book, through carefully and meticulously reproducing the variations in typography and reproducing the artwork, the materiality of the manuscript of *Blood and Guts in High School* is eroded significantly in the published work. As an experimental writer Acker meets the necessary challenge of the process of book production, working from materials that in their raw form could only ever be exhibited as art. Johanna Drucker, in her rigorous study *The Visible World: Experimental Typography and Modern Art 1909–1923*, defines the 'theme of materiality' for the various avant-garde groups working at the beginning of the twentieth century as 'the self-conscious attention to the formal means of production in literature and the visual arts'.[22] Drucker acknowledges that the practices of those writers and artists associated with Cubism,

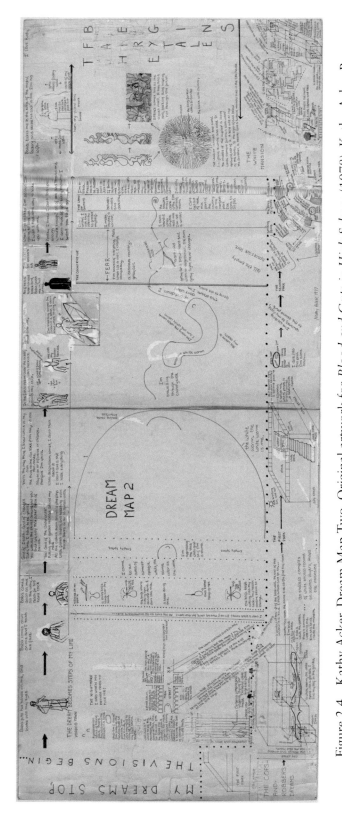

Figure 2.4 Kathy Acker, Dream Map Two. Original artwork for *Blood and Guts in High School* (1978). Kathy Acker Papers, David M. Rubenstein Rare Book & Manuscript Library, Duke University.

Futurism, Dadaism, Nunism, and Vorticism varied widely; yet, Drucker remarks, across avant-garde work in the period 'the insistence upon the autonomous status of the work of art (visual or literary) which veritably defines the founding premise of modernism was premised upon the capacity of works to claim the status of *being* rather than *representing*'.[23]

The idea of materiality gestured to here by Drucker can only be approached as a mode of nostalgia by Acker in terms of reproducing the conditions of production that drove the historical avant-garde. A larger question at stake is the degree to which Acker can resist representation, a question that similarly beset the historical avant-garde at the turn of the twentieth century. In order for the autonomous status of the work of art to be claimed, Drucker observes, 'the materiality of their form had to be asserted as a primary in-itself-condition not subordinate to the rules of imitation, representation, or reference'.[24] The Dadaist medium of photo collage is a central coordinate for the idea of collage, the resistance to imitation, and the violence enacted by the cutting and pasting technique. Acker was affiliated with the Dadaist Fluxus group in the 1960s. The earlier photomontage and collage work of the modernist German avant-garde artist Hannah Höch (1889–1978) offers an illuminating comparison with Acker's work. Höch's work *Schnitt mit dem Küchenmesser durch die letze Weimarer Bierbauchkulturepoche Deutschlands* (1919–20) (*Cut With the Kitchen Knife through the Last Weimar Beer Belly Cultural Epoch of Germany*) uses text and image. The work is an assemblage of a vast number of text and images cut from newspapers, magazines, and other materials. The reference to the kitchen knife in the title of the piece draws attention to the violence of the cut of the knife that slices modern life into pieces and reassembles the images to form a fragmentary vision of the artist's contemporary world. The attack on the false cohesion of reality (constructed by the realist paintings of the nineteenth century) through the cut and the desire to reflect social change were key aims of the Dadaist collage. Höch's work disrupted the codes that marginalised and suppressed women in twentieth-century Germany through the cut and through juxtaposition of images of women, male figures, people in sports, and images of Weimar Germany. Maud Lavin remarks that in her feminist allegory: 'Höch assigns women a catalytic role in the opposition between a revolutionary Dada world associated with Karl Marx and the anti-Dada world of the politically compromised President Friedrich Ebert.'[25] The non-organic materiality of the Dadaist photomontage and collage medium draws attention to the material cut into the whole. Fragmentation and disruption are the result of the cut, which enables the formation of new juxtapositions that offer a perception of reality more faithful to the chaos and heterogeneity of modern life and the revolutionary vision of the artist through non-organic form. The 'theme of materiality' and the disruptive cutting present in the literary collage of *Blood and Guts in High School* are similarly pivotal to Acker's work. The political climate shifted between the moment of the book's composition and the moment of publication, from Carter to Reagan. The increasingly right – wing political climate saw the reaction against the gains of the civil rights and feminist movements. Acker's collagist practice offers a material practice of disruption comparable to Höch's allegory. A central aim of this chapter is to recognise that such a primary materiality must be mediated by the printed page in the process of the book production of *Blood and Guts in High School*. The collage composition and eroded materiality nevertheless remain visible in the printed book, explicitly drawing attention to the book's non-organic status. Here I examine the materiality of *Blood and Guts in High School* as an antigrammatical discourse that runs counter to ordinary language.

The heading of Acker's typesetting notes: 'INSTRUCTIONS FOR PUTTING THIS DAMN BOOK TOGETHER' – which stands alone on its own page in the Citadel Notebook – discloses the anxiety the author experienced in the act of assembling the materials for the publisher. On the following page, under the heading 'DUMMY FOR BLOOD AND GUTS', nineteen very detailed handwritten directions stipulate exactly the way in which Acker wanted the book to be assembled. The first eleven read:

1) TITLE PAGE: typeset
2) page 1 & page 2 – PARENTS STINK: typpset [sic] to line 6 "-ply and crazy when" on page 6 of Xerox. Insert picture 1 in second page of book (original provided)
3) In layout, follow line spacing of manuscript. Will also need proofing.
4) original Merida picture included

5) Insert picture 2 "Merida" as soon as possible after sentence about the Merida marketplace (Zerox p. 18) Insert "my cunt red ugh" picture as soon as possible after same page on page 21 Xerox.

6) picture "cause she wanted to fuck love. . .) insert as soon as possible after CAUSE OF LASHES: THE SURGE OF SUFFERING IN THE SOUL CORRUPTS THE SOUL (Xerox p. 26)

7) Insert YOU ARE THE BLACK ANNOUNCERS OF MY DEATH (as soon as possible <u>before</u> the same phrase on p. 29 of Xerox.

8) Insert picture "And the man" as soon as possible before the same phrase on p. 33 top of Xerox.

9) Insert picture "TURN MY EYES INSANE" as soon as possible before same phrase on p. 37 bottom of Xerox.

10) when a sentence occurs on a separate page such as page 40 of zerox, keep it that way.

11) The dream maps occur immediately after the title page OUTSIDE HIGH SCHOOL. First the small dream map which I only have a lousy Xerox of. Stonehill have the original & they won't give it up. Then the double dream map. I have the original.[26]

Acker's typesetting requirements expose the strict arrangement of text and image and highlight the authorial intentionality present in the book at the level of experimental composition.

Blood and Guts in High School is both an illustrated book and a visual and verbal collage. At a textual level, the work is an experiment in typography. Typographic signification is a fundamental component of Acker's avant-garde practice. This aspect of the book is returned to throughout this chapter, which claims the materiality of the text as a discourse resistant to, and in flux with, linguistic meaning and traditional grammatical structures. The presentation of *Blood and Guts in High School* as a collage and the new relations generated between text and image by the work positions *Blood and Guts in High School* in a lineage of illustrated works by Charles Baudelaire, Stéphane Mallarmé, and Arthur Rimbaud. These avant-garde writers, whom Acker engages with at numerous points in her works, were the progenitors of the avant-garde experiments with text and image at the beginning of twentieth century. Renée Riese Hubert in her study *Surrealism and the Book* (1988) distinguishes between the mimetic approach to book illustration taken by nineteenth-century authors and illustrators and the anti-mimetic approach adopted by avant-garde writers and artists at the turn of the twentieth century. Hubert draws on the work of the Dadaists, as precursors to surrealism:

> The Dadaists in particular – Hans Arp in *Die Wolkenpumpe*, or Francis Picabia in *Poémes et dessins de la fille née sans mere*, Cendrars and Fernand Léger in *La Fin du monde* – sought to break down the order of textual space, the conventions of lettering, and whatever might smack of literary conformism. Pages in their books defied and challenged the reader mainly through the elimination of descriptive and narrative elements that might provide a stable identity for the author or the subject matter.[27]

Hubert's comments on the resistance of Dadaism to narrative conventions illuminate an understanding of Acker's use of illustration and experimental typography in *Blood and Guts in High School*.

On an aesthetic level, a number of Acker's illustrations for *Blood and Guts in High School* bear resemblance to the line drawings of Dada artists. The illustrations that accompany Francis Picabia's *Poémes et dessins de la fille née sans mére* (1918)[28] are one example. Some of the line drawings that illustrate *Blood and Guts in High School* have a more mimetic relation to the text than others, such as the illustration of a vulva that accompanies the text 'My Cunt Red Ugh' (*B&G*, 19). Other instances of illustration create new relations between text and image. The 'Merida' image, that Acker is keen to position as soon as possible after the occurrence of the sentence about Merida in the text, is of a phallus with women's fingers pointing towards it. The text on the previous page reads:

> Everywhere in Merida and in the countryside are tiny fruit drink stands: drinks *jugos de frutas* made of sweet fresh fruits crushed, sugar, and water. Every other building in Merida is a restaurant . . . Merida, the city, is built on the money of the hemp growers who possess one boulevard of rich mansions and their own places to go to. (*B&G*, 13)

Similar unexpected juxtapositions occur with another image of the phallus that Acker refers to in her direction, which is accompanied by a caption which is comprised of a line lifted from Acker's rewriting of

César Vallejo's *The Black Heralds* (1919), 'YOU ARE THE BLACK ANNOUNCERS OF MY DEATH' (*B&G*, 24), and an image of a bound woman titled 'Ode to a Grecian Urn' (*B&G*, 63). In each of these latter instances, unexpected juxtapositions of text and image are integral to the book's feminist critique.

The visual prosody of the dream map in Acker's work often resembles Picabia's image-text aesthetics whereby the text follows the line of the drawing. In Picabia's image 'Polygamie', text is handwritten onto an abstract image that bears resemblance to female genitalia. The words 'VAGiN PRiNTANiER' ('vernal vagina'), 'MORMONS', and 'CALEN DRIER' ('calendar') follows the visual lines of Picabia's images. 'JEUNE ZiBELiNE' ('young sable') appears in the centre of the vulva shaped space. Similar visual and verbal relations occur frequently in Acker's cartography. The first map, 'A Map of My Dreams' (*B&G*, 45; see Figure 2.5) contains a series of images of a bird in flight that Janey is escaping. The lines of Janey's flight are in part composed by verbal language that follow the line of flight, and read 'but the bird keeps following me no matter how well I fly'. A large circle maps out 'black water', the letters of which follow the visual line vertically, letter by letter, and caligrammatically. The line of the image replaces the horizontal linear line of the text. In *Blood and Guts in High School*, there is constant movement from one medium to another that signals the transformative potential of the text at the level of composition. Such mutability and instances of text/image juxtaposition offer numerous sites of interpretation, in which the image inflects the text, and the text, reciprocally, inflects the image. The book fluctuates between simultaneous readings of the visual and verbal, whereby the visual and verbal connect in a referential capacity, such as the image 'And the Man' (*B&G*, 27), the title of which is extracted from Acker's rewritten César Vallejo poem, and non-habitual text–image relations that disrupt normative referential visual/verbal relations. A visual and verbal collage that blurs the boundaries between art object and book, *Blood and Guts in High School* shares with surrealist works such as André Breton's *Nadja* (1928) what Hubert terms a Hegelian 'dialectics of paradox rather than . . . mimesis'. For Hubert, *Nadja*'s 'opposition to logic stems from the rejection of one-track argumentation or clear-cut resolutions'.[29] An early form of surrealist experimentation, collage, Hubert observes, was an 'agent both of subversion

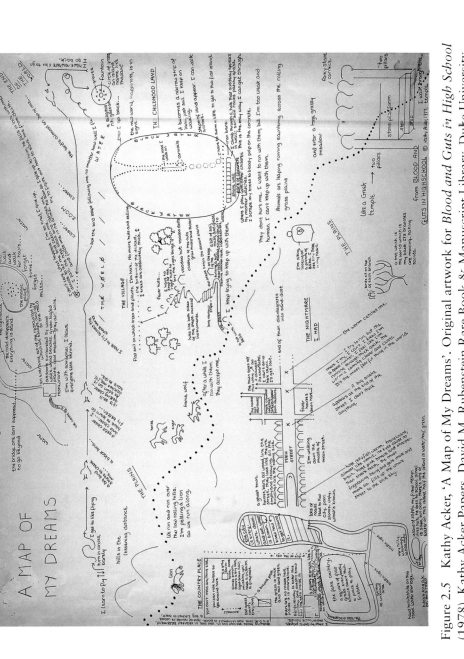

Figure 2.5   Kathy Acker, 'A Map of My Dreams'. Original artwork for *Blood and Guts in High School* (1978). Kathy Acker Papers, David M. Rubenstein Rare Book & Manuscript Library, Duke University.

and of experimentation'. Hubert points to Breton's surrealist manifesto and his attack on the conventions of the novel alongside 'the need of inventing undefined and preferably undefinable genres, of elaborating new languages and techniques capable of fulfilling the revolutionary aims of the movement'.[30] Acker's collage possesses a comparable resistance to linearity, alongside the desire to find new languages for revolutionary means.

Acker's experimental practice in *Blood and Guts in High School*, in the collaged manuscript, both resounds with Dadaist cut-up techniques of the early twentieth century, and the aesthetics of the underground press, magazines, and fanzines that emerged in the 1960s through punk. These small press publications that were improvised, published text and images, often cut and pasted, often creating primitive juxtapositions. Their compositions were reminiscent of avant-garde manifestos of the early twentieth century, and the materials of the publications were cheap paper and printing. This radical small press form went against the grain of what was considered respectable 'literature' and the marketplace, and is most likely what the Comptroller of Customs refers to when he uses the term 'underground publishers'. Acker distributed the artwork for *Blood and Guts in High School* in various forms. For instance, she created a twenty-seven page Xeroxed pamphlet of the artwork for *Blood and Guts* as a present for the artist and small press publisher Sol LeWitt.[31] This handmade book is an example of the 'copy art' medium of punk and post-punk. The materiality of these publications is found in the poor quality paper stock, and ineffective printing. Xeroxing was central to this generation of writers and artists, more than the mimeographed magazines of counterculture.[32] The works were rough copies of originals created by placing the original onto glass. This version of *Blood and Guts in High School* created for Sol LeWitt is primarily a visual collage. The final version of *Blood and Guts in High School* is a visual and verbal collage, in which the visual and verbal are held in a dialectical relation whereby neither form is subordinated to the other, though both verbal and visual prosody are reciprocally disrupted by the other. The visual book created for Sol LeWitt, and 'The Persian Poems', are testament to the mutability of the work. *Blood and Guts in High School* can be dismantled and rearranged in different configurations that maintain their independence as individual and autonomous works. When considering Acker's early experimental collage techniques, Antin's definition of collage is worth bearing in mind: 'the dramatic juxtaposition of disparate materials without commitment to explicit syntactical relations between elements'.[33] Acker's juxtaposition of materials in *Blood and Guts in High School* creates a non-organic textual collage that obstructs linear reading, and disrupts the conventional codes of language, associated by feminist theorists at the time with patriarchal discourse.

(R)écriture feminine

Blood and Guts in High School is a feminist work that should be positioned in the context of second-wave feminism in the 1970s. Acker deflects allegiance to any one strand of feminism and her works, as sites of critical engagement with feminist theory, are all the richer for their resistance to a single feminist model. The theoretical hybridity of Acker's writing offers new pathways for feminist readings. Of her contemporaries Acker singled out Hannah Arendt for offering 'a real tradition of humanism: the melding of precise feeling and reasoning.' She hailed Simone de Beauvoir for using theory 'in order to apprehend, to touch actuality, not vice versa.' For Acker the significance of de Beauvoir's work is that it permits a dialectical site, 'such theory involves the allowance of contradictions.'[34] Of Luce Irigaray the pithy statement 'Theory leads to passion'[35] sufficed to indicate Acker's regard. Here and elsewhere in her essays and unpublished notebooks, Acker shows her knowledge of the French feminist discourses emerging at the time of her writing. In her engagement with feminist theory and other threads of critical theory, Acker was very much a second wave feminist thinker. Discussing feminism in the 1980s with Jean Radford and Juliet Mitchell, Jacqueline Rose recently remarked: 'I think we were of a generation who really believed theory was going to be socially transformative.'[36] Acker was part of that generation. In the same conversation Mitchell and Rose highlight the importance of literature, that, like psychoanalysis, 'allows you to transgress.'[37] The space of literature in Acker's text offers a site of liberty in Rose's sense but also allows for the convergence of conflicting feminist discourses. In Acker's oeuvre a feminist politics of literature emerges that is able to bridge continental and American feminist threads of discourse.

Woman's ontological negation within language and within philosophical and psychoanalytic discourses was a central concern of the
feminisms arising in the post-war period. The question of a feminine
linguistics and the exclusion of the feminine from the symbolic in
Jacques Lacan's *Seminar XX: On Feminine Sexuality* (1975) was the
nucleus of Irigaray's and Cixous's writings in the mid-1970s. Luce
Irigaray understood the notion of *écriture féminine*, feminine writing,
as facilitating the disclosure of feminine desire. Within the masculine
symbolic order, Irigaray claimed in *Speculum of the Other Woman*
(1974), a year before the publication of Lacan's seminar on feminine
sexuality, 'Woman, for her part, remains in an unrealized potentiality
– unrealized at least, for/by herself.'[38] Irigaray apprehends woman's
impossibility and its corresponding relation to her ontological status:
'not only is she secondary to man but she may just as well not be as
be. Ontological status makes her incomplete and uncompletable. She
can *never* achieve the *wholeness* of her form.'[39] The resolution of
woman's aphasic condition for Irigaray resided in the creation of a
language between women.

Cixous called for woman to 'put herself into the text – as into the
world and into history – by her own movement'.[40] Her notion of an
écriture féminine and the impossibility of its realisation within the
symbolic is necessarily bound to woman's impossibility within phallocentric discourse:

> It is impossible to *define* a feminine practice of writing, and this is an
> impossibility that will remain, for this practice can never be theorized,
> enclosed, coded – which doesn't mean that it doesn't exist. But it will
> always surpass the discourse that regulates the phallocentric system;
> it does and will take place in areas other than those subordinated to
> philosophico-theoretical domination. It will be conceived of by sub-
> jects who are breakers of automatisms, by peripheral figures that no
> authority can ever subjugate.[41]

Cixous conceives the impossibility of demarcating women's writing but she does not understand this to be analogous to woman's
disappearance. Cixous's work is important for Acker in carving out
the notion of a language separate to that of phallocentric discourse.
In her 1992 essay on the work of Richard Prince, Acker reveals a
clear affinity with radical feminism: 'The fight against the patriarchal

sexist society is the fight against the refusal to allow contradiction, difference, otherness.'[42] Acker cites *The Newly Born Woman*, understanding Cixous to be concerned with *écriture féminine* as the return of the repressed, 'an explosive return, which is absolutely shattering, staggering, overturning, with a force never let loose before'.[43] Cixous's theorising of a radical form of writing not confined to, or subordinated by, patriarchal discourse is a significant early coordinate for Acker's work.

However, Acker took issue with what has been termed Cixous's and Dworkin's separatism. 'I don't think the problem is with men', Acker told Larry McCaffery. 'Take Cixous's argument against Kristeva, with Cixous saying that our problems have their source in genital difference – so that the fact that men have cocks is what makes them evil.' In this debate Acker positions herself with Kristeva. Remarking that 'Kristeva's argument that the real problem has to do with role models'[44] is compatible with her own thought, Acker makes the point that it is not men but society that is the problem. Kristeva remarked on woman's ontological negation in terms of impossibility:

> a woman cannot 'be'; it is something that does not even belong to the category of *being*. It follows that a feminist practice can only be negative, at odds with what already exists so that we may say 'that's not it,' and 'that's still not it.'[45]

Kristeva's landmark contribution in the 1970s, her doctoral thesis *Revolution in Poetic Language* (1974), addresses language as the primary site of revolution. 'In the twentieth century,' she stated in interview, 'after suffering through fascism and revisionism, we should have learned that there can be no socio-political transformation without a transformation of subjects: in other words, in our relationship to social constraints, to pleasure, and more deeply, to language.'[46] In particular Kristeva understood that it was poetic language that possessed the capacity for revolution.

Blood and Guts in High School is concerned explicitly with, in Hélène Cixous's and Catherine Clément's words, the 'subordination of the feminine to the masculine order'.[47] Yet it is also a response to what Acker viewed as 'the need for narrative and the simultaneous need to escape the prison house of the story'.[48] In *Blood and Guts in High School* Janey is imprisoned both within language and within hegemonic discourses. Crucially, she is incarcerated by her inability to move beyond those discourses because, unlike Acker's later female voices, she is unable to engage with impossibility, a condition of her existence. Like her father Johnny Smith, 'Janey Smith' is a linguistic placeholder, an element of a sentence that is required by syntactic constraints but carries little or no semantic information. Janey is then the signifier of a lack but fundamentally, like Johnny, her male correlative and her father, she exists within the patriarchal world, inscribed within phallocentric discourse. Perhaps the mathematical definition of the term 'placeholder' is as significant as the linguistic one in this instance: a symbol or piece of text used in a mathematical expression to denote a missing quantity or operator. The merger of Janey's identity with the terms that conceptually corral her within language and under the male gaze is shown throughout her narrative. In *Speculum of the Other Woman* (1974) Irigaray explores the denial of feminine identity by an explicitly patriarchal society and the enforced entry of the woman 'in contempt of her sex, into "masculine" games of tropes and tropisms'.[49] Acker explicitly shows Janey's confinement within masculine figurative and metaphorical abstractions of women. In her essay 'Reading the Lack of the Body: The Writing of the Marquis de Sade', Acker addresses the non-existence of woman: 'In the patriarchal society there are no women; there are only victims and male substitutes. And men.'[50] Her assertions resonate with Irigaray's claims: 'Nature is female because, as is the case with women, she does not exist. She does not have existence apart from the gaze which is always male or male-defined.'[51] Acker cites Irigaray directly: 'Of course what matters is not the existence of an object – as such it is indifferent – but the simple effect of a representation upon the subject, its reflection, that is, in the imagination of a man.'[52] Janey's self-definition within the terms that oppress her is evident in the first part of the book. In the theatrical dialogue between Janey and Johnny, Janey states 'I get hysterical when I don't understand' (*B&G*, 12), thus defining herself within what Acker elsewhere describes as the 'restraint-hysteria duality',[53] one of the confining dualisms that pervade Acker's patriarchal society in *Blood and Guts in High School*.

Janey's imprisonment within the symbolic is shown most explicitly in the illustrations that appear early in the book and in her dream maps. Janey's visual language clearly reveals the limitations of her imagination. In an illustration that appears in the section titled 'Outside High School', the figure of the bound woman is directly connected to the female genitals and to the constraints imposed within language and metaphor through its juxtaposition to an illustration of a vulva. Below the female genitals the title reads 'Girls Will Do Anything For Love' and on the opposite page the heading under the bound woman reads 'Ode to a Grecian Urn'. The contours of the vulva reflect that of the tied body. This visual analogy functions to correlate the two images and the reference to Keats's 'still unravished bride of quietness'[54] places the image in a lineage of literary metaphors that constrict female identity. These illustrations have a corresponding poem in the text entitled 'On the desire for love', a rewriting of Keats's 'Ode to Psyche' (*B&G*, 101).

Throughout the narrative, sections cut into the novel reveal an idea of vision and an understanding of the liberating power of the dream world. The differing linguistic registers of such sections encroach upon Janey's narrative. Some resound with Acker's conception of dreams that clearly emerges from Burroughs's work. She stated in a section of her essay 'On Art and Artists' entitled 'William Burroughs's Realism' that Burroughs fought post-bourgeois language with poetry: 'images, dangling clauses, all that lingers at the edge of the unsaid, that leads to and through dreams. As Burroughs has said: without dreams, our desires, especially sexual desires, we will die.'[55] Alex Houen has provided an insightful account of Acker's exploration of dreams in her early work *I Dreamt I Was a Nymphomaniac: Imagining* (1974).[56] David Antin's ideas on dreams are revealing in the context of Acker's work.[57] Antin remarks 'Freud was clearly modernist in his commitment to collage in his dream theory.'[58] Janey writes a letter to her dreams:

> You are the only thing that matters. You are my hope and I live for you and in you. You are rawness and wildness, the colours, the scents, passion, events appearing. You are the things I live for. Please take me over.

She then states: 'Dreams cause the vision world to break loose our consciousness' (*B&G*, 36). Yet 'dreams by themselves aren't enough to destroy the blanket of dullness. The dreams we allow to destroy us cause us to be visions/see the vision world':

> Once we've gotten a glimpse of the vision world (notice here how the conventional language obscures: WE as if somebodies are the centre of activity see what is the centre of activity: pure VISION. Actually the

VISION creates US. Is anything true?) Once we have gotten a glimpse
of the vision world, we must be careful not to think that vision world is
us. We must go farther and become crazier. (*B&G*, 37)

The parenthetical intervention in this passage announces another
narrative voice that critiques Janey's assumptions and draws attention to the discursive limitations of both conventional language and
Janey's corresponding restricted consciousness. The prioritising of
the subject is rejected by this voice, and vision is given precedence.
From this stems the epistemological doubt 'Is anything true?' The
close of parenthesis places us back within Janey's narrative.

Janey's dream maps, whilst introducing an innovative visual
device and spatialising the unconscious, in fact reveal the limitations of Janey's psychic landscapes. These limitations are a direct
result of her captivity within the psychoanalytic models of identification that de Beauvoir criticised and the confines imposed by
her sexual abuse. Janey's first dream map, 'A Map of My Dreams'
(*B&G*, 46–7), reveals her unconscious before her sexual abuse by
her father. In this dream Janey's mother is present. Janey draws a
stone wall and indicates a path of concrete where she plays with
other children. 'My mother watches', she writes. This space is
part of what Janey terms 'the childhood land'. In this space of the
maternal Janey can fly, and there are trees and animals she plays
with, a village, and musical instruments. This space is partitioned
by a dotted line from the lower section of the dream map, which is
dominated by Baba, Janey's father. Here Janey details a nightmare
she has in which she encounters a 'huge jelly fish worm', abject,
'like vomit'. In the linguistic register of a child she describes it as
'the most frightening being', and it 'gets more and more so'. Rather
than the lush grassy meadows in the upper section, the tree in this
section Janey understands as being part of the structure of her
body: 'a tree which is the world which is my back'. This corporeal
image and the threatening phallic figures of the snake and the worm
signal Janey's domination by phallic symbols. Situated just below
the border between the innocent childhood land and the nightmare
is Baba: 'I'm sitting looking at a picture of Baba. I see tiny Baba
in my heart.' On the proceeding page, however, is another dream
map (*B&G*, 48–9), announcing the beginning of Janey's vision, her
seduction by her father Baba.

Acker's mapping of the vision reveals the extent to which Janey's imagination is structured around her sexual abuse. The dream symbols that occur in this map are linked to the underworld and sex. Cerberus appears encaged 'jumping around yapping for meat', and Janey is caught and killed by the white worm. In the section headed 'The nightmare I had when my father tried to fuck me' she describes a 'possession dance' in which she experiences a frenzy: 'I'm shaking my head as fast as possible from side to side, I want my head to come off, between my rigid static hands.' However, when she calls her identity into question, she is only able to desire becoming male tropes: 'I want to be the Mermaid, the Seducer of Men, Sex.' The phallic jellyfish worm from the first map appears again. She describes the pain of her abuse metaphorically in terms of being knifed, for whilst she feels knifed her health does not change. The worm, the knifing, and the 'area of the opaque white' describe the physical process of her rape and accompanying sexual fluids through the linguistic and visual register of a child. Towards the end of the second dream map Janey identifies directly with the phallus: 'the white worm. the white worm is me.' Evidence of Janey's psychosexual development occurs in the following dream map (*B&G*, 50–1) that details 'the fairytale' in which Janey is taken to the underworld with Baba. Baba seduces her and she envisages him to be the 'huge-winged black bird' who flew over the land of her childhood in the initial dream map. She has acquired the language of sex, presumably from her encounters with Baba: 'Baba takes me to the edge of the metal factory and sticks his cock in me. I'm his wife.' Within the grey metal factory walls Janey draws an ejaculating phallus and describes it in explicit sexual terms. The fusion of Janey's child-like register with raw sexual language highlights the violence of sexual abuse. At the same time the visual symbolism in these dream maps reveals the symbolic restraints within the space of Janey's imagination.

The anxiety of self-description

Through her cut-up technique, visual materiality, and narrative interventions, Acker provides an exegesis of Janey's narrative from within the text. In the cut-up technique Acker enacts, through the use of the knife or the scissors, a literal violence against linearity. Acker stated that in *Blood and Guts in High School* she 'tried to make Janey seem like one person',[59] constructing a singular female subject in her central protagonist. This statement registers the tension between form and the content of the work that narrates Janey's life, as Acker's professed drive to make Janey a unitary subject is in conflict with the fragmentary, indeterminate and unresolved nature of the collage form. The idea of constructing a singular female subject is implicitly identified in the text when the capitalists get together and discuss 'the Janey question' (*B&G*, 135). As a number of critics have remarked, Acker's work is often in line with Judith Butler's theories and in some aspects anticipates Butler's work on gender.[60] In her essay 'Seeing Gender' (1995) Acker engages with Butler directly. Here Acker identifies a certain conception of her impossible status as a child:

> as a girl, I was outside the world. I wasn't. I had no name. For me, language was being. There was no entry for me into language. As a receptacle, as a womb, as Butler argues, I could be entered, but I could not enter, and so I could neither have nor make meaning in the world.[61]

Acker's understanding of the conflation of her impossibility with the inability to possess or make meaning holds a direct relation to her lack of a language: 'I was unspeakable so I ran into the language of others.' She then acknowledges: 'In this essay, as yet, I am only repeating those languages.' Acker also realises the paradox inherent to woman's interpellation: 'Though I couldn't be named, everyone was naming me' and she cites Butler: 'This naming of what cannot be named is itself a penetration into the receptacle that is at once a violent erasure, one that established it as an impossible yet necessary site for all further inscriptions.'[62] Recapitulating Butler's central claim Acker remarks: 'the name *female* acts to erase the presence of women'. Expressing her consequent desire to move beyond her imposed negation within the symbolic Acker states: 'When I was a girl, I wanted to do anything but be a girl, for both *girl* and *woman* were the names of nothing.'[63]

Blood and Guts in High School reveals the crisis of self-description that occurs when Janey attempts self-definition. Denise Riley's theories of language illuminate the anxiety of self-description manifested in Janey's narrative. Riley anticipates Butler's belief in woman's indeterminacy, '*woman* itself is a term in process, a becoming, a constructing that cannot rightfully be said to originate in an end'.[64] Riley, in 1988, had already suggested an alternative approach to the 'veering between deconstruction and transcendence' by positing 'that "women" is indeed an unstable category, that this instability has a historical foundation, and that feminism is a systematic fighting-out of that instability – that need not concern us'.[65] Acker's later works reveal different modes of the indeterminacy of 'women' as resistance to the 'sexed abstractions'[66] that Riley understands 'women' to have been categorised as. Janey's narrative shows no such resistance. Riley's work on the autonomy of language offers an approach to the literary work that foregrounds language in such a way that resonates with Acker's understanding of the primacy of language. In her recent study *Impersonal Passion: Language as Affect* (2005) Riley opens her first essay 'Malediction' with a discussion of verbal violence. She conceptualises the 'bad word' as a means to think through how verbal violence, such as racist speech, or sexist speech, works on those it targets. In Janey's narrative both physical and verbal violence are present. Jean-Jacques Lercercle has commented on the interrelation of the two modes: 'Violence there is, which affects bodies – the violence of murder and mutilation, rape and incest. But this violence is inseparable from language, it dwells in language.'[67] 'In its violent emotional materiality', Riley argues, 'the word is indeed made flesh and dwells among us – often outstaying its welcome.'[68] The word's ability to resonate within its target and, crucially, the resultant potential for internalisation makes it barbaric. When 'malignant speech'[69] implants itself in the listener and is internalised, 'it's no longer felt to come "from the outside"'.[70]

In the opening section of *Blood and Guts in High School* Janey compares herself to Sally, her father's new young girlfriend:

> **Janey** (*to herself*): Fresh meat, young girls. Even though I am younger, I'm tough, rotted, putrid beef. My cunt red ugh. She's thin and beautiful; I've seen her. Like a model. Just the way I've wanted to look and I never will. I can't compete against *that*. (*Out loud*) It must be wonderful (*trying to make her voice as innocent as possible*) for you to have someone you can share everything with. You've been lonely for a long time. (*Janey trying to make herself into nothing.*) (*B&G*, 18)

A number of linguistic processes occur in Janey's dialogue in this instance to reveal the crisis of self-description. Firstly, by analogising 'young girls' with 'fresh meat' through parataxis, Janey violates women through linguistic objectification. Yet this act of linguistic violence originates in misogynistic 'predatory speech'[71] which seeks to master women. It also recalls Cerberus in the third dream map who appeared hungry for meat. The violence of the sexual reduction of the female body to meat in male discourse is inflicted by Janey, disclosing her own mastery by the 'hard word'. She then defines herself within this violation and sets herself within the perimeters of the meat metaphor: 'I'm tough, rotted, putrid beef.' For Riley: 'The hard word reverberates – so much so that it holds the appeal of false etymology.'[72] In extending the metaphor, Janey develops the false etymology of the malignant word. Such brutality intensifies with the statement 'My cunt red ugh.' Janey's illustration of her vagina that appears on the page adjacent to the dialogue illustrates this utterance, and her use of the vernacular and exclamative 'ugh' collapses self-disgust and the pain inflicted by her pelvic inflammatory disease. Her use too of '*that*' objectifies Sally by merging her identity with her outward appearance. This internal speech is followed by a (false) outward expression of happiness that her father has found someone to be with, the external polite nature of which serves to highlight the violence of Janey's interior linguistic register. Following this statement a sentence, functioning as a stage direction, is set apart from Janey's speech in parenthesis and written in italics '(*Janey trying to make herself into nothing.*)' This indicates Janey's inner attempt at ontological negation, which emerges as an effect of the interiorisation of the hard word.

Janey's internal enunciations evince what Riley terms an 'extimacy'. Extimacy is twofold: it can take the positive form of the internalisation of beautiful speech within its listeners but it can also be experienced as 'linguistic hatred, felt by its object as drawn inward'.[73] Janey, having experienced the latter form, a negative extimacy, reinforces Johnny's verbal abuse through internalisation and subsequent reiteration in the form of self-description. Recalling the conversation she has with Johnny:

> He hinted that I'm a loud brassy Jewess. I'm too dependent on him and that freaks him out of his mind. What makes it worse is that even though I need help, I don't know how to ask anyone for it. So I'm

always bearing down on him and blaming him. I'm too macho (that's my favourite one).

    I repeated all these sentences in my mind. I knew that I was hideous. I had a picture in my head that I was like a horse, like the horse in *Crime and Punishment*, skin partly ripped off and red muscle exposed. Men with huge sticks keep beating the horse. (*B&G*, 20)

Self-interpellation occurs in this extract through the internalisation of the father's words. Albeit negatively, Janey undergoes subject formation and acquires epistemological verification from Johnny's description of her ('I knew that I was [hideous]'). This is extended later in Janey's tale of the 'hideous' monster and the Beaver. Her self-imagining as the mare flogged by its master Milkolka in Raskolnikov's dream in Dostoyevsky's *Crime and Punishment* reveals a self-alignment with an animal in servitude ('She belongs to me! I'll do as I like with her',[74] Milkolka cries as he beats his mare). Janey's self-interpellation in this instance is a process of self-subjection through imagining that also reveals her desire for the law. Discussing Louis Althusser's understanding of subjection to the law through interpellation, Judith Butler claims that 'the possibility of a critical view of the law is thus limited by what might be understood as a prior desire for the law, a passionate complicity with the law, without which no subject can exist'.[75] For Butler:

> For the 'I' to launch its critique, it must first understand that the 'I' itself is dependent upon its complicitous desire for the law to make possible its own existence. A critical review of the law will not, therefore, undo the force of conscience unless the one who offers that critique is willing, as it were, to be undone by the critique he or she performs.[76]

Ontological possibility in this instance is linked to subjection. Unable to accept impossibility as a condition of existence, Janey, incapable of critical questioning of the law and constituted through language, reveals the 'I''s dependency upon the law. In one of her illustrations an arrow points to a series, 'I I I I I I I I I I' and the note reads 'I wish there was a reason to believe this letter' (*B&G*, 108). Acker, however, offers the critique that Butler refers to here.

    One of Janey's capitalised statements reads 'I AM NOT ME.' Paradoxically defining herself in the negative through the use of the pronoun 'me' yet simultaneously asserting her presence 'I am', Janey negates herself through self-assertion and reveals her self-alienation. Samuel Beckett's *Not I* (1972) offers an interesting comparison to Janey's narrative in terms of self-reflexive negation. Both Janey and Beckett's disembodied mouth of a seventy-year-old woman materialise in their discursive acts a dependence on the paternal that fasten them to the symbolic. Ontological negation is tied to impossibility in their enunciations, as Kristeva recognises in her essay on Beckett: 'A missing (grammatical or discursive) object implies an impossible subject: not I. And yet', like Janey, 'it exists, she speaks; this de-oralized and frustrated mouth is nevertheless held to its trivial search.'[77] For Kristeva, Beckett's Mouth epitomises 'impossible femininity' and in this sense stands in contrast to Janey's narrative: '*Not I*', is for Kristeva 'a heart-rending statement of the loss of identity.'[78] For Elaine Scarry, Beckett's 'syntax reflects the structure of existence'.[79] She cites Keir Elam, for whom *Not I* is 'the first drama in history whose central agon has to do with a grammatical category'.[80] Janey's act of enunciation, like that of Beckett's Mouth, is paradoxically what Scarry asserts as both 'the negation and the affirmation'.[81] In Janey's narrative ellipses, incomprehensible baby language, and expletives, perform a negating function similar to the ellipses in *Not: I*. Beckett's Mouth utters:

> . . . prayer unanswered . . . or unheard
> . . . too faint . . . so on . . . keep on . . .trying . . . not knowing
> what . . . what she was trying . . . what to try . . . whole
> body like gone . . . just the mouth . . . like maddened . . . so
> on . . . keep- . . . what? . . . the buzzing? . . . yes . . . all the time[82]

In Janey's narrative the statement 'I don't know what or who's happening' heads a page in which the following words are scrawled in varying formations horizontally and diagonally across the page:

> PUKE GOOGOO ME YUMN SHIT SHIT SHITFACE ME SHIT
> SMEARS ON MY HANDS I STINK I GOOGOO I STINK REAL
> GOOD I STINK WHEN I SMEAR SHIT ACROSS MY FACE
> LOTS I'M A OFFENDER END OF ME ME ME } WHO IS THIS?
> (*B&G*, 106–7)

In this attempt at self-definition Janey can only regurgitate the hard word and indeterminate baby language. Lyn Hejinian observes that children objectify language in their play, 'in jokes, puns, and riddles, or in glossolaliac chants and rhymes'. In doing so, Hejinian claims: 'They discover that words are not equal to the world, that a blur of displacement, a type of parallax exists in the relation between things (events, ideas, objects) and the words for them – a displacement producing a gap.'[83] This process of objectification and subsequent gap is evident in Janey's discourse. The two registers that punctuate Janey's utterances of 'I' and 'me' function as sites of omission and exclusion and thus bar Janey's self-articulation. Yet the experimental typography of Janey's scrawling and the use of the page as a visual field evoke a resistance to conventional language structures. Elsewhere utterances in block capitals evoke a desperation for meaning in language that is comparable to Beckett's Mouth. In Hester's narrative the upper case letters denote an attempt to enunciate beyond the confines of the text: 'I'M ALONE. THE SHIT WITH DISTINCTIONS BETWEEN CRAZY AND SANE. DOES ANYONE KNOW WHAT'S HAPPENING?' (*B&G*, 100). Lower case letters collapse Hester's narrative back into her dependency on Dimwit: 'Dear Dimwit: There's really no plan. I don't understand what happening. I don't know how to talk to you. I like you' (*B&G*, 100). Yet the impossible feminine subject is, through negation, affirmed in such enunciations. *Blood and Guts in High School*, in revealing the limitations imposed on Janey's discourse by conventional language, exposes the anxiety of self-description.

Feminist inflections: the function of the poetic

Throughout her works, Acker engages with male avant-garde writers and situates her writing in relation to their work. The work of nineteenth-century French poets Rimbaud, Verlaine and Mallarmé, early twentieth-century poets such as Rainer Maria Rilke, and prose writers such as Louis-Ferdinand Céline, Georges Bataille, and Jean Genet have a peculiar function in Acker's work. Acker's engagement in her work is explicitly with the European avant-gardes of the nineteenth and twentieth centuries. In this respect she shares with Kristeva a belief in the revolutionary capacity of the nineteenth-century French poets. In interview with Larry McCaffery she referred to this tradition of resistance as the '"black path" or the *poète maudit* tradition – the path of "abjection" which is the way writers such as Genet and

Céline work'.[84] As I explored in the first chapter, Acker's early literary background was very much rooted in poetry and her acquaintance with poets such as Jerome Rothenberg. Her intentional move away from writing poetry in the late 1960s and early 1970s to following in Burroughs's and Antin's footsteps in writing prose encourages an interest in her use of the poetic. Ron Silliman positions Acker in a lineage of writers who write against the constraints of normative realism: Gertrude Stein, Hemingway, and Joyce. The work of these writers led, for Silliman, to the rise of what he terms 'the contemporary art-novel'.[85] Silliman apprehends Acker's works as art-novels. He writes: 'Of particular note within this vein is the appearance of a subdivision of novelists who write for, and are principally read by, poets, such as Jack Kerouac, Douglas Woolf, Paul Metcalf, Harry Matthews, Kathy Acker or Fielding Dawson.'[86] Discussing the prose poem Silliman points to the fact that Acker's *Great Expectations* (1982) was published as an example of 'language poetry' by the French journal *Change*.[87] Peter Wollen has also observed that Acker, like Stein, bridged the genres of poetry and prose.[88]

The poetic in Acker's work functions to rupture established discourse. For Riley there is an irrational element to language that poetry capitalises on:

> Poetry, you could say, is systematically 'mad language', although not at all because of its author's tendencies, but merely because that half-latent unreason endemic to all ordinary language is professionally exploited by poetry. That – not something more ethereally glorious – is what poetry does, what it is. The writer is then in a delicate position of giving her limited assent to this craziness in its infinite ramification of sound-associations and puns and affective cadence.[89]

In Riley's terms impossibility is language's difficult excess that the speaker has no control over. In many ways Riley's notion of the poetic stems from her reading of Lecercle's idea of 'the remainder', the other side to language that 'emerges in nonsensical and poetic texts, in the illuminations of mystics and the delirium of logophiliacs or mental patients'.[90] The remainder is manifested in both Acker's use of the poetic in *Blood and Guts in High School*, and in the visual materiality of the work. As Riley suggests, poetry has a relation to impossibility. For Blanchot, 'poetry might orient us toward another relation, a relation with the obscure and unknown that would be a relation neither of force [*puissance*], nor of comprehension, nor even of revelation'.[91] This is not an instance of articulation, 'poetry is not there in order to say impossibility', Blanchot argues, rather, 'it simply answers to it, saying in responding'. It is a case of 'naming the possible, responding to the impossible'. Furthermore Blanchot understands poetry's response to evade the sort of expression that would draw impossibility 'under the attraction of language'. Blanchot's suggestion is. 'It is poetry's existence, each time it is poetry, that in itself forms a response and, in this response, attends to what is addressed to us in impossibility (by turning itself away).'[92]

For Kristeva the poetic holds a relation to the semiotic which is connected to the modality that Freudian psychoanalysis signals 'in postulating not only the *facilitation* and the structuring *disposition* of drives, but also the so-called *primary processes* which displace and condense both energies and their inscription'.[93] Kristeva's understanding of the semiotic illuminates an analysis of Acker's linguistic innovation. The symbolic, in Kristeva's terms, 'syntax and all other linguistic categories – is a social effect of the relation to the other, established through the objective constraints of biological (including sexual) differences and concrete historical family structures'. The semiotic, on the other hand, includes 'genetic programmings', particularly the primary processes 'such as displacement and condensation, absorption and repulsion, rejection and stasis, all of which function as innate preconditions, memorizable for the species, for language acquisition'.[94] Kristeva reveals the semiotic rhythm within language to be manifested in Mallarmé's assertions in his essay 'The Mystery in Literature'. In this piece Mallarmé apprehends a literary space: 'Indifferent to language, enigmatic and feminine, this space underlying the written is rhythmic, unfettered, irreducible, irreducible to its intelligible verbal translation; it is musical, anterior to judgment, but restrained by a single guarantee: syntax.'[95] This site, that Mallarmé appears to situate beneath the text, is aligned with woman. The position of this Mallarméan lacuna has a resemblance to Riley's affect and Lecercle's idea of the remainder. Mallarmé sees the black mark writing over white text. While Acker's use of Mallarmé acknowledges the disruption of linear reading, and brings this into her contemporary moment, her use of Mallarmé can also be viewed as inverting his master trope, positioning the spaces between marks as dynamic rather than vacancies waiting to be delimited by inscription. A field-orientated reading of *Blood and Guts in High School* might see the white spaces as pushing and pulling the text. This approach extends the discussion of Acker's use of the page as a visual field in her early exercises discussed in Chapter 1 in relation to Olson's ideas of the open text and composition by field. When viewed as a visual composition, the relation between light and dark marks becomes an absence of marks. Acker's writing methods in *Blood and Guts in High School* and her use of the poetic point to an impossible literary space and disclose a desire to make meaning beyond the symbolic. In order to demonstrate Acker's use of the poetic to reject conventional narrative in *Blood and Guts in High School*, I will examine two modes of the poetic in her writing. Firstly there is a clear practice of *récriture* at work in the text. To illustrate this I address two instances in which Acker rewrites the work of César Vallejo and Mallarmé. Secondly, I address 'The Persian Poems' and an instance of verbal collage in the text to explore the tension in the text between conventional language and another language. This tension emerges at the points in the text when Acker uses the poetic, and experiments with typography. Acker's experiments here voice indeterminacy and point to the impossible by recognising the space as part of the composition and not subordinate to the mark.

In the first section of *Blood and Guts in High School*, Acker inserts an adaptation of a poem by the Peruvian poet César Vallejo (1892–1938) into Janey and Johnny's dialogue. Like Mallarmé, Vallejo was widely regarded by his critics as a difficult poet whose work defies straightforward explicability. In the foreword to Vallejo's complete works, Mario Vargas Llosa remarks on the primacy of language in Vallejo's poetry:

> the mystery in his poetry resides not in those existential subjects or states but, rather, in how they take shape in a language that communicates them to a reader directly more through a sort of osmosis or contagion than through any intelligible discourse.[96]

The poem that Acker adapts is Vallejo's 'September' from the collection *The Black Heralds* (1919):

September

You were so good to me
that September night . . . even to hurting me!

I do not know about the rest; and for that matter,
you shouldn't have been that good, you shouldn't have.

You sobbed that night upon finding me
hermetic and tyrannical, ill and sad.
I do not know about the rest . . . and for that matter,
I do not know why I was sad . . . so sad . . .!

Solely on that sweet September night
did I possess in your Magdalene eyes, all
the distance of God . . . and I was sweet to you!

Likewise, it was a September evening
when I sowed in your embers, as decreed,
the puddles of this December night.[97]

The emphatic use of ellipsis in this poem to communicate the force of feeling and despair in Vallejo's male lyric subject is an instance of the poet's avant-garde aesthetic and poetic performativity. As Michelle Clayton has remarked, Vallejo's poetry can be read as being 'split between avant-garde experiment and political commitment'.[98] A form of activism, Vallejo's new poetic language expressed human suffering. Acker's choice of Vallejo in many ways acts as a textual mirror for her own practice.

In her rewritten version Acker writes back to Vallejo from the position of the female addressee in his original version of the poem:

September

This September night, you fled
So good to me . . . up to grief and include!
I don't know myself anything else
But you, YOU don't have to be good.

This night alone up to imprisonment no prison
Hermetic and tyrannical, diseased and panic-stricken
I don't know myself anything else
I don't know myself because I am grief-stricken.

Only this night is good, YOU
Making me into a whore, no

> Emotion possible is distance God gave integral:
> Your hateful sweetness I'm clinging to.
>
> This September evening, when sown
> In live coals, from an auto
> Into puddles: not known. (*B&G*, 10)

The female lyric 'I' inflects the lines of the male lyric subject of Vallejo's poem. The poetic sensibility that emerges from these lines is at once complicit with woman's silent identity created by the earlier poem and reveals a form of resistance through verbal violence. The rewriting of the final lines of the second stanza in the anaphoric 'I don't know myself' asserts the alienation of the lyric subject within her poetic identity constructed by the male subject, while the grammatical disorder of the lines discloses an instance of Acker's resistance to conventional language in *Blood and Guts in High School*.

In this poem we have an early example of Acker's practice of *récriture*, or 'rewriting'. Whilst Acker rewrites 'September', she also preserves the avant-garde force of Vallejo's poem. As Lecercle notes: 'Stylistic incoherence is the aptest way of expressing linguistic violence.'[99] The linguistic violence that emerges from the jumbled line in the third stanza, 'Emotion possible is distance God gave integral', is matched with the oxymoronic pairing of 'hateful' and 'sweetness' in the following line. Yet the female voice is still imprisoned by her place within the poem, clinging to the male and ultimately fated not to exist. However, the linguistic violence inflicted creates a new poetic register that clashes with Janey and Johnny's orthodox discourse that surrounds it. In the final stanza Acker practices a poetic technique similar to H.D.'s imagism. The pronoun has disappeared and the lines are stripped down into a new economy of language and, crucially, are brought into the present tense. In an act of decentralisation, a new aesthetic reality is created that displaces time and the male lyric agency. In its place two contrasting direct images, live coals and puddles, are set alongside an oblique idea of the self ('an auto') and the state of being 'not known'. Meaning emerges that defies interpretation, while the final caesura heightens the unknowability of the female lyric self.

Acker's engagement with Vallejo continues throughout Janey and Johnny's dialogue. Many of Janey's typographical inscriptions are rewritten lines of Vallejo's poem 'The Black Heralds'.[100] These lines reveal an affect that constitutes meaning. There is a tension between Janey's imprisonment within the masculine symbolic and the affect that emerges from her typography that voices a language not confined to the symbolic strictures that corral her. Drucker remarks that modernist typographic experiment straddles the realms of art and literature, defying disciplinary distinctions. The radical potential of typography for Drucker resides in this resistance. 'The most potent aspect of typography's form' is in Drucker's view, 'its refusal to resolve into either a visual or verbal mode.'[101] Whilst there are clear instances of the corralling effect of Janey's interpellation and subsequent self-subjection in *Blood and Guts in High School*, another language emerges through typography in her narrative that runs counter to her subjection within the symbolic. In *Impersonal Passion*, Denise Riley theorises the impersonality of language, the idea that 'language as a speaking thing, neither my master nor my instrument, is amiably indifferent to me'.[102] Like Acker in her 1993 essay 'Against Ordinary Language: The Language of the Body', Riley turns to the Bulgarian-born but German-language novelist Elias Canetti as an authority on language.[103] In his 1969 essay 'Word Attacks', Canetti described being seized by violent linguistic outbursts whilst living in England after the war, outbursts in which he would retreat to his room and uncontrollably fill pages with German words. Examining his affliction by what he termed 'the agony of words, occurring independently of their meaning'[104] Canetti states, 'I viewed those word attacks as pathological.'[105] Canetti's 'agony of words' is significant for Riley, as she understands that 'tension, unease, or a feeling of dispossession can result from the ostensible content of what's said, and the affect which seeps from the very form of the words'. 'In short,' Riley states, 'unexamined rhetoricity is at stake.' Furthermore, 'It's not just a matter of the unspoken "implications" of what's said, but something stronger: of how language as the voice of its occasion can also inflect its speakers.'[106] Riley's notion of unexamined rhetoricity suggests that there are new modes of language and formations of meaning made possible by affect.

As we have seen, Janey's narrative is punctuated by illustrations and variations in typography, while her dialogue with Johnny is broken by the statements in block capitals adapted from 'The Black Heralds'. Acker's choice of Vallejo's poem that voices suffering and despair is notable. The first stanza reads:

> There are blows in life, so powerful . . . I don't know!
> Blows as from the hatred of God; as if, facing them,
> the undertow of everything suffered
> welled up in the soul . . . I don't know![107]

These blows 'are few' 'but are', and they 'open dark trenches / in the fiercest face'. Acker metonymically rewrites the poem. The full rewritten version of the poem was hand typed by Acker in block capitals and is housed in the archive as a single work titled simply 'BY CESAR VALLEJO' and is signed 'rewritten Kathy Acker 1978'.[108] The rewritten text is then cut up by Acker, and the lines invade Janey and Johnny's conventional discourse. For instance, Vallejo's blows become lashes: 'LASHES MAKE ME NO LONGER MYSELF' (*B&G*, 20), 'LASHES, AS IF THE WORLD, BY ITS VERY NATURE, HATES ME' (*B&G*, 21), 'CAUSE OF LASHES: THE SURGE OF SUFFERING IN THE SOUL CORRUPTS THE SOUL.' His trenches become ditches, 'TINY SOUNDS, BUT SOUNDS . . . OPEN DARK DITCHES IN THE FACE' (*B&G*, 23). Vallejo's God in Acker's lines becomes the secular world in which women are negated. In these instances and elsewhere, that which Riley terms a 'linguistic unease' becomes apparent in Janey's narrative. Riley positions 'on the verge of guilt': 'a condition elastic enough to encompass all too many definitions, of which one is that gnawing feeling of having failed according to rules that I did not make myself'.[109] Under these linguistic conditions Janey experiences disbelief in the letter 'I' as, in Riley's terms, 'the very constraints of language-use induce this sensation that "I" lies'.[110] By contrast, to return then to Janey's statement 'I AM NOT ME' the affect that arises from the use of majuscules asserts a presence that is in conflict with Janey's self-negation.

For Riley there is a 'linguistic emotionality'[111] at work in language, and she understands self-presentation and irony as 'kinds of affect which are embedded in some ordinary fundamental workings of language'.[112] The typography, punctuation, and layout of a sentence also carry affect 'and can be contrived to carry all of it'.[113] Acker's use of block capitals is one way in which the text of *Blood and Guts in High School* exceeds the confines of language that imprison Janey. The accompanying shift in register in these statements aligns affectual meaning with the poetic. Vallejo's lyric I speculates as to the identity of the annihilating blows: 'Perhaps they are the colts of barbaric Attilas; / or the black heralds sent to us by Death.' The methods of expansion afforded by experimental prose in this instance reveal a very different practice to the poetic condensation at work in Acker's rewriting of 'September'. In Acker's revision, the voice that interrupts Janey's narrative occupies the violent site of dissent opened up in Vallejo's lines: 'MAKE MORE FIERCE AND MAKE SEXUALITY STRONGER. THIS IS THE TIME FOR ALL PRISONERS TO RUN WILD. YOU ARE THE BLACK ANNOUNCERS OF OUR DEATH. (BE SUCH TIME YOUNG HORSES Of ATTILA THE HUN. OH ANNOUNC-ERS WHO SEND US DEATH.') (*B&G*, 23). Vallejo's third stanza develops the conflict experienced between life and religious forces:

> They are the deep falls of the Christs of the soul,
> of some adored faith blasphemed by Destiny.
> Those bloodstained blows are the crackling of
> bread burning up at the oven door.[114]

Acker adapts and interiorises these lines to resituate them in a humanism: 'ANNOUNCE THE RUINS PROFOUND OF THE CHRISTS WITHIN (US). OF SOME BELIEF CHERISHED WHICH FATE CURSES, THESE *LASHES* BLOODY SOUND THEIR CRACKLINGS OF A LOAF OF BREAD WHICH IN THE VERY DOOR BURNS US UP.' External forces are de-authoritised and instead the self is elevated (the Christs within us). In the same way, Vallejo's despair in the final stanza when 'man' is summoned and 'He turns his eyes' becomes abstracted from its religious context in Acker's rewriting and turns into a philosophical statement about women's ontological negation: 'TURN MY EYES INSANE, WHILE BEING CORRUPTS ITSELF, AS A POOL OF SHAME, IN THAT HOPE' (*B&G*, 29). The violent 'lashes' the female voice experiences are linked to pain, insanity and a pool of shame, the accompanying illustration of an ejaculating penis entitled 'TURN MY EYES

INSANE' link the summoning 'slap on the shoulder' by the God-like figure that turns all to guilt in Vallejo's poem with the repression of female desire and the infliction of shame within the phallic economy. Crucially in Acker's version it is 'being', not Vallejo's 'everything lived', that becomes a pool of shame. The affect that emerges through typographical dissent in these invasions stages a performativity that is at variance with the silence inflicted upon woman in conventional discourse. Finally Vallejo's closing lines: 'There are blows in life, so powerful . . . I don't know' become in Acker's work an ambivalent declaration of the speaker's alienation: 'PLEASE / ME NO LONGER MYSELF' (*B&G*, 31).

The first poem in a later section designated as poems written by Janey takes the title of Mallarmé's work *Un Coup de dés jamais n'abolira le hazard* (1897), translated in Janey's narrative as 'A throw of the dice never will abolish chance' (*B&G*, 105). Janey's version opens with a series of double negatives, 'I don't want nothing no more', 'I don want no cancer in my bones', and breaks into the series of expletives mixed with baby language scrawled and scattered across the page written in a child's handwriting. The language in its affect and disruption is unremittingly violent. The hard word reverberates in Janey's direct mimicry: 'Oh suck my cock honey suck my cock. That's what its all about / I love how you turn yourself / Around and upside-down inside-out' (*B&G*, 109). Later in the poem Janey moves into her 'vision of agony' (*B&G*, 113) and refers directly to Mallarmé. As Malcolm Bowie has pointed out there are two main vocabularies functioning in *Un Coup de dés*: 'on the one hand, seafaring, tempest and shipwreck and, on the other, the pursuit of knowledge and the attempt to define the mental or metaphysical conditions by which that pursuit is deflected, discredited or annulled'.[115] Furthermore he states: 'The more profound his penetration into poetic language, the more acute his sense of that language's emptiness, of the lack of correspondence between verbal fictions and being.'[116] In her rewriting of Mallarmé's *Un Coup de dés*, Acker purloins the poet's semantic devices in the interweaving of Janey's narrative with another narrative that pushes towards the 'desire to lose consciousness' (*B&G*, 112). She edges towards a peripheral vision that might in all actuality be nothing: 'go to the end / as if there's a beyond / driven beyond bodily desires into just desire, not for what, just desire / DEFIANCE born' (*B&G*, 112).

Drucker positions Mallarmé as the originator of avant-garde typographic experiment: '*A Throw of the Dice* stands as the single most striking precedent for avant-garde experiment with the visual form of poetic language.'[117] The foremost aspect of Mallarmé's practice, and part of the poet's attack on quotidian forms of language such as the media, Drucker understands to be the technique of 'visually scoring the poetic page by use of different sizes and fonts of typographic letterforms'.[118] Like Mallarmé, Acker uses shifting typefaces to produce meaning through a linguistic performativity. The use of enlarged and variable typefaces here and elsewhere to convey the writer's vision echoes the practices of Concrete poets in the 1960s, practices that Acker would have been exposed to and influenced by early in her career. Such use of typefaces, spacing, and the juxtaposition of differing linguistic registers imbue the work with texture, and, subsequently, a dynamic conflict with ordinary language. Through a similar textuality 'DEFIANCE' attains its performative dimension in the poem as Acker's inverted Mallarméan deployment of the space as well as the mark. In Acker's rewritten text Mallarmé's masculinist privileging of the black mark is offset and stripped of authority by the active recognition of the white space in the production of non-verbal meaning:

DEFIANCE SCORN BLOOD

(not just hallucination dispersed from agony – Mallarmé).

if this is the world DEFIANCE

would become the whole world DEFIANCE

the world would be a flame:

A TOTAL FLAME BURNING
ITSELF UP
BLOOD AND FEAR AND GUTS
MY VISION. (*B&G*, 113)

Earlier in a section entitled 'Hawthorne is a writer', Acker states: 'Writers create what they do out of their own frightful agony and blood and mushed-up guts and horrible mixed-up insides' (*B&G*, 100). Acker's intervallic spaces echo Mallarmé's and through feminist inflections the nothingness that transpires in Mallarmé's verse is also present in Acker's. The space of negation 'in which all reality turns into a howl and makes / itself go away' is, paradoxically, materialised.

Elsewhere Acker's poetic experimentations are more explicitly aligned with the need for a new language. As stated at the outset of this chapter, 'The Persian Poems' were published as an independent volume by Papyrus Press in 1972, six years before Acker copyrighted *Blood and Guts in High School*. The poems are positioned in the middle of Hester's narrative in the book review/appropriation of Hawthorne's *The Scarlett Letter*. Throughout this narrative and its various composite parts there is a recognition of the inadequacy of language. Hester seeks a new language but can only conceive of acquiring it through her husband's instruction: 'TEACH ME A NEW LANGUAGE DIMWIT. A LANGUAGE THAT MEANS SOMETHING TO ME' (*B&G*, 96). Janey's discovery of a new language to learn is significant, and the language she learns, Persian, offers Janey an escape from gender, since there is no grammatical gender in Persian, nor are pronouns marked for natural gender. As a result of the absence of gender in Persian, Janey's morphological examination of the language results in self-interpellation as she can only refer to herself as 'Janey'. Janey's attempt to learn the language leads to her experimentation with the Ezafe, the construction in Persian script that denotes certain relationships between Persian words, among them possession and qualification. Janey's translations in 'The Persian Poems' are not accurate Persian. Her constructions are symptomatic of her desire for meaning outside the symbolic. In her innovative use of the marks she evidences a motility, made possible by typographical inflection. However, when she drills the verb structures (*B&G*, 76), the poems reveal her confinement within grammatical structures. Houen astutely reads this as revealing Janey's need 'to order herself as a subject according to rules of syntax and vocabulary'.[119] Reading Acker's work through Burroughs's idea of 'the word as viral control' and Deleuze and Guattari's understanding of the 'order word', he argues that Janey's drilling of verb structures invariably shows her imprisonment within the confines of language and social regulations.[120] However, an antinomy can be traced between confinement and linguistic experimentation in 'The Persian Poems'. Linguistic aberrations appear in the text to undercut the authority of the syntactical rules that Janey has interiorised (and thus imposes upon her translation). For instance in 'The Persian Poems' and elsewhere, Janey's alphabetical character for the letter 'm' is skewed, an extra grapheme is added to make a new symbol. The effect of this deformation of the letter is to create what Lecercle understands as a textual excess 'that both ruins the coherence of the text and compensates for its lack'. In the instance of textual excess: 'The excess of *délire* is the expression of the excess of desire.'[121]

Acker's use of collage further reveals this textual excess. Towards the end of Janey's book report a statement on 'materialistic society and the sexual revolution' reads:

> Since the materialistic society had succeeded in separating sex from every possible feeling, all you girls can now go spread your legs as much as you want 'cause it's sooo easy to fuck it's sooo easy to be a robot it's sooo easy not to feel. Sex in America is S&M. This is the glorification of S & M and slavery and prison. (*B&G*, 99)

The narrative continues and segues into a prose poem that seems at first glance nonsensical. Taken as a whole and read as one disjointed poem, that which Lecercle terms 'the real of linguistic conjuncture'[122] materialises to violate and question the mastery of orthodox linguistic structures. Yet the poem discloses itself to be comprised of two texts, for the most part each text occurring on alternating lines:

> In this society there was a woman who
> freedom and suddenly the black night opens up and
> fucked a lot and she got tied up with ropes and
> on upward and it doesn't stop
> beaten a lot and made to spread her legs too wide
> the night is open space that goes on and on,
> this woman got so mentally and physically hurt
> not opaque black, but a black that is extension
> she stopped fucking even though fucking is the thing to do.
> This woman was really tied up. One day a
> and excitement and the possibilities of new
> man tried to fuck the woman. She loved him
> consciousness, consciousness.
> desperately so she wouldn't let him touch her
> open her find all her gooky and bloody and screaming

don't you see it?
and angry and hurt inside. Tell me how are the
right here. more important than any desperate
lobotomy children supposed to act? How are
love desperate possibility of going out farther,
the children who imbibed acid and downs and dex and
going out and out as far as possible
horse before they were born, who walk through the
going out as far as possible in freedom
radioactive rain, how are they supposed
going out as far as possible in freedom
to act? Tell me now why am I scared to fuck
going out as far as possible in freedom
you Dimwit? I'm all alone in outer space.
going out as far as possible in freedom, (B&G, 99–100)

The collage technique that combines these two voices in two very different registers stages a discordance that produces meaning at the site of the two texts' convergence. The uncomfortable discordance between the existential hope and sublimation engendered by the second poetic voice and the language of the oppressed subject in the first text points to two modalities: the external reality and the poetic. It also points once again to the idea of space as liberating for the female voice: 'the night is open space that goes on and on'. The alignment of the night (knight) with the female protagonist in Acker's later text, *Don Quixote*, extends the idea of the night as a space of feminist potential. Here, the possibilities of a new consciousness that the poetic announces are questioned by the anaphoric repetition of 'going out as far as possible in freedom'. The grammatical construction 'as far as possible' implies a limitation and the repetition of the lines create a refrain that disallows any movement beyond the linguistic construction. In this limitation the poem signifies the indescribable. The switch between registers gives voice to affect, to the impossible in these lines. This poem also reveals in microcosm the process of dilation and contraction that takes place throughout the work.

Acker stated, 'to use language is to enter the world'.[123] She also understood the 'nonnegotiable disparity between the self's version of the world and the world'[124] to be the affliction of her contemporary America. Acker's understanding of the limits of language in this regard can be considered in a historical frame. The censorship of language was to become a central aspect of the culture wars in America in 1989, a policing of creativity that Acker confronts in *My Mother: Demonology* (1993). The dualistic conception of an entity named self on the one hand and an entity named other or the world on the other, was to Acker madness. The final vignette of *Blood and Guts in High School* offers two substantial sections comprised of language and corresponding hieroglyphics entitled 'The World' and 'The Journey'. 'The World' concerns the search for the book of transformations: 'Shall we look for this wonderful book?' the voice asks, 'Shall we stop being dead people?' The final section, 'The Journey' is the quest to find that book. The verbal inscriptions in this section are handwritten. Drucker connects linguistic transparency with immateriality, and writing with materiality. The frequent use of hieroglyphics in this section empowers inscription, visual materiality, and writing over linguistic transparency. 'The Journey', which could stand alone as an autonomous piece, recovers pictorial form, and reclaims the visibility of writing, against the oppression of conventional structures of grammatical meaning that oppress Janey. Yet *Blood and Guts in High School* ends with the image of Janey's grave and an epitaph written in type that locks language back into the deadlock of schematic rhymes, Janey's sexual dependency on the male, and conventional language. Through the visual and verbal dynamics of the collage, Acker's quest for a textual site for the feminine impossible imaginary realm becomes apparent in this early work. The emergence of materiality and the non-organic text as a site of resistance, that exists counter to ordinary language, anticipates Acker's later works that manifest the languages of the body. Whilst this textual site is not realised in *Blood and Guts in High School*, the struggle of the woman writer to make meaning is apparent, and voice emerges in the book through experimental composition.

Chapter 3

Writing-through: *Don Quixote: Which Was a Dream*

Scholarship on Acker's works has paid particular attention to literary strategies of appropriation. *Don Quixote: Which Was a Dream* (1986) has been taken up by many critics as paradigmatic of Acker's technique of feminist appropriation.[1] This chapter recognises that such scholarship is valuable to an understanding of Acker's work, yet seeks to move a conception of Acker's writing away from a focus on appropriation as such in order to offer a more complex articulation of the experimental practices at work in the text.

In part, the longstanding critical focus on appropriation in Acker's work has been engendered by Acker's own comments in interviews around the time of the book's publication. In conversation with Ellen G. Friedman Acker explicitly remarked: '*Don Quixote*, more than any of my other books, is about appropriating male texts.'[2] In the same interview, she elaborated on her compositional process and the question of feminist intent:

> as a rule I haven't thought, 'I am a woman, a feminist, and I'm going to appropriate a male text.' What happens is that I frame my work way after I write it . . . In fact, I wrote the second part of *Don Quixote* first by rewriting texts, out of a Sherrie Levine-type impulse. Then I wrote the first and third parts later. The Lulu segment had been commissioned by Pete Brooks as a play. And I think I did the Leopardi part early on as well. Then I actually had an abortion. While I was waiting to have the abortion, I was reading *Don Quixote*. Because I couldn't think, I just started copying *Don Quixote*. Then I had all these pieces and I thought about how they fit together.[3]

Many scholars have highlighted Acker's reference here to a method of appropriation that is comparable to Sherrie Levine's art.[4] Levine began producing appropriative art in the late 1970s. Her work was exhibited at Douglas Crimp's 'Pictures' show at Artists Space, New York in 1977, an exhibition which, as David Evans has observed, 'launched a now pervasive art based on possession – usually unauthorized – of the images and artefacts of others'.[5] Levine photographs the photographs of renowned photographers. This practice is evident in her 1979 work *After Walker Evans*. In her 1982 'Statement' on her appropriative practice, Levine conceives of a picture as 'a space in which a variety of images none of them original blend and clash'. Comparing her work, and the work of other appropriative artists to Flaubert's copyists, Bouvard and Péchuchet, Levine states 'we indicate the profound ridiculousness that is precisely the truth of painting'.[6]

For the contemporary poet Caroline Bergvall, Acker's work also 'falls in line with broad notions of conceptual practice'.[7] Acker is regarded rightly by contemporary writers, such as Bergvall and Vanessa Place, as a progenitor of women's conceptual writing.[8] Bergvall conceives Acker's practice as 'Something like Walter Benjamin meets Sherrie Levine', referring to the Benjamin of the Arcades project.[9] Bergvall's attention to the conceptual elements of Acker's work is productive for thinking through the primacy of composition that emerges in Acker's work as a result of her early methods of textual appropriation. Bergvall apprehends Acker's writing as 'a literary mode which only exists through other texts. The writer conceives of writing as a collated and plagiarized multiplicity.' She remarks: 'Cultural pillaging provides a poetic trajectory that negates the original authorial voice.' 'The uniqueness of the work', Bergvall observes, 'is its lack of uniqueness, its negativity. It exists as a mode of textual appropriation, a process of shadowing and transference.'[10] The value of Bergvall's conception of what she terms Acker's 'literary pauperism' is that it points to the way in which the value of content is depreciated through textual appropriation. In Bergvall's words: 'Thieving denatures what it steals.'[11] However, Bergvall also understands a paradox to be apparent in Acker's works, whereby a continuity emerges 'between detached textual procedure and authorial motivation, between constricted social positioning and the not-I multiplicity of her writerly voice'.[12] Bergvall's idea that the uniqueness of Acker's conceptual work is its lack of uniqueness (its negativity) is insightful if in the second instance 'uniqueness' is taken to refer to the content of the work, the words, and the sentences. This chapter shifts the focus away from appropriation to assert that the significance of Acker's use of others' texts is to strategically devalue content as a means to foreground compositional form, thereby creating the conditions for the emergence of meaning through complex experimental linguistic practices and paratactic disjunction.

In Acker's work, appropriated material functions to shift the meaning of the text from content to form but the use of appropriated material within *Don Quixote* does not render the work itself a work of appropriation. Acker employs techniques of appropriation as part of her practice but these methods are only part of an intricate web of linguistic play and experimental forms of iteration. The impulse to appropriate may indeed have been comparable for Acker at the time of composing the preliminary materials for *Don Quixote* to Sherrie Levine's pure appropriation in works such as *After Walker Evans* (1979). In such works, the original images that are produced by Levine's lens are direct reproductions of Evans's. Having undergone no manipulation, they are presented as Levine's own. The final published text of *Don Quixote,* however, is far from an act of pure appropriation. The Levine 'impulse' was exactly that, generative but by no means formative of Acker's final work.

Writing-through

Acker's comments to Friedman point to more than a simple claim to direct appropriation in the initial stage of constructing the work. They inform an understanding of her compositional practice and the relation of that practice to the feminist concerns of the work. The idea of the experience of abortion as an impediment to thought is connected directly by Acker to the literary act of pure appropriation, a textual act of re-production but simultaneously of non-creation ('Because I couldn't think, I just started copying *Don Quixote*'). In contrast to the connection Acker makes between non-thought and appropriation, Acker's remarks also highlight the importance of composition to her textual bricolage: 'I had all these pieces and I thought about how they fit together.' In Acker's words here creative intelligence is located in the act of assemblage, rather than the act of copying, which, in Acker's view, arises from a lack of thought. The practice of putting the elements together creates the final text, and this is where thought (and feminism) intervenes. 'That middle part of *Don Quixote*', Acker noted to Friedman, 'is very much about trying to find your voice as a woman.'[13]

In 'Abortion and Logic', a subsection of Acker's 1994 essay, 'Reading the Lack of the Body: The Writing of the Marquis de Sade', Acker takes up the issue of woman's freedom in Sade's society in relation to abortion. Acker observes that in Sade's 1795 work, *Philosophy in the Bedroom*: 'The discussion about female identity narrows down to the problem of abortion.' Positioning herself with Sade's character Madame de Saint-Ange, she alludes to the female character's claim that '[w]oman's freedom . . . depends upon her ability to stop pregnancy'.[14] This present chapter argues that the voice of the woman writer emerges specifically through the experimental strategy of writing-through. When read as the predominant experiment in *Don Quixote*, writing-through transpires as a method of production and resulting literary progeny associated by Acker with the experience of abortion. John Cage and Jackson Mac Low's practices of 'writing-through' offer a productive entry into Acker's practice of rewriting in the second part of *Don Quixote*. For Tyrus Miller, Cage's and Mac Low's intertextual poems, which embody the strategy of 'citational reading/writing', 'represent exemplary demonstration of anarchist poetic (and more broadly, cultural) practice'.[15] He states:

> For the acrostic, 'mesostic,' and 'diastic' forms they often use to structure the works are themselves, first and foremost, tools for 'writing-through' already-written works. Cutting across individual texts or a corpus of texts, mesostic or acrostic forms shift the 'motivation' and 'relevance' of source texts in complex and often politically charged ways. The procedures displace the source's original claims on knowledge and authority, sometimes undercutting their basis in the work's form, diction, and rhetorical address, at other times highlighting these claims in peculiarly inflected ways or changing the tone with which they are pronounced.[16]

This idea of writing-through can be taken up with reference to Acker's practice but reconfigured to a non-procedural method. Whilst Acker does not employ acrostic, mesostic, or diastic forms in *Don Quixote*, she does cut across texts, rewriting sections in ways that transform the original text. Miller's comments on the ability of practices of 'writing-through' to dislocate the 'claims on knowledge and authority' made by the original text reveal the capacity of the practice of writing-through to de-form the epistemological structures of the original works at hand. The introduction to this book drew on the importance of the decentralisation of narrative for Acker, and, more broadly, for women's experimental writing. 'Writing-through' facilitates decentralisation, as it is able to displace and thereby depose the centralised narrative of the original source text.

The complexities of Acker's process of rewriting emerge when read as a practice of non-procedural 'writing-through'. For Steve McCaffery, the writers he cites as practising the method 'share a predilection for secondary discourses arrived at via annexation, violence and alteration'.[17] The practice of writing-through as an experimental writing strategy that de-forms the source text stands in contrast to traditional ideas of literary insemination, offering a form of thinking about the woman writer's relation to male texts. Harold Bloom's *The Anxiety of Influence: A Theory of Poetry* (1973) remains the outstanding model of literary insemination. In Bloom's account, the formation of grand narratives and literary canons are predicated on the relation of influence, between a poet and a literary forefather. Whereas the generative literary model is resolutely male to male, insemination remains grounded in the archetype of heterosexual reproduction (the male author's work is understood as the offspring of the male forefather, bred by literary insemination). When situated in an antithetical relation to the reproductive trope of literary history and canon formation, Acker's trope of abortion emerges as both intimately feminist and avant-garde. De-formation, fragmentation, and loss of order emerge as elements of the experimental text. At the level of form, Acker's methods of writing-through, and her associated use of disjunction, de-composition, transliteration, intertextuality, and paragrammatic writing, are positioned here in relation to abortion as a literary trope.[18]

In the interview with Larry McCaffery cited above, Acker motions to a distinction between strategies of appropriation and rewriting. The larger scale strategy of appropriating Cervantes' text can be demarcated from the practice of rewriting that occurs in the second part of the text, which can be read as a complex non-procedural

practice of writing-through. Discussing Jackson Mac Low's procedural practices, Miller suggests that Mac Low's configurations are
productively approached in terms of 'active rewriting'.[19] The final
manuscript of *Don Quixote*, which became the Grove Press edition
of the work, offers a tripartite composition. The first part contains
the abortion and Don Quixote's transformation into a knight. Acker
employs strategies of disjunction in this first part with the result that
Don Quixote's narrative is cut up with various inserts critiquing
American politics. The second part, 'Other Texts', consists of texts
that are rewritten male texts: Andrei Bely's *St Petersburg* (1913),
Giuseppe Tomasi di Lampedusa's *The Leopard* (1958), and Frank
Wedekind's Lulu plays, *Earth Spirit* and *Pandora's Box* (originally
titled *Lulu: A Monster Tragedy* (1892)). The third part returns to
strategies of disjunction: Acker again cuts in sections on American
politics with Don Quixote's narrative, and employs paragrammic
techniques as a means to explore what the self might be outside dualistic reasoning and the confines of classical narrative.

The paragram, theorised by Julia Kristeva in her essay 'Towards
a Semiology of Paragrams', points to poetic language as 'the only
infinity of code', the doubleness of the literary text (reading and writing), and the intertextuality of the literary work as 'a network of
connections'.[20] Steve McCaffery takes up the term 'paragrammic' to
indicate 'a material poetics of unstable linguistic systems'. He likens
the paragrammic to that which he terms 'the poetics of turbulence'
implicated in Charles Olson's remark that 'the real life in regular
verse is an irregular movement underneath'.[21] For McCaffery, there
is a fundamental socio-political dimension to the paragram that dis-
limns that which Houston Baker understands to be the fixity that
is 'a function of power'[22]: 'Pertaining as paragrams do to hidden,
nonlinear relations within texts, their disposition commits all writing
to the status of a partly self-organizing system.' For McCaffery this
makes paragrams 'unquestionably not only major agents of linguistic
instability and change' but, furthermore, paragrams 'advance a protosemantic challenge to the smooth instrumentality of linguistic par-
lance'.[23] 'Non-conventional reading habits' are able, in McCaffery's
view, to exploit the turbulence and non-linearity of 'paragrammic
disruption'. McCaffery traces a lineage of writers who practice the
method that he also terms 'written-reading': 'Ronald Johnson and
Lucrette, Charles Olson, Jackson Mac Low, and William Burroughs,

John Cage and Tom Phillips all appear . . . as contemporary-writers-of-their-unconventional-readings of others' writings.'[24] Rather than a work of plagiarism, or appropriation, Acker's *Don Quixote* can be approached as a new form of paragrammic writing-through.

An unpublished document housed in the Kathy Acker Papers, titled 'Rejects from *Don Quixote*', contains the materials that Acker excised from the vast repository of writings that originally constituted matter for the work. The 'rejects' run to 65 A4 typed pages and consist largely of plays, experimental prose, and philosophical writings on colour and perception. The opening section of Acker's file of 'Rejects from *Don Quixote*' illuminates her textual collagist practice. The piece is entitled 'Description of Female Weight-Lifter':

> 1.   on nature.
>
> Writing must be a machine for breaking down, that is allowing the now uncontrolled and uncontrollable reconstitutions of thoughts and expressions. All other kinds of writing simply express.
>
> The first given, then, or the always-present beginning or return to is nothing. I(dentity) is and does nothing. Once there's (there always is) nothingness, any event's possible. My methodology's total rigor. This or any total rigor is meaningless.
>
> Those who are driven by poverty, those who are free from material worries hunger exhausting labor a joyless existence ask the same question, the question of meaning.
>
> A language is the appearances of connections therefore language as in writing doesn't express anything: it creates.[25]

Acker's negative aesthetics in this omitted paragraph foreground her later conceptual work with bodybuilding, which is taken up in detail in Chapter 6 in relation to the aesthetics of failure. The perceived problem of expression in *Don Quixote* is that it is tied to rational knowledge. The question of meaning has a political force. The breakdown of grammatical precision is aligned with 'those who are driven by poverty, those who are free from material worries'. The voices of the socio-politically disaffected inflect the cumulative and agrammatical sequence 'hunger exhausting labor a joyless existence'. They ask the same question, 'the question of meaning'. Here Acker points to the distinction between language and writing, whereby writing 'creates' and is positioned antithetically to 'expression'. Acker's practice of writing-through in the second part of *Don Quixote* is an experimental practice that explores the 'uncontrollable reconstitutions of thoughts and expressions' that the female weight-lifter conceives of as writing.

The excised material points to the centrality of 'the question of meaning' in Acker's work. In a piece titled 'On Burroughs' Acker writes that, in Burroughs's work, 'meaning – the meaning of the self or self – lies not in what is said, in character and/or plot, but in gaps between, in the movement of one section to another'. For Acker, this recognition is revolutionary: 'Do you see how radical this is? In regard to the structuring of the novel, the conventional novel? Even more significantly, with regard to the usual understanding of meaning, that meaning is what is understood.'[26] Acker's comments provide insights into the politics of form in Burroughs's work and the experiments in structuring the novel that evidently influenced her own work. In contrast to conventional structures of meaning Acker argues that, in Burroughs's work, 'meaning resides in emptiness, in slippage, rather than what is said'.[27] Through aphasia, strategies of writing-through, translation, paragrammatics, and the protosemantic, meaning similarly emerges from compositional structure and what is not said in *Don Quixote*.

Aphasia

Entitled 'Other Texts', the prefatory statement of the second part of *Don Quixote* reads: 'BEING DEAD, DON QUIXOTE COULD NO LONGER SPEAK. BEING BORN INTO AND PART OF A MALE WORLD, SHE HAD NO SPEECH OF HER OWN. ALL SHE COULD DO WAS READ MALE TEXTS WHICH WEREN'T HERS' (*DQ*, 39). In her unpublished notes on Marguerite Duras's *The Malady of Death* (1982), Acker picks out the citation 'to silence her' and asks 'what is the relationship between speech and knowledge?'[28] In *Don Quixote* aphasia is a condition that emerges from the limitations imposed by normative grammar, and represents a form of culturally induced inexpressibility. For Don Quixote, silence impresses what cannot be said because of the limitations of language, as language is, to recall Antin's remarks cited in Chapter 1, 'the cultural matrix in which the value systems that determine politics are made'.[29] Silence evolves across Acker's oeuvre. Silence tends to denote oppression in the early works. In Acker's later work, silence becomes the site of a new language. In her 1990 essay 'Nonpatriarchal Language: The Body', Acker writes: 'Let one of art criticism's languages be silence so that we can hear the sounds of the body: the winds and voices from far-off shores, the sounds of the unknown.'[30] Chapter 6 takes up the politics of silence and its relation to the representation of pain in Acker's final works. Here I want to focus on silence and aphasia.

In *Don Quixote*, silence is related to unreason and the questioning of language that madness precipitates. Blanchot explains precisely how madness questions language:

> Madness would then be a word in perpetual discordance with itself and interrogative throughout, so that it would question its own possibility, and therefore the possibility of a language that would contain it; thus it would question language itself, since the latter also belongs to the game of language.[31]

Implicit within Blanchot's claim is a certain relation between madness and impossibility. Foucault also discerns the affiliation of the two concepts. Foucault correlates madness with impossibility in his idea of the secret nature of man, which he describes as 'impossible minds, the fruit of mad imaginings'.[32] For Foucault, Descartes' movement toward truth 'made impossible the lyricism of unreason'.[33] Foucault accordingly traces a movement whereby unreason becomes impossible around the seventeenth century. This transition of madness to a state of impossibility is a movement towards politically imposed aphasia, as the point at which unreason becomes impossible is also 'where it must begin to silence itself'.[34] Perhaps there is a parallel to be drawn between the ostracising of unreason in Cartesian metaphysics and Blanchot's apprehension of the power relations between possibility and impossibility. In the Introduction and Chapter 2, I set out Blanchot's idea of a language that escapes possibility. Blanchot extends this idea in relation to thought: 'if the thought of the impossible were entertained, it would be a kind of reserve in thought itself, a thought not allowing itself to be thought in the mode of appropriative comprehension'.[35] However, Blanchot remarks that 'the impossible is not there to make thought capitulate, but to allow it to announce itself according to the measure other than that of power'. He continues with a rhetorical statement: 'What would this other measure be? Perhaps precisely the measure of the other as other, and no longer according to the clarity of that which adapts it to the same.'[36] *Don Quixote* rigorously explores the ways in which thought, through experimental writing, can be enunciated outside the parameters of rational discourse. The unspeakable, which characterises the experience of abortion in *Don Quixote*, is figuratively expressed in the practice of writing-through.

Roman Jakobson takes up the condition of aphasia in his 1956 essay 'Two Aspects of Language and Two Types of Aphasic Disturbances'. Understanding aphasia to be 'a language disturbance',[37] Jakobson claims the authority of structural linguistics to illuminate 'the study of verbal regression', and 'the aphasic disintegration of the verbal pattern'.[38] For Jakobson, speech is a process of selection whereby 'certain linguistic entities' are selected by the speaker and combined into 'linguistic units of a higher degree of complexity'.[39] The speaker is not free in his lexical choice, however; he is bound to choose from that which Jakobson terms a 'lexical storehouse', shared by the speaker and the addressee. In *Don Quixote*, it is the Bible that is the lexical repository. Don Quixote tells her canine companion, St Simeon: 'In Our Bible or The Storehouse of Language, we tried to tell women who they are: The-Loving-Mother-Who-Has-No-Sex-So-Her-Sex-Isn't-A-Crab or The Woman-Who-Loves-That-Is-Needs Love So Much She Will Let Anything Be Done To Her. But women aren't either of these' (*DQ*, 27). Don Quixote's statement implicates the lexical field demarcated by the Bible in the corralling of female identity into either the figure of the chaste mother or the figure of the passive female. 'As long as you men cling to your dualistic reality which is a reality molded by power,' the female knight states, 'women will not exist with you' (*DQ*, 28). Within this 'reality molded by power', within these constructed social identities, women do not exist. Abortion functions in the novel as resistance to the corralling of women's identity and a transgression of the law. Don Quixote states explicitly: 'I had the abortion because I refused normalcy which is the capitulation to social control. To letting political leaders locate our identities in the social' (*DQ*, 17–18). The act of abortion, in its refusal of the role of the mother and the passive female, is directly linked to the condition of aphasia engendered by the deficiency of the lexical storehouse to provide linguistic entities for women's experience.

The condition of aphasia in *Don Quixote* is evident in Acker's experimental practice. Jakobson distinguishes between two types of aphasia. The first he terms 'the similarity disorder', or 'selection defi-ciency'.[40] People who experience this condition are entirely depen-dent upon the context of language. Jakobson states of the person affected: 'The more his utterances are dependent on the context, the better he copes with the verbal task. He feels unable to utter a sen-tence which responds neither to the cue of his interlocutor nor to the actual situation.'[41] Within this type of aphasia, Jakobson observes, the ability for code switching has been lost and thus 'the idiolect indeed becomes the sole linguistic reality'.[42] If words are not spoken in the speaker's idiolect, '[h]e considers the other's utterance to be either gibberish or at least in an unknown language'.[43] The second form of aphasia, the opposite of 'the similarity disorder', Jakobson terms 'the contiguity disorder'. This type of aphasia resonates with Acker's strategies of writing-through. In this 'contexture-deficient aphasia', Jakobson states, '[t]he syntactic rules organizing words into higher units are lost; this loss, called "agrammatism," causes the degeneration of the sentence into a mere "word heap".'[44] As a result: 'Word order becomes chaotic; the ties of grammatical coordination and subordination, whether concord or government are dissolved.'[45]

One outcome is the emergence of the 'telegraphic style', a mode of language in which words that solely function grammatically, such as conjunctions, prepositions, pronouns and articles, are the first to be omitted. Jakobson states:

> The less a word depends grammatically on the context, the stronger is its tenacity in the speech of aphasics with a contiguity disorder. Thus the 'kernel subject word' is the first to fall out of the sentence in the case of similarity disorder, and conversely, it is the least destruc-tible in the opposite type of aphasia.[46]

Drawing on Jakobson, Hannah Sullivan in her rigorous study, *The Work of Revision* (2013), suspects all modernist writers to be 'would-be aphasics, doers of different abnormal voices'.[47] Amongst other convincing examples, she notes that Joyce's 'revisions by addition' in *Ulysses* 'turn single adjectives into bound compounded forms'[48] while the 'heaped fragments' in the closing sections of *The Waste Land* resemble an instance of contiguity disorders.[49] Within the context of the final published work, Don Quixote's aphasic failure and ontological negation usher in the practice of writing-through as a response to aphasic inexpressibility. Tactics of annexation, violence, and alteration are at work in Acker's writing-through of male texts in the second part of *Don Quixote*. Acker's practice resembles both the literary condensation of Cage and Mac Low and Jakobson's 'telegraphic style'. As Craig Dworkin remarks 'by reducing voluminous texts' Cage and Mac Low 'created compressed versions of the parent text'.[50] The use of 'telegraphic style' has a similar outcome.

The grammatical paring and omission inherent to Jakobson's idea of the aphasic's 'telegraphic style' is evident in the first text in the middle section of *Don Quixote* titled 'Other Texts'. 'Russian Constructivism', the text that opens the second section of *Don Quixote*, points to the Russian avant-garde in the early part of the twentieth century, and, significantly, was titled 'Russian Constructivism and Semiotics' in the original unpublished manuscript.[51] The initial subsection of 'Other Texts' is titled 'Abstraction' and is a rewriting of Andrei Bely's *St Petersburg* (1913). Acker's choice of Bely's text is significant. Johanna Drucker remarks that the Russian Constructivists 'had the most developed theoretical stance with respect to the possibilities of formal innovation as a political tool'.[52] Acker's invocation of Russian Constructivism is worthy of attention, and can be positioned in relation to wider practices of the neo-avant-garde, and her continuation of radical modernist practice. Hal Foster comments on two radical 'returns' in art practices that occurred in the late 1950s and 1960s: the readymades germane to Duchampian Dada, and 'the contingent structures of Russian Constructivism – that is, structures, like the counter-reliefs of Tatlin, or the hanging constructions of Rodchenko, that reflect both inwardly on material, form and structure and outwardly on space, light, and context'.[53] A similar abstract aesthetics is found in 'Other Texts'. In the 1950s and 1960s, Foster observes, constructivism offered a historical alternative to 'the modernist model dominant at the time', developed by Roger Fry and Clive Bell, and later cultivated by Clement Greenberg and Michael Fried. In her choice of Bely, Acker also continues her engagement with Symbolism (that began with the rewriting of Mallarmé in *Blood and Guts in High School* and continues in her later trilogy in the narratives of Rimbaud and Verlaine in *In Memoriam to Identity*), bringing the text into the contemporary. In an act of excavation and preservation, Acker houses the radical impulse of Bely's work within the unreadable text of *Don Quixote*, the difficulty of which protects the source text from cultural reification.

Acker both rewrites Bely's work and uses techniques of disjunction to destabilise the text. In her notes on William Burroughs's *Exterminator!* (1973), Acker discusses the dream-like structure of Burroughs's work, whereby textual collage functions to disallow the reader from emerging from a fictional text into reality. In works that use this collagist strategy of disjunction Acker notes: 'The reader does come up, but only to enter an even crappier story.'[54] In what might be termed paratactic disjunction, *Don Quixote*'s layering of disjunctive texts that are often written in contrasting registers ruptures logical consequence. Acker states: 'there's no cause-and-effect cause cause-and-effect tells you what's real (this happened because of this)'.[55] Jan Corbett has described collagist practice in the middle section of *Don Quixote* as 'regressive appropriation', a composite of 'fragments of myth abstracted from the literary canon'.[56] Corbett's reading highlights the significance of Acker's detachment of texts from the literary canon, as well as underlining the process of abstraction that takes place in such experimental practice. Yet reading 'Other Texts' through the prism of techniques of writing-through reveals Acker's strategies as much more complex, and the text emerges as more than simply a collection of fragments. The change of genre between sections of the text is the key technique in creating what Acker understands to be a labyrinthian textual structure. Change of genre is also the key to Acker's version of 'writing-through'. In her essay 'Nonpatriarchal Language', Acker explores 'the dream of the labyrinth or the self that will lead us to languages that cannot be authoritarian'.[57] Writing-through a variety of texts is an early method that reaches towards this idea of the labyrinth. Acker uses, not simply appropriation, but techniques of rewriting, collage, disjunction, switching genre, and translation as part of what might be considered her practice of non-procedural writing-through.

Acker rewrites the 'Prologue' to Bely's modernist text, bringing to the forefront the idea of abstraction, which she takes as a subheading. Bely's own work employed techniques of abstraction and was designed to create a sense of disorder, a hellish vision of St Petersburg on the brink of Revolution. Set over forty-eight hours in St Petersburg, around the year 1905, the plot revolves around a father, Apollon Apollonovich Ableukhov, a Tsarist official who represents the old order, and a son, Nikolai, who marks the brewing revolution and the infiltration of Marxism into Russia. Acker condenses Bely's plot in a few lines:

> Petersburg, my city.
>   Petersburg steeples triangles bums on the streets decrepit churches broken-down churches churches gone churches used as homes for bums for children forced away from the abandoned buildings they run.
>   Son.
>   1.
>   City of people who weren't born here who decided to live here who decided to live here who're homeless, trying to make their own lives: poor refugees artists rich people. People who don't care and care too much. Homeless. You, baby crib, only you've been financially shuffled off by the USSR government. (*DQ*, 41)

Acker's selection from Bely's work reverberates with her critique of the US government and capitalist structures throughout *Don Quixote*. At the time of writing *St Petersburg*, Bely sympathised with the Bolsheviks. Bely's work is a work of textual abstraction. Textual abstraction affords both authors a method of breaking with representational qualities, creating a radical textual space that accommodates an equally radical, revolutionary politics. Acker maintains Bely's revolutionary authorial voice, bringing the text into the contemporary. She rewrites not just the text but also adopts and adapts many of Bely's techniques. John Cournos notes the similarity between James Joyce's *Ulysses* (1922) and Bely's *St Petersburg*:

> Both compress the action of their narratives, both use something of a stream-of consciousness method, both employ a variety of techniques, both describe sharply divergent characters, present flashbacks and memory associations, newspaper reports, and thoughts and emotions which overlap and interplay.[58]

However, compression, as Vladimir E. Alexandrov points out, also leads to the production of a certain illegibility in Bely's work. When Bely abridged the novel in 1922, Alexandrov observes, he reduced whole dialogues between characters, the result of which was that 'the new text contains numerous passages teetering on the edge of unintelligibility'.[59] Both *Don Quixote* and *St Petersburg* are the result of rigorous revision and excision of the original materials for the final works. Alexandrov notes

> the cuts Bely made strengthen the general impression the novel produces – that the world in it is difficult to apprehend, and that it 'flickers' between being and not being fully visible to its perceivers in the text or intelligible to its readers.[60]

Bely's prologue foregrounds the experimental nature of his text:

> If Petersburg is not the capital, then there is no Petersburg. Then its existence is merely imaginary.
> But Petersburg is not merely imaginary; it can be located on maps – in the shape of concentric circles and a black dot in the middle; and this mathematical dot, which has no defined measurements, proclaims energetically that it exists: from this dot comes the impetuous surge of words which makes the pages of a book; and from this point circulars rapidly spread.[61]

The emergence of the book (Bely's 'impetuous surge of words') from an abstract topography situates it as a text generated from a work of abstract art, Aleksandr Rodchenko's *White Circle* (1918) or Kazimir Malevich's *Black Circle* (1923), for instance, rather than as the representation of a geographical site (though Bely's work predates both of these artworks). Geometric abstraction points to non-representational space. Of his work *Black Suprematist Square* (1913), Malevich expressed his fear that the artist could be 'imprisoned in the cube'.[62] Yet abstraction also signals Malevich's other hypothesis: that this 'non-objective creation'[63] might extend into another space that as Anna Moszynska remarks 'extends beyond the circumscribed horizon'.[64] Acker's rewritten text reflects this abstract aspect of Bely's work. Through paragrammatic shifts and oblique rhyme, the text is condensed and reduced into a 'telegraphic style': 'run. Son. 1'. The disjunctive sections of text are obliquely threaded through abstract metonymy. Acker takes 'Peter', the contraction of Petersburg, as the polysemous metonymical point of transition between her texts, entering into the contemporary story of the female weight-lifter in an act of displacement: 'In Peter one morning, the female weight-lifter fell out of her loft-bed' (*DQ*, 42). This narrative shift, and switching of genre through the word Peter, is an aspect of writing-through. Acker takes a line from Bely's 'Prologue': 'Petersburg, Saint Petersburg, or Peter (it is all one)',[65] and uses it as the basis for an experimental strategy. Through semantic play and inflection Acker, in her rewriting, performs the interchangeability of terms that Bely simply states. In the female weight-lifter's story, 'Peter' is a place. After the brief interlude of a newspaper cutting entitled 'City of Passion', there is a further transposition, as 'Peter' becomes a person, the recipient of two contemporary letters from his lover. Following this epistolary section the subsequent polyphonous text opens with an account of Russian Constructivist, Vladimir Tatlin's aesthetics, alongside the relations between Bely and Alexander Blok, written in a colloquial voice. This colloquial voice is spliced and cut in with critical questions posed in an objective tone and with life writing:

> Tatlin designed a city. Tatlin took unhandlable passion and molded it.
>
> It all comes out of passion. Our city of passion.
>
> Biely wanted to fuck his closest comrade, Alexander Blok's wife until the duel between them in 1906 (which never happened), then Biely left Russia for a year. When Biely described this passion, he constructed a language as if it were a building. If architecture wasn't cool cold, people couldn't live in it. I have to find out why I'm hurting so much. Recognition: I'm really hurting. One of this hurt's preconditions is I'm in love with you. (*DQ*, 46)

The idea of a city of passion, mentioned in the earlier newspaper cutting, re-emerges in this section. The technique of disjunction, which disallows an absolute text, affects an opening here for the subsequent question: 'Is sensuality less valuable than rational thought?' (*DQ*, 46). Through disjunction and metonymical repetition, discourses of rationality and sensuality are threaded through the rewritten text so that the emergence of radical lines of enquiry such as: 'Is there a split between the mind and the body, or rather between these two types of mentality?' must be answered in the negative, as the aesthetic dialectic of the sensual and the rational created by the textual collage suggest that dualisms are not valid or, at least, are destructive, within the framework of the rewritten text.

Translations, time, and transliterations: Acker, Catullus, Zukofsky

For Julia Kristeva, poetic language escapes binaries. Acker turns to the poetic in the second part of her text as a means to move beyond dualism. The poetic in *Don Quixote* is a mode of communication that is one way of addressing issues of impossibility and non-linear time, positioned, with female identity, outside traditional grammatical structures and fixed denotation. In the third part of *Don Quixote*, the aphasic knight explains poetry to her comrades, the dogs:

> 'I write words to you whom I don't and can't know, to you who will always be other than and alien to me. These words sit on the edges of meaning and aren't properly grammatical. For when there is no country, no community, the speaker's unsure of which language to use, how to speak, if it's possible to speak. (*DQ*, 191)

The second part of the first text, 'Poems of a City', is, in the first instance, a writing-through of Gaius Valerius Catullus's eighth poem in the collection *Polymetra*. Acker held an interest in translating Latin. A copy of P. Vergili Maronis, *Bucolica et Georgica* housed in the Kathy Acker Papers reveals Acker's scrupulous annotations in the margins of the Latin poet's work. Along with the translations of individual words, Acker marks up phrases that are significant to her: 'intended prophetic obscurity'[66] for instance, and various grammatic features of the text such as 'hyperbaton'[67] (the inversion of the arrangement of common words to create sentences arranged differently, a practice Acker practised in her rewriting of Vallejo in *Blood and Guts in High School*). In rewriting Catullus, Acker aligns her work with that of her contemporary, Bernadette Mayer, whose translations and imitations of Latin and Greek poets, particularly the work of Catullus, subvert the classical text and imbue it with a feminist voice.[68] More recently, Anne Carson has taken up and translated Catullus's poem 101, in *Nox* (2009), an elegy for Carson's brother. Acker's focus on the role of translation in the act of rewriting Catullus, however, is closer to Louis Zukofsky's homophonic translations of the Latin poet in the volume *Catullus* (written 1958–66, first published 1969). Both Acker and Zukofsky translate Poem VIII. It tells of a fleeting love affair between Catullus and an unnamed girl. Zukofsky's translation is titled 'Miss Her, Catullus? Don't Be So Inept . . .' Louis and Celia Zukofsky state in their 1961 'Translator's Preface': 'This translation of Catullus follows the sound, rhythm, and syntax of his Latin – tries, as is said, to breathe the "literal" meaning with him.'[69] The conflation of breath and meaning as a performative origin is affiliated with the act of listening in the Zukofskys' work. As Charles Bernstein remarks, for their *Catullus* poems (1969) Louis and Celia Zukofsky developed what would be termed homophonic translation, 'translation with special emphasis to the sounds rather than the lexical meaning'.[70] Bernstein presents homophonic translation as a reframing device: 'Leading with the sound, homophonic translation reframes what is significant in translation, challenging the idea that the translation should focus on content or create poems that sounds fluent in their new language.'[71] The method of homophonic translation creates a new form of communication, by subordinating fixed denotation and fluency to sound, and innovative language structures.

The prioritising of sound over meaning in Zukofsky's *Catullus* poems has led some critics, such as Peter Quartermain, to apprehend Zukofsky's poems as transliterations rather than traditional translations. Referring to the Zukofskys' volume, Quartermain remarks that '*Catullus* is totally subversive of the whole academic, scholastic, and pedantic tradition of poetry practiced in the English language in the twentieth century.'[72] The first eight lines of the poem illustrate Zukofsky's technique (the original is reproduced underneath Zukofsky's poem):

> Miss her, Catullus? don't be so inept to rail
> at what you see perish when perished is the case.
> Full, sure once, candid the sunny days glowed, solace,
> when you went about it as your girl would have it,
> you loved her as no one else shall ever be loved.
> Billowed in tumultuous joys and affianced,
> why you would but will it and your girl would have it.
> Full, sure, very candid the sun's rays glowed solace.
>
> Miser Catulle, desinas ineptire,
> et quod vides perisse perditum ducas.
> fulsere quondam candidi tibi soles,
> cum ventitabas quo puella ducebat

amata nobis quantum amabitur nulla.
ibi illa multa tum iocosa fiebant,
quae tu volebas nec puella nolebat.
fulsere vere candidi tibi soles. [73]

The effect of transliteration is a displacement of grammatically centred meaning and the generation of new meanings through parataxis.
Homophonic translations of individual words render the line ungram-
matical. Yet the new lines, such as 'Billowed in tumultuous joys and
affianced' allow for the emergence of affect and generate eroticism.
Zukofsky's line in its indifference to grammatically centred meaning reveals the very nature of grammar as a law imposed upon the
sentence. Importantly then, Zukofsky's work is also a subversion of
traditional hermeneutical enquiry. Designating the work as 'an act
of great mischief', Quartermain adds 'with no knowledge of Latin
whatsoever, he is translating the entire work of the great untranslatable poet'.[74] Zukofsky's practice is in many ways a strategy of
literal non-knowledge. 'Not knowing Latin', Quartermain observes,
'enabled him to objectify its sounds.'[75] Yet lines two, four and five
look like translations. Translation aims for accuracy with regards to
the meaning and sense of the original sentence. By comparison, transliteration, being the transcription of the word into the corresponding
letters of another alphabet or language, is a language-centred practice that usurps the centrality of meaning generated from classical
grammatical structure. Quartermain refers to Zukofsky's 'generative
incoherence'[76] produced in his experimental practices. Comparing
Catullus to Joyce's *Finnegans Wake* (1939), Quartermain remarks
on the 'turbulence' and impenetrability of the work, stating 'as in
Finnegans Wake, the writing creates the situation to which it refers'.[77]

A comparison emerges with Acker's work, one that is central to
an understanding of Acker's creation of new textual conditions and
the practice of feminist translation, an auxiliary strategy to her practice of writing-through. Bergvall remarks on the conceptual nature
of translation. Tracing a long history of deviant translation, Bergvall
draws on Thomas Urquhart's additions of English games to his translation of Rabelais' *Gargantua* (1532–64). She remarks: 'In these distended translations, it is the parasitical endlessness of the associative
stimuli that is arresting, the virtuoso display of a task unfaithfully
executed.' The task 'is executed along the lines of structure, rather

than verbal correspondence'. For Bergvall in this instance: 'The translation exercise becomes more diffuse and opaque. The calque is no longer a one-to-one, but a one-to-one intercepted and recirculated via a different register.'[78] Similar to Bergvall's conception of 'distended translations', which use tactics of 'deviation and redirection' to 'displace the expectations of translation',[79] Acker's translation of Catullus skews traditional notions of translation. Like Zukofsky's transliterations, Acker's rewriting of Catullus offers no stable textual coordinates and inscribes the translator's voice as the creator of language-centred meaning in the text.[80] Bernstein highlights the agency of the translator in *Catullus*, and suggests that transliteration is an act of defamiliarisation. He comments that 'Zukofsky insists that the mark of the translator be pronounced, and that in making the translation strange, we may provide a way to come closer to its core.'[81] Transliteration, specifically in relation to the act of transcribing the words of male texts, is a strategy used by Acker to find a voice as a woman, which takes the form of a mark, a feminist inscription, a non-verbal stamp, an alteration of the male poet's language that is both inside and outside language.

Acker's rewriting and glossing of Catullus's poem is a subversion of the literary model of insemination. Her new text permeates the original but fragments and de-forms it. Acker's rewritten text of Catullus's poem takes a bipartite structure and renames the poem 'On time'. In the left column multilingual text runs parallel to the commentary in the right column. Here the breaking of logical consequence is central to Acker's writerly practice, as she uses fracturing to call into question the reason of the actual world. The experiment also points to the capacity of the practice of writing to disrupt language in a way that speech cannot. The first poem in 'Poems of a City' (metonymically recalling the St Petersburg of the previous section) concerns the subjunctive and its relation to the imaginary:

> *On Time*

desinas ineptire et quod vides perisse perditum ducas.	The subjunctive mood takes precedence over the straightforward active. The past controls the present.
fulsere quondam candidi tibi soles,	The past.

cum it hurts me to remember I
  did act up today, a way of
  saying 'I'm not perfect,' forgive
  my phone call, ventitabas quo
  puella ducebat (on a leash:
  leather Rome)
amata nobis quantum amabitur   The first future tense. What
  nulla.   do words really say: does this
                                  future propose future time?

ibi illa multa kisses on kisses
  between us
you hands your flesh unending
  time into time
the past wasn't past – how do I
  transform the past: that awful
  prison cause it ends?
fulsere vere candidi tibi soles.   By repeating the past, I'm
                                  molding and transforming
                                  it, an impossible act. (*DQ*, 47–8)

In this poem Acker's innovative poetic practice relates to Don Quixote's claim: 'An alteration of language, rather than of material, usually changes material conditions' (*DQ*, 27). Acker's linguistic experimentation produces textual indeterminacy through penetrating the original text and infiltrating the text with a contemporary voice.[82] Again, Quartermain's analysis of Zukofsky's *Catullus* is illuminating. He states that an invitation to translate and the simultaneous revoking of that invitation by the text is inherent to both Joyce's and Zukofsky's practice: 'A salient feature of *Finnegan's Wake* is that the very punnish nature of the book invites us to translate whilst ensuring that translation is impossible; a similar punishment lies in store for the reader of *Catullus*.'[83]

A comparable play is at work in *Don Quixote*. The annotative structure both points to a translation of the text, yet it does not offer a translation but a grammatical exegesis. Acker's initial linguistic commentary on the poetry of Catullus in the right column privileges the subjunctive, the mood of verbs expressing what is imagined, over the indicative, the mood of verbs expressing statements of facts. The lines 'desinas ineptire et quod vides perisse perditum ducas' are traditionally translated as 'you should stop fooling / And what you know you've lost admit losing.'[84] Acker comments on these lines: 'The subjunctive mood takes precedence over the straightforward active.' The subsequent commentary on language self-reflexively remarks on the act of appropriation as well as the confining historicist cultural narrative: 'The past controls the present.' Acker's comment on the line 'fulsere quondam cadidi tibi soles' ('The sun shone brilliantly for you, time was') is simply 'The past.' Later, the Latin original of Catullus's poem reads: 'amata nobis quantum amabitur nulla', and is translated conventionally as 'Loved by us as we shall love no one' (literally· '(she is) loved by us as no body {female} will be loved'). As Acker notes, it is the first use of the future tense in Catullus's poem.[85] Calling into question the indicative truth of the statement, 'What do words really say: does this future propose future time?' affirms the subjunctive turn Acker practices and destabilises the authority of the proposition. Fracturing the poem, inserting contemporary lines between Catullus's lines, such as 'how do I transform the past: that awful prison cause it ends?', the left column solicits a rhetorical relation with the right. Parallel to Catullus's line 'fulsere vere candidi tibi soles' (the sun shone brilliantly for you truly), the commentary responds to the despair in the previous lines of the left column. Literally writing through Catullus's poem, Acker performs what she understands to be an 'impossible act', moulding and transforming the past by repeating it.

Here, and in her subsequent poems on time, Acker's experimental practices can be positioned in relation to Kristeva's articulation of 'cyclical' time in her pioneering essay 'Women's Time' (1981). Kristeva understands two modes of temporality, 'cyclical and monumental', to be 'traditionally linked to female subjectivity'.[86] These two temporal modalities stand in contrast to 'the time of linear history, or *cursive time* (as Nietzsche called it)'.[87] Again referencing Nietzsche, 'monumental time' is 'the time of another history, thus another time . . . which englobes . . . supranational, sociocultural ensembles within even larger entities'.[88] Positioning cyclical and monumental temporalities in relation to the second phase of feminism, women who approached feminism after 1968, and those women 'who had an aesthetic or psychoanalytic experience', Kristeva marries the refusal of linear temporality with 'an exacerbated distrust of the entire political dimension'. She states: 'Essentially interested in the specificity of female psychology and its symbolic realizations, these women seek to give a language to the intrasubjective and corporeal experiences left mute by culture in the past.' '[T]his feminism', she states, 'situates itself outside the linear time of identities which communicate through projection and revindication.'[89] Acker's new model of time realised through her act of writing-through can be positioned in relation to Kristeva's feminist temporalities.

Having announced the 'impossible act' that her rewriting is carrying out, a new section is introduced. Until this point in the poem, the commentary has been in line with the Latin accompaniment to the left. In the new section Acker bleeds the past into the present:

nec quae fugit sectare, nec miser
  vive
good advice sed obstinata mente
  perfer, obdura.
vale, puella. (My awful telephone
  call. This's my apology, Peter.
Do you accept?) *iam* (ha ha)
  Catullus obdurat,
nec te requiret nec rogabit
  invitam:
     I'm a good girl
I have, behave perfectly.
at tu dolebis. The imaginary
  makes reality, as in love, cum
  rogaberis nulla
scelesta. Scelesta nocte. My
  night. quae tibi manet vita
  without me?
quis nunc adibit? without me cui
  videberis bella?
quem nunc amabis? with me you
  fuck whoever you want.
Let the imagination reign
  supreme. quem you now
fucking? cuius esse diceris
  huh!
quem basiabis a stupid question?
  cui labella labula mordebis?
  (allied to death?)
at tu, Catullus, destinatus obdura
to facts, for only the imagination
  lives.

My present is negative.
This present becomes
imaginary: The future of
amabitur and the
subjunctive at the
beginning of the poem?:

The imagination is will. (*DQ*, 48–9)

Through the fusion of languages and semantic disruption, '[t]his present becomes imaginary'. This pataphysical abstraction of time is a consequence of the 'impossible act' that takes place in the first half of the poem; such an act elicits a move into an imaginary space through experimentation and performs on a linguistic level Don Quixote's quest for love. The future of 'amabitur', the phrasal future verb 'will be loved', and the subjunctive at the beginning of the poem might indeed be imaginary. Acker's disjunctive writing-through of Catullus creates an illegible text and opens up an affective field.

There is a form of seduction at work in both the Zukofskys' trans-literations and Acker's experimentalism. As Riley remarks: 'seduction entices whatever is latent to make itself overt'.[90] In Acker's discursive construction the intervention of the contemporary lines transform the original text, turning Catullus's pentameter into a free-form affective syntax. In fact, splicing contemporary lines into the Latin imbues Catullus's lines with an evident sonorous lack of control. In the above excerpt for instance, the lower case Latin, with its lyrical hendecasyllabic rhythms, is for the most part subordinated through hypotaxis to the upper case of the contemporary feminine lines:

> at tu dolebis. The imaginary
>   makes reality, as in love, cum
>   rogaberis nulla
> scelesta. Scelesta nocte. My
>   night. quae tibi manet vita
>   without me?

Illegibility deposes denotative meaning and empowers the materiality of language. The punning on 'cum' intersects and collapses the Latin and the contemporary vernacular. Functioning as both an abstract preposition, meaning 'combined with' in both Latin and English, and a contemporary noun referring to semen or vaginal fluid, the word folds the past into the present. The loss of control affected through the syntax of the Latin gestures to the latter definition. What Riley terms linguistic affect, which I discussed in Chapter 2, occurs in this rewriting of Catullus in an active form, and is instrumental to Acker's practice of *récriture féminine*. The act of writing-through and the strategies of dis-junction provide the conditions for the emergence of linguistic affect, that which Riley understands to be complicit with both 'a grammar of the emotions' and 'emotional grammar'.[91]

Feminist paragrammatics and the protosemantic

The poems that follow Acker's rewriting of Catullus adhere to the non-reason of the subjunctive: 'subjunctive tenses grammatically reflect the new model of common time: change is time' (*DQ*, 51). Writing through Catullus's poem allows Acker to question the future tense within the present, replacing the indicative conditional with the counterfactual conditional. Acker's experimentation creates a counterpossible space and temporality obverse to the specific mode of temporalisation through which, as Steve McCaffery observes, grammatically centred meaning is realised.[92] These issues were sketched in Chapter 1. Within this counterpossible space of Acker's textual collage, it is absolute meaning that is rendered impossible. The mode of temporalisation – that is, time as metamorphic – is realised through disjunctive structure. The remainder of the first text explores the relation between this new model of time, desire, and death. In a poetic section titled 'Loneliness', Acker practises a method of unworking in which the lines of the poem are not given but the commentary is offered instead. A further comparison arises here between Acker's piece and Zukofsky's '*Mantis:* An Interpretation' (1934), Zukofsky's free verse annotation to his sestina 'Mantis' (1934). Bernstein has remarked that Zukofsky's 'commentary-in-verse' implies 'the insufficiency of *the* poem and the necessity for interpretation – not as closure but as a dialectical method for opening the word's work into a social world'.[93] Within the section 'Loneliness', the omission of the original text that the lines are commenting on suggests not just the insufficiency of the poem but the impossibility of writing.

In these poems Acker struggles with two temporal models, that which she terms 'common time' and that of death and the imaginary. The temporal model to which the latter relates is the temporality realised in the experimental text and accords to Kristeva's cyclical time. If being born is entry into cursive time, linguistic unity, and linear history, the non-linear time of the de-formed text can be positioned in relation to the literary trope of abortion that opens *Don Quixote*. In a subsection in the first part of *Don Quixote*, titled 'History and Women', Don Quixote positions the time of death as antithetical to the time of history, from which women are excluded: 'It's not history, which is actuality, but history's opposite, death, which shows us that women are nothing and everything' (*DQ*, 31). The narrative voice states:

                                                            Love
destroys common time and reverses subject and object; the
verb acts on itself; I'm your mirror; identity's gone because
there's no separation between love and death. Line twelve. The
final model of time is that the mirror reflects the mirror, time is
our love. (*DQ*, 51)

In the final lines the voice reaches what is termed the 'absolute present':

              all the verbs are now subjunctives; all
verbs are change. Again: loving you is making me feel pain.
The final verb, *is changed*, grammatically reflects its opposite
in content: the mirror. Time: love or fusion exists side by side
with change:

Time is desire: 'I want you. That's all I can think. This is our absolute present. Line twenty-six' (*DQ*, 51). The annotations, which are
the substance of Acker's text, gloss the unpresentable. Appropriately
enough, two poems follow that are an attempt to write desire: 'Time
is Pain' and 'Time is Made by Humans'.

Three sections of experimental prose follow the poetry sections that
are a collage of disjunctive writings on semiotics and samplings of erotic
prose. The first section of the second part takes male texts, and through
dis-structures of unreason produces non-absolute rewritings in which
woman finds a voice in the negation of language. The concern with time
and non-linear narrative in *Don Quixote* reflects Acker's interest in
issues of time and the philosophy of language. Like Stein's experiments
with language and the creation of a continuous present that were influenced by the teachings of William James,[94] Acker's experiments with
language and time emerge from her interest in the philosophy of language. In an unpublished document, 'Commonsensical / Philosophical
Use of Words', Acker explores notions of the 'specious present' and
'Ideal Languages' in the work of Wittgenstein, Gustav Bergmann, and
William James. The works' significance as influences on Acker's experiments and her struggle with articulating a new narrative temporality
are worth noting. Put very simply, the notion of an Ideal Language for
Gustav Bergmann is a language free from context. Laird Addis sum-
marises the concept as follows:

the ideal language, in contrast to all natural languages, is context
free. In all natural languages the truth or falsity of some utterances

or dicta depends on where or when and by whom they are uttered or written. The ideal language removes this 'limitation' and still says everything that can (or perhaps 'must') be said.[95]

The philosophical idea of a language free from context resonates with Acker's desire to find a language outside ordinary language. The temporality of such a language would necessarily be free from any tense. In *The Principles of Psychology* (1890), William James states: 'The only fact of our immediate experience is what Mr E. R. Clay has well called "the *specious* present".'[96] Acker points to the specious present as the temporality of experience, and she discusses its relation to the notion of the ideal language in her notes. She poses 'the problem of time' and asks: 'How are commonsensical statements containing an explicit or implicit reference to time, such as the statement that a certain individual has a certain duration, to be transcribed into, or, reconstituted in, the ideal language.' 'The specious present', she notes, 'is a duration. The specious present is the (temporal) span of a man's duration.'[97] The quandaries that Acker points to here in her notes (that run to thirty-five pages) signal her working through the difficulties of using a language that is both in and out of time, her attempt to make language present. Her methods of writing-through in *Don Quixote*, and her poetics on time, can be read as endeavours to realise a contemporary model of time, an absolute present, that may be a narrative time rendered in the specious present.

As the outset of this chapter suggested, Acker's experimental tactics in *Don Quixote* can be positioned in relation to Kristeva's semiology of paragrams and, concomitantly, to Steve McCaffery's recent work on protosemantics. For McCaffery:

> the protosemantic is more a process than a material thing; a multiplicity of forces, when brought to bear on texts (or released in them), unleash a combinatory fecundity that includes those semantic jumps that manifest within letter shifts and verbal recombinations, and the presyntactic violations determining a word's position: rupture, reiteration, displacement, reterritorialization.[98]

Kristeva does not consider the poetic to be confined to the genre of poetry. Instead, she states in her essay 'Towards a Semiology of Paragrams', 'the operation of the poetic ... means the language of both "poetry" and prose'.[99] In what she calls '*Transformative* semiotic practice', Kristeva explains the sign 'becomes blurred: "signs" are disengaged from their denotation'. In contrast to the symbolic system, Kristeva claims that 'transformative practice' 'is changing and seeks to transform, it is not limited, explanatory, or logical in the traditional sense'.[100] Transformative practice and paragrammatic writing are complementary: 'Paragrammatic writing', Kristeva states, 'is a continuous reflection, a written contestation of the code, of the law and of itself.' Designating the writing of Dante, Sade, and Lautréamont as illustrative of the practice, she states, 'it is the contestatory philosophical enterprise become language'.[101] *Don Quixote* is replete with paragrammatic writing. Don Quixote's opening statement in part three offers a neat example:

> Don Quixote: 'He whom I love is my eyes and heart and I'm sick when I'm not with him, but he doesn't love me. He's my eyes; he's my I's; I see by my I's; he's my sun. My son lets me see and be. Thus he's my and the Ⓐ. I've said it in every book, mainly porn or poor books, I've ever written Ⓐd nauseam even in nauseam, for love hurts badly. I'll say it again: without I's, the I is nothing. (*DQ*, 101)

The 'I' here is multiple, inflected by its homophone, 'eye', denoting perception and sight. McCaffery takes up homophony in his chapter 'Zarathrustran "Pataphysics"'. 'Homophony', he writes, 'registers a certain autonomy of language outside of referential constraint and systematic relations but also unleashes a *dynamis* of vertiginous, uncontrollable transformations. The homophone is a conjunctional force, not a thing: Jarry's syzygy between similar sound and dissimilar meaning.' McCaffery refers to Lecercle who draws the connection between the multiplicity of meaning at the site of the homophone and the subsequent 'loss of mastery by the subject who is compelled to give into this proliferation'.[102]

This passage is paradigmatic of Acker's use of punning throughout the text. The use of punning in the latter part of the text is a recurrence of the form of wordplay that brought the protagonist of the text into existence. Echoing Cervantes's delusional protagonist's request to the innkeeper to dub him a knight, Acker's female Don Quixote, punning on medical instruments, deems 'catheter' to be the glorification of 'Kathy'. '[B]y taking on such a name which, being long, is male,' the narrator states, 'she would be able to become a female knight or a night-knight' (*DQ*, 10). The birth of the female knight, occurring in an instance of paranomasia, also takes place at the site of linguistic indeterminacy, aligning the emergence of the female self with paragrammatics. This anarchic poetic writing is inflected here by the circled A, a reference both to the politics of the passages of the text that critiques American politics and to the paragrammatics of the text. The text has an ambivalent status. On the one hand, Acker's experimentation is evidently intentional and implies a certain amount of textual control that deliberately gives rise to the protosemantic. Yet the fraught energy of the composition gestures to what Riley sees as exceeding the dexterous hand of the poet, who creates 'the familiar critical idea of an "ambiguity of meaning"'. She delineates this other force as 'a far less malleable affair, a continuous white noise, an anarchic whirring-away, unstoppable, relentless'. Homophony is just one example, she asserts, words 'so congenitally at risk from the interference of their double or triple meanings', so that the reader of the poem is at risk of 'dissolving through a plurality of possible meanings'.[103] This other force of writing inheres in the sections of repetition that unnerve, displace, and destabilise meaning. In a section in which the narrator converses with a teacher each piece of the dialogue is repeated four times, a conceptual practice that disrupts meaning through the protosemantic gesture:

> '"That," said my teacher, "'s what we're going to find out. It's not simply the case that we can't know anything. We do know."
> '"That," said my teacher, "'s what we're going to find out. It's not simply the case that we can't know anything. We do know."
> '"That," said my teacher, "'s what we're going to find out. It's not simply the case that we can't know anything. We do know."
> '"That," said my teacher, "'s what we're going to find out. It's not simply the case that we can't know anything. We do know."
> '"This is something new."
> '"This is something new."
> '"This is something new."
> '"This is something new." (*DQ*, 167)

The use of repetition destabilises meaning. The reiteration of 'we do know' with no denotation, suggests the very opposite. Similarly, the repetition of 'This is something new' violates the very concept of newness and originality. Through such asemantic features, *Don Quixote* questions the rational, displaces any notion of a central-ised narrative, and moves towards a new form of language and temporality. The formation of a new sense of female time is evi-dence of the creativity at work in Acker's experimental practice of non-procedural writing-through and protosemantic play. The forging of a new narrative temporality emerges through the turbu-lence of the text as the creative force of experiment. The new mode of creativity in *Don Quixote*, aligned by Acker with the trope of abortion, can be situated in a counter-position to the idea of liter-ary influence as insemination and offers new pathways to thinking about the progeny and the process of making meaning in the work of the experimental wrier.

Chapter 4

Intertextuality and Constructive Non-identity: *In Memoriam to Identity*

On 5 December 1991, Fred Jordan at Pantheon Books sent William Burroughs the proofs of Acker's *Portrait of An Eye*, the collection of early texts comprising the final manuscripts of the three novellas *The Childlike Life of the Black Tarantula by the Black Tarantula* (1974), *I Dreamt I was a Nymphomaniac: Imagining* (1975), and *The Adult Life of Toulouse Lautrec by Henri Toulouse Lautrec* (1973). In a letter dated 7 January 1992, Burroughs's agent, James Grauerholz, penned a taut reply, pointing to the irony that Acker had been one of his clients in 1977, and that he had, in fact, offered the books to Fred Jordan in the same year, when Jordan was at Grove Press. Grauerholz includes in his letter a quote from Burroughs:

> A writer's 'I' is often the least interesting aspect of his artistic consciousness, and Kathy Acker beautifully resolves this problem by having no 'I', and having many 'I''s . . . her 'author' moves and shifts before you can know who 'you' are, and that gives her work the power to mirror the reader's soul.[1]

Burroughs's observations here commending the shifting nature of Acker's 'I' and the text's subsequent ushering in of multiple identities in her early trilogy are mirrored in Acker's comments in interview with Ellen G. Friedman in 1989. Regarding her early trilogy she states: 'The major theme was identity, the theme I used from Tarantula through *The Adult Life of Toulouse Lautrec by Henri Toulouse Lautrec*, the end of trilogy. After that I lost interest in the problem of identity.'[2] In response to Acker's turning away from the problem of identity, critics such as Christopher Kocela have referred to Acker's 'post "identity"' work.[3] *In Memoriam to Identity* (1990), the first work in Acker's later trilogy, is a reticulation of four protean narratives, 'Rimbaud', 'Airplane', Capitol', and 'The Wild Palms'. This chapter argues that disjunction gives way to topology in *In Memoriam*. Chapter 3 revealed Acker's experimentation in *Don Quixote* to be a practice whereby the reader does emerge from the varying texts but only to enter another text. The strategy in *Don Quixote* is paratactic disjunction. Whilst there is no escape from the texts, no space as such between the texts, the alternative texts remain distinct from one another, particularly in their registers, despite Acker's overarching metonymical play in her practices of writing-through. The transition from disjunction to topological intertextuality embodies a correlative modulation from textual plurality to textual mutability. Acker's experimental practices in *In Memoriam* differ from her disjunctive methods through a text-level and sentence-level topological form that enables mutability, transformation, and continuous change. The use of the term 'topological' here refers to the way in which the constituent parts of the experimental text are arranged. A topology designates a continuity of surface, the paradigmatic example of the topological form being the Möbius strip, which has no inside or outside by the fact of it being one surface. The concept is used to distinguish the experimental practices in *In Memoriam* from disjunctive practices. In mathematics, the term 'topology' is used to denote the study of geometrical properties and spatial relations that are not affected or altered by the continuous shape or size of figures. Acker's narratives in *In Memoriam to Identity* can be read as topological, as they are not disjunctive but fold in and intersect in such a way that creates continuity whilst the narratives remain non-linear. As a countable noun, 'topology' denotes a family of open subsets of an abstract space in which two of the subsets are members of the family, and this collective includes the space itself and the empty set. In his study of the modernist transformation of mathematics, Jeremy Gray comments on the field of topology and the modernist nature of objects such as knots. Tracing work on topology back to Jules Henri Poincaré's papers on topology published in 1895, Gray observes that the examination of loops in the three-dimensional space developed as a prominent mathematical field of study. 'Two loops are considered equivalent', he remarks, 'if one can deform into the other.'[4] In the study of new topologies,

Gray discerns a 'modernist shift'[5] from the world of 'genuine three-dimensional objects manipulated in the natural way' to 'artificially defined "spaces" studied by the groups that describe some of their cruder geometric features'. This was, Gray remarks, the birth of 'algebraic topology'.[6] The properties of topologies inform an understanding of Acker's intertextual practice in *My Mother Demonology*, which is a method that creates a fluid textual space in which narratives are not subject to rupture and paratactic disjunction but intersect and flow through the folds of the text.

Chapter 1 addressed Acker's engagement with the $L=A=N=G=U=A=G=E$ poets, the resistance of language-centred writing to monosemy. Writing against the repression of language into a single meaning, Acker's early poetic works experiment with creating irreducible polysemy. The polysemy made possible by the unshackling of language discussed in Chapter 1 has a comparative property in the multiplicity of selves propagated by the topological structure of *In Memoriam to Identity*. Intertextual writing enables the resistance to fixed identities and a singular self within the text. The work constructs an experimental fictive site, a web of interwoven non-causal *récits*, which intersect to create a reintegrative topological textual space for the decentred subject. *In Memoriam to Identity* is an obituary to identity. Yet rather than denoting nostalgia it upholds textual indeterminacy as the site of the protean self and reveals the way in which the experimental text can dislimn self-fixity through experimental practice.

Topological revolutions

In an unpublished notebook entitled 'Ulysses Backwards', Acker remarks of Burroughs's *The Wild Boys: A Book of the Dead* (1971), 'this book that, coming after Burroughs' cut-up or anti-narrative period, leads me into wonder by means of narrative'.[7] For Acker, Burroughs's narrative entails a loss of identity on the part of the reader: 'when I reread WB [sic] The Wild Boys, take over and I, miraculously as Rimbaud says, am one of them'.[8] The 'purity' of Burroughs's work takes Acker by surprise. She writes that she is 'Shocked by how the narratives refuse to provide a good read, comfort, security, sanitary – all the qualities literary critics most prize in these anti-literary, anti-intellectual days.'[9] Burroughs's work is placed in an antithetical position to mainstream literature, which Acker understands to be problematically aligned with ease, repose, and to stand in contrast to literary and intellectual culture. In her essay 'A Few Notes on Two of My Books', Acker states: 'A writer makes reality.'[10] The experience of reading *The Wild Boys* reaffirms Acker's apprehension of the relation between the experimental text and reality, and hence the importance of her own writing, as she states that she is 'shocked out of my desires to hide my desires to be anything but a controversial experimental writer'.[11] Acker's use of the term 'controversial' is synonymous here with the modernist idea of difficulty, the incoherence that the Comptroller of Customs took issue with in *Blood and Guts in High School*, rather than the idea of controversial as sensational. Acker simultaneously reports being 'shocked into reality'. 'Shock', repeated by Acker to express the affect of reading Burroughs's narrative, is equivalent to the rupture the marvellous is able to produce, according to Breton. Acker continues:

> As in his other books, Burroughs' interest, his only interest, thus the purity of his writing, is in reality. I'm not using this word lightly. My pen slips: instead of writing 'word', I scribble 'world'. In the WB, tho [sic] more narrative than his earlier more cut-up novels, B has no interest in creating a world. He has disinterest. As a writer, his job is to cut through stories, myths, facts, to show that all accounts are fabrics, fabricated. And yet, there is nothing else. No ground. The writer is both fabricator & fabric, clone. "the real", as another of his generation has said "slips through the cracks." The real is neither this story nor that & both. In other words, every world, story, film scene is political.[12]

The slip of Acker's pen, whereby 'word' becomes 'world', registers the question of fiction and ontology, and the avant-garde goal of the sublation of art and life, a recurring concern of her later trilogy. Yet the acknowledgement of Burroughs's 'disinterest' in such a creative project indicates the negation of the world as constructed out of linear history, a mode of negation that is idiomorphic to the experimental writer's work. Acker's comments here also point to her interest in 'unworking'. Understanding Burroughs's purpose to be to cut through stories, myths and facts, as a means to reveal both the fictionality and the materiality of all accounts, rendered in Acker's notes in the play of the noun and verb, 'fabric' and 'fabricated', Acker aligns experimental literary creation with 'unworking'. Despite apprehending all accounts as inherently fictional, Acker's analysis of Burroughs reinstates the terms 'reality' and 'narrative', an alignment this chapter takes up in relation to Acker's own avant-garde practice.

In a set of unpublished teaching notes on Marguerite Duras's 'The Malady of Death', Acker constructs an exercise on what she terms 'unworking'. Tracing a genealogy of 'unworking', her notes read: '(The recit: p. xxii, Lineage: surrealism to the recit [sic]. But before that, Rimbaud.)'[13] Acker here brings to light a line of experimental practice that runs from Rimbaud, through surrealism, to the *récit*. Acker's understanding of the *récit*, from her references in these notes, evidently stems from Blanchot and it underpins her use of the term 'narrative'. In the first chapter of *The Book to Come* (1959), Blanchot distinguishes between the novel and the *récit*, a term which (in Charlotte Mandell's translation) is translated synonymously as 'narrative'.[14] Using Ulysses's encounter with the Sirens as paradigmatic of the point of indeterminate narrative within the wider framework of *The Odyssey*, Blanchot positions the song of the Sirens as the encounter with the imaginary. 'There is', Blanchot claims, 'an obscure struggle underway with any narrative and the encounter with the Sirens, that enigmatic song that is powerful because of its defect.'[15] A struggle takes place, in Blanchot's account, between the prudence of Ulysses and his attempts to circumvent the dangers of the Sirens' song. Caution is aligned with linear narrative: 'the power of the technique that always plays safely with unreal (inspired) powers'.[16] Blanchot states:

> With the novel, the preliminary voyage is foregrounded, that which carries Ulysses to the point of encounter. This voyage is an entirely human story; it concerns the time of men, it is linked to the passions of men, it actually takes place, and it is rich enough and varied enough to absorb all the strength and all the attention of the narrators.[17]

Conceived by Blanchot as set in real time and as depicting events that could be actual, the novel here is depicted as closely related to the genre of realism. By contrast, and making reference to Nerval's *Aurélia*, Rimbaud's *Une Saison en enfer* and Breton's *Nadja*,

Blanchot apprehends the *récit* to be 'the narrative of an exceptional event that escapes the forms of daily time and the world of ordinary truth, perhaps of all truth'. 'That is why', Blanchot claims, 'it could reject all that could link it to the frivolity of a fiction (the novel, on the contrary which says nothing but what is credible and familiar, wants very much to pass as fiction).'[18] For Blanchot indeterminacy differentiates narrative from the novel: 'Narrative is the movement toward a point – one that is not only unknown, ignored, and foreign, but such that it seems, even before and outside of this movement, to have no kind of reality.'[19] Acker's idea of unworking speaks to this element of the *récit*. Both unworking and the *récit* are positioned counter to linearity and history, elements of the novel. In Blanchot's account the indeterminate 'point' of the *récit*, however, is not recessive but authoritative. As Daniel Just observes, the *récit* in Blanchot's formulation, in contrast to the novel that 'imposes functionality on both the quotidian and the story about it', is 'neither fictional nor familiarly factual'.[20] The non-novelistic nature of the *récit*, which resists storytelling, in Blanchot's theory is closely related to a non-referential language. Just explicates the relation between the absence of fixed content and structure in the *récit* and the erasure of denotative meaning:

> Since the *récit* has no fixed content or structure, and since what happens in it falls out of describable daily occurrences, instead of designating a set of rules, this genre ... simply stands for a type of narrative language that suspends deixis.[21]

The suspension of deixis, that is, the erasure of context dependent meaning, is a key attribute of the *récit*. So too is the creation of a new language. Just remarks:

> The *récit* has to invent a new type of language, one that would have to circumvent the denotative power that narrative language always exerts. Where the novel turns away from the devastating lure and describes other events, the *récit* perpetuates the Siren's lure without portraying everyday comings and goings.[22]

In Memoriam to Identity is an experiment with the *récit* form. Acker's work can be read as a complex engagement with the politics and the aesthetics of the *récit* form, which, through intertextual practice, offers the fluctuating form of the text as a site for constructive non-identity. In 1987, Denise Riley took Sojourner Truth's declarative question at the 1852 Ackron Convention, 'Ain't I a Woman?', and reconsidered it in light of her own contemporary moment. Riley, writing at the end of the twentieth century, hoped for another Sojourner Truth to issue a new if linguistically awkward plea, 'Ain't I a fluctuating identity?'[23] In this early essay, Riley makes a case for the need to circumvent the 'fictive status' of woman inherent to some of Lacan's followers and sees a similar need to elude Derrida's notion of the 'undecidability' of woman, as set out in *Spurs: Nietzsche's Styles* (1978).[24] In *The Words of Selves: Identification, Solidarity, Irony* (2000), Riley extends her earlier work to dispel the assumed connection between solidarity and identity. 'Not only is an identity no sound foundation for empathy', she argues, 'but some strong attachment to it may run counter to the development of effective fellow feeling.'[25] Solidarity in fact entails a renunciation of fixed identity, as rigid self-definition forecloses empathic relations with others:

> Jettisoning any keen interest in my categorisation may be a prerequisite for much interest in others who don't share my defining condition. The more rigorously I adhere to my own name, the less empathetic interest I'll extend. The contented gleam of the fully rounded subject need have no connection with what lies outside it. Identities may first have to be loosened and laid aside for the sake of solidarity.[26]

Within the framework of Riley's theory, non-identity is constructive, as non-identity possesses 'the virtue of deferring to the ordinarily protean shape of identities, and it mimics their projected nature'.[27] Acker's topological intertextuality in *In Memoriam to Identity* creates textual conditions that are able to harbour 'nonidentity'.

The notes that Acker jotted down for her lecture on 'unworking' align the question of identity with the *récit* form: 'This will clearly show how structure is content in literature. Now look at theory behind recit [sic] or behind unworking. That is, we will be considering identity.'[28] In *Don Quixote* it was the act of writing-through the collagist practice that emerged as voice. *In Memoriam to Identity* constructs a web of interwoven non-causal narratives that produce the narrative conditions for metamorphosis through polysemy. The topological form of the narratives and the decentralised structure is imbricated with the content of the work. Form is content. The idea that writing offers a reality not governed by imposed temporal or narrative logic but rather one that adheres to chance, indeterminacy, and perception is at the core of Acker's later work. Rimbaud's narrative points to the problem of determinism and fixity in a section that questions Marxism and Freudianism:

> Marxism is irrevocably tied to certain rationalist and positivist tenets of nineteenth-century thought. Mechanistic determinism lies at its heart. The same could be said of Freudianism. The problem now is that the theory dependent on absolute models can't account for temporal change. What is given in human history and through human history is not the determined sequence of the determined, but the emergence of radical otherness, immanent creation, nontrivial novelty.
>
>   In the world of time there is only ex-nihilo creation simultaneous with causality.[29]

Acker is writing against 'ex-nihilo creation simultaneous with causality' in *In Memoriam to Identity*. Literary creation (out of nothing) in *In Memoriam to Identity* is not bound to causality, and correlatively not bound to linearity. The compositional practices of intertextuality produce a decentralised narrative but it is an intertextuality that clearly has its roots in modernism. Acker's experimental practice echoes the mythical method of Joyce's *Ulysses* (1918), where a day in Dublin is built upon a system of thematic parallels, the narrative of which is disinvested of authority by other mythic patterns – such as Shakespeare's *Hamlet* or tales from the *Arabian Nights* that function to decentralise it. In her extensive work on practices of intertextuality in the work of Joyce, Scarlett Baron remarks on the ability of strategies of intertextuality to challenge traditional ideas of literary genealogy. Intertextuality, she argues, 'takes a bird's eye view of the relations between texts, exploding the binary and diachronic structures that sit at influence's conceptual heart'.[30] Acker's text too works to negate binary and diachronic structures as a means to divest literary influence of power.

In Acker's work, influence is closely related to determinism and centralisation. In an unpublished essay dated 1997, deceptively titled 'Bruce Willis and Me', Acker discusses Borges' essay 'Pascal's Sphere' (1951). Aligning emotion and cognition, Acker writes:

> my feelings, and so thoughts, are moved most deeply when Borges quotes Pascal explaining: "It (nature) is an infinite sphere, the center of which is everywhere, and the circumference nowhere" and then states that what Pascal actually wrote, if one looks at the manuscript, but was too scared to leave as penned, was ". . . a frightful [not *infinite*] sphere, the center of which is everywhere, and the circumference nowhere."[31]

Acker's reading of Borges' essay discloses an anxiety of centralisation, via her emphasis on Pascal's substitution of 'infinite' in place of 'frightful'. In the original lines, Pascal's fright is of the omnipresence of the centre. In the tempered emendation the replacement 'infinite' erases the anxiety, suggesting that the pervasive centre is not repressive, but rather liberating in its boundlessness. Acker's essay also reveals her concern that the writer or artist might self-censor, a concern taken up most notably in her subsequent work, *My Mother: Demonology*. Acker shares with Borges the belief that writing matters. She understands that for Borges: 'To write is to form perceptual reality, to form the ground for the emergence of the material.'[32] The relation between writing and the formation of perceptual reality, as Chapter 1 has shown, is a central preoccupation of Acker's writings since her juvenilia. By 1990, Acker's exploration of this relationship has developed to the point of scrutinising what a model of reality might be which lies outside language. In an essay written for *Marxism Today* dated 1990, Acker posits: 'If reality or that which lies outside language is itself a discourse, this model of reality must also incorporate both truth and falsehood. With regard to human perception. In other words: we see through a glass darkly.'[33] The practice of topological intertextuality enables the coexistence of truth and falsehood.

Acker gestures to *In Memoriam to Identity* as an act of rewriting in a note at the end of the work: 'All the preceding has been taken from the poems of Arthur Rimbaud, the novels of William Faulkner, and biographical texts on Arthur Rimbaud and William Faulkner'

(*IM*, 265). Faulkner's *The Wild Palms* (1939) consists of two inter-woven stories, each of which contains five chapters. The final story of *In Memoriam* takes the title of Faulkner's work, while the first story, 'Rimbaud', is five sections long, echoing the structure of Faulkner's work. Acker's narrative strategy in *In Memoriam* absorbs the mate-rial that she is working with. Her practice resembles in form Rim-baud's own intertextual writing, which James Lawler delineates as involving 'that typically anxious modernist ambition to consume rather than echo the texts of the past'. Commenting on Rimbaud's poem 'Le Bateau Ivre', Lawler remarks that Rimbaud's poem is 'not a patchwork of quotations but a coherent whole that encompasses a vast lexicon of words and figures'.[34] Lawler's comments here point to the intertextuality of Rimbaud's work, whilst differentiating it from techniques of collage. Acker synchronously reads and writes Rimbaud, and in doing so can be seen to move away from her earlier cut-up techniques, whereby the textual materials remained hetero-geneous and largely separate on the page, to an integrated technique whereby multiple narratives become fluid. The 'Easter' section of Rimbaud's narrative is a paradigmatic example of the practice of intertextual weaving that is typical of *In Memoriam* as a whole. The section opens with an epigraph from Rimbaud's 'Song from the Highest Tower' (1872) that signals the narrative event, the love affair between Rimbaud and Verlaine:

R:
Idle youth enslaved to everything
let the time come when hearts feel love. (*IM*, 26)

The narrative at the forefront of the 'Easter' section, and the pre-ceding section 'The Beginning of the Life of Rimbaud', is written in the contemporary idiom, a neutral American vernacular, and tells of R's (Rimbaud's) love affair with V (Verlaine) and R's comings and goings with de Banville and other Parnassian poets. The epi-graph functions to displace the foregrounded narrative. The con-temporary rendering of Rimbaud's voice is complemented by the original poetic voice of the source text, which is a direct citation from Rimbaud's 1872 poem. Yet equally Rimbaud's words written in the late nineteenth century are distanced, by both the paratextual positioning of the citation as an epigraph but also by the switching into a contemporary register.

The movement and progression of the contemporary narrative which the section enters at the outset of the 'Easter' section is hindered by short staccato declarative sentences: 'V told R to get out. R wandered down the dog-shitted streets; R had nowhere to stay' (*IM*, 26). Narrative accumulation is further obstructed by the repetition of 'R thought to himself' at the beginning of the third and fourth paragraphs. As the material of each paragraph is comprised of R's thoughts, the staging of those thoughts through the voice of the third person narrator obstructs R's voice. The dissimilarity between Rimbaud's poetic voice in the source text and the 'R' of the text is heightened by the child-like historical précis of the Franco-Prussian war:

> R thought to himself: After the Germans won the war, some of them wandered to South America. The French, especially the French in charge of their black colonies, missed them. Some Germans left South America to work for these offices. Just recently the Germans pierced France and killed lots of French; now the French colonists hire ex-top German military. When there are no values, it's hard for me to find a reason to live.
>
> R had nowhere to live. 'The suffering's enormous,' he wrote Izambard, a friend of his. This statement described nothing because a statement can mean something only to someone who knows. Provincials, like married people, aren't homeless. Every morning R woke up next to no one on concrete. Human flesh needs human flesh. Because only flesh is value. R continued: I'm increasing my suffering cause I have to be stronger to be a writer. I'm training myself.'
>
> Humans always look for a reason for their suffering.
>
> If humans are inescapably subject to inscrutable yet inflexible natural and/or historical laws, utopianism is absurd.
>
> Several days after V had thrown him out, V found R in a pile of dog shit. R was picking his nose without seemingly being disgusted. R spat at V and told V V was too disgusting, bourgeois, married for R to touch him. (*IM*, 26–7)

The colloquial register of R's mental account of the war functions to strip historical narrative of objective authority and portrays its absurdity. R's final thoughts ('When there are no values it's hard for me to live') are given emotive value by the preceding lines. So too does the final line inflect the previous lines, as R's despondency is the ascription of despair to the futility of war. The repetition of 'to live' across R's final cognitive statement ('it's hard for me to find a reason to live') and the first line of the succeeding paragraph 'R had nowhere to live' at once connects the first person and third person statements and highlights the asymmetry of third and first person accounts. For R, 'to live' means to exist, whereas in the third person statement, 'to live' is the empirical use of the verb that denotes making a home in a particular place. Yet negation metonymically speaks across the lines, as R has neither a reason to live, nor a place to live. No longer distanced paratextually, R's original voice proceeds to break through the contemporary narrative in the following line in direct speech. The source text of Rimbaud's letter to Georges Izambard, Charleville, 13 May 1871[35] is cited in Acker's text as a three word statement: 'The suffering's enormous'. Rimbaud's letter to Izambard in 1871 criticises Izambard for his self-confinement within the parameters of academia, a self-corralling that Rimbaud understands to remove any radical socio-political value from Izambard's work. Rimbaud writes: 'Deep down, you only see in your principle a subjective poetry: your insistence on getting back to the university feeding-trough – forgive me! – proves it.'[36] Rimbaud insists that he will see the objective poetry in Izambard's principle and his words connect the objective poetry to the insurrection of the Commune that was taking place at the time:

> I shall see objective poetry in your principle, I shall see it more genu-
> inely than you would! – I shall be a worker: that's the idea that holds
> me back, when my mad rages urge me towards the battle of Paris –
> where so many workers are dying even as I write to you![37]

Acker's citation is taken from Rimbaud's declarative statements of what it is to be a poet: 'The thing is to arrive at the unknown by a disordering of *all the senses*. The suffering is enormous, but you have to be strong to be born a poet, and I've recognized I'm a poet.'[38] As Martin Sorrell observes, objective poetry for Rimbaud is 'one in which the poet transcends the psychology of the self and overcomes egoism, either deliberate (as in Romanticism) or unintended'.[39] Rimbaud's words in Acker's narrative reflect this: 'The issue is always the self: *I* am going to die' (*IM*, 15). Acker's excision of Rimbaud's statement

'The suffering's enormous' from the original letter initially decontextualises the citation from its specific context, what it is to be a poet. Yet Acker's abstracting of Rimbaud's words does not dispossess the words of meaning but, rather, functions, compositionally, to continue the poet's avant-garde project of objective poetry within her experimental prose.

By displacing Rimbaud's words, Acker recontextualises Rimbaud's 'suffering' within her contemporary moment. Rimbaud's suffering is deployed throughout the text metonymically. The opening section for instance references Rimbaud's literal desire to self-mutilate:

> In school, R contemplated suicide more times than he had before. He was too shy to have friends. Cold knives, he wrote, city of knives all of which are interior and stick into the ice of the mind. The knives are my nerves and they're hurting me. (*IM*, 9)

The comment on Rimbaud's statement (cited above): 'This statement described nothing because a statement can mean something only to someone who knows' devalues universal denotation. The following line gains political depth, as it writes against bourgeois conceptions of destitution. The seemingly simple declarative sentence: 'Every morning R woke up next to no one on concrete' acquires resonance from its paratactic positioning to the previous line ('Provincials, like married people, aren't homeless'), and this textual relation is empathic. So too is the line inflected by two sentences that follow: 'Human flesh needs human flesh. Because only flesh is value.' The lines that enclose the image of Rimbaud homeless and alone point both to Rimbaud's intellectual isolation (his statement is not understood) and his empirical isolation (he is homeless, and alone with no lover). The sentence 'Human flesh needs human flesh' is performative, and produces affect in its linguistic intimacy, in the proximity of 'human flesh' to 'human flesh'. Human flesh is joined to human flesh via the verb 'need' and held in the closed frame of the sentence. Meaning is generated through experimental composition. Rimbaud's suffering is contextualised more specifically in the final lines through a further citation from the 1871 letter to Izambard. The two fragmented sentences that follow the paragraph – 'Humans always look for a reason for their suffering' and 'If humans are inescapably subject to inscrutable yet inflexible natural and/or historical laws, utopianism is absurd' – both adopt the distance of scientific or anthropological discourse through the use of the word 'humans'. The narrative then moves back into the foregrounded third person account of R and V's love affair.

The practice of decentralisation in this passage reveals the way in which Acker does not allow the foregrounded narrative to hold authority over other auxiliary lines. The asymmetric patterning of the lines yields metonymical refractions and reflections that produce new non-verbal meanings through intertextual composition. The narrative of R and V is further displaced, yet simultaneously reflected, in the weaving of a Japanese story, and four accompanying illustrations.[40] Acker's use of illustration in *In Memoriam to Identity* is a tool of intertextuality. Each illustration accompanies a line from a Japanese story, the narrative of which is threaded intermittently through the narrative of V and R:

> V didn't approve of R's living in de Banville's maid's room.
>
> In a Japanese story, the path of life is but a dream. The length of this path is but a dream. Storms pass us by. How many dreams must we dream in search of real love? A student who's travelling loses his way. He sees men killing each other. Then he arrives in a city whose brutal police are arresting as many of the poor as they can.
>
> The next six months, V couldn't or wouldn't decide between his wife and R. He was weak. V and R could have waited forever in limbo. (*IM*, 30)

The images are inserted into the text, which continues to weave Rimbaud's narrative with the Japanese story. The first illustration accompanies the line 'the path of life is but a dream' (Figure 4.1). The image is of a fox in grass. The moon, disproportionate to the fox, looms large in the background. The aesthetics of the image point to the aesthetics of the text. The moon and the fox are both foregrounded on a single plane, and the intersecting lines of the grass are abstract strokes.[41] The image has narrative power and diverts the course of Rimbaud's narrative. As the artist and early twentieth-century scholar of Japonisme Sadakachi Hartmann noted, foxes in Japanese sculptures 'create a strange impression of mythological conceptions; they have something ghostly about them.'[42] The interplay of text and image functions to visually foreground the brief lines that

... the path of life is but a dream.

Figure 4.1   Kathy Acker, 'The Path of Life is But a Dream'. Original artwork for *In Memoriam to Identity* (1990). Kathy Acker Papers, David M. Rubenstein Rare Book & Manuscript Library, Duke University.

are excised from the text and captioned below the images. A second image (Figure 4.2) of two Japanese women and an elder Japanese man attacking a Samurai warrior accompanies the lines 'How many dreams must we dream in search of real love?' The image embodies resistance to oppression. There is a disconnection between the caption and the image; the words do not directly denote the image. Rather the images mirror the aesthetics of the narrative of the surrealist Japanese story:

> The sun is full and absolutely round. At the end of the day. Wild dogs become wolves in the forest of the night. There's no light. The new

How many dreams must we
dream in search of real love?

Figure 4.2   Kathy Acker, 'How Many Dreams Must We Dream in
Search of Real Love'. Original artwork for *In Memoriam to Identity*
(1990). Kathy Acker Papers, David M. Rubenstein Rare Book &
Manuscript Library, Duke University.

tax collector doesn't have a lamp. The wolves chase him to the edge
of a ruined temple. Religion is dead. At this edge he sees two men
who might not be real, fighting. The men have been battling for seven
years. (*IM*, 32)

The line 'he sees two men who might not be real, fighting' is excised
from the narrative and used as a caption for the third image that
depicts a Japanese fighter eating a man's head (Figure 4.3). In the
original image a bright red ink is used for the blood, which functions to imbue the image with corporeality. Intertextually, the images

Figure 4.3   Kathy Acker, 'He Sees Two Men Who Might Not
Be Real Fighting'. Original artwork for *In Memoriam to Identity*
(1990). Kathy Acker Papers, David M. Rubenstein Rare Book &
Manuscript Library, Duke University.

expand the auxiliary narrative of the text and offer another non-verbal narrative that intersects with the text, topologically folded into the narrative via the captions. The final image illustrates the final section of the Japanese story in Rimbaud's narrative:

> R wrote back to V that he had to see V if their relationship was to continue.
>
> In the Japanese story, when the new tax collector entered the temple of ruins, he saw a girl. One of the fighters bandaged his own wounds. The girl, naked, bathed in the river. The fighter and the girl fucked. The temple is decayed.
>
> V wrote: Of course we're going to see each other! Soon! I'm planning our next meeting right now. (*IM*, 38)

The fourth illustration, 'The fighter and the girl fucked' (Figure 4.4) is a complex illustration in which the bodies of the fighter and the girl are conflated. The bright red blood in the original image now symbolises both conflict and desire. The lines of the drawing blend the bodies, so that the image becomes a protean space. The undulating lines and patterns of the illustrations reflect and refract the layers of *In Memoriam to Identity*. The capacity of the image to aesthetically embody simultaneity and conflict, mythical and contemporary space, is used by Acker to metonymically accentuate the themes that the textual narratives share. The images relate to the system of thematic parallels in *In Memoriam*, creating new forms of non-linear relations.

'A Japanese Interlude' is then subsequently foregrounded as a section. A rewriting of Murasaki Shikibu's work, *The Tale of Genji* (1008), the aesthetic associations of the text speak across the sections in back projection to the narrative of Rimbaud. *The Tale of Genji* is an illustrated book. Often considered the first novel, the work tells of life in court in Japan in the early years of the eleventh century. *In Memoriam to Identity* echoes *The Tale of Genji* in its composition. Richard Bowring remarks that Genji 'contains digressions, parallel plots, stories within stories, and shifts of view' often being read as 'not really a narrative but a series of more or less independent stories'.[43] The work is comprised of 54 chapters and contains 795 poems. Some of the illustrations are simply of objects, such as 'Veranda and railing'; others are scenes excised from the narrative, 'Gentleman Wearing a Stone Belt', for example, or 'Peering out through Standing Curtains'. Yet there is always an excess to the images that is not present in the text, a detail present in the image not signified by the text. For example,

The fighter and the girl fucked.

Figure 4.4   Kathy Acker, 'The Fighter and the Girl Fucked'. Original artwork for *In Memoriam to Identity* (1990). Kathy Acker Papers, David M. Rubenstein Rare Book & Manuscript Library, Duke University.

the illustration for 'Veranda and railing', men play the flute on the veranda;[44] there are two men in the image 'Gentleman Wearing a Stone Belt',[45] one holding the other's belt, and a theatricality to the three women peering out through the standing curtains.[46] Whilst the images of a Japanese story appear in the 'Easter' section of Rimbaud's narrative, there are no illustrations in 'A Japanese Interlude', thus the source text links aesthetically to the Japanese story in the previous section. Structurally the text undulates topologically between sections as the focal depth of the narrative shifts and foregrounds the Japanese story and Rimbaud's narrative becomes auxiliary. Such undulations, and shifts of focal depth, are characteristic of *In Memoriam to Identity* as a whole. These textual folds serve structurally to enable textual metamorphosis and, in creating a protean textual form, offer a site for constructive non-identity.

Constructive non-identity

Acker's collagist work, *Blood and Guts in High School*, was read in Chapter 2 as disclosing the anxiety of self-description. Chapter 3 traced the way in which excision, re-formation and practices of writing through in *Don Quixote* offer a (de)compositional non-verbal voice through experimentation. *In Memoriam to Identity* manifests the protean nature of non-identity in form and content. The works in Acker's later trilogy are experiments in writing the 'languages of the body'.[47] Acker lists mutability as the primary aspect of the ten elements of the languages of the body: '1. The languages of flux. Of uncertainty in which the "I" (eye) constantly changes. For the self is "an indefinite series of identities and transformations."'[48] The fluidity of language here is associated with the fluctuation of both the 'I' and the perceptual faculty (eye), and correlated to the indeterminacy and plurality of the self. A comment on Faulkner set apart from Airplane's narrative in parenthesis, in the final section of *In Memoriam to Identity*, states 'a critic who perhaps does not like women has said . . . women have shifting identities [perhaps it is men who do not recognize the shifting nature of identity]' (*IM*, 220). Here the protean nature of the self is not gendered, though the apprehension of identity as fixed and immutable is understood as a patriarchal concept. There is a marked transition from Janey's wrestling with the anxiety of self-description, the desperate scrawling of the 'I' over the original manuscript of *Blood and Guts in High School*, to Airplane, who 'had decided, after considering the facts of herself, that women don't have shifting identities, but rather they roam' (*IM*, 220). The experimental form of each of these works reflects this differentiation. The topological structure of *In Memoriam to Identity* allows for the mutability of the self in the text. Expression emerges through the thematic parallels across the narratives, rather than being fixed to one named voice. Naming in *In Memoriam* compounds this further. Rimbaud becomes Verlaine, the female voices are distanced from their names, which function in part to negate interpellation, as they take the form of objects, 'Airplane', and 'Capitol'. Yet *In Memoriam to Identity* is no seamless representation of the mutable self. Rather the text registers the tension between postulated identity and the mutable self. Identity, understood by Bauman and Riley as 'a critical projection of what is demanded and/or sought upon "what is" with the added proviso that it is up to the "what is" to rise, by its own effort, to the sought/demanded'[49] reinstates the binary inner and outer that obstructs transformation. The topological form of *In Memoriam* is the first instance in the later trilogy of an experimental practice that seeks to dislimn the boundary of the dualism inner/outer through textual composition.

At the level of the narratives, fixed identity is deceased in *In Memoriam*. Acker elaborated on her understanding of the relation between *creative* language and identity in her interview with Larry McCaffery:

> when you're writing you aren't using language (with all its problematics) to 'express identity' at all. What I realized was that language doesn't *express* anything, it *creates*, it makes, it creates something that didn't exist before. This goes back to Joyce.[50]

In Memoriam is a topological site for the protean self, created through linguistic experimentation. Previous studies have addressed Acker's work in terms of identity politics. Charles J. Stivale in his 1998 essay 'Acker/Rimbaud: "I"-dentity games' examines the creative resonance of Rimbaud in Acker's text. Stivale argues that Acker's work 'is in many ways an enactment of the young poet's elusive, yet powerful statement, "JE est un autre" (I is an other")'. 'This phrase', Stivale contends, 'is arguably the most succinct definition of the "I"-dentity games, i.e. the destabilization of identity, poetic as well as human.'[51] Stivale draws on Airplane's evocation of Rimbaud:

> Rimbaud had said: 'I am an *other*.'
> Airplane: 'But Rimbaud wasn't a woman. Perhaps there is no other to be and that's where I'm going.' (*IM*, 226)

Rimbaud's statement is modified in Airplane's recollection. 'I *is* an other' becomes I *am* an *other*'. In the first statement 'I' is objectified and gestures to self-alienation, whereby the self is alienated into the position of other within the binary 'I' and 'other'. In Airplane's rewriting, Rimbaud's statement owns the 'I' and 'I' and 'other' are conflated. Airplane's subsequent feminist response to Rimbaud can be read in divergent ways. Her postulation can be read as there is no other, the other does not exist. It can also be read as an affirmation of non-identity, against the prevailing belief that to exist is to have a singular fixed identity. This idea is articulated by Bauman, when he states that 'identity has the ontological status of a project and a postulate'.[52] Riley takes up Bauman's analysis as a claim that 'identity' is in fact 'the name given to attempts at escape from the uncertainty of not quite belonging'.[53] Positioned in relation to such an understanding of identity, *In Memoriam to Identity* emerges as a site for 'the uncertainty of not quite belonging'. Within the framework of non-identity, there is 'no other' 'to be' – a future ontological position whereby no other comes into existence (to be). Here, Acker's dialogue with Rimbaud in *In Memoriam to Identity* reveals the way in which Rimbaud's statement ultimately reinforces a binary, the 'I' and the 'other', which associates identity with a dualistic structure of difference. This reading of Rimbaud is reinforced when Capitol defines herself through the statement, in reference to her relation with the given world:

> The lawmakers of this world (lawyers, judges, dealers) who were the rich sculptor demanded that Capitol not only destroy this doll, but also publicly apologise for using a rich famous person's work, for hating ownership, for finding postcapitalist and Newtonian identity a fraud, for all her years of not only publicly hating an ignorant and therefore unjust society but also of trying to make someone of herself. ('I am an *other*.') (*IM*, 261)

In this instance Capitol, who understands postcapitalist and Newtonian identity to be fraudulent, occupies the place of 'other' when encountering the external world. In contrast to the corralling notion of identity in the given world, the experimental narrative has the capacity to hold non-identity. Both Rimbaud's statement, and Capitol's reference to herself in contemporary socio-political space remain acts of self-description whilst gesturing to an alienation from the 'I'. Such self-descriptions run counter to the instances in which the voices of the text locate their selves within the unsayable and the non-actual:

> What matters, Capitol didn't have to learn, and she could have been condemning not her own sexuality but her own conjunction of sexuality need and heart, is what perhaps according to actuality cannot ever be said, 'I will not be nothing'. (*IM*, 260)

The statement gestures to a future state of becoming, a condition of non-identity, 'I will not be', and a resistance to ontological negation: 'I will not be nothing'. Non-identity is constituted in the statement 'I will not be nothing' as distinct from being 'something'.

In content and form, *In Memoriam* offers a communal fictional site of what Riley understands to be 'anti-identity politics'.[54] 'Anti-identity politics' would offer a framework within which: 'Instead of being spoken for or glossed over, the misnamed, the forgotten, or the oppressed would speak their own truths, would articulate their common situation, would gain power through their own consolidation of their obliterated or travestied needs or interests.'[55] Language is capable of harbouring non-identity. The text is a site of escape and emancipation for the female voices of the text from the subjection inherent to being identified. Capitol remarks: 'Men told me they remembered who they fucked: they brought out memories for display, notches cut into a belt, to name identity. Being female I didn't and don't have to prove that I don't exist' (*IM*, 204). The notches on the men's belts that signify the women they have had sex with, a violent gesture of ownership and capital accumulation, are instances of the subjection of the female through identification complicit with the structures of postcapitalist and Newtonian identity. These structures Capitol rejects in her contemporary avant-garde art practices: 'Now in her work she smashed up dolls and remade these pieces, as one must remake oneself, into the most hideous abstract nonunderstandable conglomerations possible which certain people saw as beautiful' (*IM*, 249). Capitol's art reveals visually the practice of constructing non-identity at work in Acker's text. At the level of form, the intersecting narratives have an artistic counterpart in Capitol's abstract configurations that resist comprehensibility.

The ethics of decentring

The overarching topological weave of *In Memoriam to Identity*, and the constituent practice of narrative polysemy, can be read as harbouring an ethics of decentring at the level of the text, in form and content. In the advent of a renunciation of identity, it is not, in Riley's view, a new identity that is formed, but, rather, 'a confirmation of my rigorous separateness with some common dilemma or painful fix, together at last, though far apart'.[56] From this new understanding of the post-identity condition emerges 'an ethics of decentring' and it is 'one that pertains to solidarity'.[57] Importantly, Riley rescues the idea of the decentred subject from being understood as an 'anaemic spectre of a conservative postmodernism', suggesting that in place of this tired conception the decentred subject can be considered in a contemporary context as 'the pulsating and elastic creature of a million circulating words, vulnerable to history while it speaks history'.[58] For Riley the split that inevitably occurs when a new being is articulated, 'this subject constituted in division', is not solely a 'psychic phenomenon', as psychoanalytic discourse tends to purport, nor can it be reduced to a 'purely philosophical partition'.[59] Here Riley notes the intimacy of identity and distinctiveness that Hegel avows. Furthermore, she contends, 'this disintegration of the names of selves need not hint at any mournful lack. It is also reintegrative'.[60]

In *Empire of the Senseless* (1988) Abhor cries for the world to 'use fiction, for the sake of survival, all of our survival'.[61] Abhor's call echoes Acker's comments in 1989: 'the artist, though politically and socially powerless, must find the ways for all of our survival'.[62] Throughout *In Memoriam to Identity* the voices of the narratives gesture to both their alienation from the lived world, and their subsequent asylum in non-actual states. Airplane explains: 'When the world in which you live is sick, you have to live in the imaginary' (*IM*, 141). Story and fiction are closely aligned with the protean self. Echoing and negating Breton's quest for self-knowledge at the opening of *Nadja* (1928), Capitol enquires at the outset of her narrative, '*Who am I?* That's not quite the question I keep asking myself over and over. *What's my story?* That's it. Not the stories they've been and keep handing me. My story' (*IM*, 154). Here Breton's epistemic enquiry within the framework of identity, 'Who am I?' is replaced by 'What's my story?' Capitol reiterates this assertive fictive ontology: 'We're not nothing, we're our stories' (*IM*, 156). Through such declarations, the decentred self is implicated with narrative. Capitol rejects the notion of a fixed identity alongside narrative as it is handed down and encoded within a literary culture of influence. Neither identity nor narrative should be adopted. The plural self, characteristic of the decentred subject, can be brought into being only through experimental literary practice that is able to maintain the coexistence of intersecting narratives.

Acker's works, in particular her early work *Blood and Guts in High School*, which portrays Janey's linguistic anxiety, reveal the psychic conflicts inherent to the subject confronted with the limitations of ordinary language. *In Memoriam to Identity* takes up the social forms of negation that differentially produce subjectivity both in content and form. The protean text undoes, or 'unworks' the coherence of traditional narrative and temporal structures. Negativity exists within the form of the experimental text, and is constitutive of the text's aesthetic politics, as it is the resistance of the voices of the narratives to their lived experience and social negation that is frequently referenced in the text. The voices of the narratives repeatedly gesture to their political and social negation within social space. Capitol states: 'I remembered that what existence was for me was that there was nowhere to escape' (*IM*, 194). Airplane's conflict with lived experience is expressed in a scene in which she is attempting to communicate with a man in the lived world:

> Now she was listening. Sound and silence had become inverted.
> "I could hear the silence. 'No, I'm not dead,' I said. Inside. Inside my head. I'm curious."
> "This tall man is my death," she said to herself.
> "He's got hands and a coat. There's reality. I need reality. Things. 'Hi!' I said this to him in my mind, but the words weren't coming out. There was a dislocation somewhere.
> " 'Hi, mister, you don't want to be so tall and frightening.' My mind swerved. Or something in my mind swerved. 'All of me doesn't want this thing to happen. This bigness.' All of me was screaming, but nothing was coming out of the mouth like an asshole that doesn't work. The body of the world is dislocated. (*IM*, 112)

Airplane's narrative registers the relation between the inside/outside dualism. The dislocation that Airplane refers to signals an aphasic condition of social alienation. The form of the dialogue collapses the third and first person, vacillating from 'I said' to 'she said to herself', back to 'I said' with no change in voice. Yet Airplane's words are not a straightforward case of interior monologue or stream of consciousness, as the words, in a form that echoes Stein's experiments, are framed in the text as direct speech. The form of the text in staging Airplane's words as a dialogue that is unheard, and indeed unspoken, in the lived world ('the words weren't coming out'; 'nothing was coming out of the mouth') gives voice to silent speech.

The text progresses toward reintegration in the later sections. At the end of Capitol's narrative, self-presence is situated in a necessary counter-position to presence in the lived world: 'Afterwards vanished but no more to myself' (*IM*, 212). Non-existence at other points appears as a socio-political imposition. Airplane reports in the final section 'The Wild-': '(The judge told me not to exist and that my mother had stopped existing.)' (*IM*, 233). The ruling is placed in parenthesis, paratextually isolating the social negation that Airplane experiences in the lived world. Enclosing and excising, and therein marginalising Airplane's devaluation in the given world within the space of the experimental narrative, the narrative offers Airplane voice and existence within the text. Carla Harryman perceives Acker's 'use and consideration of language as connectedness, a language that is and makes reality'.[63] *In Memoriam to Identity* registers the tensions surrounding the avant-garde objective of the sublation of art and life. Toward the end of the book, Airplane understands there to be a new life in fiction and form. Airplane's survival emerges as the product of a reciprocal devaluation of the lived world:

> Though it no longer mattered returned to her life which was mainly work and some friends. (As if she had ever left.) By returning to a reality which no longer mattered or existed for her, work or art criticism (the old New York art world was dead) [. . .] she was actually building a new life. Not in terms of content, but form. Fiction. Realized that fiction, only as reality, must work: life begins in nothingness.
> The world of nothingness. (*IM*, 244–5)

Airplane's understanding of a new life in fiction and form emerges here at the end of *In Memoriam to Identity* as a mode of ex-nihilo creation simultaneous with non-causality and non-linear time, and functions to enact a negation of the lived world. The textual slippage found in the omission of the third person singular pronoun 'she' between 'mattered' and 'returned' signals non-identity. The *récit* in *In Memoriam to Identity* becomes an essential reserve that is able to overcome social alienation by offering a non-actual space of existence and a topological site of reintegrative textual politics.

Acker's practice of reintegrative intertextuality, whereby intertextuality functions to create communal relations between the voices of the narratives, operates on three levels in the text. The first, as has been discussed, involves non-identity and the topological intersections of the narratives of Rimbaud, Capitol, and Airplane (voices are folded into other voices). Two other experimental strategies create new forms of textual relationality: the practice of *récriture*; and topological revolutions at the level of the experimental sentence, whereby narratives continuously evolve into a new textual aesthetics. This non-deictic textual aesthetics offers a new perceptual reality that runs counter to the lived reality of the voices frequently referred to throughout the work. Airplane refers to her 'life of disease and sex show' (*IM*, 133). In the doctor's room she points to the distance between her perceptual reality and reality. Airplane reports a conversation that takes place '"You're not crazy," my doctor-to-be or not doctor-to-be decided' and then states 'Something had been decided in reality' (*IM*, 134). This 'reality' stands in contrast to the perceptual reality of the voices of the narratives.

Bound to her feminist negative aesthetics, Acker's rewriting of Rimbaud, and of other sources, such as Murasaki Shikibu's work, is a gesture of intimacy, textual relationality, and solidarity. *Récriture* in *In Memoriam to Identity* is counterposed to the crisis of relationality that the voices of the text experience in the lived world. Acker's rewriting of Rimbaud is both a reading of Rimbaud and a dialogue with Rimbaud. *Récriture* in *In Memoriam* harbours this metamorphic potential. For instance, in a section of Rimbaud's narrative, 'The End of Poetry', Acker rewrites the section of Rimbaud's *A Season in Hell* entitled 'Delirium II: Alchemy of the Word', with only minor alterations, which are largely additions. The original reads:

> I dreamed of crusades, voyages of discovery that were never recorded, republics with no history, suppressed wars of religion, revolutions in manners, a ferment of races and continents: I believed in each and every form of magic.

I invented colours for the vowels! – *A* black, *E* white, *I* red, *O* blue, *U* green. – I presided over the form and movement of every consonant and, making use of instinctive rhythms, I imagined I might invent a poetic language that would one day be accessible to all the senses. I would be the sole translator.[64]

Unlike her practice of excision and writing through in *Don Quixote*, Acker's rewriting of Rimbaud is expansive, rather than reductive:

"And I dreamed of the Crusades, voyages of discovery unknown to our history books, dreamed of nations who exist outside documentation, of suppressed religious wars, revolutions of this society, major shifts of races and actual masses even continents – topological revolutions: I have believed in every desire and myth.

"This was my childhood.

"Language is alive in the land of childhood. Since language and the flesh are not separate here, language being real, every vowel has a color. *A* is black; *E*, white; *I*, red; *O*, blue; *U*, green. The form and direction of each vowel is instinctive rhythm. Language is truly myth. All my senses touch words. Words touch the senses. Language isn't only translation, for the word is blood.

"At first, this is all just theoretical.

"But I wrote silences, nights, my despair at not seeing you and being in a crummy hotel next to you. I saw wrote down the inexpressible. I fixed vertigo, nothingness. My childhood. (*IM*, 89–90)

In Acker's text, Rimbaud's 'voyages of discovery that were never recorded' become 'unknown to our history books'. '[R]epublics with no history' are transformed into 'dreamed of nations who exist outside documentation'; while Rimbaud's 'revolutions in manners' are dilated in rewriting to encompass 'revolutions of this society, major shifts of race and actual masses even continents'. In the final phrase ('topological revolutions'), Acker combines Rimbaud's notion of revolution, and contemporary interest in continental drift, with its more abstract meaning: metamorphosis, transformation, and innovation. Setting the idea off from the preceding text with a dash that both connects and separates it, the amalgam of 'topological' and 'revolution' points to the wider structure of the book. 'Topological' indicates abstract space. Revolutions that concern topologies concern the properties of space. Acker's interwoven textual configurations in

In Memoriam correspond to the idea of a topological revolution of and within the narrative.

Having indicated the metamorphic potentiality of a topological conception of the text, Acker continues to rewrite Rimbaud, substituting his 'every form of magic' for 'every desire and myth'. She adds in the myth of childhood, places Rimbaud's narrative within that space, and connects this interstice with the tactility of language. This is followed by the construct of an abstract causal link: 'Since language and the flesh are not separate, language being real, every vowel has a colour', Acker concretises Rimbaud's emphatic 'I invented colours for vowels!' through the causal structure, effectively creating a textual space wherein abstract consequence can occur. Rimbaud's colour-vowel creations are located within this new topological space. Acker augments Rimbaud's paratactic clause '*A* black' with 'is', the third person singular present of 'to be'. '*A* is black', and as such, Rimbaud's imagined associations are imbued with ontological weight. In Acker's text, Rimbaud's 'I' is removed from the space apart from the possessive adjective 'my': 'All my senses touch words.' Within this space, itself a topological revolution synecdochic of the book as whole, 'Language is truly myth.' In Acker's text, it is not Rimbaud who manipulates instinctive rhythms, there is no poetic mediation between the body and the word, '[t]he form and direction of each vowel is instinctive rhythm'. A reciprocal relation emerges between words and senses, as indicated in the semantic construction: 'All my senses touch words. Words touch senses.' A somatic relation, a textual intimacy is created: senses touch words and words touch senses in the material form of the text, connected by the unmediated 'touch'. Rimbaud's imagined poetic language, in Acker's text, is made real and it is reiterated across the topological form of the text. In Capitol's narrative a voice echoing Rimbaud states: 'Childhood. The whole of poetry is there. I have only to open my sense and then to fix, with words, what they've received' (*IM*, 192). The final causal phrase of Acker's rewriting of Rimbaud that asserts the caution against reducing language to translation, on account of the somatic nature of language, is a self-reflexive comment on Acker's own practice of *récriture*. The sentence points to an understanding of the potential limitation of the abstract space created, that initially it is just theoretical. Here the relation between sight, writing, and negation is direct: 'I saw write down the inexpressible. I fixed vertigo, nothingness.' Rimbaud's writing the inexpressible is accompanied by the concretising of negation, so that 'nothingness' becomes tangible through language, fixed experientially as vertigo and located within the space of *In Memoriam to Identity*.

At the level of the sentence, *In Memoriam to Identity* enacts transformation through the undulation of one register into an abstract aesthetics, a sentence-level topological revolution:

> "Taking my medicine and holding my clothes about me, my arm linked through the rapist's arm, as if we were the figures in a tarot card, I walked into light which was either twilight or the beginning of dawn. A mirror, a quick movement of the metal bars of a stretcher on the outside: I saw myself as a ghost who wasn't going to die, not a ghost but only semiopaque flesh. Pale shadows move only in the uttermost profundity of shadows. (*IM*, 132)

For Acker, 'poetic discourse and sex are processes of transformation'.[65] In this passage, a section of Airplane's direct speech in which she is narrating her experience in an abortion clinic, the text oscillates between the realism of the description of the hospital room, Airplane's perception, and abstract imaginary space. Causality is negated and inverted in the passage. The colon between 'outside' and 'I' marks the shift into the poetic. The narrative, however, does not mark a shift into interior space but rather there is a move into the language of obscurity and contradiction: 'I saw myself as a ghost who wasn't going to die, not a ghost but semiopaque flesh.' Airplane's narrative then mutates into abstraction and moves towards non-meaning: 'Pale shadows move only in the uttermost profundity of shadows.' The distinction between poetry and prose collapses in these linguistic oscillations, and the binary inner/outer is dislimned through the movement from ordinary language to abstraction. Here the experiment with the *récit* is apparent. Each interwoven narrative leads to the imaginary through linguistic mutation.

Paradoxically, for Blanchot, the event towards which the *récit* edges disrupts and overturns the linearity of time but simultaneously 'asserts time', by which Blanchot means 'a particular way for time to be accomplished, time unique to the narrative that is introduced to the lived life of the narrator in a way that transforms it'. The *récit* is able to accommodate, and produce, the 'time of metamorphosis'.[66] Narrative temporality is formed in *In Memoriam to Identity* that accords to the non-linear temporality of the *récit*. The movement of the lines into non-meaning is related to the conception of an else-where that the voices point to throughout the text. Cixous pointed to this 'somewhere else' in 'Sorties' (1975): 'There has to be somewhere else, I tell myself . . . That is not obliged to reproduce the system.' For Cixous this place is writing: 'a somewhere else that can escape the infernal repetition, it lies in that direction, where *it* writes itself, where *it* dreams, where *it* invents new worlds'.[67] In *In Memoriam to Identity*, the voices repeatedly refer to an unknown elsewhere. Airplane states at one point: 'I didn't understand why I was saying what I was saying, but my consciousness had gone somewhere' (*IM*, 116). At other times, language is acknowledged, in line with the self, as having the capacity to bring that elsewhere into existence: 'There is nowhere else to go. I have to go somewhere, I said to myself, there-fore, there has to be somewhere' (*IM*, 205). Simultaneity is achieved in the form of the text. In Airplane's narrative at the outset of 'The Wild-', in another instance of the imbrication of the lived world with abstract textual aesthetics, the binary inner/outer is eroded through the asymmetry of subject and verb:

> The street was bare on both sides. Now. On both sides buildings all alike made up of tiny square brown compartments were begging for food. Life here on came out on Saturdays. Came out from the dark brown tangles of the intellect. Having come out, clothes were sold direct from Italy at half price (half price being the same as full price in uptown department stores). (*IM*, 233)

At sentence level, the asymmetry of the subject 'buildings', and misapplied verb, 'begging', operates to open up a non-actual space within a description of the lived world. The repetition of the predi-cate 'came out' initially ascribed to life topologically folds the outer and inner, as life 'came out' from abstraction, 'the dark brown tan-gles of the intellect'. Acker uses colour in her later work to concre-tise abstract space, as colour, like abstract states such as pain, has no single intentional object. Here Acker's use of the colour brown impresses the non-material intellect with abstract materiality. The movement back into the description of street life, with the repetition of 'came out' completes the topological fold. Narrative metamorphosis mirrors the plasticity of non-identity, of the subject constituted in division. Acker's comments on the need for the model of reality that lies outside language to incorporate truth and falsehood in terms of representing human perception are realised here in the topological form of *In Memoriam to Identity*.

Airplane, echoing Rimbaud's words 'language and the flesh are not separate' (*IM*, 89), makes the connection between the languages of the body and non-verbal understanding with reference to Wittgenstein: 'The flesh must be the mind. What did some philosopher I read at university ask? Wittgenstein. I never understood questions except deep down, where understanding can't be verbal' (*IM*, 118). The closing lines of *In Memoriam to Identity* are spoken by no specified voice in the text. They signal the move into a new abstract territory that is sexuality and issue a call into the unknown: 'It's as if there's a territory. The roads carved in the territory, the only known are memories. Carved again and again into ruts like wounds that don't heal when you touch them but grow. Since all the rest is unknown, throw what is known away.' The final lines gesture to the transition to sexuality as form in the subsequent work of the trilogy: '"Sexuality," she said, "sexuality"' (*IM*, 264).

Chapter 5

Montage and Creative Cutting: *My Mother: Demonology*

Acker produced a number of notebooks as preliminary materials for *My Mother: Demonology* (1993). In one, a note reads: 'Cut into very short beautiful sections.'[1] Acker's textual instruction to herself reveals the significance of the cutting technique to the production of literary aesthetics in the work. Acker programmatically adopts montage composition as the apparatus of *My Mother: Demonology*, as both a continuation of her experimentation with producing indeterminacy, and, related to this literary experiment, as a form of aesthetic resistance to the climate of cultural censorship in the US that was brought about by the Bush administration from 1991 to 1993.[2] As Chapter 2 observed, cutting and montage are crucial to modernism. For Walter Benjamin, montage, in particular the 'epic' theatre of Bertolt Brecht, was testament to the avant-garde work of art's capacity to use fragmentation and the discontinuous form for progressive means. In montage, Benjamin states, 'the superimposed element disrupts the context in which it is inserted'.[3] Benjamin explains that montage: 'emerged around the end of the war, when it became clear to the avant-garde that reality could no longer be mastered'. For Benjamin montage enabled 'reality to have its say – in its own right, disordered and anarchic if necessary'.[4] The importance of montage for Benjamin was, as I stated at the outset of this book, its ability to preserve, through discontinuous form, the progressive elements of the avant-garde work of art. 'The Author as Producer', given as an Address at the Institute for the Study of Fascism in 1934, has a political urgency. Benjamin believed that the organic work of art posed a risk in instating a false illusion of reality and of a harmonious social whole. In the early decades of the twentieth century, film emerged as the quintessential medium of montage practice, most notably in the work of the Soviet avant-garde filmmaker Sergei Eisenstein. In film montage, Benjamin understood the juxtaposition of elements to have the capacity to meet 'a new and urgent need for stimuli'. The radical juxtaposition of elements in film was able to establish 'perception conditioned by shock [*chockförmige Wahrnehmung*][5] as a formal principle. Michael Levenson comments on the ability of montage to collapse objective reality with the perception of the filmmaker: 'The individual shot, the photographic image, represented the given reality – the "granite" truth of the world – but the arrangement of shots achieved the montage effect, the reconstruction and interpretation of the world.'[6] Montage was important to early twentieth century experiment for its ability to offer a new mode of perception.

This sense of montage as politically progressive is vital to Acker. First published in 1993, *My Mother: Demonology* was written at the height of the culture wars in America. Acker revealed an anxiety concerning the risk of assimilating oppressive cultural forces in an interview with Lawrence A. Rickels in *Artforum* in February 1994. She explains that at the time of writing *My Mother: Demonology* her 'writing freedom' was a central concern. Acker was close friends with many of the artists, such as Karen Finlay, who had had their National Endowment for the Arts (NEA) grants vetoed in 1990 as a result of government measures. Referring to the experience of writing in a climate of cultural censorship by the Republican elite, Acker remarks: 'When I began writing *My Mother: Demonology*, I was worried that I was internalising certain cultural censorships.' Aligning aesthetic liberty with sexual writing she explains:

> I used to go to sexual writing for my freedom. That place was no longer available, due to the changes in our society and my own writing history. All writers are scared of internalising restrictions; we're looking for the places of freedom that take you by surprise.[7]

This chapter argues that experimental composition is the means by which such restrictions can be circumvented and 'writing freedom' sustained. Textually, through the cutting up and juxtaposition of different narrative segments, *My Mother: Demonology* offers a site in which narratives corresponding to the political climate of the US at the time Acker was writing are brought into play with appropriations of the epistolary correspondence between Bataille and Laure (Colette Peignot), ekphrastic literary renditions of various sequences from Dario Argento's *Suspiria* (1977), Radley Metzger's *Therese and Isabelle* (1968), Samuel Goldwyn's *Wuthering Heights* (1939), and Luis Buñuel's *L'Age d'Or* (1930), as well as sections that appear to be life writing, and the work of Ingeborg Bachmann and Paul Celan. The juxtaposition of narrative elements, not the content of those elements alone in *My Mother: Demonology*, produces meaning. The text reverberates with the political concerns of the materials of the text. Acker's engagement with the work of Bataille and Laure in *My Mother: Demonology* has been analysed by a number of scholars.[8] In interview with Rickels, Acker accounts for her engagement with the work of Bataille and Laure on political grounds, remarking that for Bataille and Laure democratic and post-Leninist models were redundant. Acker views Bataille and Laure as taking up anthropological work in the 1930s as a means of exploring myth and sacrifice in order to 'devise a new ground for a new social model'.[9] In the later sections of *My Mother: Demonology*, Acker cites the poetry of Paul Celan and Ingeborg Bachmann, poets associated with the post-war literary group *Gruppe 47*. Led by Hans Werner Richter and Alfred Andersch, the objective of the group was to realise the ideal of democracy after 1945. The group's weekly publication, *Der Ruf* (*The Call*), was deemed politically radical and proscribed by the US military government in 1947. In both cases the writers' works incorporated in *My Mother: Demonology* resonate on both an aesthetic and a political level.

The significance of filmic montage of the 1920s and 1930s in addressing Acker's experiment resides in the practice of juxtaposition. Montage as a compositional form offers the aesthetic means by which a new social model can be manifested in a work. Montage is anti-form form. Central to the cinematographic practices of the golden age of Soviet cinema in the 1920s, montage was viewed by Soviet filmmakers as a tool capable of altering perceptions, and as a form that could give voice to the new social values of the Russian Revolution. In his 1935 essay, 'The Principles of Montage', the Russian filmmaker and theorist Lev Kuleshov states: 'The artists' relationship to his surrounding reality, his view of the world, is not merely expressed in the entire process of shooting, but in the montage as well, in the capacity to see and present the world around him.'[10] Kuleshov observes that there are two 'technological elements' to every art form: 'material itself and the methods of organising that material'.[11] Kuleshov asserts that the quality of films is in part determined by montage, and in part by the material itself 'since the material of cinema is reality itself, life itself, reflected and interpreted by the class consciousness of the artist'.[12] Montage is able in this way to reflect the Marxist principles of the Revolution. By Kuleshov's evaluation, the politics of a film is imbricated with form. Kuleshov's contemporaries – Sergei Eisenstein, Dziga Vertov, and V. I. Pudovkin – shared the understanding that 'the specifics of the material were contained in the organization of the cinematic material (which meant separate shots and separate scenes), in the joining and alteration of the scenes amongst themselves, in other words, in montage'.[13] Kuleshov's most renowned discovery was the principle of meaning-making through juxtaposition. Commonly referred to as 'the Kuleshov effect', in 1918 the filmmaker discovered that juxtaposing the same image of the actor Ivan Mozhukin with different objects produced different perceptions of the actor's expression. For instance, the juxtaposition of Mozhukin's face with the image of a bowl of soup made him appear hungry, when the same image of the actor was juxtaposed with the image of a reclining woman his face was perceived as lustful. The essence of making meaning in film montage for Kuleshov is engendered by the practice of juxtaposition, a key experimental practice deployed by Acker in *My Mother: Demonology*.

Eisenstein, Kuleshov's student, regarded film as possessing the capacity to reflect a different mode of consciousness. This dimension of montage is film's resistance to the pressures of wider culture and forces of reification and is central to Acker's literary experiment. Through the formation of a new mode of consciousness, film is able to circumvent the tendency of other art forms to become complicit with the system they were critiquing. For Eisenstein, before film only art forms existed that 'were inevitably distorted and blurred by being reflected in the consciousness typical of a system to which they were knowingly antagonistic but which their minds could not help reflecting'.[14] Such a danger, to which writing is evidently susceptible, is precisely the source of the anxiety that Acker expresses to Rickels surrounding the risk of internalising cultural restrictions in her works. Eisenstein understands the form of montage as enabling the creation of perception through motion. He apprehends the structures of film aesthetics as embodying: 'the creation of motion out of the two motionless forms – we are not dealing with natural, physical movement but with something that has to do with the way our perceptions work'.[15] Eisenstein here points to the creation of perception in film. For Eisenstein, it is the separate fragments of montage that function 'not as depiction but as *stimuli that provoke associations*'. He draws the connection between the practice of assemblage in montage and perception. The partialness of the fragments, he sees as being a key element of the production of stimuli because it is the partialness of fragments that 'forces our imagination to add to them and thereby activates to an unusual degree the spectator's emotions and intellect'.[16] Eisenstein's link between the practice of montage and the formation of perception offers insights into Acker's literary montage. Like Kuleshov's understanding of the interrelation of montage and the class consciousness of the artist, Eisenstein states that the creation of perception in film conflates artistic creation and compositional form. 'This is not only the primary phenomenon of cinematic technique,' he asserts, 'it is above all a primary phenomenon of the human mind's capacity to create images.'[17] Significantly, the apprehension of movement is, strictly speaking, an illusion. What occurs, rather than being actual movement, is the ability of consciousness 'to bring together *two separate phenomenon* into a *generalised image*: to merge two motionless phases into an image of movement.'[18] This 'image of movement' is integral to Eisenstein's apprehension of montage as a radical aesthetic form, as the movement of the cells of montage are aligned with the individual units of a social collective, and meaning arises from the relations between the elements. As such Eisenstein positions the polyvalent nature of montage in a counterposition to the stasis of bourgeois culture and the status quo. Acker's issue with the fixity of 'rationalist positivist tenets of nineteenth-century thought' (*IM*, 52) to which she understands Marxism to be tied is perhaps resolved in the conception of montage as theorised by Eisenstein. Underlining the politics of his aesthetic principle of montage, Eisenstein remarks

> It is no coincidence that cinema has flourished most in the country where [Marx's] principle of base and superstructure, in its clearest and most consistent form, underlies the social and political structure enshrined in the historic document of the Soviet Constitution.

To further consolidate his claim, Eisenstein cites Schiller: 'The most perfect of all the works to be achieved by the art of man [is] the construction of true political freedom.'[19] The idea that political freedom can be achieved through montage form resounds throughout Acker's literary experiment. I argue that through creative cutting and montage Acker is able to embody the sexual realm in her work. These compositional strategies, alongside the smaller scale experimental practice of writing through the image, create the conditions for the emergence of a poetic vertical axis that creates a new mode of consciousness and perception in the work.

Creative cutting

Cutting is the foundational procedure of film montage. Acker's practices of cutting and juxtaposition of material, and the subsequent transformation of the archival materials from their raw form to the published page, can be considered a literary form of 'creative cutting'. The late modernist experimental filmmaker Maya Deren develops this concept in her essay 'Creative Cutting', first published in the magazine *Movie Makers* in May and June, 1947.[20] Cutting, in Deren's theory, is capable of producing new forms of knowledge. For Deren, the practice of cutting by the film director is directly related to the epistemic, cognitive dimension of the film. 'If the function of the camera can be spoken of as the seeing, registering eye,' she states, 'then the function of cutting can be said to be that of the thinking, understanding mind.' Here Deren's connection between cutting and the thinking mind has a comparison with Eisenstein's remarks on montage and perception. For Deren, 'the meaning, the emotional value of the individual impressions, the connections between individually observed facts, is, in the making of the film, the creative responsibility of cutting.'[21] This interrelation between the creative practice of cutting, meaning, and the associations that emerge through juxtaposition between the independent elements is characteristic of Acker's practice.

The notebooks for *My Mother: Demonology* housed in the Kathy Acker Papers reveal the significance of cutting to Acker's experimental practice. Heavily linear in places, the draft notebooks contain long passages of ekphrastic literary diegeses of the film material she was working with, particularly Dario Argento's *Suspiria* and Radley Metzger's *Therese and Isabelle* (a cinematic adaptation of Violette Leduc's 1966 erotic novel *Thérèse et Isabelle*). The term 'ekphrastic' is used here as Acker's literary narratives that arise from the films she is working with do not simply directly appropriate the film script (or in the case of Buñuel's *L'Age d'Or*, the intertitles). Rather, Acker describes the cinematic images and sequences. James A. Heffernan offers a brief definition of ekphrasis as a 'verbal representation of a visual representation'.[22] Chapter 6 addresses Acker's practice of ekphrasis in more detail in her later work, 'From Psyche's Journal' (1997). In *My Mother: Demonology* the practice of ekphrasis involves film, rather than sculpture. A simple example of this practice occurs in the paraphrase of the opening of *L'Age d'Or* in the 'Maggots' section of 'Clit City' (*MMD*, 54). Other parts of the notebooks are filled with life writing, experimentations with Persian sentences and translations, and notes on William Burroughs. Much of the material is crossed out by diagonal lines and frequently the pages are annotated with notes for assembling the material for the final manuscript. The notebook titled 'Clit City' for example is largely a literary diegesis of Metzger's *Terese and Isabelle*. The literary narrative that emerges from the film consists partly of Acker's ekphrastic verbal description of sequences in the film and partly of pure appropriation of Terese's verbal narrative, which in Metzger's film tells her story in hindsight and overlays the visual narrative in the film. Various remarks in the notebooks refer to the changes Acker planned to make in the course of redrafting, cutting, and regrouping the material. Several pages contain the annotation 'CUT' at the top of the page. One notebook opens with the numbered instructions: '1. cut-up bio 2. WLTY 3. now turn to book'.[23] Acker's annotation invokes a comparison between creative cutting and the practice of cutting inherent in excision. Acker's editorial injunction 'cut' most likely refers to the act of excision. Acker's practice brings two versions of 'cutting' together, which are linked through the act of experimental composition. The director's 'cut' is the filmmaker's composition, it is the act of putting things together. The editorial 'cut', the act of taking something out, in Acker's practice is closely related to the creative 'cut'. This is revealed in Acker's direction to 'cut-up bio'.

The long notebooks, often filled with just one narrative, read very differently to the final versions of Acker's works. They are devoid of the creativity inherent in the compositional 'cut', as they exist prior to this practice. An annotation at the top of a page, twenty-three pages into the 'Clit City' notebook, reads 'START'. This page is typical of the notebook as a whole. The first section is crossed out and is an example of the vast amount of handwritten material that did not make the final cut of *My Mother: Demonology*. Whilst the material has been excised by Acker in the process of editing, the writing remains closely related to the themes and images that occur across the final composition:

> By imagining the city in which I really am I make the real city: mythic figures who live under so militaristic a government it's as if they live without one. The poets & artists who are so large as to be monstrous. Bikers and knife wielding women. Where <u>will</u> has come to equal <u>desire</u> – there is nothing else. And so a kind of desert lion-dust of desert: green & citron giving to gun-mental [sic], to a single plum-dark sail. The sailor has changed.[24]

The writing and the desert imagery echo Juan Goytisolo's experimental novel *Juan the Landless* (1975), a work that Acker refers to in the notebooks for *My Mother: Demonology*.[25] The use of colour to symbolise heterogeneous elements, the idea of desire as liberation, and the body as a topographical site permeate Goytisolo's narrative:

> the desert beckons to you once again, as vast and stubborn as your desire, and you will penetrate the dense configuration of implacable copper-colored breast: mountainous arms will wall off the line of the horizon, mercifully isolating you from the fertile and hostile world: striding step by step across the sheath of its smooth abdomen.[26]

Acker's writing in the notebooks, which blends Burroughs's-style dystopic visions with Goytisolo's desert landscapes, was largely not included in the final manuscript of *My Mother: Demonology*. Yet, Goytisolo's fusion of landscape and body, and his love for the Muslim world and intimacy with Persian as a language, do have a significant place in Acker's work. These themes are clearly echoed in the very carefully and strategically placed sections such as 'A Farsi Lesson' that is positioned in the final work as a brief single page section just before 'Clit City'.

The sections from the notebooks that do appear in the final published version of 'Clit City' are the ekphrastic accounts of the openings of Argento's *Suspiria* and Metzger's *Terese and Isabelle* that follow the excised section in the original notebooks. The sequences follow one another in Acker's work (both in the notebook and in the final piece) and are placed in the final published manuscript after the opening sequence of life writing in 'Clit City'. Acker does lift one word from the excised piece in the notebook in her final piece, and adds it into her literary paraphrase of the opening sequence of Argento's *Suspiria*:

> Inside the taxi, where it was warm, though I couldn't see through the rain, I watched the other red door open and a girl who looked like me race past it. I couldn't see clearly.
>
> When I tried to see more definitively, I saw only the rain and the colors of gunmetal. (*MMD*, 41)

The adjective 'gunmetal' has been lifted from the omitted section (and modified from 'gun-mental') and incorporated into the final piece. Instances of such small-scale practices of cutting are prevalent across the notebooks and reveal the way in which Acker worked scrupulously with her raw materials, selecting sometimes just a word from long passages of prose to include in the final work to augment the linguistic patterning and word families of the final piece.

In their raw form, the notebooks are comprised of unassembled material. Cutting is the underlying aesthetic practice that engenders the compositional design of the final text. For the surrealist writer and filmmaker Luis Buñuel, cutting is an essential part of *découpage*, which he defines as 'an authentic moment of creation in film . . . one in which the ideas of the filmmaker are defined, roughly subdivided, cut up, regrouped, and organized'.[27] According to Buñuel it is in the process of *découpage* that '[T]he intuition of film, its cinematic embryo comes to life.' Cutting is a procedure that produces transformation: 'Segmentation. Creation. Excising one thing to turn it into another. What before was not, now is.' It is for Buñuel: 'The simplest and the most complicated way to reproduce, to create. From the amoeba to a symphony. An authentic moment in film is its segmentation.'[28] The slicing open of Simone Mareuil's eye in the opening sequence of *Un Chien Andalou* (1929) suggests that the film that follows is germinated by the cut of vision. Buñuel understood the camera to afford vision freed from cultural restraints. 'The lens' he delineates as '"that eye without tradition, without morals, without prejudices, but nonetheless able to interpret by itself" – sees the world'. Acker's cutting is evidently a process in her compositional practice that takes place after the initial writing stage. The opening section of the final manuscript, 'My Mother', appears on the eighth and ninth pages of a notebook titled 'The Dead Meat of Sailors / I learn Dialectic'. The notebook opens with a segment titled 'The Labyrinth of Language' which consists of experiments with language and meaning. Some sections are given titles in the draft notebooks that are carried over to the final piece but the majority of the intertitles and possible intertitles are jotted down at the back of the notebooks along with the page numbers to which they refer:

26–34 DREAMING ABOUT YOUNG GIRLS
  34 RED/ MEMORY INSERT / RED
  44 WORMS – THE
  49 LABYRINTH OF LANGUAGE
     – THE ERADICATION OF
50 – WORMS FROM CUNTS
  54 – BEYOND ESTROGEN THERE
  – 60 ARE MURDERERS[29]

Many of these intertitles are used unaltered in the final text. Others are adjusted: 'Worms' in line with Argento's *Suspiria* become 'Maggots' (*MMD*, 53), similarly, 'The Eradication of Worms from Cunts' becomes 'The Eradication of Maggots' (*MMD*, 56). Other parts of the notebooks signal Acker's experimentation with narrative voice. A number of annotations read 'into first person', other notes gesture to Acker's practice of doubling, 'Ellen as Beatrice', for example. Acker's notations often indicate her continuing struggle with making meaning and the limitations of language. A collection of remarks that are crossed out reveals Acker's compulsion to break with her given language. A self-reflexive fragment reads: 'If you write in the future, it will be in another language. From this point on, break the language that was yours, begin by writing in accordance with simple phonetics.' She then refers to 'the practices of a bodie language, of a worde made trulie fleshe'. In other places notes read:

'What are the words but the words don't make any sense', and 'THE EXPERIMENT IS CALLED FREEING THE IMAGINATION.'[30]

Freedom of the imagination, Acker's 'writing freedom', is arrived at through experiment with form in *My Mother: Demonology*. The notebooks are comprised of large chunks of continuous writing. By comparison, the final published version of the work is consciously designed, possessing a semantic and compositional complexity and resolution not present in the notebooks. It is the work of Acker's revision. More precisely: the work emerges from creative cutting. The act of cutting and regrouping, the process of segmentation and juxtaposition, engenders the indeterminacy of the text. John Cage's account of the composition of his lecture 'Indeterminacy' gestures to the relation between an indeterminate assemblage of materials and a plural depiction of actuality that offers a new understanding of the complex relationality between beings. In *Silence*, the lecture is composed of fifty-four stories. Cage states:

> My intention in putting the stories together in an unplanned way was to suggest that all things – stories, incidental sounds from the environment, and, by extension, beings – are related, and that this complexity is more evident when it is not oversimplified by an idea of a relationship in one person's mind.[31]

Acker's practice is more controlled than Cage's. Acker's technique is a process of cutting into texts, rather than the unintentional juxtaposition of a number of whole narratives. Yet *My Mother: Demonology* creates indeterminacy comparable to Cage's. The narrative voice of *My Mother: Demonology* states: 'The history of the century can be seen as defined by the struggle between a model of, or desire for, an absolute reality, and a model, or recognition, of reality as indeterminate' (*MMD*, 108). Acker's practice of cutting and assemblage and the overarching montage form of *My Mother: Demonology* enable the creation of a reality in fiction that is indeterminate.

Acker's intertextual assemblage of the pieces of narratives creates the non-logical patterning that yields meaning across the montage. The first section of *My Mother: Demonology* cuts the appropriated narrative of Laure's 'Story of a Little Girl'[32] into sections of a narrative that appears to be life writing, and these are cut in and integrated with the narrative 'My Mother', which echoes the strained and incestuous relationship between Terese and her mother in Metzger's

Terese and Isabelle, as well as Bataille's intimate relationship with his mother in *My Mother* (published posthumously in 1966). The second section, 'Letters from My Mother to My Father', juxtaposes segments of narrative on Acker's present-day America and the Gulf War with appropriations of the epistolary correspondence between Bataille and Laure. In this section the juxtaposition of elements is shocking:

> (A sun declines in front of you. The sunless air'll make your
> fingers grow red, and there spots will swell. Every possible color
> in the world'll sit in this sky until evening black spreads over
> the air or your pupils, and you will never be able to know which.
>   (JOIN THE U.S. ARMY
>   GET KILLED)
> (Solitary, mad, deprived of community, depraved and proud
> of all your depravity, you dream, no longer of a lover, but solely
> of sex the way a rat desires garbage. (*MMD*, 19–20)

Here the personal is interrupted with the parody of the recruitment slogan for the US Army that intervenes violently, set apart from the text in block capitals. 'A Farsi Lesson' is positioned between the section 'Letters from My Mother to My Father' and section three, 'Clit City'. 'A Farsi Lesson' conflates the language of Farsi with the imagery of the body. The didactic implication of the title, and the placing of Farsi as the first language, with the English translation in parentheses beneath it imbues 'A Farsi Lesson' with a discursive relation with the segments of text that point to the need for a new language. 'Clit City' opens with a piece of assumed life-writing collapsed with the voice of Laure. This piece makes reference to the Gulf War:

> according to all the American media, a war had just broken out
> between the United States and several of the Arab nations. The media
> was presenting this war as my old school had presented the problem
> of pain. I decided to go back to school. A school that this time could
> teach me about pain. (*MMD*, 34)

A Farsi poem appears a little later in 'Clit City' cut into the Argento narrative and preceding the critique of the Moral Majority in America. Pain also occurs frequently, within different contexts, in such a way that the word 'pain' becomes a site for accumulative meaning and associations. In the opening sequence of 'Clit City', the narrator states: 'Just as I wonder how a bodiless person can go anywhere, so at that time I thought that I could not feel pain without a body. Dead people don't know pain' (*MMD*, 34). In the subsequent section, 'Two Girls', pain is referred to in the third person voice: 'She thought about the pain, then played being a dead animal' (*MMD*, 39). Through patterning and non-logical sequencing, verbal occurrences create layers of association in the text that generate non-linear narratives across the work as a whole.

Within the body of the segments, cutting and assemblage are crucial to the creation of non-linear textual movement that gives signification to dream, memory, and the structures of desire. A comparable continuity is evident between the continuous nature of many of the narratives in the notebooks and the raw uncut film reel. Deren highlights two aspects of her practice of creative cutting that are fundamental to the creation of 'oneiric time' in her films. The first is the technique of 'cutting into action'. Deren discusses this method as it functions in her film *A Study in Choreography for the Camera* (1945). In the image of the dancer leaping in the film, the image of leaping is given a longer duration than is possible in actuality. The duration is achieved, Deren explains, through 'cutting into action':

> the first shot was cut off just at the point where the dancer began to descend, the second shot similarly, and the third was cut off just before the landing. In the second and third shots the ascent is also cut off, since once he has levelled off, to show him rising again would have implied a fall between shots. In other words, no single action was completed, and, consequently, the subsequent action was understood not as new and independent but the continuation of the one which has not yet been completed. In this sense, movement or action is carried 'across the splice'.[33]

Cutting, in Deren's practice, creates a movement and an action not possible in actuality. This practice of cutting contrasts to the montage practices of Eisenstein and Buñuel, which aim to break continuity and, in doing so, to bring unexpected elements together. Eisenstein and Buñuel's work intentionally reveals the juxtaposition of elements through making the cut visible. Splicing in Deren's films works to make the cut invisible, so that the break between elements cannot be seen.

In Acker's literary practice of cutting there is a comparable practice of 'cutting into action' that exists alongside the other forms of cutting that make the juxtaposition of elements visible. This practice is in part enabled in *My Mother: Demonology* by Acker's literary diegesis of films. Through creating narratives from films, Acker instils in her raw narratives the movement that is intrinsic to the succession of images inherent to film. Hypothetically, this might explain in part Acker's selection of material, as the ekphrastic film narratives are conducive to such a technique in a way that the disjunctive literary narratives, such as the desert segment cited above, are not. In this vein is it significant that Acker produced the *Wuthering Heights* narrative that comprises segment four of *My Mother: Demonology* from Samuel Goldwyn's 1939 film adaptation, rather than appropriating Emily Brontë's 1847 novel. Acker's literary practice of 'cutting into action' is evident in the 'Murder' section of 'Clit City':

I had found the school for which I had been looking.

Found in that pouring rain.

To the taxi driver, I said, 'Wait for me.'

The blue and red rain soaked me.

When one of the red double doors opened, a gray head appeared and asked, 'Do you want something?'

I replied that they were expecting me.

In no uncertain terms she told me to go away.

No matter how long I knocked, the door wouldn't open again.

The rain fell down more heavily than it had before. According to my memory.

Inside the taxi, where it was warm, though I couldn't see through the rain, I watched the other red door open and a girl who looked like me race past it. I couldn't see clearly.

When I tried to see more definitively, I saw only rain and the colors of gunmetal.

I have always wanted my dreams to be like that of childhood or of Radley Metzger's film of the book, *Therese and Isabelle*.

A woman returns to her school.

A private school like mine.

I had wandered away from the others to the lavatories. The sound of Baudelaire still in my ears. An odour hung inside the cubicle. . . .

A tenderness defined my hairs. I leaned over the bowl.

My best friend came into the toilet.

'Kiss me on the mouth.'

'No. It's too soon.'

I hadn't wanted to go to school in the first place. My mother made me do it so she could be alone with her new husband. I told her to her face, while he was standing with her, that he married her only for her money. They both denied that.

So I was forced to attend boarding school.

Memories do not obey the laws of linear time. (*MMD*, 40–1)

The cut into action occurs here between the line ending 'the colors of gunmetal' and the line beginning 'I have always wanted my dreams to be like that of childhood'. The first narrative is the paraphrase of the opening of Argento's *Suspiria*. Acker's literary account aestheticises Argento's film at the level of the literary surface. The opening line 'I had found the school for which I had been looking' is a straightforward account of one of the early scenes in the film. Acker's subsequent description of the blue and the red rain is a direct ekphrastic account of Argento's highly stylised film and use of Technicolor, but in the literary account, rain becomes abstracted from the image and attached to the perception of the narrative voice. Rain cannot be blue or red, yet the literary account literalises the image in the film. What Acker's literary narrative of the film offers is the perception that the film generates.

The narrative is carried across the splice into the account of Metzger's *Terese and Isabelle* through reciprocal verbal relations that create a textual landscape indigenous to the two narratives. The insert of 'According to my memory' foregrounds the narrative of *Terese and Isabelle*, which is told entirely from Terese's memory. The narrative 'I' too is carried across the cut. Cutting the Argento narrative at the point that the narrator reaches the school and cutting this narrative in with the first memory scene in which Terese and Isabelle are at school creates an illusion of movement across the narratives. The lines, 'I had wandered away from the others to the lavatories. The sound of Baudelaire still in my ears', are lines taken directly from Terese's narrative, evoking, in line with Metzger's film, Baudelaire's poem 'L'Invitation au voyage' ('The Invitation to the Voyage') from *Les Fleurs du Mal* (1857). Baudelaire's poem, which centres upon the imagined union with his lover, brings together memory and desire at an imagined site where 'all is order and leisure, / Luxury, beauty, and pleasure'.[34] The sentence 'Memories do not obey the law of linear time' is synecdochic of the structure of *My Mother: Demonology*, which also skews the time of the films that it is appropriating. The movement of the fluid narrative voice through the segments creates in literary montage what Deren viewed as 'a relativistic universe'[35] in which the individual moves through variables of time and space as a continuous rather than a fixed identity. A powerful visual instance of such continuity across disparate elements of the film occurs in Deren's film *At Land*. The protagonist, played by Deren, moves from a natural landscape into a dinner party scene. Climbing a pile of driftwood on a beach and emerging from her ascent in the natural environment in a new and unrelated sequence in which she is moving across a table at a dinner party on her hands and knees, Deren literally crawls out of one sequence into the other.

A similar continuation of the narrative voice occurs across the sequences in Acker's literary montage. The voice of the first section, 'My Mother', which appropriates Laure's *Story of A Little Girl*, states of her childhood 'I'd do anything to find out about my body, investigated the stenches arising out of trenches and armpits, the tastes in every hole' (*MMD*, 9). Here once more the body is collapsed with war imagery through the rhyme of 'stenches' and 'trenches'. The voice of 'Clit City' echoes these words creating continuity across the sections. In the subsection titled 'Period' the voice states: 'I can't find out who I am. I know nothing about my body. Whenever there's a chance of knowing, for any of us, the government, Bush, if you like, reacts to knowledge about the female body by censoring' (*MMD*, 62). Cutting into action and using verbal patterns and repetition to move the narratives across the splice gives narrative motility to the montage text in *My Mother: Demonology* that is not found in Acker's earlier collagist experiments, *Blood and Guts in High School* and *Don Quixote*. Deren puts the 'stuttering tempo of amateur films'[36] down to the failure to master the technique of cutting into action. The disjunctive nature of collage similarly does not carry narrative elements across the splice, though in literary terms this is no failure. As Chapters 2 and 3 showed, literary collage produces a mode of meaning that precisely hinges on disjunction. Carrying narrative elements across the splice in *My Mother: Demonology* through thematic patterning and verbal play facilitates Acker's creation of non-linear sequences that manifest the structure of dreams, memory, and desire through a form of condensation. For Deren, in experimental film, the process of 'intercutting' is able to create an 'order of simultaneity'[37] that is not possible in actuality. 'Intercutting' Deren defines as 'a very careful and dextrous manipulation of interruptions'. The method 'assumes that the action is understood to be continuous even during the period when it is not being shown'.[38] Acker employs devices of doubling to give rise to simultaneity. There is a complex pattern of pairings of interchangeable lovers in the text: Laure and Bataille; Terese and Isabelle; Cathy and Heathcliff; Paul Celan and Ingeborg Bachmann; and Beatrice and Dante. Simultaneity is also created at the level of composition and the parallels and patterns of the central leitmotifs of the films in the literary diegeses. The paralleling and continual movement from one narrative into another in *My Mother: Demonology* creates a literary order of simultaneity. This simultaneity in the work is crucial, as it creates movement in the non-linear work. Acker's practice of creative cutting generates the discontinuous structure of montage in *My Mother: Demonology*, and is key in the emergence of meaning through the association and juxtaposition of elements. In *Don Quixote* Acker forged a new sense of present time in which: 'Time is desire' (*DQ*, 51). Laure's words in the first section of *My Mother: Demonology* suggest that narrative drive is connected to desire: 'From now on I'm going to decide for myself and live according to my decisions – decisions out of desire' (*MMD*, 17). Later, the narrative voice states: 'every text is text of desire' (*MMD*, 40). Desire is fundamental to the movement of *My Mother: Demonology* and montage facilitates the composition of a text structured by desire.

The structures of desire

In a section of her essay 'The Language of Sex the Sex of Language' headed 'Why Poetry is the Proper Discourse for the Representation of Sexuality', Acker states: 'In the sexual realm, many, if not all, of the human intercourses meet: fantasy, the imagination, memory, perhaps especially childhood memory, desire, need, economy, power.'[39] Through creative cutting and juxtaposition, the montage apparatus of Acker's *My Mother: Demonology* can be read as creating a textual site for the confluence of human intercourses, and thereby manifesting the sexual realm. *My Mother: Demonology* brings together aspects of Eisenstein's montage practices and surrealist montage practices, in particular the work of Luis Buñuel. Eisenstein had very little regard for the surrealists, describing automatic writing as 'purposeless meditation', and his work on montage utterly eliminated questions of desire. Eisenstein comprehended the aim of surrealism to be 'aimed at dispersing unity and wholeness'.[40] The surrealist aesthetic appeared to Eisenstein to be diametrically opposed to 'the collectivist conception of the way human beings should combine in a Socialist state'.[41] In a way that is more akin to surrealist practices and aims, Acker's work brings ideals of socialism into dialogue with the revolutionary capacity of desire to disrupt the political status quo. Acker's practice of montage in *My Mother: Demonology* maps on to the versions of desire found in her previous works. For instance, *The Burning Bombing of America* voiced the relation between 'nonlanguage' and desire. The rebels in *Blood and Guts in High School* state that desire is capable of 'PUTTING INTO QUESTION THE ESTABLISHED ORDER OF A SOCIETY' (*B&G*, 125). In *Empire of the Senseless* Abhor voices the liberating and limitless nature of desire: 'My sexuality was ecstasy. It was my desire which, endless, was limited neither by a solely material nor by a solely mental reality.'[42]

For Acker, the significance of surrealism for her work in *My Mother: Demonology* resides in the conviction that desire has the power to liberate. Hugh J. Silverman observes that the twentieth century was concerned with two formulations of desire: the Freudian idea of libidinal desire, and the Hegelian conception of desire as power. The early apprehension of the latter is found in the work of Machiavelli (1469–527). Silverman remarks that Machiavelli understood desire to 'take the form of a will to control, to maintain power, to use every means available to achieve such ends'.[43] This desire to dominate others is political desire, and is related conceptually to knowledge and determinacy. By contrast, the idea of libidinal desire that emerges from Freud's work on sexuality aligns desire with the unconscious, characterised by latency and unknowability, but with the capacity to move and manifest obscurely in images and words with disruptive force. Indeterminacy is the power of libidinal desire. In Freud, and in Lacan's work, desire has no fixed meaning, it is indeterminate, and the paradigm of ambiguity. For Freud, desire is always obscured by censorship, yet knowledge of desire and the instinctual drives is akin to self-knowledge. In *The Interpretation of Dreams* (1900), Freud frequently offers examples of what he understands to be the obscuring of desires in dreams. In his dream of the three

Fates he points to the impossibility of representing desire, as he understands his dream to 'make use of an innocent desire as a screen for a more serious one which could not be so openly displayed'.[44] For Lacan, 'The object of desire, in the usual sense, is either a fantasy that is in reality the support of desire or a lure.'[45] A prohibited discourse, unconscious desire is unnameable, detectable in language only in violations of speech, in slips of the tongue for example, or as the latent, obscured content of metaphor.

Acker brings the ascription of desire to social transformation into dialogue with the question of sexual censorship in an undated and unpublished piece entitled 'Sexual Censorship'. Taking up the issue of censorship and control, Acker writes 'The issue isn't sex, sex isn't an issue. The issue is control on all levels.'[46] For Acker, control inflicted on sexual desire by rationality enacts a problematic reduction: 'Rationality when it controls sexual desire causes fear and degenerates sexual desires into their weak, ugly forms: rape, feelinglessness, all appearances of bourgeois swinging, manipulation after manipulation.'[47] For the surrealists, desire was a pathway to self-knowledge. Similarly, in *My Mother: Demonology* desire is aligned with realisation of the self, and knowledge of the body is aligned with self-knowledge and the irrational. In the first section of *My Mother: Demonology* the narrative voice states: 'Perusing *The One Hundred Twenty Days of Sodom* exulted and horrified me; horror because I recognised myself, or desire' (*MMD*, 15). In the vein of Sade and Bataille, Acker states: 'The problem of sexual censorship is, finally, the problem of human identity: We are deeply irrational.'[48] Acker positions sexual censorship and the corralling of sexual desire as contiguous with the limitations imposed upon identity by rationality. When Acker published the section of *My Mother: Demonology* titled 'Clit City' as an entire issue of the journal *New Censorship* in 1992, the work was not a matter of simply fighting sexual censorship with the exposure of sexually explicit material. For Acker, advocates of sexual censorship do not apprehend the complex relation between sexuality and language. Rationality forecloses knowledge of that which lies beyond its strictures. In judging and condemning sexuality Acker suggests: 'Perhaps we are condemning our unknowable humanity.'[49] 'Clit City', the title of which brings eroticism into relation with the external world through juxtaposition, is paradigmatic of Acker's experimentalism in *My Mother: Demonology* as a whole, which rejects the denotative relation between sex and language, and manifests the irrational in experimental form.

By juxtaposing sections that parody the moral and political rhetoric of the US Republican administration, such as 'Bush on Abortion', with narratives that manifest desire, such as the accounts of Terese and Isabelle, and the narrator's sexual experience with monks (*MMD*, 152), Acker explicitly positions libidinal desire as a counternarrative to political desire as power. The repression of libidinal desire in *My Mother: Demonology* is connected to war and centralised power. The fortune teller's remarks at the end of section two relate the repression of desire to the political climate:

> "Your problem is desire. You've tried unsuccessfully to resolve, dissolve desire through work. As a result of this repression, either you must go to war, or you are at war. The cards are unclear on this temporal point. You are now moving through the negative part of that dialectic; there'll be synthesis when your centralized power has died". (*MMD*, 25)

Whilst Eisenstein repudiated surrealist forms, Acker's late modernist experimental practice brings Eisenstein's conception of the image of movement and the political force of the relations between the elements of montage together with a surrealist understanding of desire. In Acker's work the tensions between Eisenstein's idea of montage and the surrealists' form of montage are held dialectically, and productively, in the text and worked out to an extent through textual experimentation. Acker's experiment brings Eisenstein's understanding of montage as a new form of perception and Buñuel's idea of montage as the structure of desire into dialogue. Perception and desire are conflated in *My Mother: Demonology*. The political value of montage in Eisenstein's formulation and the liberating power of montage in Buñuel's work are both present in Acker's montage.

At the level of literary composition *My Mother: Demonology* adopts structural elements of surrealist cinematic montage. Acker alludes explicitly to Buñuel in the 'Maggots' section of 'Clit City', a segment of the text that is itself a literary paraphrase of the opening scene of Buñuel's *L'Age d'Or*. For Buñuel, montage is the structure of desire. Linda Williams remarks that *L'Age d'Or* is 'a continuation of the Surrealist exploration of the structure of desire begun in *Un Chien Andalou*'.[50] Williams observes that, partly, the surrealists' turn to film was engendered by an effort to rid themselves of the 'the rigid codifications of verbal language', so that they might 'encounter the relative freedom of a seemingly more direct expression of desire'.[51] The structure of montage, the juxtaposition of contrasting elements and the power of the image to act as a site of condensation, enable the creation of an oneiric actuality in film. These aspects of surrealist film are also found in *My Mother: Demonology*. For the surrealists the creation of this oneiric actuality was crucial, as film in this regard was able to bring the unconscious into the everyday. Williams points to a key distinction between *Un Chien Andalou* and *L'Age d'Or*. The former film, Williams argues, 'is a questioning of society and of the illusory unity of the self'. The latter is 'a questioning of society and the illusory unity of the social body, once more through the disruptive force of erotic desire'.[52] Initially screened privately as a silent film on 27 May 1930, at the estate of the Vicomte de Noialles, *L'Age d'Or* was subsequently prohibited on 3 December 1930 by Jean Chiappe, the anti-communist Prefect of Police, who also banned Eisenstein's *The General Line* in the same year. The radical force of *L'Age d'Or* emerges from the juxtaposition of sequences. Audiences were shocked by the political implications of the visual juxtapositions that aligned Bishops with skeletons, and the interruptions of scenes such as that of a religious ceremony with a sequence that shows the lovers (Lya Lys and Gaston Modot) frolicking in mud,[53] with all its connotations of excretion, a visual metaphor that is carried across the sequences. The mud is just one of a multitude of visual leitmotifs that are found throughout the film. There is a comparison to be made here with the scene in Eisenstein's *The General Line* in which a cream separator is used for the first time. Where mud in Buñuel's work has overtones of excretion, the cream in Eisenstein's work suggests both sexual fluids and breast milk. The erotic implications and associations that such visual metaphors generate harboured, for the surrealists, the power of the unconscious, and registered latent desire which the medium of film montage rendered to the viewer in the manifest content of the images, such as mud and, in Eisenstein's *The General Line*, cream. Such visual patterning across disparate sequences produces associational montage in which the juxtaposition of elements creates meaning and disrupts the conventional aesthetic of the prevailing culture at the time of the film's making.

Acker's work is carefully structured, crafted through a process of cutting and juxtaposition, yet the movement of the text and the relation between elements is brought about through repetition, metaphor, and metonymic patterning. In the first section an instance of metonymical patterning occurs within a few lines. The patterning associates the narrative voice with the appropriation of Laure's narrative in italics. It is also a site of erotic pairing of the narrative voice and the figure of the man. The narrator recalls a memory of her childhood, in a store with her mother: 'As soon as she was about to leave the store, as quickly as possible, I'd pay the man behind the counter. My face flamed as if struck by the sun' (*MMD*, 9). A few lines later, the text moves into Laure's narrative: '*Trying to become a wall, I hide against one. Sooted ivy and begonias are crushed. Another man rises up; his face, burning, and lips too red*' (*MMD*, 9). The narrator's 'flamed' face has a pairing with the man's 'burning' face and 'red' lips, carrying sexual desire across the two narratives and between the narrator and the male figure. The voice of the second section 'Letters from my Mother to My Father' states: 'I've always been on fire for the sake of fire' (*MMD*, 19). The patterning and instances of family resemblance surrounding bodily heat and sexual desire continue across the text. Other patterns are more obscure and often occur in the repetition of colours; this patterning is taken up later in this chapter. Through such non-linear movement across the sections the experimental text through condensation becomes the place of desire, and desire becomes a key component of indeterminate unity. To return to Acker's ekphrastic account of *L'Age d'Or*, Acker takes the opening scene of *L'Age d'Or* and fuses it with a rewriting of one of the opening scenes of *Suspiria* in which Suzy spends her first night in the ballet school. Suzy has a dream 'based on a Buñuel film':

> One scorpion of every possible color was perching on a rock in order to get a suntan. These were the years, as in World War II, when criminals were still romantic. A criminal rose way up above the scorpions and rocks. When he looked down, he saw a gaggle of Christian missionaries.
>
> As fast as he could, the Steven Tyler look-alike raced back to the joint in which he was doing something like living so that he could tell the other hoodlums that the Christians had arrived.
>
> Christians don't come. (*MMD*, 53–4)

Acker excises the anthropological detail in her ekphrastic account of Buñuel's opening scene. She aestheticises the scene and points to the limitations of Buñuel's black-and-white representation by remarking on the colours of the scorpions. The account infuses the scene with a contemporary vernacular, and the final play on words: 'Christians had arrived. / Christians don't come' continues Buñuel's political-religious critique. The excerpt also illustrates one instance of Acker's use of repetition. The phrase 'every possible color' is repeated from Bataille and Laure's exchange in the first section ('Every possible color in the world'll sit in this sky'). Repetition functions to create non-sequential relations and patterning between the discontinuous sections of the text, destabilising fixed meaning and generating sites of condensation.

The broader apparatus of *My Mother: Demonology* illustrates Acker's literary compositional montage techniques. The structure of *My Mother: Demonology* manifests the irrational through a non-linear literary form of associational montage and this functions as compositional resistance to the corralling of sexual desire by rationality and sexual censorship. The text is divided into two parts. The first part, titled 'Into That Belly of Hell Whose Name is the United States', is divided into five further subsections: 'My Mother'; 'Letters From My Mother to My Father'; 'Clit City'; 'Obsession'; and 'Dreaming Politics'. The second part of the text, titled 'Out (In the Form of Healing)', is divided into two sections: 'Redoing Childhood' and 'The Dead Man'.[54] Four of the seven subsections, 'Clit City', 'Obsession', 'Dreaming Politics', and 'The Dead Man', contain intertitles. Many of the intertitles are used as disruptive elements such as 'Preparation of the Unmentionable Based on a Pun' (*MMD*, 63). The intertitle has no direct meaning. Alluding to the rhetoric of censorship, the noun is 'unmentionable' and the 'pun' is not given. The section heading has no relation to the text that follows, which blends life writing with the rewriting of *Suspiria*. Other intertitles refer to images from the films that Acker appropriates in her practice of ekphrasis, such as 'Maggots', which refers to the scene in Argento's *Suspiria* in which maggots fall from the ceiling of the school, and 'I Enter the School's Body', which fuses both the school of Argento's *Suspiria* with the school of Metzger's *Terese and Isabelle*. Other intertitles have political implications: 'Getting Rid of Bush through Rock 'n' Roll' (*MMD*, 170) and 'Bush on Abortion' (*MMD*, 173). Many of these intertitles do not refer directly to the content that follows, thereby disrupting the expected denotative relation between content and title, and further underpinning the subversion of causal logic at work in the text. In this technique, *My Mother: Demonology* has a comparative relation to Buñuel's *Un Chien Andalou* (1929), the intertitles of which misinform the viewer and skew linear temporality ('Once upon a Time'; 'Eight Years Later'; 'Around Three in the Morning', 'Sixteen Years Before'). Through the use of non-logical non-denotative intertitles, Acker sustains the irrational composition of *My Mother: Demonology* and the radical force of desire. Structurally, and through juxtaposition, the text stages opposition to rationality.

Writing through the image

Acker understands desire as the site for a new language in *My Mother: Demonology*. In the final section of the text, Acker includes citations from Bachmann's *The Thirtieth Year* (1961) to signal the political significance of the quest for a new language:

> Language must begin in desire.
> "The elimination of injustice, of oppression, all mitigation of harshness, every improvement of a situation still maintains the disgraces of the past. The disgraces, maintained by the continued existence of the words, may therefore be reestablished at any moment.
> "No new world without a new language." (*MMD*, 224)

Acker brings the idea of desire as a catalyst for language into association with Bachmann's post-war call for a new language that would liberate her present from the past. In *My Mother: Demonology* the distinction between factual language, the language of objective reality, and the language of desire is apparent at the points in which the narrative register becomes abstract. Poetic language occurs at the places at which the text gestures to the unknown of desire. The narrative voice of 'My Mother', speaking of the loss of her virginity, states: 'I didn't and don't know what this desire means other than itself' (*MMD*, 14). A textual movement into poetic imagery and metaphoric language follows this line: 'In me dead blood blushed crimson into the insides of roses and became a living colour that's unnameable'

(*MMD*, 14). Poetry and visual metaphor rendered in language are capable of harbouring desire, and of making 'the body's imaginings actual' (*MMD*, 10). Throughout *My Mother: Demonology*, in such instances, the text undulates into composite poetic language, revealing an intricate sentence level practice of textual cutting. At other points the poetic emerges in short interruptions that function to derail the conventional denotative relations in the factual language surrounding the lines. An instance of this method occurs in the latter part of 'Clit City': 'I managed to free myself from the remaining bandages. The smoke obscured my exit. *Exit* means *rose*. During the following days, a public controversy ensued' (*MMD*, 115). Here the statement '*Exit* means *rose*' points to a metaphorical discourse, the intervention of which in the section of life-writing undermines the factual language. Through ambiguity and the non-logical association of 'exit' and 'rose' the density and materiality of language increases, a mode of composition that is one of Acker's experimental practices of creating opacity through thickening the materiality of language.

For Acker, the image has a material relation to language. In her essay 'The Language of Sex the Sex of Language', she takes up the work of the Cuban poet and literary critic Severo Sarduy, in particular his work on metaphor in his essay 'Góngora: Squaring Metaphor' in his collection of writings *Written on the Body* (1989). Acker cites the opening of Sarduy's short essay: 'Metaphor is that zone where the texture of language thickens, that higher relief in which the remainder of the sentence is returned to its original simplicity, its innocence.'[55] In her essay, Acker offers a reading of Sarduy's work: 'So in language truth and lie (hyperbole, image) are interdependent. Sarduy states that in language truth lies exactly where the hyperboles, the images built by the imagination meet.'[56] For Acker: 'The so-called factual language of the essay cannot begin to represent such complexity. The ambiguities of the language which is most metaphorical, which is continually slipping into falsity, represent the breadth and depth of the possibilities of the sexual world.'[57] Acker, in her move towards a language of the body 'against ordinary language', evades conventional relations between word and object, and the act and the word. Crucially, this is not a Lacanian or Derridean poststructural or deconstructive turn to the play of the signifier. Rather, it is a play with both verbal and visual opacity that points to the unrepresentable.

For Metzger, the use of verbal metaphor is central to his portrayal of Terese's and Isabelle's sexual encounters. In the 1968 film, metaphor enables the representation of eroticism, the visual portrayal of which would have been considered obscene. Terese narrates the verbal account of her affair over the film's sequences. Terese and Isabelle are first together as lovers in a church. The older Terese narrates in hindsight as she enters the empty chapel of the school and remembers her encounter with Isabelle. Visually the scene remains that of an empty chapel with the older Terese walking through it. The verbal narrative that overlays it tells of her encounter with Isabelle:

> I dug her neck into my teeth her lips tried to find mine and my hair and my neck in the folds of my uniform I pushed her against the floor I nailed her hands against it with the palms of mine I helped her with all the strength of my repentance breathed her in. I pulled her tight against my belly and made a loin cloth for myself she was melting my ankles and knees into delicious decay. I burst with warmth like a fruit I was running with that same liquid sweetness there were pincers softly tearing at me (oh so softly) I was following everything inside her I could see with my inner eyes the light in her flesh in my head . . . we rode intertwined down a slope of shadows we held our breath so that life and death should come to a halt. I stormed her mouth as one storms a beleaguered city. I was hoping to plunder and destroy both her entrails and my own.[58]

Metaphor is used by Metzger as a device for representing the unrepresentable and to eroticise the unseen sequence between the lovers. Acker draws specifically on these scenes in *My Mother: Demonology*. Her turn to the visual produces literary reductions of the narrative that permeate the book:

> I dug her neck into my teeth. Then I nailed her hands against the floor. Her pincers tore at me. I followed everything inside me. From now on her legs would always be spread open. I stormed her openings as if she was a beleaguered fortress. (*MMD*, 44)

Another scene in Metzger's film in which Terese and Isabelle make love in the bedroom at the school is accompanied by the following verbal account by Terese:

> she was discovering the little male organ all of us have . . . I felt stigmata open my entrails . . . a maddening eel battering itself to death

against my inner walls my eyes hurt my ears sore . . . the rubbing was burning and painful my limitations were even more painful still . . . I transformed it into the sex of a dog red and naked.

In *My Mother: Demonology* the following passage refers to the scene:

> I don't remember. Don't describe what can't be remembered. What will never be seen. What's between the legs, I and I. She was discovering the little organ that the cock imitates. My limitations are too painful. I transformed into the sex of a dog, red and unbearable to my own eyes. (*MMD*, 44)

Acker's account is distinguished from Metzger's through the foregrounding of the motif of doubling that runs throughout *Terese and Isabelle*. In Acker's feminist rewriting, Metzger's Freudian reference to the 'little male organ' becomes 'the little organ that the cock imitates'. Acker's rewritten text abstracts Metzger's use of metaphor. The substitution of 'it' for 'I transformed into the sex of a dog' enacts a surreal metamorphosis through the change of pronoun. Acker cuts and rearranges the sequences in Metzger's film. *My Mother: Demonology* ends on a repetition of the scene in which Terese meets Isabelle in the lavatories:

> The room I was in was so tiny I couldn't stand back up. I looked up. Above me, the roll of white toilet paper was covered with specks of black hairs . . .
>
> It was a reflection of my face before the creation of the world. (*MMD*, 268)

The cinematic narrative of *Terese and Isabelle* functions in *My Mother: Demonology* as a site of metaphor and a site of textual thickening.

In 'The Language of Sex the Sex of Language' Acker states, 'Poetry eludes messages because its words break down as they approach meaning.'[59] Such textual thickening and the transformation of factual language into the language of desire occur more frequently in the second part of *My Mother: Demonology*, 'Out (in the Form of Healing)'. In the fifth section, 'Dreaming Politics', the narrator relates an experience walking down a sidewalk in the city:

> **My descent into the slums:** while I was walking the way you do when you're so scared you don't want to seem to be running, down the same sidewalk, across the street I saw a store that fascinated me.

I crossed the wide street in order to see more clearly.
This sidewalk was narrow and both descended and turned sharply.
　　The store had a double, or doubled, windows. One window was black: white leaves and white frost appeared through the black. The other half of the window was unseeable.
　　Drawn through a rotting narrow black door into an even narrower dark hall: here the walls, or air, I couldn't tell the difference, were the colour of smoke. Pierrots who were the colors of both windows and both sexes were slipping into the walls; the white and black of Halloween; leafy branches, against one wall, the same but larger than those in half of the window, had melded into part of a Pierrot's body.
　　I knew that I was now where I belonged. Mutability gorgeousness darkness depths that lead only to other depths. (*MMD*, 156)

Here the use of colour and the visual brings into existence an impossible space. The movement into this space is signalled in form by the shift from conventional narrative structures ('I crossed the wide street in order to see more clearly') to language-centred writing and non-conventional grammatical constructions, which is a correlative shift from conventional narrative to the literary rendering of authentic perception. Montage functions in these instances in the juxtaposition of two narratives, the first a factual account, the second, the rendering of the narrator's imaginary. Colour is the primary mode of representation in this passage. The imagistic lines: 'One window was black: white leaves and white frost appeared through the black' calls to mind Ezra Pound's 'In a Station of the Metro' (1913):

The apparition of these faces in the crowd;
Petals on a wet, black bough.

Pound's critics have pointed to the poem as an instance of montage. Robert Scholes apprehends the poem as 'a montage of two images, superimposed'.[60] In her study of Pound, Rebecca Beasley highlights the significance of colour in the formation of Pound's poem. In Pound's account of the composition of 'In a Station of the Metro', he gestured to the inexpressible nature of his experience in the Paris Métro of encountering 'a beautiful face, and then turning suddenly, another and another'. As Beasley remarks, it was what this experience made

Pound feel that was the site of the struggle with expression.[61] She cites Pound's account of his return journey along the rue Raynouard:

> I found, suddenly, the expression. I do not mean that I found words, but there came an equation . . . not in speech but in little splotches of colour. It was just that – a 'pattern,' or hardly a pattern, if by 'pattern' you mean something with a 'repeat' in it. But it was a word, the beginning, for me, of a language in colour.[62]

Colour and the figurative enable Acker to achieve mutability in language: 'Pierrots who were the colours of both windows and both sexes were slipping into the walls.' The association of the colours of the windows, and of the leaves, with the colours of the Pierrots (that are concrete, set images) builds and condenses a material apprehension of the transmuting space. This linguistic and aesthetic density is also a site of opacity, whereby the impossible idea of the colours of 'both sexes' is brought into existence and is affirmed in the text.

Crucially there is a reciprocal aesthetic relation between the primacy of the visual and the primacy of the verbal. The verbal is not possible without the visual. Yet 'the colours' of 'both sexes' remains an abstract attribute of language, as it is unrepresentable in a visual depiction, as is the abstract linguistic aesthetics of: 'Mutability gorgeousness darkness depths that lead only to other depths.' On the back of one of the preliminary notebooks for *My Mother: Demonology*, Acker wrote: 'My mother speaks thru [sic] the images of Argento.' The visual engenders the verbal in *My Mother: Demonology*. Acker's choice of preposition in her note, 'through' rather than 'from', suggests that the image functions as a filter, not merely a position of enunciation from which the literary narrative emerges then departs. This primacy of the image in Acker's experimental montage is a continuation of a modernist aesthetic legacy. P. Adams Sitney, with whom Acker was well acquainted, suggests in his study *Modernist Montage: The Obscurity of Vision in Cinema and Literature* (1990) that the 'antinomy of vision' is a modernist paradox. 'Modernist cinematic works', Sitney writes, 'stress vision as a privileged mode of perception, even of revelation, whilst at the same time cultivating opacity and questioning the primacy of the visible world.'[63] Sitney understands one of the dimensions of modernism to be 'the apparent need to keep producing allegories of these fundamental antinomies'.[64] This variance with regards to privileging the visual is found in Acker's later works, which often accord the visual precedence over the signifying capacity of language, whilst simultaneously imbuing the visual with abstract language and revealing the limitations of the visual mode of perception. In this instance cited above in 'Dreaming Politics', which is paradigmatic of a literary aesthetics that occurs throughout Acker's later works, the visual functions to represent the unrepresentable, but, simultaneously, the slip into poetic language does, in Deren's words, 'create the visible and auditory forms for something that is invisible'.[65] Here is the antinomy of vision in Acker's work, wherein the poetic questions the primacy of the visual whilst being fundamentally imbricated with the visual.

The visual image, as both a catalyst and a prism through which the verbal narrative continually passes in *My Mother: Demonology*, is integral to Acker's creation of a new perceptual reality in her work. At the level of form, images function alongside creative cutting and experimental montage in *My Mother: Demonology* to imbue the text with movement and dynamism, thereby creating the textual conditions for mutability and metamorphosis. Eisenstein remarks that 'the method of images' is 'a method concerned with becoming, a process',[66] and positions this 'coming-into-being of the image' in a counter-position to 'static, representation depiction'.[67] Deren commented on the metamorphosis of the image made possible by film. In her own work, she stated, 'there is a constant metamorphosis; one image is constantly becoming another'.[68] The text of *My Mother: Demonology* offers verbal narratives that are in part generated by the image in film. The image governs many of the complex language patterns in Acker's literary montage. The opening words of 'My Mother', the first section of *My Mother: Demonology*, revolve around the colour that saturates Argento's *Suspiria*:

I'm in love with red. I dream in red.

My nightmares are based on red. Red's the colour of passion, of joy. Red's the colour of all the journeys which are interior, the color of the hidden flesh, of the depths and recesses of the unconscious. Above all, red is the colour of rage and violence. (*MMD*, 7)

Here, in allocating to colour the same representational status as an object, Acker subverts conventional denotative relations by disinheriting the noun of its primacy and elevating perception. Acker's

practice of ekphrasis in *My Mother: Demonology* generates a reciprocal abstruse relation between word and image whereby colour
generates the verbal narrative and colour is generated by verbal
play. In 'My Mother' the statement 'Moral ambiguity's the colour
of horror' (*MMD*, 8) generates the colour red through associational
montage. So too is the colour red generated in the appropriated narrative of Laure: 'The first colour I knew was that of horror' (*MMD*,
8). At other points, red is given a more empirical status but such
concreteness is undermined by the non-logical association that follows: 'All children come red out of the womb because their mothers
know God' (*MMD*, 8). In her performance of the work Acker used
colour in its direct visual form. Acker's annotations on an early,
unpublished, typescript of 'My Mother' marked 'Reading Version'[69]
reveal planned colour changes during her performance of the text.
In the right hand column of the script, Acker frequently marks
the text up with the handwritten directions: 'color change', 'color',
and one note reads 'slight colour changes' (the precise colours are
not indicated).

Colour in Acker's work, as in the work of William Burroughs, is a
means to express the impossible and indefinable. Acker's experiment
with the representational capacity of colour is taken up again in
Chapter 6, in the discussion of the representation of pain in Acker's
later works. The multiplicity in the representative power of colour,
signalled in the opening passage of *My Mother: Demonology* wherein
red is the colour of nightmares, passion, joy, interior journeys, hidden flesh, the unconscious, rage and violence, allows Acker to represent desire and impossibility, which have no set visual objects. Such
denotative plurality also avows colour as a site of simultaneity, the
meaning of which is relative to perception. Wittgenstein's comments
on colour are apposite here:

239. How is he to know what colour he is to pick out when he hears
'red'? – Quite simple: he is to take the colour whose image occurs to
him when he hears the word. – But how is he to know which colour
it is 'whose image occurs to him'? Is a further criterion needed for
that? (There is indeed such a procedure as choosing the colour which
occurs to one when one hears the word '. . .'.)

'"Red" means the colour that occurs to me when I hear the word
"red"' would be a *definition*. Not an explanation of what signifying
something by a word *essentially* is.[70]

The word 'red' here generates an image relative to the receiver of the word 'red', yet, as Wittgenstein remarks, this is a definition rather than an adequate articulation of the essence of the process of signifying something by language. Acker's earlier unpublished work on colour vividly reveals her interest in the relation between perception and colour. A section of one of her plays in the unpublished document 'Rejects for *Don Quixote*' is titled 'The Personal (on Perception)'. Discussing her perception of a piece of paper with coloured writing on it she states: 'I see white and blue which ends. The end of these colors makes the form.' Here Acker crosses out the sentence 'I can't distinguish between change of color a' and continues: 'But, if the end of color makes the form, why does the paper end when the white and blue end and not when the blue line ends? The relation between form and color confuses me.'[71] Acker's incertitude here, and her material on colour echoes Wittgenstein's *Remarks on Colour* (1977).[72] When Acker looks again, she is made aware of the relative properties of colour, that colour changes in relation to what it is in proximity to, that colour has no uniformity or fixed denotative property in relation to the word that names it. Reflecting further on colour Acker asks:

> What is this white? It's lighter than every other colour. But: I look to my right. The black sock on my right foot isn't the black leg-warmer around my right leg's lower half. What is black? That is, why'm [sic] I distinguishing between black and black? That is, why now am I distinguishing form change?[73]

Colour is brought into play in *My Mother: Demonology* as a means to elicit perceptual ambiguity and relativity. As with the image, and the anti-form of montage, colours generate different perceptions through juxtaposition. Colour operates as a non-verbal language.

A vertical axis: Acker, Celan, Bachmann

The transformative capacity of poetry and metaphor was central to the works of New American Cinema in the late 1960s, and to experimental montage techniques practised by late-modernist filmmakers such as Maya Deren, Stan Brakhage, Willard Maas, and Parker Tyler. Sitney takes the practice of poetry in avant-garde cinema as the subject of his recent study *The Cinema of Poetry* (2015). Discussing the Cinema 16 symposium on 'Poetry and Film' held 28 October 1953, Sitney cites Deren who proposed a concept of cinematic poetry. At this gathering of filmmakers and theorists Deren distinguished between the 'horizontal' and 'vertical' forms of temporality in cinema. Sitney explains that the *horizontal* temporal axis for Deren is 'the development of plot over sequential time'.[74] Deren aligned the vertical axis with poetry:

> Poetry, to my mind is an approach to experience . . . a 'vertical' investigation of a situation, in that it probes the ramifications of a moment, and is concerned with its qualities and its depth, so that you have poetry concerned, in a sense, not with what is occurring but with what it feels like or what it means.

She continues: 'A poem, to my mind, creates visible and auditory forms for something that is invisible, which is the feeling, the emotion, or the metaphysical content of the movement.'[75]

What might be understood as the vertical axis of *My Mother: Demonology* that is juxtaposed with objective reality and 'probes the ramifications of a moment' on an emotional and metaphysical level is evidenced in the account of the Pierrots in 'Dreaming Politics' and further underpinned by Acker's engagement with the poetry of Paul Celan and Ingeborg Bachmann, two poets affiliated with the post-war literary group, *Gruppe 47*. In a section toward the end of 'Clit City' Acker cuts in and juxtaposes lines from Celan's poem 'Snow-Bed' (1959) into a sequence detailing one theory of how the HIV epidemic began in America. Celan's original poem reads as follows:

> Eyes, world-blind, in the fissure of dying: I come,
> callous growth in my heart.
> I come.
>
> Moon-mirror rock-face. Down.
> (Shine spotted with breath. Blood in streaks.
> Soul forming clouds, close to the true shape once more.
> Ten-finger shadow, clamped.).[76]

In alluding to Celan in her work, Acker draws on a poet whose work pivots on ambiguity. Celan's work addresses the impossibility of poetry in post-war Germany, and the problems of expression and enunciation when writing of the Holocaust. Celan takes up the issue of 'obscurity' in post-war poetry in his speech upon receiving the Georg Büchner Prize, titled 'The Meridian', delivered on 22 October 1960. In response to the rhetorical question 'Then what are images?' Celan states 'What has been, what can be perceived, again and again, and only here, only now. Hence the poem is the place where all tropes and metaphors want to be led *ad absurdum*.'[77] Acker takes the first two lines of Celan's 'Snow-Bed' and positions these lines between a critique of the Bush administration and a short biography of Celan:

> Father told me that the mayor hired female prostitutes for the purpose of kicking them down flights of stairs.
>
> Eyes, world-blind, in the fissure of dying: I come,
> callous growth in my heart.
>
> The poet who wrote these lines was a Jew. Russians then in 1941 German and Romanian forces, had occupied the town in which he had been born. The latter herded Jews into ghettos.
> In 1942 they deported his parents to an internment camp. His father, there, died from typhus: his mother, murdered.
> He escaped by traveling to Vienna. Then Paris. When he was forty-nine years old, by jumping into the Seine he killed himself.
> Darker night.
>
> HAVING LOST TRACK, THE GIRL PAUSES.
>
> On the platform that he'd raise New York out of economic poverty, Mayor – won his first election. He fulfilled this promise by transforming the city's real estate. (*MMD*, 90)

The lines from Celan's 'Snow-Bed' break through and interrupt the factual language, functioning as a point of condensation. In the 'Introduction' to his recent volume of Celan's later work, Pierre Joris comments on Celan's break with his earlier verse in the volume *Sprachgitter*, of which 'Snow-Bed' is a part. In this volume, he remarks, Celan uses a compound word alone for the title for the first time. He comments: 'the language has now given up nearly completely the long dactylic lines and rhymes of the first three books, while the brief, foreshortened, often one-word lines have become more frequent'. He states that the most significant element of the volume is 'what has been called

Widerrufe: attempts at retracting, countermanding, disavowing previous poetics – those of other poets but also his own earlier stance'.[78] Celan offers an important coordinate for Acker in the move to a minimalist language and the call for a new poetics. Joris observes: 'What all of Celan's *Widerrufe* have in common is a deep dissatisfaction with traditional (and that includes modernist) poetics, and a need to push toward a new vision of writing and the world, and of the relation between those two.'[79] In aligning her work with Celan, Acker shares the poet's understanding of a new vision of writing and a new relation between writing and the world. It is also significant that she chooses these specific lines from 'Snow-Bed'. 'Callous growth in my heart' is an instance of what Joris perceives as Celan's transformation of the 'near classical topos' of the imagery of the heart and circulation. Joris claims Celan 'transforms it in such a way that it becomes vital poetic imagery at the end of his century'.[80] In Acker's work the vital imagery, condensed, irreducible to a single meaning forms a rupture in the text that surrounds it, from which a new language emerges.

My Mother: Demonology evidences the disparity between writing and the world. The cutting technique and the juxtaposition of the political critique and the poetic have the effect of heightening the objectivity of the factual language. Within this compositional structure the poetic becomes a site for the expression of the perception of Acker's contemporary world under scrutiny. The lines from Celan and the line in block capitals that points to the movement of the girl create an order of simultaneity through intercutting, interrupting and undermining the narrative concerning the Mayor with other narratives. The narrative critiquing the Mayor and the associated social and economic demise of the city then continues after the interruptions. In the earlier section, 'Clit City', in the creative cutting of the film narratives, Acker's compositional technique created semantic and image patterning across the splice, in such a way that the narratives were blended and attained a non-logical fluidity. Here there is no continuation or patterning across the cut. Instead, the juxtaposition of the account of the gentrification of the city and the poetic creates a site of conflict and critique. The poetic emerges as embodying the emotional experience and functions to expose the conflict between the human voice of suffering and the external world. Acker's use of the poetic here recalls Bernstein's remarks on Shklovsy's idea of defamiliarisation and the capacity of poetry to 'make the metaphoricity of our perception in and through language more palpable'. The next cut into the narrative of gentrification rewrites the final lines of Celan, expanding the lines into prose: 'Celan said: My flesh is named *night*. Than night as, if not more complex. Whether or not you touch me, my flesh'll feel desire to such an extent, it'll be named *desire*' (*MMD*, 91). Acker's rewriting of Celan aligns desire with freedom from suffering. The third intervention writes through, excises, and appropriates Celan, offering a condensation of 'Snow-Bed', reducing the poem to a five word line:

> In a way history had proved Marx wrong. The leftover artists, by necessity rich, relied, nevertheless, totally on the controllers of money for patronage.
>
> Desire mirror steep wall. Down.
>   – Celan
>
> Steam heats the inhabitants and the city all through the dead winters. A trust fund had been established for the maintenance of the water pipes when they had first been built. (*MMD*, 91)

The minimalism of the poetic line and the succession of concrete obscure words employ a form of imagism. The lone adverb 'Down', isolated, negated, and displaced, creates a void in the sentence. Positioned between the linear accounts of the external reality, the poetic line forms the vertical axis of the text.

In the context of struggling to write in a climate of social oppression Acker brings the work of Ingeborg Bachmann into *My Mother: Demonology*, allowing Bachmann's *Songs in Flight* (*Leider auf der Flucht*) (1978) to infiltrate the final section of the work titled 'The Dead Man' (*MMD*, 217). Bachmann's work appeared in Jerome Rothenberg's small anthology of German poets, *New Young German Poets* published by City Lights in 1959, a collection that Acker would likely have been familiar with. The final section of *My Mother: Demonology* opens with a tarot reading. The intertitles veer between references to the narrator's time in Germany (in which the seventh section is loosely set) such as 'BITS FROM THE DIARY I WROTE IN GERMANY – I WAS JUST COPYING PORN NOVELS' (*MMD*, 218), references to Eliot's *The Waste Land*, 'THE FIRE SERMON' (*MMD*, 220), 'THE RETURN OF WATER TO THE EARTH' (*MMD*, 246), titles which establish textual relations with the opening section, 'B SPOKE' (*MMD*, 260) and 'MY MOTHER SPOKE' (*MMD*, 261) and an intertitle that references the concerns of *Gruppe 47*, 'REDREAMING GERMANY'

(*MMD*, 239). Bachmann published just two collections of poetry in her lifetime, along with a few individual poems. Highly interested in the work of Wittgenstein, Bachmann's work explores problems with language and expression. Her decision to stop writing poetry in 1964 has been regarded by critics as an enactment of Wittgenstein's final statement in the *Tractatus*: 'What we cannot speak about we must pass over in silence',[81] a statement to which Bachmann directly referred in a 1973 interview. It is possible that reading Bachmann was instrumental in the formation of Acker's exploration of silence in her later works. Bachmann's work embodies anxiety surrounding expression, and the recognition that a new language is needed in the post-war world. Mark Anderson, in his introduction to Bachmann's work, cites the often-quoted poem 'Exile' as evidence of Bachmann's nomadic status. In a permanent state of exile he understands that for Bachmann: 'The poet's only home must be built from vowels, images, rhythms – from the poet's language.'[82] Anderson observes that most readers of Bachmann agree with the early critic of her work, Günter Blöcker, who understood Bachmann to have created her own categories with regards to poetry and language. For Anderson: 'Part of this originality was her characteristic fusion of abstract language with powerfully concrete images, or what was termed a "philosophical language of images"'. Anderson reads Bachmann's work as traversing the temporal and the spatial border. 'In her poems', he writes, 'the temporal mode always seems on the verge of dissolving into the spatial, whereas a precise spatial image often stands for a temporal or philosophical abstraction.'[83] Anderson's comments articulate an abstract aesthetic that Acker shares with Bachmann.

The anxiety of writing that which is inexpressible permeates the final section of *My Mother: Demonology*. Lines are cut in, not with other narratives, but with ellipsis:

> I will do anything to talk. That one thing which is impossible.
>   Because I cannot will it. I will be taken. Here is the beginning
>   of necessary violence . . .
>   When the flesh is torn (incarceration is broken and language
>   emerges) . . .
> . . . . (*MMD*, 219)

The use of ellipsis opens up a textual space of non-expression, found only in the final part of the text. The use of ellipsis is a later technique that extends Acker's earlier experiments with the visual field of the page. Acker carves out an impossible topography. The narrator states of the landscape that surrounds her:

> Then began another stretch, whose name was *Unknown*, where all was disappearing. Standing away from the motorcycle, when I looked across waters, which now ran considerably, I saw a second mass of land, more mysterious than the one I was on. (*MMD*, 222)

This topography Acker develops in the final work of her trilogy, *Pussy, King of the Pirates* (1996). In *My Mother: Demonology* the exploration of this territory remains curtailed due to the narrator's limitations: 'Where could I go in all this freedom? But I didn't know anything . . . the roads . . . the language . . . so I had no idea where I might go: that lack stopped me' (*MMD*, 222). The limitations of the narrator's knowledge negate her capacity for perception: 'Not knowing anything, I saw nothing' (*MMD*, 222).

Acker does not translate or cite a translation of Bachmann's work, thereby preserving Bachmann's original language. The voice of *My Mother: Demonology* frequently refers to her inability to understand German, an allusion perhaps to the unique language that Bachmann writes in. As Anderson remarks, like Wittgenstein and Canetti, whose works Acker also alludes to across her oeuvre, Bachmann wrote

> what might be termed a 'minority' German (which must not be confused with regionalism or dialect): a subtle, ironic, nuanced language different from the High German of northern Germany. Averse to dogmatic or sweeping generalizations . . . musical and yet clear-headed, rarely mystical and yet not without a trace of the uncanny – this language is also 'Austria'.[84]

Like the instances of Farsi in the text, Acker takes care not to offer a mere translation which would enact a subordination of the original language to English. For our purposes here a translation of the lines cited by Acker (*MMD*, 223) reveals the relation of Bachmann's poetry to the literature of the body:

> initiated into love
> but only here –
> when the lava bolted down

and its breath hit us
at the foot of the mountain,
when at last the exhausted crater
revealed the key for these locked bodies –

We stepped into enchanted chambers
and lit the darkness away
with our fingertips.[85]

Bachmann's poetry reinforces the vertical axis of Acker's work. Here obscure images are made concrete, and given materiality by the physical anthropomorphising of nature, the 'breath' of the lava, the 'foot' of the mountains. Alluding to the Holocaust, Bachmann's poetry traverses the real and imagined through the creation of abstract yet precise poetic images.

To return to Acker's citation of Bachmann's *The Thirtieth Year*, the passage reveals the use of montage to signal a new language:

> Language must begin in desire.
> "The elimination of injustice, of oppression, all mitigation of harshness, every improvement of a situation still maintains the disgraces of the past. The disgraces, maintained by the continued existence of the words, may therefore be re-established at any moment.
> "No new world without a new language."

> > Innen ist deine Hufte ein Landungssteg
> > für meine Schiffe, die heimkommen
> > von zu grossen Fahrten.

> > Das Glück wirkt ein Silbertau,
> > an dem ich Defestigt liege. (*MMD*, 224)

Acker's citation of the seventh poem of 'Songs of Flight' points to a language of the body. The text augments the patterning of erotic images also found in the text's references to Metzger's *Terese and Isabelle*, and establishes an association with the corporeal desert landscapes of Goytisolo's *Juan the Landless*. Just as Bachmann turns to nature, so the narrator of the final section of *My Mother: Demonology* finds solace in nature: 'Nature is a refuge from myself, from opposition, from the continuing impossibility of me.' The narrator then adds: 'Nature's more than just a refuge but it's impossible to speak about it directly. For nature can only be spoken about in dream' (*MMD*, 249). Bachmann's images in this section of her poem conflate the body with nature through metaphor, particularly the sea. In translation the citation reads:

> Within, your breast is a sea
> that pulls me to its bed.
> Within, your hip is a landing pier
> for my ship, coming home
> from too long a voyage.
> Happiness twines a silver rope
> to which I lie moored.[86]

For Bachmann in exile, the body and language offer home. When the narrator of *My Mother: Demonology* visits the playwright Bachmann's voice enters the narrative again. The translated poetry reads: 'Within, your mouth is a downy nest for my fledgling tongue. / Within your flesh . . . that I wash with my tears / and one day will outweigh me', and after a two line entry back into the main narrative then reads (in translation) 'Within, your bones are bright flutes / from which I charm melodies / that enrapture even death . . .'[87] The images in Bachmann's work function in Acker's text as linguistic sites that conflate inexpressibility and the language of the body.

These lines of introspection are cut into a narrative detailing the narrator's time in Germany whilst on a book tour. There are distinct allusions to the life of Bachmann. The narrator spends time with the playwright Georg Büchner in the narrative. In structure and themes *My Mother: Demonology* alludes to Büchner's work, particularly his 1837 play *Woyzeck*. At the time of its posthumous publication (1879), *Woyzeck* was an innovative and radical work. An early influence for Bertolt Brecht and his development of Epic Theatre, the play bears the hallmark features of montage, and is often considered the first montage drama. Moving away from the three- or four-act traditional structure, the play is composed of twenty-four short episodic scenes that have no clear continuity. The poetic fragments of Celan and Bachmann in *My Mother: Demonology* function in a similar way to the evocative fragments of folksongs that punctuate *Woyzeck*. In *Woyzeck*, an unknown force is alluded to, that is present throughout the play, yet eludes representation. In the third scene Woyzeck states to Marie: 'It followed me right to the edge of town. Something we can't grasp, something we can't understand, something that drives us mad.'[88] In *My Mother: Demonology* a dialogue takes place between Büchner and the narrative voice:

> I asked him what I could do about desire.
> He replied that in front of him there were black branches cracking in a black sky. "Desire isn't a problem because life revolves around desire."
> Here were the beginnings of desire. (*MMD*, 228–9)

Here desire is aligned with the poetic, and is given voice to by Büchner. The 'beginnings' of desire echoes the earlier statement 'language must begin in desire'. The image of 'black branches cracking in the black sky' integrated as reported speech in Büchner's dialogue with the narrator echoes 'the white and black of Halloween; leafy branches' (*MMD*, 156) of the earlier image of the transmuting Pierrots. Unlike the critical juxtaposition of the work of Celan and the political critique of capitalism and the climate of gentrification, Acker's creative cutting in the final section of *My Mother: Demonology* creates textual relations between the prose narrative and the poetic interruptions.

The vertical axis of poetry is brought into relation with the instances of poetic prose in the final section in such a way that the fusion of the poetic with reality gestures to a domain in which imaginings are made actual. For Acker, this is the acknowledgment of a place outside language. The final interruption from Bachmann aligns this domain with both the negation and the affirmation of the 'I'. The narrative voice states: 'I'm discussing the realm known as *the loss of language*.' The following section of the eighth poem of 'Songs in Flight' follows. Cited in the original by Acker (*MMD*, 237), the passage translates as follows:

I am still guilty. Raise me.
I am still guilty. Raise me.

Free the ice from the frozen eye.
Break through with your glances,
seek the blue depths,
swim, look and dive.

It is not I.
It is I.[89]

A clear instance of Bachmann's 'philosophical language of images', there is a precision of perception embodied in these lines. The nouns 'eye' and glances' are brought together with kinetic verbs associated with perception and freedom: 'free', 'break through', 'seek', 'look'. Yet, the images remain abstract. The insertion of the text into *My Mother: Demonology* reverberates with the narrator's struggle with meaning. The narrator of the final section declares: 'I am a woman who's alone, outside the accepted. Outside the Law, which is language.' She asserts:

> My life's disintegrating under me so I'll not bear the lie of meaning.
> My inability to bear that lie is what's giving me strength.
> Even when I believed in meaning, when I felt defined by opposition and this opposition between desire and the search for self-knowledge and self-reclamation was tearing me apart, even back then I knew that I was only lying, that I was lying superbly, disgustingly, triumphally.
> Life doesn't exist inside language, too bad for me. (*MMD*, 253)

The lines echo Baudelaire's poem cited in *Therese and Isabelle*, bringing together the desire, the rejection of conventional meaning, the search for the self, and the loss of language. Towards the end of the work, two lines indicate the site of meaning in the text, next to which in the draft typescript, Acker has written 'great' in pen:[90]

> It's necessary to cut life into bits, for the butcher store nor the bed of a woman who's giving birth is as bloody as this.
> Absurdity, blessed insolence which saves, and connivance are found in these cuts, the cuts into "veracity."' (*MMD*, 267)

Acker's practice enacts such cuts. Meaning in *My Mother: Demonology* is not found in language alone, but in experimental composition. Writing on her short film, *Meshes of the Afternoon* (1943), Deren explained that the work reveals 'the inner realities of the individual' which includes 'the way in which the subconscious will develop, interpret, and elaborate an apparently simple and casual experience into a critical emotional experience'. For Deren the final scene, in which the protagonist of the film witnesses herself dead, is an instance in which the imagined culminated with 'such force that it became reality'.[91] The act of cutting, and the juxtaposition of given reality with the imaginary in *My Mother: Demonology*, constructs a relativistic reality in fiction comparable to Deren's in film, which operates as an antidote to the socio-political climate in which Acker was writing. The creative practice that emerges in *My Mother: Demonology* whereby poetic language emerges from opacity reveals Acker using montage to generate new forms of language that are situated in a counter-position to ordinary language.

Ekphrasis, Abstraction, and Myth: 'From Psyche's Journal', *Eurydice in the Underworld*, 'Requiem'

From 1993 to 1997, Acker developed her interest in the capacity of the artwork to offer new modes of literary experiment. Acker's essays, 'Running through the World: On the Art of Kiki Smith' (1995) and 'From Psyche's Journal' (1997) are testimony to the writer's engagement with the work of contemporary women artists, whose primary medium is sculpture. Acker explores the relation between writing and sculpture within the context of the work of Kiki Smith, Cathy de Monchaux, and the late modernist artists who influenced them, Eva Hesse, Louise Nevelson, Lee Bontecou, and Louise Bourgeois. Acker's later compositions reveal an imbrication of the practice of ekphrasis with the reappropriation of mythology, as a means to represent the unrepresentable. Murray Krieger, in his work *Ekphrasis: The Illusion of the Natural Sign* (1992), examines at length the relation between the visual and the verbal in the practice of ekphrasis. For Krieger, ekphrasis has an intrinsic relation to the impossibility of representation. 'Ekphrastic ambition', Krieger argues, 'gives to the language art the extraordinary assignment of seeking to represent the literally unrepresentable.'[1]

The ekphrastic impulse enables Acker to access the materiality of sculpture in language. This chapter draws conceptual links between Acker's ekphrastic experiments in her later essays and her experiments with writing and bodybuilding. Krieger reveals the relation between ekphrasis and the crisis of the referent when he sketches varying modes of 'doubleness in language as a medium of the visual arts'.[2] One of these modes of 'doubleness' Krieger conceives as follows: 'language in poems can be read as functioning transparently, sacrificing its own being for its referent; and it can be viewed as functioning sensuously, insisting on its own irreducible there-ness'.[3] This study has traced the production of opacity as a means to preserve the materiality of language in a number of Acker's works. Acker's move towards abstraction evidently emerges from her experimentation with linguistic opacity, as a counter to linguistic transparency. Krieger's sensuous 'irreducible there-ness' of language is comparable to opacity as it has been taken up in Acker's works in previous chapters. For Krieger, the 'ekphrastic principle' for the Western imagination has been a means by which it 'has sought – through the two-sidedness of language as a medium of the verbal arts – to comprehend simultaneity, in the verbal figure, of fixity and flow, of an image at once grasped and yet slipping away through the crevices of language'.[4]

Acker's ekphrastic engagement with abstract sculpture, and the subsequent production in Acker's work of a literary form of abstraction, is achieved through writing from the materiality of the art object. Ekphrasis in Acker's work is brought into dialogue here with Acker's work on bodybuilding, her literary calisthenics, and her reappropriation of mythology. In her unpublished notes titled 'Outlines for Kiki', housed in the Kathy Acker Papers, Acker discusses a series of Kiki Smith's sculptural works. Smith's work *Siren* (1994) is a female torso made of muslin with beads in the place of genitals, and birds in place of the head. Acker highlights in her notes the relation of materiality to myth in Smith's work. A note to Smith's work *Reina* (1993) reads 'on Myths and Icons, the stories by which we live'. Of *Siren*, she writes 'emphasis always on reality, the physical the materiality'.[5] Smith takes Sirens, Harpies, and key mythical and religious female figures such as Lilith and the Virgin Mary as her subject matter. Citing Smith, Acker's notes read: 'ON BODY STUFF, ON THE MATERIAL: in sculpture all you have is the material world, the body, and each material has its histories, its cultural baggage, each material has certain physiological effects on its perceiver.'[6] Once again, Acker's notes reveal her preoccupation with perception and with the effect of a work on the recipient of the work. Acker emphasises in her comments the perceiver-centred nature of Smith's sculpture. For Smith, the move away from figurative sculpture to abstract work was a way of approaching the body freed from the constraints of cultural preconceptions. She states: 'in figurative sculpture, there has been a very limited recognition of what people are – in general, their bodies have been represented in a lustful or heroic manner'. Smith explains: 'I just want to talk about other things that are happening with the body because my life is neither lustful or heroic enough.'[7]

For Eva Hesse (1936–70), an artist who greatly influenced Kiki Smith, the abstract artwork is the site 'where art and life come together'. Hesse began making large-scale sculptures in 1965. She stated of her work:

> it's only the abstract qualities I'm working with, which is to say the material, the form it's going to take, the size, the scale, the positioning or where it comes from in my room – if it hangs on the ceiling or lies on the floor.

Importantly, however, Hesse states: 'I don't value the totality of the image on these abstract or aesthetic points.' Rather, 'it's a total image that has to do with me and life. It can't be divorced as an idea or composition or form'.[8] Crucially, for Hesse, the abstract artwork is able to embody 'the total absurdity of life'.[9] Absurdity in Hesse's work is what cannot be represented. Hesse related the absurd in her work to that which she described as the 'complexity' of her life: her turbulent past, and her experience in 1969 of being diagnosed with, and suffering from a brain tumour.[10] Acker's later works that take up the issue of her breast cancer can be brought into dialogue with Hesse's conception of absurdity. James Meyer eloquently outlines the absurd in Hesse's work: 'The absurd for Hesse is the product of formal tension. It cannot be described. Even the word "absurd" is too loaded with specific allusions to suggest the quality, or feeling that Hesse sought.' Meyer's observations underline the tangible impossibility at work in Hesse's sculptures:

> The 'absurd,' in Hesse's sense, is an effect of exaggeration or in-betweenness. It is not a 'thing' but, 'the sensation of the thing.' It is what *happens* when a shape is joined with another, enlarged, repeated. An effect cannot be depicted; it can only be implied, never stated, never shown.[11]

Hesse's mature work, *Expanded Expansion* (1969), made of fibreglass, polyester resin, latex, and cheesecloth, is paradigmatic of the artist's practice, which creates an aesthetic space that dialectically holds opposites. Meyer comments of Hesse's work:

> The interesting question here is not that a difficult life inspired an 'extreme art', but how Hesse gives form to this perception . . . Her skeins of string and rubber sheets and coils brim with allusion, yet what these materials are pointing *to* is not easy to say.[12]

A comparable aesthetic is found in Acker's mature work. In 'From Psyche's Journal', ekphrasis offers Acker access to a liminal aesthetic space that is able to dialectically hold opposing elements: inside/outside and life/death. In an unpublished notebook titled 'Persephone Grown Up' Acker writes: 'It is now necessary to see everything: in this seeing the distinction between inside & outside isn't operative.'[13] This transitional space, that aligns perception with the bringing together and dissolving of opposites in Acker's writing, is also the space of the reappropriation of mythology. In the draft of the final article on Kiki Smith, Acker remarks: 'myths, icons are alive because we internalize and remake them'.[14]

Ekphrasis and abstraction: 'From Psyche's Journal' (1997)

On 3 March 1997, the British sculptor, Cathy de Monchaux, faxed Acker twenty-three drawings, accompanying notes, and floor plans for a series of artworks that were to appear in the first major exhibition of her work at the Whitechapel Gallery in London, held from 30 May to 20 July 1997. De Monchaux's sculptural works gesture at once to the form and shapes of the female sex organs and to labyrinthian structures and intricate patternings found in nature: coils, snail shells, the tails of seahorses, the wings of birds, intestines. The sculptures, all of which fit with de Monchaux's single description of 'Swallow' (1994) as an 'imaginary object',[15] are composed of multiple materials: leather, metals, chalk, ribbon, glass, paper, and muslin. The aesthetics of the pieces are intricate and harbour multiplicity: undulating folds of leather framed by sharp ornamental metal frames that gesture simultaneously to flora, armoury, and brooches; nature, machinery, violence, and adornment. The original fax housed in the

Kathy Acker Papers shows Acker's annotations to these works. In the margins of de Monchaux's plan for the installation, Acker has written notes that detail both her aesthetic responses to the work, and her rewriting of the myth of Psyche. The experimental short prose essay, 'From Psyche's Journal' (subheaded in the original manuscript 'For Cathy de Monchaux') emerged from these notes, and was included in the catalogue for de Monchaux's 1997 exhibition.[16]

'From Psyche's Journal' brings together and conflates the practice of ekphrasis and reappropriation at the site of the experimental text. Acker, in her practice of ekphrasis, joined her contemporaries in the poetry world, John Ashbery, Frank O'Hara, and Barbara Guest. Unlike Ashbery's engagement with painting in *Self-Portrait in a Convex Mirror* (1974), however, Acker chose the most classical form of ekphrasis, the verbal representation of a visual object. 'From Psyche's Journal' develops the ekphrastic technique practised in *My Mother: Demonology* in Acker's literary accounts of the films that she used as source materials for her narratives. Within the ekphrastic text, the myth of Psyche is reappropriated, yet it is not resituated into contemporary cultural conditions. By imbibing the myth within the space of ekphrasis, Acker succeeds in creating an abstract contemporary space that exists outside culture, in the field of a verbal representation of de Monchaux's imagined objects. Alongside ekphrastic writing, 'From Psyche's Journal' rewrites 'The Most Pleasant and Delectable Tale of the Marriage of Cupid and Psyche', which comprises Books IV to VI of Lucius Apuleius's *The Golden Ass* (AD 170). The work also references the myth of Persephone, and there are lines taken from Aristophanes' *The Frogs*. The references to de Monchaux's art appear as annotations in Acker's original manuscript of 'From Psyche's Journal'. In the final piece, the titles of the artworks are placed in an indented text box that protrudes from the left hand margin into the reappropriated text. Spatially this instils the text with a three dimensionality, in such a way that creates a literary *trompe l'œil*: the works penetrate the text in a similar manner to de Monchaux's wall installations. The objects in the 1997 exhibition of de Monchaux's work were mounted onto the gallery wall. Their dimensions protruded into the gallery space. The text of 'From Psyche's Journal' is a space curated by Acker, a verbal depiction of de Monchaux's floor plan.[17] The multiform nature of de Monchaux's sculptures, the multiplicity of the materials out of which they are constructed, have a literary counterpart in the collagist structure of Acker's text. The language constantly shifts genre between the poetic, the contemporary vernacular, appropriated citations from Apuleius's *The Golden Ass* (referred to as 'The Sacred Book' in Psyche's narrative), and the philosophical. Against the composite elements of de Monchaux's sculptures, language emerges in all its materiality. That which might be termed the intermateriality of de Monchaux's work functions to mirror, highlight, and inflect the intertextuality of Acker's experimental text.

De Monchaux's sculptures offer Acker access to a visual and material form of eversion: the body is turned inside out. In *Suck Violets* (1996) (Figure 6.1) the flesh-like swelling folds of red leather emerge from the constraints of the metallic body of the piece that takes the shape of a seahorse's tail. De Monchaux's notes to the piece read: 'Seahorse like thing with top section opened out to reveal brain-like red leather fruit like this. Brass, copper, leather, chalk.'[18] In Psyche's journal, Acker highlights the aesthetics of eversion in de Monchaux's piece:

> To be beautiful is to be a seashell, so open that all the oceans and fluids of the earth, of the body, are heard through you. Openness so open that it turns itself inside-out and makes a snail-shaped labyrinth that leads to the future.[19]
>
> in memory of *Suck Violets* (1996)

The sea imagery found in *My Mother: Demonology* that embodied female sexuality and the agency of the sexual organs recurs in 'From Psyche's Journal'. So too do the associated themes of openness and radical vulnerability. Eversion is found in the early works of Kiki Smith that Acker wrote on. The female figure of Smith's *Blood Pool* (1992) is lying in a foetal position. She appears to be covered in blood and her vertebrae along the spine of her back are exposed, as if they are breaking through the skin. A comparable practice of eversion is found in *My Mother: Demonology* written one year after *Blood Pool*, in Acker's images of menstrual blood and disembodied sexual organs: 'Let your cunt come outside your body and crawl, like a snail, along the flesh. Slither down your legs until there are trails of blood all over the skin.'[20] Yet there is a move away in Acker's final works from a feminist aesthetics of eversion grounded in corporeality found in *My Mother: Demonology* and *Pussy, King of the Pirates* to an aesthetics

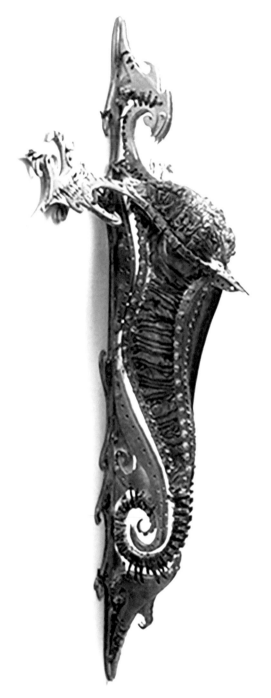

Figure 6.1   Cathy de Monchaux, *Suck Violets* (1996). Brass, copper, leather, ribbons, bolts, French chalk. 60 × 40 × 13 cm. © Cathy de Monchaux. All Rights Reserved, DACS 2015.

of eversion that emerges from the material of the art object. The shift parallels a shift from figuration of the body to abstraction. In Psyche's passage cited above, the language of the body is abstracted, referenced through the aural language of the seashell, the aesthetics of eversion emerges from the sculpture. Later in Psyche's narrative, the violet becomes the space of transformations and the art object is placed within the space of the myth:

> *Suck violets.* In this picture, found halfway between the river (or the doorway) and the mirrors (or the windows at the back of the room), there are flowers all around me. I must be in a new world, a world which is a sort of violet, cause everything is continually changing into everything else, animals into minerals, into vegetables, and these vegetables are seahorses and they're not. They eat the bits of river that trickle to them through the ground only they are made of dead animal and their brains are split open.[21]

Transformation takes place at the site/sight of the visual object, which is capable of embodying metamorphosis in a way that language is not. In her handwritten notes on de Monchaux, Acker notes 'abstraction flows into representation and back again. Within the no-longer closed circuit of representations, female genitalia turn into mineral & animal entities, hard turns into soft, all is movement.'[22] The multiplicity of de Monchaux's work engenders an unconditional space that harbours indeterminacy. The initial section of Psyche's journal accompanying *Suck Violets* manifests a mode of eversion that turns the body inside out, inside is outside. Yet it is also an abstraction of flesh into the materials of the sculpture: brass, copper, leather, chalk. Eversion here gestures toward the inanimate and reaches towards death both in the material form of the art object, and the transformation inherent to decay, animals become minerals, vegetables, sea-life. In her annotations to de Monchaux's work *Cogent Shuddering* (1997),[23] Acker pens the notes 'life & death intermix' in the margins. Beside *Confessional* (1997) she jots 'life/death/self/other', and her notes accompanying de Monchaux's sketches for *Making a day for the dead ones* (1997) and 'floor piece in progress' (1997) read 'life/death' (Figure 6.2).[24] De Monchaux's notes to 'floor piece in progress' state: 'lead covered rectangular boxes held down with metal clasps idea of contained poisonous substance which is lead but very seductive'.[25] Louisa Buck, discussing de Monchaux's *Clearing the tracks before they appear* (1994–7), draws on

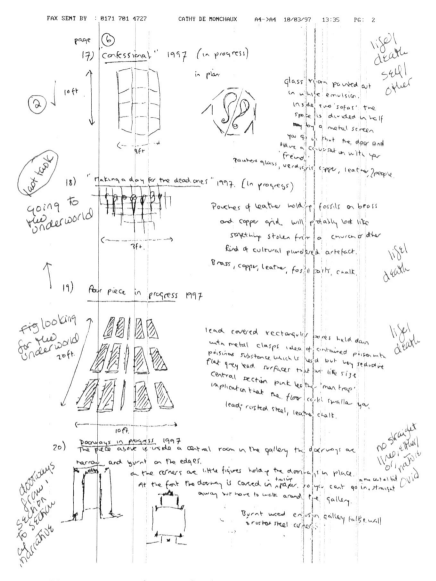

Figure 6.2   Fax from Cathy de Monchaux to Kathy Acker (3 March 1997), showing Acker's annotations. Kathy Acker Papers, David M. Rubenstein Rare Book & Manuscript Library, Duke University.

Primo Levi's assertion in *The Periodic Table*, that 'Lead is actually the metal of death: because it brings on death, because its weight is a desire to fall, and to fall is a property of corpses, because its very colour is dulled-dead . . .'[26] The material of the art object enables the coexistence of death and desire. Through ekphrasis Acker situates Psyche in this liminal state between life and death. The form of the text mirrors this state. In *My Mother: Demonology*, through the appropriation of the experimental film techniques of Buñuel, Deren, and Argento, divergent narratives yielded to fluidity through creative cutting. By contrast, in 'From Psyche's Journal', the syntax is structured, material, and unyielding. Like de Monchaux's sculptures, the images created in the text gesture to the presence of desire: the abundance of red, the fluids of the body. Yet as with the sculptures, the body is not fluid. Psyche states: 'I knew that the earth was my body.'[27] The grammatically structured sentences, in their architecture, point to the materiality of the sentence.

This is not to say, however, that Acker reverts to that which McCaffery refers to as 'grammatically centred meaning'.[28] For whilst 'From Psyche's Journal' often employs the structures of that which Andrews terms 'normative grammar',[29] meaning is abstracted. Writing remains language-centred, a 'writing of diminished referentiality'.[30] Like de Monchaux's imagined objects, Acker's ekphrastic writing is both material and immaterial. In her notes Acker refers to de Monchaux's sculptures as 'Objects at the edge of the visible handwritings that appear & then don't. All we have with Cathy de Monchaux's is a map that doesn't exist.'[31] Acker's comments on the appearance and disappearance of language in de Monchaux's work resound with the radical nature of abstraction. In an essay titled 'Disfiguring Abstraction', Bernstein argues that what is most radical in modernist abstraction, 'is not the actualization of "pure abstraction" but the oscillation of figure and nonfigure, a fort-da of appearance/disappearance'.[32] In Acker's work, this fort-da of visibility/invisibility opens up a site of new perception: 'You can see & you can't. There is separation & there isn't. As in self and other.'[33] This phenomenological site of embodied abstraction is a site of pure eversion:

> Persephone, not knowing whether she loved or detested her kidnapper, finally became so hungry in the land of a death that she bit into a red fruit. Into what lay between her lips. Her mouth biting into her own mouth. This red was the center of the seashell. Red so open, so visible, that all that lay inside, the self, and all that lay outside, the world, became the same.[34]

The merger of the practice of ekphrasis and the strategy of *récriture* recontextualises the myth of Persephone into the aesthetics of de Monchaux's contemporary sculptures. Eversion here is not fluid but takes place at the site of colour, visible, yet non-denotative, which is also the site of the self. The verb 'lay' materialises that which is inside and outside as it implicates an object, materiality. The self then becomes material, yet remains abstract, and inside and outside become one. In her notes Acker expressed the desire to 'talk about palpability, the body'. She compares de Monchaux's objects to shrines: 'Every shrine', she writes, 'attests to the presence of the unapproachable.' She understands each map to be 'a shrine that leads to the unapproachable'. 'If de Monchaux's object and mappings hover at the edges of form & invisibility', Acker reasons, 'they turn the usual hierarchy of spirit over physical, mental over physical'. Crucially, 'the shrine, physical, doesn't matter except that it leads to what otherwise cannot be reached. The snail trail, the sexual juice that doesn't exist.'[35] Examining the issue of palpability, Acker poses the question 'What if all that is palpable is contiguous rather than dependent on that which isn't?'[36] This contiguous relation is realised in the clausal structure of Persephone's narrative, whereby the palpable act of biting into the fruit, an act as visible, discernible, and as tangible as her lips are physical, borders the intangible, the red, the non-dualistic site of the self, and eversion, a space accessed through ekphrasis.

The process of ekphrasis allows Acker's writing to move towards non-meaning. 'As abstract turns into representation', she observes, 'so meaning turns into non-meaning.'[37] For Bernstein abstraction resides on the borders of the visible and invisible, resisting meaning. Asserting that the relation between one abstract work and another is, in Wittgenstein's terms, through 'family resemblance', Bernstein states 'the harder we try to define abstraction, the more it slips away'.[38] Ekphrasis enables the verbal figuration of that which is inexpressible. The abstract aesthetics of de Monchaux's work facilitate rather than preclude representation in Acker's work. This precipitation of de Monchaux's sculptures stands in contrast to the problematics encountered by classical sculptors in their adherence to the classical law of art. Gotthold Ephraim Lessing's landmark 1766 work, *Laocoön: An Essay on the Limits of Painting and Poetry* took the ancient Greek sculpture, *Laocoön* (excavated in Rome in 1506), showing the three figures in the pain throes of death as his starting point for a study of the relations between sculpture and poetry. As Lessing observed in 1766, in works such as Timanthes's painting of the sacrifice of Iphigenia the representation of the father's pain is 'subjected to the first law of art, the law of beauty',[39] and thereby sacrificed. He points to the impossibility of representing pain in classical sculpture and applies this to the case of Laocoön. He says of the sculptor, '[t]he master was striving to attain the greatest beauty under the given conditions of bodily pain. Pain, in its disfiguring extreme, was not compatible and must therefore be softened.'[40] Thus within the 'necessary limitations'[41] of sculpture, '[s]creams must be reduced to sighs, . . . because they would often deform the countenance to a repulsive degree'.[42] In de Monchaux's work representation is not limited by aesthetic rules of representation. *Balming Rusty Wounds* (1966) is made of rusted steel, leather and chalk. The light pink leather dusted with chalk appears as a flesh pipe, its vulva-like folds held together tautly by rusted steel clasps bound in place by nails. At intervals the light pink leather breaks open, straining against the rusted steel that binds it. The leather in the centre is red. Yet the sculpture, whilst embodying pain alludes to the decorative traditions of the late nineteenth and early twentieth centuries, imbuing the work with an abstract beauty. Pain and beauty coexist, neither subordinated to the other. De Monchaux's imagined objects subvert classical laws of aesthetics and open up an abstract space and a composite field for Acker's experimental writing.

Acker provides an illustration of a floor plan of a building in her reappropriated text. It occurs directly before the reappropriation of the end of Book IV of *The Golden Ass*, when Psyche is brought to an appointed rock, at the command of Apollo's prophecy, to be left to die, clothed in mourning apparel. In Acker's illustration, at the entrance of the building there is a plaque. On the opposite wall to the entrance there are 'windows mirroring all that lies in front of them' and, in the middle, Acker has sketched two vertical lines that she labels 'lines of perception (time)'. On the following page Acker offers an ekphrastic account that begins by referring to de Monchaux's large-scale installation piece: 'Over the only doorway, huge enough to be one of its shorter sides, a plaque read "wandering about in the future, looking forward to the past."'[43] The text mirrors the architecture that Acker perceives in de Monchaux's work. De Monchaux describes the work as a 'very large wall piece two windows bricked up with white painted glass central section pink scar like image – covered in chalk lots of black ribbons'. Acker annotates de Monchaux's sketch and description: 'BUILDING:

Windows in building – name of building cause can't see outside, self so inside is outside.'[44] In the reappropriation of the myth of Psyche, this text becomes a threshold that ushers in the transition into interior space:

> As soon as I had crossed the threshold, I started thinking about these words. In front of my eyes were two windows embedded in the room's back wall. Instead of revealing whatever might be behind them, whatever lay in the back of the building, these eyes, as if all of the world and so time was existing in the building, mirrored whatever lay in front of them. Especially the doorway in which I had just been standing.
>
> Now I found myself inside an architectural snail or conch, for the rooms within rooms, insides in insides, as I passed through them, led me to where I wanted to be. To the future. Outside was inside; insides were insides: perception opened to all. The more I saw, the farther I could travel.
>
> As I looked on the buildings walls, I saw what was to come. I understood the words on the plaque.[45]

This movement into the synecdochal space of the snail-shaped labyrinth that Psyche experienced in the encounter with *Suck Violets* at the outset offers a new site and a new perception. Through a reference to the description of Cupid's house in 'the sacred book', this perception is conflated with Cupid's house that Psyche enters in Book V of *The Golden Ass*. Psyche's experience of the space gestures to the experience of inhabiting the exhibition and Psyche offers here her own ekphrastic rendition of the artworks she encounters:

> There are tiny photos in one of the corners. Each shows a fruit or a tree or a flower. Animals, each one different from all the others, look down at every vegetable, twine into every one; vegetable turns mineral turns live animal turns dead animal. Apart from logic or reason. Nature lives inside this room or building: that which used to be outside rests inside.
>
> As I walk through the rest of the space, I see different objects. Each object is a picture because it's representational as well as abstract. In both photos and pictures/object, the genres of nature are continually transmuting in and out of each other. Phenomena is constantly being born and dying. As I look at each object, I see all there is to be:[46]

Transformation is located at the point of perception of the artwork, in a space 'apart from logic or reason'. The art object holds the capacity to represent transmutation. The text, in its repetition and patterning is itself abstract. Bernstein offers a definition of abstraction:

> Marks in space. Perhaps protolanguage, perhaps protoart, no doubt something outside of the categories we now understand. Abstraction and patterning – visual marks unmoored from utility or representation – is a recurring impulse in the history of inscription whether we frame it as the unconscious or primitive.[47]

The abstract space that Psyche encounters is an ontic space, offering a vision of 'all there is to be'. Through the placing of the colon, the text opens onto expansion but in the absence of any words following the colon, the expansion is also negation. Such an aesthetics of negation calls to mind Hesse's remarks on her abstract objects: 'As a thing, an object, it acceeds [sic] to its non-logical self. It is something, it is nothing.'[48]

The bridging of abstraction and representation in Acker's work is significant. For Bernstein writing in 2013, the tendency in contemporary culture is for artworks not to sustain an 'aesthesis of abstraction', and thus contemporary artworks cease to 'enact the fierce struggle against representation that at one time animated them'.[49] In Acker's experimental piece that conflates ekphrasis and reappropriation, and in de Monchaux's sculptures, an 'aesthesis of abstraction' persists, and it is the traversing of abstraction and the representation of non-meaning within the abstract form that perpetuates the radical force of abstraction. 'From Psyche's Journal' is a performative act of perception that, in creating an abstract space of inscription, embodies the 'epistemological potential'[50] that Bernstein understands to be inherent to the abstract work. In doing so, Acker represents an impossible site, in which self and other are conflated. At this point a paradox arises, whereby the site of impossibility is simultaneously the performative potential of the text. The composite field opened up accommodates impossibility. In her later texts Acker's experimentalism opens up a textual site that escapes power and fringes the obscure. Responding to *Confessional*, Psyche voices palpability, abstracted, reaching towards the unknown: 'This night I see is the disappearance of the world, of my life and my death. Touch is left. I have no fear.'[51]

Literary calisthenics

Acker's works open up a discursive realm in which an interplay between the text and classical mythology takes place. The 'language of the body' that occurs in her work is a language of self-expression. In her artistic and literary practices, the production of this language is contingent upon the text reabsorbing mythological formations. Acker's conception of language as bodybuilding is pertinent here. In Acker's works we find a use of the materiality of form to reinscribe the classical body. Acker wrote her essay 'Against Ordinary Language: The Language of the Body' in 1993. She explains that she had been bodybuilding for ten years, and attempting to write about bodybuilding for five years. In her essay, Acker details her failure to write about bodybuilding and theorises the relationship between this failure and the emergence of 'the language of the body' which 'resists ordinary language'.[52] This resistance of the body to ordinary language in the act of bodybuilding possesses a parallel in Elaine Scarry's assertion that 'ordinarily there is no language for pain . . . it (more than any other phenomenon) resists verbal objectification'.[53] In both Acker's experimental writing that takes up the pain of her breast cancer and Scarry's understanding of the inexpressibility of pain we can detect a paradox of representation by which elements are unveiled that resist ordinary language, and thus resist cultural expressibility.

Acker met this paradox in a writing experiment: her essay on bodybuilding. Acker's languages of the body might be termed 'literary calisthenics' after David Antin's experimental writing practices in 'The November Exercises' (1971). In 2001, Antin reflected on the techniques employed in his early work:

> 'The November Exercises' was just what it claimed to be – a series of exercises undertaken several times a day – the time markings tell how many. It was November 1971 and I was in a down mood. So they functioned as a cross between calisthenics and spiritual exercises, operating on the events of the daily news, or my personal life by means of a handbook for foreigners, *Essential Idioms of English*. I started on November 1st and ran out of steam by November 27th.[54]

Acker's literary calisthenics are comparable to Antin's but involve specifically experimenting with the body as the site of language. The term 'calisthenics' is used distinct from 'exercises' for the rhythmic element the term implies, along with the desire of those practising calisthenics to achieve grace of movement. Calisthenics consists of the use of the body alone without equipment or apparatus to transform the body. Bodybuilding is calisthenics. As Acker states: 'Bodybuilding is a process . . . by which a person shapes his or her body.'[55] Bodybuilding involves a tension between stasis and movement. 'I always want to work my muscle, muscular group, until it can no longer move: I want to fail.'[56] The relation to the material is fundamental: 'Bodybuilding is about failure because bodybuilding, body growth and shaping, occurs in the face of the material.'[57] Acker's plan in her bodybuilding experiment was to attend the gym (Acker herself was a bodybuilder) and then to describe everything she had experienced after each workout in a series of diary entries. This, she believed, would 'provide the raw material' for the essay. However, recognising the failure of her method she stated '[a]fter each workout, I forgot to write. Repeatedly. I . . . some part of me . . . the part of "I" who bodybuilds . . . was rejecting language, any verbal description of the language of bodybuilding.'[58] During the course of her experiment, Acker realised that the only way she could conceive of writing about bodybuilding was by 'analyzing this rejection of ordinary or verbal language'.[59] The act of bodybuilding has an affinity with Acker's own literary practice of appropriation. Bodybuilding, Acker writes,

> is a process . . . by which a person shapes his or her own body . . . The general law behind body-building is that muscle, if broken down in a controlled fashion and then provided with the proper growth factors such as nutrients and rest, will grow back larger than before.[60]

Once she had recognised muscular destruction in bodybuilding as vital to muscular growth, she was able to analogise her experience to art, asking: 'Is the equation between destruction and growth also a formula for art?'[61]

In Acker's experimental writing this destruction–growth formula becomes immediately apparent in both her feminist revisions of male texts and in her use of repetition within those texts. As I have shown in earlier chapters, Acker takes the frames of texts such as Cervantes' picaresque novel *Don Quixote* (1605) and Dickens'

Great Expectations (1861) only to repeat them within her experimental appropriations. As I illustrated in Chapter 3, this technique, which effects a distortion, repetition, and consequent fracture of classic male texts, facilitates Acker's displacement of traditional narrative structure and imbues her novels with a non-verbal voice that emerges from experimental composition. This method of feminist framing and appropriation is repeated in microcosm within the body of Acker's recontextualisations. The symbolic confinement of conventional syntax is aligned with institutional oppression. Acker uses repetition to strip syntax of meaning. She does this in her earliest work, *Blood and Guts in High School* (1978), in Janey's Persian poems. 'The Persian Poems', as Chapter 2 remarked, are a series of grammar exercises that through repetition expose the constraints of language that educational institutions impose. Janey's desire to rid herself of the semiological structure is paradoxical as it takes the form of drilling a verb structure 'to get rid of language' (*B&G*, 76). Janey, in these constructions, refers to herself in the third person: there is no 'I'. Her desire to move beyond language is disempowered by the very means through which she expresses that desire. Conventional language in Acker's work is imprisoning. Breaking the confines of that language, her work embodies a movement both towards death and myth, and towards a liberation of the self: 'the closer we are living to total human death', one of Acker's female voices states, 'the weaker the socio-political restraints on us' (*DQ*, 164).

Acker views the world of mythology as antithetical to the suppression of the individual under capitalism. The consequence of political and cultural oppression is the turning of the individual away from a dead reality toward myth, which Acker understands as a new reality. Acker's earlier texts such as *Blood and Guts in High School*, in which her female protagonists are trapped within the confines of socio-political constraints, are precursors to her later texts such as *Pussy, King of the Pirates* (1996) in which her protagonists find a language for the self and escape repression through recourse to mythology. In her brief introduction to Fabre and Mapplethorpe's collaboration *The Power of Theatrical Madness*, entitled 'Opera: The Actual Working of Terror and Ecstasy', she writes:

> Confronted with an exorbitant unapproachable that casts its alien shadow over him, the individual feels an affinity with the world of

myth. What he shares with it is the gesture of falling silent. Not only the inability but also the refusal to believe in or speak the truth, the recourse to myth which turns a theatrical or communicatory gesture into opera is a phenomenon of the world in which there is cause to fear everything.[62]

Mythology in Acker's works such as *Don Quixote* is associated with the double motif night/knight, that which escapes the fear induced by cultural censorship. Yet as this passage shows Acker also apprehends myth as a sublimating force. The use of mythology enables Acker to find a language for feminine subjectivity and for desire that exceeds and invalidates conventional cultural tropisms of identity.

This can be seen in the case of Pussycat and the pirates in the final novel in Acker's trilogy, *Pussy, King of the Pirates* (1996). As well as Pussycat being an unknown and ephemeral Eurydice figure ('She disappeared as fast as she had come'[63]), Acker's prostitutes/ pirate girls are a punk appropriation of Ovid's Propoetides. Book X of Ovid's *Metamorphoses* tells the story of the 'loathsome Propoetides'; as a result of their denial of the divinity of Venus, 'they were visited by the wrath of the goddess, and were the first women to loose their good names by prostituting themselves in public'. Then, 'as all sense of shame left them, the blood hardened in their cheeks, and it required only a slight alteration to transform them into stony flints'.[64] Acker restores the corporeality of the Propoetides in her appropriation of Ovid's myth. The pirate girls represent all that the male has suppressed in the female and all that a reactionary society fears in female sexual corporeality: menstrual blood, discharge, odour, and an active female desire as opposed to sexual passivity. In her reappropriation of mythology 'the many faults which nature has implanted in the female sex'[65] that Pygmalion was so revolted by when he encountered the Propoetides are the very elements that construct Acker's pirates and become the building blocks of a radical female agency.

Acker states that part of the technique in breaking down a muscle group in bodybuilding is 'to make that group work up to, even beyond, capacity'. To do this Acker explains that it is necessary to 'visualize the part of the body that is involved. Mind and thought . . . [are] always focussed on number or counting and often precise visualizations.'[66] Acker's description of the process of breaking down muscle in bodybuilding in order to allow the growth of new larger muscle voices the destruction–growth equation:

> Bodybuilding can be seen to be about nothing but *failure*. A body-builder is always working around failure. Either I work an isolated muscle mass, for instance one of the tricep heads, up to failure. In order to do this, I exert the muscle group almost to the point that it can no longer move.
>
> But if I work the same muscle group to the point that it can no longer move, I must move it through failure. I am then doing what I call 'negative reps', working the muscle group beyond its power to move. Here is the second method of working with failure.[67]

A visual and linguistic space is opened up in Acker's appropriations of mythology between the act of repetition and the failure of replication. Acker enacts this process in her repetition of the frame of male texts as well as her repetition of classical myths. In the visual and linguistic elliptical spaces that are created in this process, avant-garde cultural elements emerge within a neoclassical context.

Acker's language of the body that she reads as being produced in the act of bodybuilding is correlatively the emergence of a language that conflates meaning and essence. It contrasts with and indeed rejects ordinary language. Commenting on the antithesis between meaning and essence that Wittgenstein unfolds at the end of his *Tractatus Logico-Philosophicus*, Acker asks: 'If ordinary language or meanings lie outside essence, what is the position of that language game which I have named *the language of the body*?' 'Bodybuilding', Acker conceives as being a language of the body, which at once 'rejects ordinary language' yet 'itself constitutes a language, a method for understanding and controlling the physical which in this case is also the self'.[68] Acker recalls the Bulgarian-born but German-language novelist Elias Canetti's description of the beggars of Marrakech 'who possess a similar and even simpler language game: they repeat the name of God. In ordinary language', Acker argues,

> meaning is contextual. Whereas the cry of the beggar means nothing other than what it is; in the city of the beggar, the impossible (as the Wittgenstein of the *Tractatus* and Heidegger see it) occurs in that meaning and breath become one.

Acker claims that this is the site of the language of the body 'in which meaning and essence no longer oppose each other'.[69] Acker's decontextualising of classical mythology by repeating the configurations of mythology within a new contemporary context provides the conditions for the emergence of the language of the body, as it is through the act of recontextualisation that meaning and essence are conflated. The techniques of appropriation and rewriting in Acker's earlier work foreground the production of the silent languages of the body, which in her later work give voice to pain and death.

Falling silent: *Eurydice in the Underworld* (1997) and 'Requiem' (1997)

The representation of ulterior space through the reappropriation of mythology in Acker's later works, *Eurydice in the Underworld* (1997) and 'Requiem' (1997), is a performative act that ultimately enables the representation of pain. Acker's narrative structure in *Eurydice in the Underworld* and 'Requiem' is based on the Greek tragedy. The act of resituating the classical female figure within a contemporary framework is a process of abstraction. More specifically, Acker, in her later works, re-evaluates mythology to represent pain. The transgression of political inexpressibility in Acker's early works in many ways facilitates the transcendence of the inexpressibility of pain in her later works. Elaine Scarry in her study *The Body in Pain: The Making and Unmaking of the World* (1987) divides the single subject of bodily pain into three different subjects: '*first*, the difficulty of expressing physical pain; *second*, the political and perceptual complications that arise as a result of that difficulty; and *third*, the nature of both material and verbal expressibility, or, more simply, the nature of human creation'.[70] Reading *Eurydice in the Underworld* through Scarry's study brings to light the way in which Acker addresses these three problematics of the representation of pain in her reclaiming of mythology. Scarry acknowledges the topological relationship between these three subjects when she states '[p]hysical pain has no voice, but when it at last finds a voice, it begins to tell a story, and the story that it tells is about the inseparability of these three subjects, their embeddedness within one another'.[71] It is through the reinscription of the body of classical mythology into the contemporary text and image in Acker's later works that this narrative of pain finds a voice.

In her chapter 'Pain and Imagining', Elaine Scarry attends to the idea of the world's construction and reconstruction through the relation between physical pain and imagining. In the first part of her study, Scarry looks at the infliction of pain in torture and war and this involves what she theorises as the 'unmaking' of the world. She states that 'it is impossible to speak of either torture or war without attending to the destruction of the artefacts of civilization in either their interior and mental or exterior and materialised forms'.[72] More significantly, Scarry states that 'the infliction of pain in torture is inextricably bound up with a political "fiction" just as the injuries of war are bound up with a process of conferring facticity on unanchored cultural "constructs"'. Scarry reinstates her point that 'physical pain is exceptional in the whole fabric of psychic, somatic, and perceptual states for being the only one that has no object' in the external world. For Scarry, the only state that is as anomalous as pain is the imagination. Pain is remarkable owing to the fact that it has no object whereas imagination is remarkable, according to Scarry, on account of it being the only state that is wholly its object. Scarry's speculations then lead her to assert that 'physical pain . . . is an intentional state without an intentional object; imagination is an intentional object without an experienceable intentional state'.[73] However, Scarry acknowledges that it is most probably an error to state that physical pain in isolation is an intentional state, insofar as only by having an object does it exist as an intentional state. Pain then, in Scarry's formula, only becomes an intentional state 'once it is brought into relation with the objectifying power of the imagination'.[74] It is through the relation of pain and imagining as 'framing events' in Acker's work that pain, as an intentional state, is represented and emerges as a (de)creative force. This intentional state is expressed through the language of the body in which meaning and essence are conflated in a performative representational act.

Acker takes the mythical figure of Eurydice as her narrative voice for her final published text *Eurydice in the Underworld* (1997). The title immediately reconfigures the original version of the myth, which positions Orpheus as the subject of the tale. Acker appropriates Eurydice's name in the stage directions, shortening it to 'YOU', effectively instating the second person singular as her identity and thus the reader's identity as the narrative voice. This assimilation is important, as when Eurydice becomes YOU the reader enters Eurydice's identity, and only through assuming this narrative position can the reader effectively travel as Eurydice into the underworld. For Nicole Cooley, writing about Acker's text, Eurydice's 'status as a mythic icon is subverted by the reality of her suffering body'.[75] At the outset Eurydice occupies an apartment in Algiers. She is dislocated from her classical background and situated in contemporary space. Orpheus is with her, who is 'the spitting image of Hades'. YOU is vomiting, unable to eat and in pain, still bandaged up from her recent mastectomy. The first part of the play details Eurydice's physical pain and diagnosis. Much of the material of this section is taken directly from an article that Acker wrote for the London *Guardian Weekend* magazine entitled 'The Gift of Disease' (18 January 1997) in which she detailed her rejection of conventional medicine to treat her breast cancer. She describes the horror of the treatment and the loss of self that she experienced. In the process of being prepared for her mastectomy she recalls: 'I was being reduced to something I couldn't recognise.'[76] Acker explained: 'conventional cancer treatment was reducing me, quickly, to a body that was only material, to a body without hope and so without will'.[77] Act Three of 'Requiem' also depicts Electra's diagnosis with breast cancer (Electra is synonymous with Eurydice in Acker's work). At the point of diagnosis Electra reports '[w]hat I had believed to be reality / had just been taken away from me'.[78] In the external world of reductive materialism and institutional oppression, Eurydice's pain strips her of identity until she becomes 'the thing under the cap'[79] in the hospital room. The reductive power of institutional repression that leads to a loss of self within the physical (institutionalised) body is the inversion of the process of bodybuilding in which Acker experiences the physical as self. Pain, in Acker's work, is perhaps more analogous to the dynamics of bodybuilding. Like the practice of bodybuilding, the experience of pain rejects ordinary language, resisting representation and defying verbal language. It has a relation to the reduction of language discovered by Acker in the gym. The language-game that Acker names the 'language of the body' is a bodybuilder's language: 'a minimal, even a closed, set of nouns and numerical repetition'.[80] In her earlier list of ten languages of the body, the fourth entry reads: 'the language of this material body: laughter, silence, screaming'.[81] Silence and screaming are two of the minimal non-verbal languages of pain.

Myth allows Acker to bring pain into relation with 'the objectifying power of the imagination' through having Eurydice move into and speak from the underworld. At the end of the eighth scene, YOU goes into the operating theatre/the underworld and leaves Orpheus wandering around the hospital grounds, lamenting on the outside, singing: 'Can anyone tell me: / Oh, where is Eurydice?'[82] Acker's contemporary equivalent of Eurydice's fatal snakebite, the anaesthetic administered to YOU, provides the means by which Eurydice makes the transition from institutional space to mythological space. Whereas Ovid's tale tells of Orpheus's plight to find Eurydice in the underworld, Acker's play tells the story of Eurydice after the snake bite/anaesthetic. When YOU wakes up she is in the land of the dead. This passage from the external world to the internal world places Eurydice/YOU in the site of her pain and disease, which is inexpressible in the external world. This movement away from the socio-political constraints of institutional space is central in facilitating Acker's representation of pain.

The architecture of Eurydice's imagined space is a mirror of the body. Again it is with reference to Canetti's description of a 'typical house in the geographical labyrinth of Marrakech' that Acker articulates this space in her essay 'Against Ordinary Language'. 'The entire construction of this house,' she states, 'windows, etc., is directed inward, to the central courtyard where only openness to the sun exists'. She explains:

> Such an architecture is a mirror of the body. When I reduce verbal language to minimal meaning, to repetition, I close the body's outer windows. Meaning approaches breath as I bodybuild, as I begin to move through the body's labyrinths, to meet if only for a second, that which my consciousness ordinarily cannot see.[83]

This internal space of the body becomes textual space in *Eurydice in the Underworld*. Eurydice's breast cancer places her in an interior space, a non-signifying realm of silence and the imagination that hitherto in Acker's texts has been the site of female desire. In *Eurydice in the Underworld* this intentional state of pain is the product of the convergence of pain, imagination, and textual space.

In the section 'Diary Written by Eurydice When She's Dead' Eurydice states: 'Silver here is everywhere an object . . . in this place objects and colours have the same status.'[84] As Chapter 5 explored, colour in *My Mother: Demonology* plays an important role as a means to express the impossible and the indefinable. Colour functions in Acker's later work as the intentional property by which pain is brought into existence as an intentional state. Colour disrupts the subject–object relationship presupposed in the external world. Derek Jarman used a single colour as a representational device to address the political and perceptual complications of representing pain in his film *Blue* (1993). Jarman's film realises the intentional state of his pain through the persistence of the blue screen. This cinematographic device forces his viewer into a position of watching a blue screen for the duration of his narrative. The viewer is absorbed into the otherwise non-signifying presence of the colour blue, which situates her/him both in the pain of Jarman's blindness, his AIDS-related illness, and beyond it. In Jarman's words: 'Blue transcends the solemn geography of human limits'.[85] Colour in this instance acts as the medium through which Jarman communicates the interior of his thought process disallowing any specific image to correspond to his thought, and this connects the interior state of his pain to the viewer's imagination without recourse to sentimentality or polemic. Jarman's blue, like Acker's red, is capable of holding conflict. For whilst 'Blue protects white from innocence / Blue drags black with it / Blue is darkness made visible',[86] it is also '[t]he fathomless blue of Bliss'.[87] Crucially, in his cinematography, colour allows Jarman to decontextualise his mind from his physical body. Jarman's use of blue as a representational property within language allows the film-maker to signify the multiplicity of inexpressible elements within his consciousness. The persistence of blue allows Jarman to narrate his vision against his illness.

A similar narration takes place in Acker's work. Physical pain and imagining occur in Eurydice's underworld in what Scarry terms a 'forward form' that has 'a shape necessitated by the exceptional place that each has within the psychic arrangements of intentional states and their objects'.[88] The transcendence that takes place in Eurydice's underworld is performative. The text is the object created through Eurydice's speech act from the space of her imagination but in it Eurydice also transcends materiality and it becomes a protean space of creation and transformations:

I'm a seedling. It's Winter and all the plants are stripped. Whatever of them is able to rise above the earth waves branches in the air.

I am starting from nothing. So slowly.

I can see that the sky is gray today. There's some clarity because the white wall of the empty building. Behind it, a derelict red brick building. Blue plastic on a dead-leaf-covered roof, over a red door, windows through which nothing can be seen. Two white roses rise out of the small squares of wet soil placed in the concrete.

    I see ivy is crawling fungus-like over the nearest roof. There's no more difference between what I'm seeing and who I think I am.

    Reality has been reduced.

    Somebody said 'nobody reads anymore'. Nobody is anymore. Time is being reduced because plants must spring up. I can see them, roses, I once said 'a rose is my cunt'. I want to do more than just see.[89]

The narrative 'I' is in a state of becoming. Yet the passage expresses the pain of becoming in a decaying space. As in bodybuilding, Acker breaks down language in this space and this reduction of language to a minimum parallels the reduction of reality. The exiguous use of language and movement towards abstraction, however, produces meaning. In 'Against Ordinary Language' Acker compares the journeying into the body that takes place in bodybuilding to 'that geography that is without the world's languages' found by the man who 'unlearns the world's languages' in Canetti's work.[90] 'The small loss of language', Acker writes, 'occurs when I journey in and to my own body.'[91]

Rather than a space of corporeality, this internal space has been reconfigured through the use of colour and the reduction of language as a non-objective space, which is found in abstract art. In lines such as '[t]here's some clarity because the white walls of the empty building' Acker can be read as writing against ordinary language. In omitting either the preposition 'of' between 'because' and 'the' or omitting the continuation of the sentence via a verbal clause, Acker both rejects the prepositional relationship of belonging between two entities common to conventional syntax and also the syntactical demand for the continuation of a sentence. The two spaces of ellipsis this creates point to a syntactical disruption and it is within these spaces of absence that Acker's Wittgensteinian language emerges, 'a language game which resists ordinary language'.

Eurydice's alienation is expressed in the imagery of the dereliction of the architecture, which parallels the generative elliptical spaces of her language in this scene. In this space the two white roses rise out of the only squares of soil in the concrete. Acker's conflation of the self with perception enacts the symphysis of meaning and essence. Erasing the difference between that which she sees and who she thinks she is, Eurydice's writing becomes the language of her body. This space of Eurydice's imagination is an ontological space. Acker's language of the body is performative, as it is, in Judith Butler's terms, 'the vehicle through which ontological effects are established'. Performativity, Butler stated in interview with Peter Osborne in 1994, is something like 'the discursive mode by which ontological effects are installed'.[92]

In the narratives of Eurydice and Electra, Acker explores and exposes the change that takes place in perception with the advent of terminal illness. In 'Requiem' Electra points to what 'we, / mistakenly / call "time"' and the act of 'trying to find meaning where there is none'. Electra narrates a similar movement towards a language of the body to Eurydice's. Although she does not go into the underworld, Acker uses the monologue to have Electra voice an internal narrative, which is cut off from the external world. In her monologue at the beginning of Act Three, she states that at the moment when her disease became unbearable 'thought died in my brain. Something larger than me rose up inside me / and screamed without using my voice, / No more of death. Again / no more of death'.[93] This silent language that comes from within Electra is important. In Eurydice's narrative she states she wants to do more than just see. In Acker's play, Electra places this ontological birth in the idea of 'acting':

It must be
that every finger, ring and stone,
every single possible thing,
the song and she who sings
is caused
and that each cause is precise.
If this is true, then to descend
to the causes of all things
to the factory of the self,
is to begin to act.[94]

'Act' here is both the performative and for Electra (being the protagonist of a play) the self-reflexive meaning of 'act', as well as the idea of taking action as opposed to remaining passive. The beginning of both is located here in the descent to the 'factory of the self'. There is a clear parallel between Eurydice's imagined space as a result of her descent into the underworld and Electra's descent, which takes place whilst she is alive. Electra opens her final song with a quotation from Rainer Maria Rilke's first Duino Elegy: 'Who, if I cried out, would hear me among the angels?' Electra's final song is a discourse with Rilke in which she moves from fear to an acceptance of death. The idea of the possibility of creation within a space of decreation is articulated by Electra: 'because I have met my death, I give myself birth',[95] and she fortifies this statement by referring to classical mythology:

> Remember that Persephone
> raped by Hades
> then by him brought
> into the Kingdom of Death
> there gave birth
> to Dionysius[96]

Acker's reminder of the birth of Dionysius echoes Rilke's idea that grief is the Source of Joy[97] and that to be full of life is to be full of death. By repeating Rilke's lines within Electra's speech, Acker's appropriation of the Electra myth here fuses her protagonist's identity with Rilke. Simultaneously she appropriates Rilke, who was dressed up as a girl by his mother when he was younger, in one of the final instances of that which Carla Harryman has called the 'ventriloquy of childhood'[98] in Acker's work. In her final lines she banishes the mother/Clytemnestra of the Electra complex and citing Rilke's tenth Duino Elegy Electra sings:

> 'Emerging at last from violent insight
> 'Sing out in jubilation and in praise',
> To the angels who terrified away the night.
> Let not one string
> of my forever-child's heart and cunt fail to sing.
> Open up this body half in the realm of life, half in death
> and give breath.[99]

These lines are central to Acker's representation of pain and death and her transcendence of the external world that disallows her becoming. Here the opening of the body within the liminal space between life and death is the space of ontological birth. This is the production of the language of the body in which meaning and essence become one. Echoing Acker's comments on Canetti's beggars, Electra sings: 'For to breathe is always to pray. / You language where language goes away.' In her equation of breath and silence, Acker approaches Bataille's inner experience. For Bataille, silence is a 'slipping' word, it is 'the abolition of the sound which the word is; among all the words it is the most perverse, or the most poetic'. The word 'silence', Bataille states, 'is the token of its own death':

> Silence is given in the sick delectation of the heart. When the fragrance of a flower is charged with reminiscences, we linger alone over breathing it in, questioning it, in the anguish of the secret which its sweetness will in an instance deliver up to us: this secret is only the inner presence, silent, unfathomable and naked, which an attention forever given to words (to objects) steals from us, and which it ultimately gives back if we give it to those most transparent among objects. But this attention does not fully give it up unless we know how to detach it, in the end, even from its discontinuous objects, which we do by choosing for them as a sort of resting place where they will finally disappear, the silence which is no longer anything.[100]

Acker's experimentation in her final texts, through abstraction, the poetic, and language-centred writing, detaches from the denotative attention given to words, of which Bataille writes. Drawing on Hindu philosophy, Bataille brings silence into relation with breath. For Hindus, breath is the resting place. Bataille remarks that breath is 'no less inner' than silence: 'just as a "slipping" word has the property of capturing the attention given in advance to words, so breath captures the attention which gestures have at their command, the movements directed towards objects'. However, Bataille observes, 'of these movements breath alone leads to interiority'. Both breath and silence shelter negation, and through negation have a relation to the impossible: 'Silence is a word which is not a word and breath an object which is not an object',[101] Bataille states. Bernstein interprets Ginsberg's 'latterday insistence on breath / &clarity, &the focus that meditation can bring', 'as an attempt to hone in on the essential / &

separate out the beclouded'.[102] Acker's idea of breath as a language of the body recalls Stein's equation of language and breath discussed in the introduction of this study, in which, Acker states 'language was primary, so that it would have the power of breath'.[103] Charles Olson's work on breath also resonates here. Olson expounded his ideas concerning breath in his 1950 manifesto 'Projective Verse': 'the line comes (I swear it) from the breath, from the breathing of the man who writes, at the moment that he writes'.[104] 'A projective poet', in Olson's understanding, will go 'down through the workings of his own throat to that place where breath comes from, where breath has its beginnings, where drama comes from, where, the coincidence is, all act springs'.[105] Electra's performative breath, and her falling silent at the end of 'Requiem' is also the birth of her self expressed in a silent language of the body that is created in the absence of ordinary language.

It is Acker's unintentional foregrounding of the state of pain's inexpressibility in her earlier work through the disclosure of the prohibited body that in many ways facilitates her later reappropriations of classical mythology to represent pain. Scarry acknowledges that 'pain and death . . . are radical and absolute, found only at the boundaries they themselves create'.[106] Here we have an interesting paradox and one that can be linked to the ontological effects of Acker's 'becoming' and the associated opacity of the experimental text. In her early works Acker transgresses cultural boundaries, enforcing the body's corporeality and its eroticism as a response to its denial by the external world and liberating it from socio-political constraints. Body breaks through materiality. It is the turning away from this body and celebration of corporeality towards non-sentient representations that allows Acker to invert and reappropriate her own representations, moving towards abstraction and a detachment from the body. This inversion enables Acker to reveal the radical and absolute nature of pain and death and the boundaries that pain and death create. Her earlier works, through her *récriture féminine*, exhibit the process of creation. Through repetition her reappropriations move through the failure of replication to the production of a language in which meaning and essence are one. Acker's later works, 'From Psyche's Journal', 'Requiem', and *Eurydice in the Underworld* are processes of decreating the body. Through the silent language of the body they express the intentional state of pain by bringing it into relation with the self-effacing nature of the imagination. The 'intense form of negation' that Scarry attributes to pain and death is made vivid in Acker's work. The experimental compositional practices of ekphrasis, literary calisthenics, and reappropriation of mythology move Acker's work towards a larger understanding of representing the indescribable, or inexpressible. Ekphrasis and literary calisthenics are both contingent on a relation with the material, whereby depiction emerges through the encounter with the material. In each practice Acker confronts a formal tension between something that cannot be described and the need to ascribe the unpresentable presence. Both too involve visualising. Ekphrasis is the visualising of the artwork; bodybuilding involves visualising and counting. Meaning emerges from these experimental practices that is non-verbal. As the abstract artwork embodies the absurdity of life for Hesse, for Acker, abstraction, silence, and breath offer languages not tied to context or denotative meaning but instead are able to voice those states such as desire, pain, and death, which resist ordinary language.

Conclusion

Reflecting in 1990 on her early adult years immersed in the New York art world, Acker remembered 'being taught that it's not an art work's content, surface content, that matters, but the process of making art. That only process matters.'[1] Attention to the manuscript practice and compositional processes of Acker's works, alongside the question of experimental practice and meaning, brings to light the new forms of creative practice that Acker's works embody. This book opened with Acker's declaration 'FORM HAS MEANING' and the importance of the imbrication of form with content to modernist and late modernist experimental writers. Acker's experimental practices – exercises in writing asystematically, collage, topological intertextuality, montage, ekphrasis, and literary calisthenics – reveal a body of compositional strategies that continue to uphold this distinctive feature of early twentieth-century experiment and preserve the radical force of her writings.

Acker's creative practice and the new forms of non-restricted meaning that arise from her works demand critical attention. The obstruction of normal reading in Acker's work is often recognised at a general level when critics perceive Acker's works as unreadable, or fragmented, or senseless. Less frequently recognised are the intricate practices of experimentation, which are innumerable and require more scholarly attention. Acker's early procedural practices, field-orientated experiments with the page, and practices of rewriting, as well as her use of non-referential language, innovative typography and modes of textual inscription, illustration, writing-through, deviant translation, various modes of cutting-up, cutting in, excising, juxtaposition, writing through the image, the instituting of opacity, and obscuring situate her in a lineage of radical modernisms. Each of the chapters of this book have traced Acker's continuation of the modernist concern with the crisis of language, and the yearning for a new language and a new revolutionary way of writing. One question that arises in a study of Acker's work is the extent to which Acker was successful in creating new languages using the tools of her experimental practice, or whether her efforts result in merely a frustrating impasse. It is my contention that Acker succeeds in creating new non-verbal languages, through experimental composition and experimental writing practices that culminate in her final works in a new form of literary abstraction.

The chapters of this book have exposed the ways in which Acker's experimental practices yield modes of defamiliarisation that offer new forms of perception. Acker's early poetic exercises show her creating perceiver-centred fields. *Blood and Guts in High School* offers new modes of feminist inscription through collage and rewriting as alternatives to Janey's confinement within the parameters of ordinary language. *Don Quixote* succeeds in forging a new sense of female time through the practice of writing-through and protosemantic experiment. *In Memoriam to Identity*, through a reticulation of narratives, generates sites of perception that conflate fiction and reality. *My Mother: Demonology* uses montage and creative cutting both to create the narrative conditions for a vertical axis that holds 'the feeling, the emotion' and 'the metaphysical content of the movement', and to dialectically enfold the quotidian and the poetic. In Acker's final works, her practices of ekphrasis and literary calisthenics enable the emergence of silent languages that give voice to unrepresentable states. This study opened by drawing on the potential insights into experimental practice when considered in light of Blanchot's idea of impossibility. Read within the framework of Blanchot's thoughts, Acker's work preserves, through experimental practice, textual sites of impossibility and the unknown. These radical literary spaces are protected from being assimilated by possibility and the powers of comprehension by the new textual conditions. This safeguarding of aesthetic space through experimental practice is the avant-garde pulse of Acker's works. It recalls the distance of the writer that she spoke of in 1979, cited at the outset of this book: 'The difference between a writer and its world gives the reason for writing.'[2] It also accords with Adorno's idea that art 'criticizes society just by being there'.[3]

When approached chronologically, the development and evolution of various experimental techniques become apparent across Acker's body of works. Early poetic exercises, such as 'Journal Black Cat Black Jewels', in their experimentation with incantatory repetition, hold the seeds for Acker's later conceptual experiments. These reach their apogee in her series of experiments with bodybuilding and literary calisthenics, and the discovery of a language that rejects ordinary language. Experiments with procedure in her homages to LeRoi Jones written in the 1970s, in their dialectical reduction and expansion of the text, are echoed in Acker's practices of non-procedural writing-through and a telegraphic style of writing in works such as *Don Quixote*. The complex use of the image and illustration in Acker's early works, particularly in *Blood and Guts in High School*, can be followed into Acker's later language experiments that write through the image, use the image as a catalyst for language, and exploit colour as a means to cultivate opacity in language. Strands of experimental practice such as these, their unfolding and refinement over the course of Acker's works, testify to the intricacies of Acker's writings and trace the trajectories of her experiments. In the continuous development of her practice, the extent of her experimental body of work, and her commitment to experiment, Acker's work has the rigour and scale of her modernist predecessors, Stein and Joyce.

Kathy Acker's legacy, like Gertrude Stein's, extends into the contemporary. Her work is being recognised by scholars in the twenty-first century from perspectives perhaps not possible in the twentieth century. As Wollen remarks, even the poets of the St Marks poetry project in New York in the 1970s, which was 'an avant-garde mecca for modernists', were utterly 'baffled'[4] by Acker's writings. A number of scholars and writers have taken up Acker's works recently. The experimental author and critic Chris Kraus is writing a critical biography of Acker, and Jason McBride is working on an extensive biography of Acker's life and work. It is also significant that Acker continues to engender experimental practices in the works of contemporary poets, writers, and filmmakers. Barbara Casper's 2008 documentary *Who's Afraid of Kathy Acker?* offers a portrait of Acker's life and work. The experimental artist and filmmaker Laura Parnes's video installation *Blood and Guts in High School* (2004–9) re-imagines Acker's work, bringing the political element of the book into the contemporary. Such works reveal Acker's legacy to be re-emerging in contemporary avant-garde culture. Les Figues Press recently set up the Kathy Acker Fellowship for an emerging writer or artist, literary editor, or art curator/organizer.

As a key figure of the American avant-garde in the 1970s, Acker continued the experimental work of radical modernism in the post-war years through to her death in 1997. She is also very much a contemporary avant-garde writer whose legacy remains present in the twenty-first century, with an immediacy that demands our attention. Stein's words in 1938 resonate here: 'A creator is contemporary, he understands what is contemporary when the contemporaries do not yet know it.'[5] Acker's and Stein's writings remain fresh, radical, and new, precisely because of the antiabsorptive nature of their writing. Forrest-Thompson's articulation of the need for the reader of the work of artifice 'to use his imagination . . . to free himself from the fixed forms of thought which ordinary language imposes on our minds'[6] is pertinent to the reader of Acker's experimental writing. The reception of Acker's works has shifted since the publication of *Blood and Guts in High School* in 1984, through new readers, and in response to the changing socio-political climates. Scholarship must now also respond to the divergent compositional elements of Acker's practice. Acker's comments on art and its criticism are equally applicable to literature: 'The homogeneity of the criticism dissimulates the heterogeneity of the art.'[7]

Notes

Introduction

1. Acker, 'Notebooks for *My Mother: Demonology*'. Unpaginated, Kathy Acker Papers, David M. Rubenstein Rare Book and Manuscript Library, Duke University, Box 3.
2. This distinction is made by critics of Bürger and is one that Bürger subsequently reiterates in his defence of *Theory of the Avant-Garde* in his recent essay 'Avant-Garde and Neo-Avant-Garde: An Attempt to Answer Certain Critics of *Theory of the Avant-Garde*', *New Literary History*, vol. 41, no. 4, 2010, pp. 695–715. However, Bürger's original thesis in *Theory of the Avant-Garde* did not use 'modernism' as a term. David Cunningham made this observation in his introduction, 'Lost in Translation: Surrealism's Theoretical Afterlives', at the 'Surrealism. Post-War Theory and the Avant-Garde' symposium at the Courtauld Institute, London, 27 November 2009. The divide that is drawn on so frequently by Bürger's critics is in some part a result of the text's Anglo-American reception and subsequent translation.
3. Bürger states: 'The avant-gardists propose the sublation of art – sublation in the Hegelian sense of the term: art was not simply to be destroyed, but transferred to the praxis of life where it would be preserved, albeit it in a different form.' See Peter Bürger, *Theory of the Avant-Garde*, trans. Michael Shaw. Minneapolis: University of Minnesota Press [1974], 2009, p. 49.
4. Richard Murphy, *Theorizing the Avant-Garde: Modernism, Expressionism, and the Problem of Postmodernity*. Cambridge: Cambridge University Press, 1998, p. 32.
5. Acker, 'NOTES ON WRITING – from THE LIFE OF BAUDELAIRE', p. 1, Kathy Acker Papers, Box 4.
6. Tyrus Miller, *Singular Examples: Artistic Politics and the Neo-Avant-Garde*. Evanston: Northwestern University Press, 2009, p. 6.

7. Walter Benjamin, 'The Author as Producer', in *The Work of Art in the Age of Its Technological Reproducibility and Other Writings on Media*, trans. Edmund Jephcott et al. Cambridge, MA: Harvard University Press, 2008, pp. 79–95. I take up Benjamin's discussion of montage in Brecht's 'epic' theatre in more detail in Chapter 5.

8. Theodor Adorno, *Aesthetic Theory*, trans. Robert Hullot-Kentor. London: Bloomsbury [1970], 2013, p. 198.

9. Murphy, *Theorizing the Avant-Garde*, p. 18.

10. Ibid. Carla Harryman makes a related point regarding Acker's work in her essay 'Acker Un-formed'. She writes that Acker's characters do not '*lack* character / subjectivity' but that they are in circumstances 'in which subjectivity, the illusory hallmark of character, is not a concern'. See Harryman, 'Acker Un-formed', in *Lust for Life: On the Writings of Kathy Acker*, ed. Amy Scholder, Carla Harryman and Avital Ronell. New York: Verso, 2006, p. 36.

11. Kathy Acker, 'Against Ordinary Language', in *Bodies of Work: Essays by Kathy Acker*. London: Serpent's Tail, 1997, pp. 143–51.

12. See Peter Wollen's essay 'Death (and Life) of the Author', reprinted as 'Kathy Acker', in *Lust for Life*, ed. Scholder et al., pp. 1–12. Carla Harryman's rigorous and insightful essay 'Acker Un-formed', pp. 35–44, offers a brilliant exegesis of Acker's experimental practices.

13. See for instance Susan E. Hawkins, 'All in the Family: Kathy Acker's *Blood and Guts in High School*', *Contemporary Literature*, vol. 45, no. 4, Winter 2004, pp. 637-58, and Suzette Henke, 'Oedipus Meets Sacher-Masoch: Kathy Acker's Pornographic (Anti)Ethical Aesthetic', *Contemporary Women's Writing*, vol. 2, no. 2, December 2008, pp. 91–110. These articles are valuable but tend towards a heavily theoretical reading of Acker's work. The extent of Acker's experiment with form in such analyses is often given less attention than the content of her work.

14. Wollen, 'Kathy Acker', p. 7.

15. Charles Bernstein, 'Artifice of Absorption', in *A Poetics*. Cambridge, MA: Harvard University Press, 1992, p. 9.

16. Ibid.

17. Veronica Forrest-Thomson, *Poetic Artifice: A Theory of Twentieth Century Poetry*. New York: St. Martin's Press, 1978, p. 132, cited by Bernstein in *A Poetics*, p. 10.

18. Ibid. pp. 10–11.

19. Ibid. p. 52.

20. Ibid. p. 56.

21. Ibid. p. 11.

22. Marianne DeKoven, *A Different Language: Gertrude Stein's Experimental Writing*. Madison: University of Wisconsin Press, 1983, p. xv.

23. Ibid.
24. Murphy, *Theorizing the Avant-Garde*, p. 24.
25. Acker, 'A Few Notes on Two of My Books', in *Bodies of Work: Essays*, p. 9.
26. Acker, 'Preface', in *Bodies of Work: Essays*, p. viii.
27. Ibid.
28. Ibid. p. ix.
29. Ibid.
30. Charles Bernstein, 'The Expanded Field of *L=A=N=G=U=A=G=E*', in *The Routledge Companion to Experimental Literature*, ed. Joe Bray, Alison Gibbons and Brian McHale. London and New York: Routledge, 2015, p. 284.
31. Wollen, 'Kathy Acker', p. 6.
32. Kathy Acker, 'The Path of Abjection: An Interview with Kathy Acker', in Larry McCaffery, *Some Other Frequency: Interviews with Innovative American Authors*. Pennsylvania Studies in American Fiction, Philadelphia: University of Pennsylvania Press, 1996, p. 34.
33. Kathy Acker, 'Kathy Acker: Top Ten', *Women's Review, Number Three*, January 1986, p. 13. I return specifically to Acker's concern with breath in my final chapter.
34. Acker, 'The Path of Abjection', p. 34.
35. See Ellen G. Friedman and Miriam Fuchs, 'Introduction', in *Breaking the Sequence: Women's Experimental Fiction*. Princeton: Princeton University Press, 2006, pp. 3–51.
36. Ibid. The origins of the methods of decentralisation that Acker adopts in her work can clearly be traced in the work of William Burroughs. Acker states: 'In terms of content and formally, William Burroughs's works are those of discontinuity and dislocation.' See 'On Art and Artists', in *Bodies of Work: Essays*, p. 2. Alex Houen provides a rich analysis of Acker's work in light of Burroughs's understanding of the word as virus, and argues that Acker's work functions to link Foucault and Burroughs 'on the basis that "language controls virally"'. See Houen, 'Novel Biopolitics', in *Powers of Possibility: Experimental American Writing Since the 1960s*. Oxford: Oxford University Press, 2012, p. 149.
37. Acker, 'The Path of Abjection', p. 35.
38. Ellen G. Friedman, 'Where Are the Missing Contents? (Post)Modernism, Gender, and the Canon', *PMLA*, vol. 108, no. 2, 1993, p. 240.
39. Ibid. p. 241
40. Ibid. p. 242.
41. Ibid.
42. Ibid. p. 244.

43. Acker, 'Preface', in *Bodies of Work: Essays*, p. viii.
44. Acker, 'Commonsensical / Philosophical Uses of Words', Kathy Acker Papers, Box 3.
45. Acker, The Black Tarantula, 'Conversations'. Unpaginated, Kathy Acker Papers, Box 4.
46. Ibid.
47. Ibid.
48. Ludwig Wittgenstein, *On Certainty*, trans. Denis Paul and G. E. M. Anscombe. London: Blackwell, 1975, p. 15.
49. Acker, The Black Tarantula, 'Conversations'.
50. Acker, 'Lecture on *Unworking*' (undated), p. 2, Kathy Acker Papers, Box 2.
51. Ibid. p. 2.
52. Bernstein, 'Artifice of Absorption', in *A Poetics*, p. 17.
53. Friedman, 'Where Are the Missing Contents?', p. 247.
54. Acker, 'A Few Notes on Two of My Books', in *Bodies of Work: Essays*, pp. 6–7.
55. Ibid. p. 7.
56. Acker, 'The Path of Abjection', p. 19.
57. Ibid.
58. Acker, 'Against Ordinary Language: The Language of the Body', in *Bodies of Work: Essays*, p. 148.
59. Kathy Acker, *Pussy, King of the Pirates*. New York: Grove Press, 1996, p. 177.
60. Maurice Blanchot, *The Infinite Conversation*, trans. Susan Hanson. Minneapolis: University of Minnesota Press [1969], 1993, p. 43.
61. In reading Acker as writing the impossible in this way, this study is in line with, rather than in contrast to, Alex Houen's important recent work on literary potentialism. Houen understands experimentation in Acker's work to 'be synonymous with establishing new possibilities of conjoining form, content, and affective power.' See Houen, *Powers of Possibility*, p. 20.
62. Kathy Acker, *The Adult Life of Toulouse Lautrec by Henri Toulouse Lautrec*. New York: TVRT Press [1975], 1978, p. 3.
63. Blanchot, *The Infinite Conversation*, p. 43.
64. Ibid. p. 44. Emphasis in the original.
65. Ibid. p. 45. Emphasis in the original.
66. Ibid. Emphasis in the original.
67. Ibid. pp. 45–46. Emphasis in the original.
68. In his rigorous study *Powers of Possibility*, Houen theorises the 'performative potentiality' that Derrida ascribes to language. Houen's discussion of the 'iterative potential' and the possibility engendered by experimental literature is significant, particularly when the

performative effects of Acker's work are taken into account. Read within the framework of Foucault, Butler, and Burroughs, Houen's study indeed reveals this potentialism in Acker's work. I engage with the tension between the two terms, possibility and impossibility, as a means of thinking through the capacity of experimental works to create new forms of meaning. The term 'impossibility' is preserved in my account as designating that which is unrepresentable but is nevertheless given presence through experimental composition. Houen, *Powers of Possibility*, p. 246.

69. Studies that incorporate chapters on Acker's work include Lidia Yuknavitch, *Allegories of Violence: Tracing the Writing of War in Late Twentieth Century Fiction*. London: Routledge, 2001; Richard Walsh, *Novel Arguments: Reading Innovative American Fiction*. Cambridge: Cambridge University Press, 1995; John Kuehl, *Alternate Worlds: A Study of Postmodern Antirealist American Fiction*. New York: New York University Press, 1991; Houen, *Powers of Possibility*.

70. See for example David James, *Modernist Futures: Innovation and Inheritance in the Contemporary Novel*. Cambridge: Cambridge University Press, 2012.

71. Jeffrey Ebbesen's chapter on Acker is an example. Ebbesen provides a detailed analysis of Acker's experimental practice, positioning these practices firmly within a postmodernist and poststructuralist frame. See Ebbesen, 'Combative Textualities: Kathy Acker's *The Adult Life of Toulouse Lautrec by Henri Toulouse Lautrec*', in *Postmodernism and Its Others*. London: Routledge, 2010, pp. 62–132.

72. Robert Siegle, 'Postmodernism', *Modern Fiction Studies*, vol. 41, no. 1, Spring 1995, pp. 165–94.

73. Joseph M. Conte, 'Discipline and Anarchy: Disrupted Codes in Kathy Acker's *Empire of the Senseless*', in *Design and Debris: A Chaotics of Postmodern American Fiction*. Tuscaloosa and London: University of Alabama Press, 2002, pp. 54–75.

74. Svetlana Mintcheva, 'The Paralyzing Tensions of Radical Art in a Postmodern World: Kathy Acker's Last Novels as Exploratory Fictions', in *Devouring Institutions: The Life Work of Kathy Acker*, ed. Michael Hardin. Calexico, CA: San Diego State University Press, 2005, pp. 47–69.

75. Kuehl, *Alternate Worlds*.

76. Katy R. Muth, 'Postmodern Fiction as Poststructuralist Theory: Kathy Acker's *Blood and Guts in High School*', *Narrative*, vol. 19, January 2011, pp. 86–110.

77. Hawkins, 'All in the Family', p. 632.

78. Nicole Pitchford, *Tactical Readings: Feminist Postmodernism in the Novels of Kathy Acker and Angela Carter*. Bucknell, PA: Bucknell University Press, 2002, p. 17.

79. Alex Houen, 'Sovereignty, Biopolitics, and the Use of Literature: Michel Foucault and Kathy Acker', in *Foucault in an Age of Terror: Essays on Biopolitics and the Defence of Society*, ed. Stephen Morton and Stephen Bygrave. London: Palgrave, 2008, pp. 63–87.

80. Carol Siegel, 'The Madness Outside Gender: Travels with Don Quixote and Saint Foucault', in *Devouring Institutions*, ed. Michael Hardin, pp. 3–27.

81. Barrett Watten, 'Foucault Reads Acker and Rewrites the History of the Novel', in *Lust for Life: On the Writings of Kathy Acker*, ed. Amy Scholder, Carla Harryman and Avital Ronell. New York: Verso, 2006, pp. 58–77.

82. Spencer Dew, *Learning for Revolution: The Work of Kathy Acker*. San Diego: San Diego State University Press, 2011, p. 21.

83. Judith Ryan, *The Novel after Theory*. New York: Columbia University Press, 2012, p. 8.

84. Ibid. p. 187. Ryan is citing Acker, 'Devoured by Myths: An Interview with Sylvère Lotringer', in Acker, *Hannibal Lecter, My Father*. New York: Semiotext(e), 1991, pp. 1–24.

85. Acker, 'Gender in Art'. Unpaginated, Kathy Acker Papers, Box 7.

86. Acker, 'The Malady of Death'. Unpaginated, Kathy Acker Papers, Box 6.

87. Acker, 'Devoured by Myths', p. 10.

88. Ibid.

89. Ryan, *The Novel after Theory*, p. 8.

90. Recently Kaye Mitchell has positioned Acker in the body of contemporary experimental women's writing in her introductory essay 'The Gender Politics of the Experiment', *Contemporary Women's Writing*, special issue 'Experimental Writing', vol. 9, no. 1, March 2015, 1–16.

91. Caroline Bergvall, 'The Conceptual Twist: A Foreword', in *I'll Drown My Book: Conceptual Writing by Women*, ed. Caroline Bergvall, Laynie Browne, Teresa Carmody and Vanessa Place. Los Angeles: Les Figues Press, 2012, pp. 18–22.

92. P. Adams Sitney, *Modernist Montage: The Obscurity of Vision in Cinema and Literature*. New York: Columbia University Press, 1990, p. 2.

93. Maya Deren speaking at the Cinema 16 Symposium on 'Poetry and Film', 28 October 1953, cited by P. Adams Sitney in P. Adams Sitney (ed.), *Film Culture Reader: The Essential Companion for Filmmakers and Festival Goers*. New York: Cooper Square Press [1970], 2000, p. 174.

94. James Meyer, 'Non, Nothing, Everything: Hesse's "Abstraction"', in Eva Hesse, *Eva Hesse*, ed. Elisabeth Sussman. New Haven and London: Yale University Press, 2002, p. 60. This citation is taken up and discussed in Chapter 6.

95. Acker was invited by the editors to list the women writers she most revered. She placed Stein fourth. Acker's list began with three female writers that she prefaced as 'The Older Ones': 1. Jane Austen; 2. George Sand; 3. George Eliot. Acker, 'Kathy Acker: Top Ten', p. 13.

Chapter 1

1. Gertrude Stein, 'Poetry and Grammar' (1935), in *Look at Me Now and Here I Am: Selected Works 1911–1945*. London: Peter Owen, 2004, p. 123.
2. Acker, 'NOTES ON WRITING – from THE LIFE OF BAUDELAIRE', pp. 1–3.
3. Bernstein, 'The Expanded Field of $L=A=N=G=U=A=G=E$', p. 284.
4. Acker's early poetry has recently been published in a small chapbook edited by Gabrielle Kappes in The CUNY Poetics Document Initiative Series. Kappes offers a rich selection of Acker's early works, sensitively edited with careful attention to precise reproduction of the experimental form of the works. This chapter references the original documents housed in the archive, as some of the early poetry discussed is not included in Kappes's volume. See Acker, *Homage to LeRoi Jones and Other Early Works*, ed. Gabrielle Kappes. Lost and Found: The CUNY Poetics Document Initiative, Series 5, Number 1. New York: CUNY Poetics Document Initiative, Spring 2015.
5. Donald Allen's, *New American Poetry, 1945–1960* was one of the most influential anthologies published in the U.S after World War II, containing the work of Charles Olson, Robert Creeley, Barbara Guest, Frank O'Hara and many others. See Allen, *New American Poetry, 1945-1960*. Berkeley: University of California Press, 1999.
6. Jerome Rothenberg, 'Preface', in *Revolution of the Word: A New Gathering of American Avant-Garde Poetry 1914–194*. Boston: Exact Change Books, 2004, p. xv.
7. David Antin, 'A Few Words', in *Selected Poems: 1963–1973*. Los Angeles: Sun and Moon Press, 1991, p. 14.
8. Rothenberg, 'Preface', in *Revolution of the Word*, p. xv.
9. Ibid. p. xvi.
10. Charles Bernstein and Bruce Andrews (eds), $L=A=N=G=U=A=G=E$, no. 9/10, October 1979, p. 1.
11. Acker, 'NOTES ON WRITING – from THE LIFE OF BAUDELAIRE', p. 1.
12. Ibid.
13. Bernstein, 'The Expanded Field of $L=A=N=G=U=A=G=E$', p. 286.

14. Bruce Andrews, 'Writing Social Work & Political Practice', *L=A=N=G=U=A=G=E*, no. 9/10, October 1979, p. 3. Emphasis in the original.

15. Ibid. p. 4.

16. Ibid. p. 3. Charles Bernstein stresses that the dollar value of poetry is 'transferable and instrumental'. Bernstein, 'The Dollar Value of Poetry', *L=A=N=G=U=A=G=E*, no. 9/10, October 1979, p. 8.

17. Steve McCaffery, 'From the Notebooks', *L=A=N=G=U=A=G=E*, no. 9/10, October 1979, p. 29.

18. Cheek's work was part of a wider field in poetics that took up art's institutional critique of galleries. The most notable instance of this critique is perhaps Lucy R. Lippard's work *Six Years: The Dematerialization of the Art Object from 1966–1972*. Berkeley: University of California Press, 1997.

19. Cris Cheek, Kirby Malone and Marshall Reese, 'TV TRIO Present CAREER WRIST', *L=A=N=G=U=A=G=E*, no. 9/10, October 1979, p. 14.

20. Andrews, 'Writing Social Work & Political Practice', p. 4. Underlining and abbreviations Andrews' own.

21. Andrews' idea of the 'anarchic liberation of energy flows' was evidently influenced by the work of Wilhelm Reich. See Reich, *The Mass Psychology of Fascism*, trans. Vincent R. Carfagno. Harmondsworth: Penguin [1933], 1983; and *The Function of the Orgasm: Sex-Economic Problems of Biological Energy*, trans. Theodore P. Wolfe. London: Panther Books, 1968.

22. Andrews, 'Writing Social Work & Political Practice', p. 4

23. Ron Silliman, *The New Sentence*. New York: Roof Books [1977], 2003, p. 8.

24. Ibid. p. 10.

25. Ibid.

26. Bernstein, citing Simone Weil's *Oppression and Liberty* in 'The Dollar Value of Poetry', p. 7.

27. Ibid.

28. Ibid. p. 8.

29. Ibid.

30. A number of studies form the background context for the re-evaluation of the medium of writing that occurred in the poetry and poetics of the poets associated with *L=A=N=G=U=A=G=E*, such as Saussure's structural approach to language, which asserted the primacy of writing in the field of language and linguistics. The school of Russian Formalism, which emerged in 1915, with its emphasis on literary device and form as elements that make literary language distinctive from ordinary language,

was a key influence on L=A=N=G-U=A=G=E poetry, in particular the work of Viktor Shklovsky and Roman Jakobson. Ron Silliman's 1977 work, *The New Sentence* had a significant impact on the avant-garde poets working in the 1970s. Silliman argued that a poem is 'inextricably involved with thought' and 'thinking is a ground for social practice'. In Silliman's understanding: 'Writing itself is a form of action.' See Silliman, *The New Sentence*, p. 4.

31. McCaffery, 'From the Notebooks', p. 29.
32. Ibid.
33. Ibid.
34. Ibid. p. 30.
35. Ibid. p. 29.
36. Bernstein, 'The Expanded Field of L=A=N=G=U=A=G=E', p. 287.
37. Andrews, 'Writing Social Work & Political Practice', p. 4.
38. Ibid. p. 5.
39. Bernstein further remarks on the relation of this approach to Brecht's 'alienation' or 'distancing' effect (*Verfremdungseffekt*): 'the idea that one can look aslant at what one is experiencing, to get glimmers of its means of production'. Bernstein points out the evident influence of Marx on such ideas and Louis Althusser's 'Ideology and Ideological State Apparatuses' (1970). See Bernstein, 'The Expanded Field of L=A=N=G=U=A=G=E', p. 286.
40. Viktor Shklovsky, 'Art as Technique', in *Theory of Prose*, trans. Lee T. Lemon and Marion J. Reis. Lincoln, NE: University of Nebraska Press, 1965, p. 11.
41. Ibid. p. 13.
42. Ibid. p. 12.
43. Ibid. p. 21.
44. Andrews, 'Writing Social Work & Political Practice', p. 4.
45. McCaffery, 'From the Notebooks', p. 30.
46. Ibid. p. 31.
47. Ibid.
48. Bernstein, 'The Dollar Value of Poetry', pp. 7–8. Emphasis in the original.
49. Ibid. p. 9.
50. Barrett Watten, 'Writing and Capitalism', L=A=N=G=U=A=G=E, no. 9/10, October 1979, p. 46.
51. Bernstein, 'The Expanded Field of L=A=N=G=U=A=G=E', p. 288.
52. Ibid.
53. Ibid.
54. Wendy Mulford, 'Afterword', in *Out of Everywhere: Linguistically Innovative Poetry by Women in North America & the UK*, ed. Maggie O'Sullivan. London: Reality Street Editions, 1996, pp. 240–1.

55. R. R. Rhees 'Introduction' (March 1958), in Ludwig Wittgenstein, *The Blue and the Brown Books: Preliminary Studies for the 'Philosophical Investigations'*. Oxford: Blackwell [1958], 1969, p. vi.
56. Wittgenstein, *The Blue and the Brown Books*, p. 17.
57. Miller, *Singular Examples*, p. 45.
58. Acker, 'Bodies of Work', in *Bodies of Work: Essays*, p. 148.
59. Ibid.
60. Stein, 'Poetry and Grammar', in *Look at Me Now and Here I Am*, p. 131.
61. Acker, 'Journal Black Cats Black Jewels', p. 1, Kathy Acker Papers, Unprocessed Box 4.
62. This is in the tradition of visual display using the page-space established by Charles Olson's pioneering essay 'Projective Verse' (1950). Here Olson asserts the primacy of the text as an 'OPEN' or 'COMPOSITION BY FIELD, as opposed to – line, stanza, overall form', which is, for Olson, 'the "old" base of the non-projective'. See Olson, 'Projective Verse', in *Collected Prose*. Berkeley and Los Angeles: University of California Press, 1997, p. 239.
63. Ibid. Peter Wollen has acknowledged Acker's debt to Olson, which he rightly observes has been overlooked in the body of scholarship on Acker's work. See Wollen, 'Kathy Acker', p. 6.
64. Acker, 'Journal Black Cats Black Jewels', p. 1.
65. Ludwig Wittgenstein, *Philosophical Investigations*, trans. G. E. M Anscombe, P. M. S. Hacker and Joachim Schulte. London: Blackwell, 2009, p. 35.
66. Ibid. p. 36.
67. Acker, 'Journal Black Cats Black Jewels', p. 2.
68. Ibid.
69. Ibid. The apparent spelling error 'ffot' appears in the original text.
70. Ibid. p. 3.
71. Ibid.
72. Ibid.
73. Andrews, 'Writing Social Work & Political Practice', p. 4.
74. Kathy Acker, *The Burning Bombing of America: The Destruction of the U.S.* [1972]. New York: Grove Press, 2002, p. 173.
75. Ibid.
76. Jackson Mac Low, 'Poetry and Pleasure', in *Thing of Beauty: New and Selected Works*, ed. Anne Tardos. Berkeley and London: University of California Press [1999], 2008, p. xxi. Emphasis in the original.
77. Mac Low further explains: 'The neologism "diastic" was coined on analogy with "acrostic" from the Greek word *dia*, through, and *stichos*, line. The writer "spells it out" in linguistic units successively drawn

from the source text in corresponding positions.' Ibid. Emphasis in the original.

78. Ibid. p. xxxi.
79. Ibid. p. xxxii. The note in parenthesis '[Buddhist skandas]' is my own.
80. Ibid. p. xxi. Emphasis in the original.
81. Charles Bernstein, 'Jackson at Home', in *Contents Dream: Essays 1975–1984*. Evanston: Northwestern University Press, 2001, p. 252. Emphasis in the original.
82. Ibid. p. 254.
83. Jackson Mac Low, 'An Afterword on the Methods Used in Composing & Performing *Stanzas for Iris Lezak*', in *Stanzas for Iris Lezak*. Barton, VT: Something Else Press [1971], 1981, p. 400.
84. 'Call me Ishmael. Some years ago – never mind how long precisely – having little or no money in my purse and nothing particular to interest me on shore, I thought I would sail about a little and see the watery part of the world. It is a way I have of driving off the spleen, and regulating the circulation. Whenever I find myself growing grim about the mouth; whenever it is a damp, drizzly November in my soul; whenever I find myself involuntarily pausing before coffin warehouses, and bringing up the rear of every funeral I meet; and especially whenever my hypos get such an upper hand of me, that it requires a strong moral principal to prevent me from deliberately stepping into the street, and methodically knocking people's hats off – then, I account it high time to get to sea as soon as I can. This is my substitute for pistol and ball. With a philosophical flourish Cato throws himself upon his sword; I quietly take to the ship. There is nothing surprising in this. If they but knew it, almost all men in their degree, some time or other, cherish very nearly the same feelings towards the ocean with me.' From Herman Melville, *Moby Dick*. Oxford: Oxford University Press [1851], 2008, p. 1.
85. Mac Low, 'Call Me Ishmael', in *Stanzas for Iris Lezak*, p. 16. Used with the permission of the Estate of Jackson Mac Low.
86. Miller, *Singular Examples*, p. 43. The terms paragrammatic (Kristeva, Miller) and paragrammic (McCaffery) occur a number of times in this study. Each term arises from Julia Kristeva's pioneering essay 'Towards a Semiology of Paragrams' published in *Tel Quel* in 1967. Taking up Saussure's work on 'Anagrams', Kristeva sets out her understanding of 'paragrammatics'. Kristeva contends that a 'paragrammatic conception of language' (and she notes that the term 'paragram' is Saussure's own) suggests three central theses. Firstly, 'Poetic language is the only infinity of code.' Secondly, 'The literary text is double: writing and reading', and finally, 'The literary text is a network of connections.' Kristeva understands these three aspects of poetic language to 'put an end to the

isolation of poetic discourse (considered in our hierarchized society, as "ornament", as "superfluous", or "anomalous") and accord it a status as a social practice which, when seen as paragrammatic, is manifest at the level of the text's articulation as well as at the level of its explicit message'. Kristeva's essay is valuable here for highlighting the primacy of the poetic as social practice for the *Tel Quel* group, and for drawing attention to the poetic as a mode that can be present in the text without recourse to designating writing as poetry or prose. The revolutionary capacity of the poetic Kristeva would take up seven years later in her ground-breaking work, *Revolution in Poetic Language* (1974). Here those theoretical seeds are sown in the retrieval of poetic discourse from the marginalised rubric of 'ornament', 'superfluous', or 'anomalous'. This context is central to a consideration of Acker's language-centred experimental works that embody the primacy of the poetic and its radical capacity. I return to the paragrammatic in Chapter 3. Kristeva, 'Towards a Semiology of Paragrams', in *The Tel Quel Reader*, ed. Patrick ffrench and Roland-François Lack. London: Routledge [1967], 1998, pp. 25–6.

87. Acker, 'Homage to LeRoi Jones'. Unpaginated, Kathy Acker Papers, Box 4.
88. LeRoi Jones, 'The Alternative', in *Tales by LeRoi Jones*. New York: Grove Press, 1967, p. 5.
89. Acker, 'Homage to LeRoi Jones'.
90. Stein, 'Poetry and Grammar', in *Look at Me Now and Here I Am*, p. 125.
91. Ibid.
92. Stein, 'Bernard Faÿ' (1929), in *Look at Me Now and Here I Am*, p. 223.
93. Jones, 'The Alternative', p. 6.
94. Shklovsky, 'Art as Technique', in *Theory of Prose*, p. 18.
95. Lyn Hejinian, 'The Rejection of Closure', in *The Language of Inquiry*. Los Angeles: University of California Press, 2001, p. 43. Alex Houen offers a brilliant analysis of the significance of Hejinian's work to Language Poetry in his chapter 'Making a Person Possible: Lyn Hejinian and Language Poetry', in *Powers of Possibility*, pp. 193–231.
96. Hejinian, 'The Rejection of Closure', in *The Language of Inquiry*, p. 42.
97. Ibid. p. 43.
98. Bernstein, 'The Expanded Field of $L=A=N=G=U=A=G=E$', p. 287.
99. Hejinian, 'The Rejection of Closure', in *The Language of Inquiry*, p. 47.
100. Ibid.
101. LeRoi Jones, *The System of Dante's Hell*, First Evergreen Black Cat Edition. New York: Grove Press, 1966, p. 9.

102. Steve McCaffery, 'Mac Low's *Asymmetries*', in *North of Intention: Critical Writings, 1972–1986.* New York: Roof Books, 1986, p. 47.
103. Acker, 'MURDERERS-CRIMINALS JOIN SUNLIGHT', Kathy Acker Papers, Box 4.
104. The title here is as it appears in the original document. It is unclear if the title contains an unintentional error, or if the misspelling is Acker's own intentionally. See Acker, 'Writing Asystematicaaly', p. 8, Kathy Acker Papers, Box 4.
105. Ibid. p. 10.
106. Jackson Mac Low, 'H U N G E R- ST r i kE', in *Revolution of the Word*, p. 175.
107. Acker, Exercise 6: 'Transformation of Sentences', in 'Exercises Writing Asymmetrically', p. 1, Kathy Acker Papers, Box 4. The page numbers to the documents restart with some exercises.
108. Craig Dworkin, *Reading the Illegible.* Evanston: Northwestern University Press, 2003, p. xxiii.
109. Acker, 'Entrance into Dwelling in Paradise', Kathy Acker Papers, Unprocessed Box 4.
110. Robert Irwin and Malcolm Lyons (eds), *The Arabian Nights: Tales of 1,001 Nights*, trans. Malcolm Lyons. London: Penguin Classics, 2010, p. 261.
111. See Susan Howe, 'Scattering as Behaviour towards Risk', in *Singularities.* Middletown, CT: Wesleyan University Press, 1990, pp. 61–70.
112. Amy Scholder remarks that *Rip-Off Red, Girl Detective* was Acker's first novel in the prefatory note to the 2002 Grove Press edition of *Rip-Off Red, Girl Detective* and *The Burning Bombing of America*. The novels were published for the first time in the 2002 edition. Alex Houen provides an insightful account of *Rip-Off Red*. See Houen, *Powers of Possibility*, pp. 156–9.
113. Susan Orlovsky's note attached to Acker, 'The Destruction of the U.S. The Burning Bombing of America', Kathy Acker Papers, Box 3.
114. Acker, *The Burning Bombing of America.* The first pages are unpaginated.
115. Recently, Vanessa Place has practised a similar experimental strategy in her work *Dies: A Sentence* (2005). The work consists of one sentence over 127 pages. See Place, *Dies: A Sentence.* Los Angeles: Les Figues Press, 2005.
116. Steven Barber, 'Introduction', in Pierre Guyotat, *Eden, Eden, Eden*, trans. Graham Fox. London: Creation Books, 1995. The first pages are unpaginated.
117. Danielle Marx-Scouras, *The Cultural Politics of Tel Quel: Literature and the Left in the Wake of Engagement.* University Park: Pennsylvania State University Press, 1996, p. 54.

118. Ellen G. Friedman, 'A Conversation with Kathy Acker', *The Review of Contemporary Fiction*, vol. 9.3, Fall 1989, p. 17. Acker carried out a series of writing experiments using masturbation as a means to access a new language of the body. This material is utilised in Acker's later work *Pussy, King of the Pirates*. Lulu states: 'While I masturbate, my body says: Here's a rise. The whole surface, ocean is rippling, a sheet that's metal, wave after wave. As *it* (what's this *it?*) moves toward the top, as if towards the neck of a vase, *it* crushes against *itself* moving inwards and it increases in sensitivity. The top of the vase, circular, is so sensitive that all feelings, now circling around and around, all that's moving is now music' (Acker, *Pussy, King of the Pirates*, p. 32). Carla Harryman reads *Pussy, King of the Pirates* as a literary process in which 'Acker repeatedly practices masturbating to produce language for the novel' (Harryman, 'Roles and Restraints in Women's Experimental Writing', in *We Who Loved to Be Astonished: Experimental Women's Writing and Performance Poetics*, ed. Cynthia Hogue and Laura Hinton. Tuscaloosa: University of Alabama Press, 2001, p. 122). Acker's work on masturbation also appears in her short piece 'The Language of the Body' (1993) collected in Margaret Reynolds, (ed.), *The Penguin Book of Lesbian Short Stories*. London: Penguin, 1994, pp. 399–411.
119. Roland Barthes, 'Preface', in Guyotat, *Eden, Eden, Eden*. Unpaginated.
120. Ibid. Emphasis in the original.
121. Ibid. pp 162–3.
122. Acker, 'Burroughs 2', Kathy Acker Papers, Box 1.
123. Acker, *The Burning Bombing of America*, p. 139.
124. Guyotat, *Eden, Eden, Eden*, p. 1.
125. Acker, *The Burning Bombing of America*, p. 140.
126. Acker, *The Burning Bombing of America*, p. 173.
127. Ibid.
128. Ibid. p. 182.
129. Ibid. p. 193.
130. Ibid.
131. Ibid. p. 196.
132. Ibid. p. 190.

Chapter 2

1. Report of the Hearing at Wellington on 8 November 1984. The documents are contained in the file of 'Blood and Guts Book Banning

Documents' kept by the NZ Justice Court, sent to Acker by Ling-Yen, 20 March 1992. The book was still banned in 1992, as Ling-Yen's cover letter to Acker concerns getting the book unbanned, with the backing of the English Department of Auckland University. 'Blood and Guts Book Banning Documents', Kathy Acker Papers, Box 7.

2. Ibid.

3. Ibid.

4. 'Submission by the Comptroller of Customs In the Matter of the Indecent Publications Act, 1963 and In the Matter of an Application by the Comptroller of Customs in Respect of the Publication – "Blood and Guts in High School Plus Two"'. Ibid.

5. For a detailed history of the censorship of *Naked Lunch* see Michael B. Goodman, 'The Customs' Censorship of William Burroughs' *Naked Lunch*', *Critique: Studies in Contemporary Fiction*, vol. 22, no. 1, 1980, 92–104.

6. Customs Act 1966 No. 28 of 1966. An Act to repeal section 141 of the *Customs Act 1901–1965*, and to amend that Act in relation to Decimal Currency. [Assented to 24 May, 1966]. The First Schedule of the Act is inclusive of the document of the Indecent Publications Act 1963. The section 11 (2) to which the Comptroller makes reference is, in line with the Customs Act, to the Indecent Publications Act 1963, No. 22, 'An Act to consolidate and amend certain enactments of the General Assembly relating to Indecent Publications', 16 October 1963, http://www.nzlii. org/nz/legis/hist_act/ipa19631963n22243/ (last accessed 24 February 2016).

7. 'Submission by the Comptroller of Customs'. 'Blood and Guts Book Banning Documents'.

8. Ibid.

9. C. H. Rolph, *The Trial of Lady Chatterley: Regina v. Penguin Books Limited*. London: Penguin, 1961, p. 187.

10. Ibid.

11. Ibid. p. 191.

12. 'Submission by the Comptroller of Customs'. 'Blood and Guts Book Banning Documents'.

13. Jean-Jacques Lecercle, *The Violence of Language*. London: Routledge, 1990, p. 6.

14. Ibid. p. 258.

15. Ibid. p. 267.

16. See Denise Riley's two studies *The Words of Selves: Identification, Solidarity, Irony*. Stanford: Stanford University Press, 2000 and *Impersonal Passion: Language as Affect*. Durham, NC and London: Duke University Press, 2005.

17. The hippy girl in the bakery uses this phrase to describe Janey, the Lousy Mindless Salesgirl, in the East Village bakery. See Kathy Acker, *Blood and Guts in High School*. New York: Grove Press, 1984, p. 39.
18. Acker, 'The Path of Abjection, p. 26.
19. Ibid.
20. Acker, '*Blood and Guts in High School* Manuscript', Kathy Acker Papers, Box 1.
21. 'The Persian Poems', in the folder 'Blood and Guts Original Artwork'. Unpaginated, Kathy Acker Papers, Box 9.
22. Johanna Drucker, *The Visible World: Experimental Typography and Modern Art, 1909–1923*. Chicago: University of Chicago Press, 1994, p. 9.
23. Ibid. Emphasis in the original.
24. Ibid. p. 10.
25. Maud Lavin, *Cut with the Kitchen Knife: The Weimar Photomontages of Hannah Höch*. New Haven and London: Yale University Press, 1993, p. 19.
26. Acker, '*Blood and Guts in High School* Original Manuscript'.
27. Renée Riese Hubert, *Surrealism and the Book*. Berkeley: University of California Press, 1988, p. 5.
28. Francis Picabia, *Poèms et dessins de la fille née sans mère* (Lausanne, 1918).
29. Ibid. p. 25.
30. Ibid. pp. 25–6.
31. 'Xerox of *Blood and Guts* for Sol Le Witt'. Unpaginated, Kathy Acker Papers, Box 9. As Wollen remarks, Sol Le Witt had published Acker's first chapbook editions of *The Childlike Life of the Black Tarantula by the Black Tarantula*, and *The Adult Life of Toulouse Lautrec by Henri Toulouse Lautrec*, illustrated by William Wegman. See Wollen, 'Kathy Acker', p. 5.
32. The mimeograph was a mode of self-publishing technology that was popular, particularly in the production of zines, from the 1950s onwards. It was a form of printing that used a typed stencil in the process of production.
33. Antin, cited by Jerome Rothenberg in 'Preface', in *Revolution of the Word*, p. xvii.
34. These comments were made by Acker in her 'Top Ten' list, p. 13.
35. Ibid.
36. Jacqueline Rose, 'Psychoanalysis, Politics and the Future of Feminism: A Conversation, Juliet Mitchell and Jacqueline Rose with Jean Radford', *Feminist Futures, Women: A Cultural Review*, vol. 21, no. 1, p. 101.

37. Ibid. p. 97.
38. Luce Irigaray, *Speculum of the Other Woman*, trans. Gillian G. Gill. New York: Cornell University Press [1974], 1985, p. 165.
39. Ibid. Emphasis in the original.
40. Hélène Cixous, 'The Laugh of the Medusa', in *New French Feminisms*, ed. Elaine Marks and Isabelle de Courtivron. Cambridge, MA: University of Massachusetts Press [1975], 1981, p. 245.
41. Ibid. p. 250. Emphasis in the original.
42. Kathy Acker, 'Red Wings: Concerning Richard Prince's "Spiritual America"', in *Bodies of Work: Essays*, p. 59.
43. Ibid. Acker is citing Hélène Cixous and Catherine Clément, *The Newly Born Woman*, trans. Betsy Wing. London and Minneapolis: University of Minnesota Press [1975], 1986, p. ix. See *Bodies of Work: Essays*, p. 60, n. 9.
44. Acker, 'The Path of Abjection', p. 35.
45. Julia Kristeva, 'La femme ce n'est pas jamais ça', in *New French Feminisms*, p. 137. Emphasis in the original.
46. Ibid. p. 141.
47. Cixous and Clément, *The Newly Born Woman*, p. 65.
48. Acker, 'Preface', in *Bodies of Work: Essays*, p. ix.
49. Irigaray, *Speculum of the Other Woman*, p. 141.
50. Kathy Acker, 'Reading the Lack of the Body: The Writing of the Marquis de Sade', in *Bodies of Work: Essays*, pp. 70–1.
51. Ibid. p. 71.
52. Irigaray, *Speculum of the Other Woman*, p. 207.
53. Kathy Acker, 'Good and Evil in the Work of Nayland Blake', in *Bodies of Work: Essays*, pp. 36–7.
54. John Keats, 'Ode on a Grecian Urn', in *Keats: The Complete Poems*, ed. Miriam Allott. London and New York: Longman, 1995, p. 533.
55. Acker, 'On Art and Artists', in *Bodies of Work: Essays*, p. 3.
56. Houen, *Powers of Possibility*, pp. 155–6.
57. See Antin's remarks: 'I seemed to have started dreaming again or started to remember dreams back around 1990, and I began collecting them, mainly for their narrative interest – about the same time I started reconsidering Freud's *Traumdeutung* as a theory of narrative. In January 1990 I gave a talk at Northwestern on "the sociology of dreams" and in March 1990 I gave a talk at Getty on the tension between narrative and anti-narrative in Freud's work on dreams.' David Antin and Charles Bernstein, *A Conversation with David Antin*. New York: Granary Books, 2002, p. 93.
58. Ibid. pp. 93–4.
59. Acker, 'The Path of Abjection', p. 26.

60. Alex Houen makes this point in relation to *The Child-Like Life of the Black Tarantula*: 'Acker effectively foreshadows Judith Butler's argument in *Gender Trouble* (1990) about how drag highlights the constructedness of "straight" sexuality as being made up of "words, acts, gestures and desire."' See Houen, *Powers of Possibility*, p. 154. Christopher Kocela has also addressed Acker's work in light of Butler in 'Resighting Gender Theory: Butler's Lesbian Phallus in Acker's *Pussy*', *LIT*, vol. 17, no. 1, 2006, 77–104.

61. Kathy Acker, 'Seeing Gender', in *Bodies of Work: Essays*, p. 161.

62. Ibid., citing Judith Butler, 'Bodies That Matter', in *Engaging With Irigaray*, ed. Carolyn Burke, Naomi Schor and Margaret Whitford. New York: Columbia University Press, 1994, p. 143.

63. Acker, 'Seeing Gender', in *Bodies of Work: Essays*, p. 161. Emphasis in the original.

64. Judith Butler, *Gender Trouble: Feminism and the Subversion of Identity*. London: Routledge, 2006, p. 45. Emphasis in the original.

65. Denise Riley, *Am I That Name? Feminism and the Category of 'Women' in History*. London: Macmillan, 1988, p. 5.

66. Ibid. p. 17.

67. Lecercle, *The Violence of Language*, p. 259.

68. Riley, *Impersonal Passion*, p. 9.

69. Ibid. p. 11.

70. Ibid.

71. Ibid. p. 13.

72. Ibid. p. 12.

73. Ibid. p. 13.

74. Fyodor Dostoyevsky, *Crime and Punishment*, trans. David McDuff. Harmondsworth: Penguin Classics, 2003, p. 70.

75. Judith Butler, '"Conscience Doth Make Subjects of Us All": Louis Althusser's Subjection', in *The Psychic Life of Power: Theories in Subjection*. Stanford: Stanford University Press, 1997, p. 108.

76. Ibid.

77. Julia Kristeva, 'The Father, Love and Banishment', in *Desire in Language: A Semiotic Approach to Literature and Art*, trans. Leon S. Roudiez. Oxford: Columbia University Press, 1980, p. 153.

78. Ibid. p. 154.

79. Elaine Scarry, *Resisting Representation*. Oxford: Oxford University Press, 1994, p. 98.

80. Scarry is citing Keir Elam, '*Not I*: Beckett's Mouth and the Ars(e) Rhetorica', in *Beckett at 80 in Context*, ed. Enoch Brater. New York and Oxford: Oxford University Press, 1986, p. 136. See *Resisting Representation*, p. 9.

81. Scarry, *Resisting Representation*, p. 91.
82. Samuel Beckett, *Not I*, in *Complete Dramatic Works*. London: Faber and Faber, 1986, p. 382.
83. Hejinian, 'The Rejection of Closure', in *The Language of Inquiry*, p. 48.
84. Acker, 'The Path of Abjection', p. 28.
85. Silliman, *The New Sentence*, p. 14.
86. Ibid.
87. Ibid. p. 95.
88. Wollen, 'Kathy Acker', p. 6.
89. Riley, 'Linguistic Unease', in *The Words of Selves*, p. 73.
90. Lecercle, *The Violence of Language*, p. 6. Lecercle and Riley collaborated on a project, *The Force of Language: Language, Discourse, Society*. New York: Palgrave Macmillan, 2005.
91. Blanchot, *The Infinite Conversation*, p. 48.
92. Ibid.
93. Julia Kristeva, *Revolution in Poetic Language*, trans. Leon S. Roudiez. Columbia: Columbia University Press [1974], 1984, p. 25. Emphasis in the original.
94. Ibid.
95. Kristeva citing Mallarmé's 'The Mystery in Literature', in ibid., p. 11.
96. Mario Vargas Llosa, 'Foreword', in César Vallejo, *The Complete Poetry: A Bilingual Edition*, trans. Clayton Eshelman. Berkeley: University of California Press, 2007, p. ix.
97. César Vallejo, 'September', in *The Complete Poetry: A Bilingual Edition*, ed. and trans. Clayton Eshelman © 2007 by the Regents of the University of California. Published by the University of California Press, p. 63. Used with permission.
98. Michelle Clayton, *Poetry in Pieces: César Vallejo and Lyric Modernity*. Berkeley: University of California Press, 2011, p. 2.
99. Lecercle, *The Violence of Language*, p. 245.
100. César Vallejo, 'The Black Heralds', in *The Complete Poetry*, p. 25.
101. Drucker, *The Visible World*, p. 4.
102. Riley, *Impersonal Passion*, p. 7.
103. See Acker, 'Against Ordinary Language', in *Bodies of Work: Essays*, pp. 143–51. Acker's engagement with Canetti is discussed in Chapter 6.
104. Ibid. p. 64.
105. Elias Canetti, 'Word Attacks', in *The Conscience of Words and Earwitness*. London: Picador, 1987, p. 63.
106. Riley, *Impersonal Passion*, p. 2.
107. Vallejo, *The Complete Poetry*, p. 25.
108. Acker, 'By Cesar Vallejo', Kathy Acker Papers, Unprocessed Box 4.

109. Riley, *The Words of Selves*, p. 17
110. Ibid.
111. Ibid. p. 2.
112. Ibid.
113. Ibid. p. 3.
114. Vallejo, *The Complete Poetry*, p. 25.
115. Malcolm Bowie, *Mallarmé and the Art of Being Difficult*. Cambridge: Cambridge University Press, 1978, p. 116.
116. Ibid. p. 2.
117. Drucker, *The Visible World*, p. 50.
118. Ibid. p. 51.
119. Houen, *Powers of Possibility*, p. 163.
120. Ibid.
121. Lecercle, *The Violence of Language*, p. 5.
122. Ibid. p. 246.
123. Acker, 'Preface', in *Bodies of Work: Essays*, p. ix.
124. Acker, 'On Art and Artists', in *Bodies of Work: Essays*, p. 2.

Chapter 3

1. Issues of plagiarism, appropriation, and intellectual property have been a central focus of many studies on Acker. One of the earliest articles to appear in this area of Acker studies was Naomi Jacobs's article, 'Kathy Acker and the Plagiarized Self', *The Review of Contemporary Literature*, vol. 9, no. 3, Fall 1989, pp. 50–5. David Galef and Ellen G. Friedman articulated a transition that many critics observe in Acker's oeuvre from methods of plagiarism in her early writings to a practice of appropriation in her middling and later works. See Galef and Friedman, 'From Plagiarism to Appropriation', *PMLA*, vol. 108, no. 5, October 1993, pp. 1174–5. Other studies in this area include Jan Corbett, 'Words Hurt! Acker's Appropriation of Myth in *Don Quixote*', in *Devouring Institutions*, ed. Michael Hardin, pp. 167–88; Lidia Yuknavitch, *Allegories of Violence*; Ankhi Mukherjee, 'Missed Encounters: Repetition, Rewriting, and Contemporary Returns to Charles Dickens's *Great Expectations*', *Contemporary Literature*, vol. 46, no. 1, Spring 2005, pp. 108–33; Richard House, 'Informational Inheritance in Kathy Acker's *Empire of the Senseless*', *Contemporary Literature*, vol. 46, no. 3, Autumn 2005, pp. 450–82; Caren Irr, 'Beyond Appropriation: *Pussy, King of the Pirates* and a Feminist Critique of Intellectual Property', in *Devouring Institutions*, ed. Michael Hardin, pp. 211–35. The subject of Acker's techniques of plagiarism and appropriation constitute a

distinct part of the broad consideration of Acker's literary techniques. Both Dew and Hardin emphasise the perfunctory nature of simply asserting that Acker deconstructs texts. See Dew, *Learning for Revolution*, and Hardin, 'Introduction', in *Devouring Institutions*, ed. Michael Hardin.

2. Friedman, 'A Conversation with Kathy Acker', p. 13.

3. Ibid.

4. See Marilyn Randall's discussion of Levine and Acker's 'plagiarism', in *Pragmatic Plagiarism: Authorship, Profit, and Power*. Toronto: University of Toronto Press, 2001, p. 249. Randall discusses Acker and Levine's works as instances of 'explicit postmodern appropriation' (p. 242). Marcus Boon also refers to the 'appropriation art' of Cindy Sherman, Sherrie Levine, Jeff Koons, and Richard Prince alongside Acker. See Boon, *In Praise of Copying*. Harvard: Harvard University Press, 2010, p. 162.

5. David Evans, 'Introduction: Seven Types of Appropriation', in *Appropriation*. London: Whitechapel Gallery and MIT Press, 2009, p. 12.

6. Sherrie Levine, 'Statement', in Evans, *Appropriation*, p. 81.

7. Bergvall, 'The Conceptual Twist: A Foreword', in *I'll Drown My Book*, p. 18.

8. Craig Dworkin includes an excerpt from Acker's 1983 work *Great Expectations* in his recent anthology with Kenneth Goldsmith, *Against Expression: An Anthology of Conceptual Writing*. Evanston: Northwestern University Press, 2011, p. 28.

9. Bergvall, 'The Conceptual Twist: A Foreword', in *I'll Drown My Book*, p. 18.

10. Ibid.

11. Ibid.

12. Ibid.

13. Friedman, 'A Conversation with Kathy Acker', p. 13.

14. Acker, 'Reading the Lack of the Body: The Writing of the Marquis de Sade', Kathy Acker Papers, Box 4. This essay was published in Acker, *Bodies of Work: Essays*, pp. 66–81.

15. Miller, *Singular Examples*, p. 67.

16. Ibid.

17. Steve McCaffery, *Prior to Meaning: The Protosemantic and Poetics*. Evanston: Northwestern University Press, 2001, p. xvii.

18. At the level of content, Acker's remarks in interview point to abortion as an event in her own life. In this regard, the creative practice of writing-through folds abortion as a literary trope into biographical material.

19. Miller, *Singular Examples*, p. 55.

20. Kristeva, 'Towards a Semiology of Paragrams', p. 26.

21. McCaffery, *Prior to Meaning*, p. xvii. McCaffery is citing Charles Olson and Ezra Pound, *Charles Olson and Ezra Pound: An Encounter at St Elizabeth's*. New York: Grossman Viking, 1975, p. 10.

22. McCaffery is citing Houston A. Baker, Jr., *Blues, Ideology, and Afro-American Literature* (Chicago: University of Chicago Press, 1984), p. 202.

23. Ibid. p. xvi.

24. Ibid.

25. Acker, 'Rejects from *Don Quixote*', Kathy Acker Papers, Unprocessed Box 4.

26. Acker, 'On Burroughs', p. 5, Kathy Acker Papers, Box 4.

27. Ibid.

28. Acker, 'The Malady of Death'.

29. Antin, 'A Few Words', p. 14.

30. Acker, 'Nonpatriarchal Language: The Body', in 'Writings 1990-1991', Kathy Acker Papers, Box 4, p. 15.

31. Cited by Bernard Tschumi in *Cinégramme folie: le Parc de La Villette, Paris nineteenth arrondissement*. Sevenoaks: Butterworth Architecture, 1987, p. 1.

32. Michel Foucault, *The History of Madness*, trans. Jonathan Murphy and Jean Khalfa. London: Routledge [1961], 2009, p. 19.

33. Ibid. p. 521.

34. Ibid. p. 541.

35. Blanchot, *The Infinite Conversation*, p. 43.

36. Ibid. pp 43–4.

37. Roman Jakobson, 'Two Aspects of Language and Two Types of Aphasic Disturbances', in *On Language*, ed. R. Waugh and Monique Manville Burston. Cambridge, MA: Harvard University Press [1956], 1990, p. 116.

38. Ibid. pp. 116–17.

39. Ibid. p. 117.

40. Ibid. p. 121.

41. Ibid.

42. Ibid. p. 124.

43. Ibid.

44. Ibid. p. 126.

45. Ibid.

46. Ibid.

47. Hannah Sullivan, *The Work of Revision*. Cambridge, MA: Harvard University Press, 2013, p. 151.

48. Ibid. p. 150.

49. Ibid. p. 151.

50. Dworkin and Goldsmith, *Against Expression*, p. 64.

51. Acker, 'Original Manuscript (Vols 1 & 2) for *Don Quixote*', p. 43, Kathy Acker Papers, Box 1.
52. Drucker, *The Visible World*, p. 65.
53. Hal Foster, *The Return of the Real: The Avant-Garde at the End of the Century*. Cambridge, MA: MIT Press, 1996, p. 5.
54. Acker, 'Burroughs 2', p. 1.
55. Ibid.
56. Corbett, 'Words Hurt!', p. 168.
57. Acker, 'Nonpatriarchal Language: The Body', p. 13.
58. John Cournos, 'Introduction', in Andrei Bely, *St Petersburg*, trans. John Cournos. New York: Grove Press, 1994, p. xv.
59. Vladimir E. Alexandrov, *Andrei Bely: The Major Symbolist Fiction*. Cambridge, MA: Harvard University Press, 1985, p. 101.
60. Ibid. p. 101.
61. Bely, *St Petersburg*, p. xxii.
62. Malevich, 'From Cubism and Futurism to Suprematism: The New Realism in Painting', cited by Anna Moszynska in *Abstract Art*. London: Thames and Hudson, 1990, p. 58.
63. Ibid.
64. Moszynska commenting on Malevich in *Abstract Art*, p. 58. I first made these remarks on abstraction in an essay. See Georgina Colby, 'The Reappropriation of Classical Mythology to Represent Pain: Falling Silent in the Work of Kathy Acker and Robert Mapplethorpe', *Comparative Critical Studies*, vol. 9, no. 1, 2012, p. 31.
65. Bely, *St Petersburg*, p. xxi.
66. Acker, 'Annotations of Virgil's Bucolics and Georgics', Kathy Acker Papers, Unprocessed Box 7. Acker's edition is Vergili Maronis, *Bucolica et Georgica*. This annotation is found on p. 11.
67. Ibid. p. 19.
68. Mayer experimented with Greek and Latin classics throughout her career. Her most extensive engagement with Catullus can be found in her later work. See Bernadette Mayer, *The Formal Field of Kissing*. New York: Catchwood Papers, 1990.
69. Catullus, *Catullus (Gai Valeri Catulli Veronensis Liber)*, trans. Celia and Louis Zukofsky. London: Cape Goliard Press, 1969. Unpaginated. In their invocation of breath as a form of language, the Zukofskys' comments echo Olson's work on breath, which I return to in Chapter 6 when I discuss the language of the body as a form of literary calisthenics. Olson states: 'If I hammer, if I recall in, and keep calling in, the breath, the breathing as distinguished from the hearing, it is for cause, it is to insist upon a part that breath plays in verse which has not (due, I think, to the smothering of the power of the line by too set a concept of foot) has not been sufficiently observed or practiced, but which has

to be if verse is to advance to its proper force and place in the day, now, and ahead. I take it that PROJECTIVE VERSE teaches, is, this lesson, that the verse will only do in which a poet manages to register both the acquisitions of his ear *and* the pressures of his breath.' See Olson, 'Projective Verse', in *Collected Prose*, p. 241.

70. Charles Bernstein, 'Introduction', in *Louis Zukofsky: Selected Poems*, ed. Charles Bernstein. New York: Library of America, 2014, p. xxiii.
71. Ibid. p. xxiv.
72. Peter Quartermain, *Stubborn Poetries: Poetic Facticity and the Avant-Garde*. Tuscaloosa: University of Alabama Press, 2013, p. 61.
73. Catullus, Poems VIII (original) and 8, in *Catullus*. Unpaginated.
74. Quartermain, *Stubborn Poetries*, p. 61.
75. Peter Quartermain, *Disjunctive Poetics: From Gertrude Stein and Louis Zukofsky to Susan Howe*. Cambridge: Cambridge University Press, 1992, p. 120.
76. Ibid. p. 116.
77. Ibid.
78. Bergvall, 'The Conceptual Twist: A Foreword', in *I'll Drown My Book*, p. 22.
79. Ibid.
80. This practice has been taken up by Tim Atkins, Peter Hughes, Peter Manson, Sean Bonney, and Harry Gilonis in recent volumes.
81. Bernstein, 'Introduction', in *Louis Zukofsky: Selected Poems*, p. xxiv.
82. Catullus is an apt source for Acker to appropriate in *Don Quixote*. Out of the 116 poems in Catullus's body of work that The Scholars collated, just twenty are without a trace of obscenity. Poem VIII in Catullus, *Catullus: The Complete Poems*, trans. Guy Lee. Oxford: Oxford University Press, 2008, pp. 8–9.
83. Quartermain, *Disjunctive Poetics*, p. 118.
84. Catullus, *Catullus: The Complete Poems*, p. 9.
85. Ibid.
86. Julia Kristeva, 'Women's Time', trans. Alice Jardine, *Signs*, vol. 7, no. 1, Autumn 1981, p. 17.
87. Ibid. p. 14.
88. Ibid.
89. Ibid. pp. 19–20.
90. Riley, *The Words of Selves*, p. 43.
91. Ibid. p. 37.
92. McCaffery, 'From the Notebooks', p. 29.
93. Bernstein, 'Introduction', in *Louis Zukofsky: Selected Poems*, p. xxi.
94. Stein's *Three Lives* is widely regarded as an experiment in creating the continuous present in language. See Gertrude Stein, *Three Lives*. London: Penguin, 1990.

95. Laird Addis, 'Time, Substance, and Analysis', in M. S. Gram and E. D. Klemke, *The Ontological Turn: Studies in the Philosophy of Gustav Bergmann*. Iowa City: University of Iowa Press, 1974, pp. 153–4.
96. William James, *The Principles of Psychology Vol. I*. London: Dover Publications, 2000, p. 607.
97. Acker, 'Commonsensical / Philosophical Use of Words'. Unpaginated.
98. McCaffery, *Prior to Meaning*, p. xvii.
99. Kristeva, 'Towards a Semiology of Paragrams', p. 26
100. Ibid. p. 40.
101. Ibid.
102. McCaffery, *Prior to Meaning*, p. 29. McCaffery is citing Jean-Jacques Lecercle, *Philosophy through the Looking-Glass*. La Salle, IL: Open Court, 1985, p. 38.
103. Riley, *The Words of Selves*, p. 72.

Chapter 4

1. Letter from James Grauerholz to Fred Jordan, Kathy Acker Papers, Box 3. Grauerholz remarks that in 1977 he was trying to place the novellas with a larger publisher than Sol LeWitt's outfit. The letter discloses the gap between Acker's literary production of her early works and their reception by a larger readership. With the publication of works such as *A Portrait of an Eye* by larger presses such as Pantheon Books, Acker's work became visible to a wider readership.
2. Friedman, 'A Conversation with Kathy Acker', p. 17.
3. Christopher Kocela, 'A Myth beyond the Phallus: Female Fetishism in Kathy Acker's Late Novels', *Genders*, no. 34, 200, p. 2.
4. Jeremy Gray, *Plato's Ghost: The Modernist Transformation of Mathematics*. Princeton: Princeton University Press, 2008, p. 238.
5. Ibid. p. 239.
6. Ibid.
7. Acker, 'Ulysses Backwards'. Unpaginated, Kathy Acker Papers, Unprocessed Box 6. The notebook is undated but *The Wild Boys* was first published in 1969 by Grove Press.
8. Ibid.
9. Ibid.
10. Acker, 'A Few Notes on Two of My Books', in *Bodies of Work: Essays*, p. 9.
11. Acker, 'Ulysses Backwards'.
12. Ibid. In this citation 'WB' refers to *The Wild Boys*, 'Burroughs' is abbreviated to 'B'.
13. Acker, 'The Malady of Death'.

14. Maurice Blanchot, *The Book to Come*, trans. Charlotte Mandell. Stanford: Stanford University Press [1959], 2003.
15. Ibid. p. 5.
16. Ibid. p. 4.
17. Ibid. p. 5.
18. Ibid. p. 7.
19. Ibid.
20. Daniel Just, 'The Politics of the Novel and Maurice Blanchot's Theory of the Récit, 1954–1964', *French Forum*, vol. 33, no. 1–2, Winter/ Spring 2008, p. 124.
21. Ibid. p. 123.
22. Daniel Just, *Literature, Ethics, and Decolonization in Postwar France: The Politics of Disengagement*. Cambridge: Cambridge University Press, 2015, p. 46.
23. Denise Riley, 'Does Sex Have a History? "Women" and Feminism', *New Formations: A Journal of Culture, Theory and Politics*, no. 1, Spring 1987, p. 35. This early essay also forms the first chapter of *Am I That Name?*
24. It is worth noting here Catherine Malabou's feminist work that takes up this question specifically in relation to the woman philosopher. See Malabou, *Changing Difference*, trans. Carolyn Shread. Cambridge: Polity Press, 1988.
25. Riley, *The Words of Selves,* p. 177.
26. Ibid.
27. Ibid. p. 178.
28. Acker, 'The Malady of Death'.
29. Kathy Acker, *In Memoriam to Identity*. London: Pandora Press, 1990, p. 52.
30. Scarlett Baron, 'Joyce, Genealogy, Intertextuality', *Dublin James Joyce Journal*, no. 4, 2011, p. 51.
31. Acker, 'Bruce Willis and Me', pp. 2–3, Kathy Acker Papers, Box 1.
32. Ibid. p. 2.
33. Acker, 'The Language of Sex the Sex of Language'. Unpaginated, in 'Writings 1990–1991', Kathy Acker Papers, Unprocessed Box 4.
34. James Lawler, *Rimbaud's Theatre of the Self*. Cambridge, MA: Harvard University Press, 1992, p. 12.
35. For the full text of Rimbaud's Letter to Georges Izambard in English translation see Arthur Rimbaud, *Arthur Rimbaud: Selected Poems and Letters*, trans. Jeremy Harding and John Sturrock. London: Penguin Books, 2004, pp. 236–7.
36. Ibid. p. 236.
37. Ibid.
38. Ibid.

39. Martin Sorrell, 'Introduction', in ibid. p. xviii.
40. In the archive, the illustrations are housed in a separate box to the manuscript. The images reproduced here are reproductions of the four original works of art in the file 'Artwork for *In Memoriam to Identity*', Kathy Acker Papers, Box 6.
41. In the original illustration, the picture has been cut out and pasted onto the page.
42. Sadakichi Hartmann, *Japanese Art*. Boston: L. C. Page, 1903, p. 52.
43. Richard Bowring, 'Introduction', in Murasaki Shikibu, *Murasaki Shikibu: Her Diary and Poetic Memoirs*, trans. John Bowring. Princeton: Princeton University Press, 1982, p. xi.
44. Murasaki Shikibu, *The Tale of Genji*, trans. Royall Tyler. London: Penguin [1008], 2003, p. 468.
45. Ibid. p. 140.
46. Ibid. p. 141.
47. In the archive Acker's essay 'Nonpatriarchal Language: The Body' is a separate essay, in the folder 'Writings 1990–1991'. The essay is published as the latter part of a larger essay titled 'Critical Languages' (1995), in *Bodies of Work: Essays*, pp. 81–92.
48. Acker, 'Critical Languages', in *Bodies of Work: Essays*, p. 92.
49. Riley, *The Words of Selves*, p. 131. Here Riley is citing Zygmunt Bauman, *Life in Fragments: Essays in Postmodern Modernity*. Oxford: Blackwell, 1995, p. 82.
50. Acker, 'The Path of Abjection', p. 23. Emphasis in the original.
51. Charles J. Stivale, 'Acker/Rimbaud "I"-dentity Games', *Angelaki: Journal of the Theoretical Humanities*, vol. 3, no. 3, 1998, p. 137.
52. Bauman, *Life in Fragments*, p. 82, cited by Riley in *The Words of Selves*, p. 131.
53. Ibid.
54. Ibid. p. 11.
55. Ibid.
56. Ibid. p. 178.
57. Ibid. Here Riley inserts a note that points to Deleuze's mention of this in his study of Foucault. Gilles Deleuze, *Foucault*, trans. Seán Hand. London: Continuum, 1999.
58. Ibid.
59. Ibid.
60. Ibid.
61. Kathy Acker, *Empire of the Senseless*. New York: Grove Press, 1988, pp. 133–4.
62. Acker, 'A Few Notes on Two of My Books', in *Bodies of Work: Essays*, p. 11.
63. Harryman, 'Acker Un-formed', p. 37.

64. Rimbaud, 'Delirium II. Alchemy of the Word', in *Arthur Rimbaud: Selected Poems and Letters*, p. 165.
65. Acker, 'The Language of Sex the Sex of Language', p. 4.
66. Blanchot, *The Book to Come*, p. 10.
67. Hélène Cixous, 'Sorties', in Hélène Cixous and Catherine Clément, *The Newly Born Woman*, trans. Betsy Wing. London and Minneapolis: University of Minnesota Press [1975], 1986, p. 72.

Chapter 5

1. Acker, 'Notebooks for *My Mother: Demonology*'.
2. Elsewhere, in a related article, I have addressed the issue of censorship in *My Mother: Demonology* and Cindy Sherman's 'Sex Pictures' through the prism of Julia Kristeva's work on intimate revolt. See Georgina Colby, 'Radical Interiors: Cindy Sherman's "Sex Pictures" and Kathy Acker's *My Mother: Demonology*', *Women: A Cultural Review*, vol. 23, no. 2, 2012, pp. 182–200.
3. Benjamin, 'The Author as Producer', in *The Work of Art in the Age of Its Technological Reproducibility and Other Writings on Media*, p. 90.
4. Benjamin, 'Garlanded Entrance: On the "Sound Nerves" Exhibition at the Gesundheitshaus Kreuzberg', in *The Work of Art in the Age of Its Technological Reproducibility and Other Writings on Media*, p. 60.
5. Walter Benjamin, 'On Some Motifs in Baudelaire', in *Selected Writings, Volume 4: 1938–1940*, ed. and trans. Michael W. Jennings and Howard Eiland. Cambridge, MA: Harvard University Press, 2003, p. 328.
6. Michael Levenson, *Modernism*, trans. Raymond Rosenthal. New Haven: Yale University Press, 2011, p. 241.
7. Lawrence A. Rickels, 'Body Bildung – Lawrence A. Rickels Talks with Kathy Acker', *Artforum*, 1 February 1994, p. 62.
8. See Terry Engbretson, 'Re-educating the Body: Kathy Acker, Georges Bataille, and the Postmodern Body in *My Mother: Demonology*', in *Devouring Institutions*, ed. Michael Hardin, pp. 69–84. See also Harryman, 'Acker Un-formed', pp. 35–45.
9. Rickels, 'Body Bildung', p. 61.
10. Lev Kuleshov, 'The Principles of Montage', in *Critical Visions in Film and Theory: Classic and Contemporary Readings*, ed. Timothy Corrigan and Patricia White. New York: St. Martin's Press, 2011, p. 137.
11. Ibid. p. 139.
12. Ibid. p. 144.
13. Ibid. p. 140.

14. Sergei Eisenstein, 'Laocoön', in *Selected Works Volume II: Towards a Theory of Montage*, ed. Michael Glenny and Richard Taylor, trans. Michael Glenny. New York: I. B. Tauris, 2010, p. 118.
15. Ibid. p. 119.
16. Ibid. p. 134. Emphasis in the original.
17. Ibid.
18. Ibid. Emphasis in the original.
19. Ibid. p. 193. Eisenstein is citing Friedrich Schiller, *On the Aesthetic Education of Man, in a Series of Letters*, trans. Elizabeth M. Wilkinson and L. A. Willoughby. Oxford: Clarendon Press, 1967. This citation is from the first paragraph of the second letter, p. 7.
20. Nayland Blake points to the potentially lucrative comparison of Acker's and Deren's works. He details Acker's involvement with P. Adams Sitney and the New York Avant-Garde film scene: 'As much as Acker's work is indebted to the cut-ups of Burroughs, it also resembled the found footage of Bruce Connor, Ken Jacobs, and Peter Kubelka.' He writes: 'Indeed, her heroines, questing for self-knowledge, could easily have stepped out of Maya Deren's *Meshes of the Afternoon*, a film where the female protagonist embarks on an ambiguous journey of self-definition / destruction.' See Blake, 'Because I Want to Live Forever in Wonder', in *Lust for Life: On the Writings of Kathy Acker*, ed. Amy Scholder, Carla Harryman and Avital Ronell. London: Verso, 2006, p. 103.
21. Maya Deren, 'Creative Cutting', in *Essential Deren: Collected Writings on Film by Maya Deren*, ed. Bruce R. Macpherson. New York: McPherson, 2005, pp. 139–40.
22. James A. Heffernan, *Museum of Words: The Poetics of Ekphrasis from Homer to Ashbery*. Chicago: University of Chicago Press, 1993, p. 3.
23. Acker, 'Notebooks for *My Mother: Demonology*'. It is unclear what Acker is abbreviating with the acronym WLTY.
24. Acker, 'Notebooks for *My Mother: Demonology*'.
25. In the published version of *My Mother: Demonology*, Acker refers to Goytisolo's use of plagiarisms in *Count Julian* (1970). Citing the teacher in a class on theory the narrative voice states: 'Count Julian, I mean Goytisolo, subverts, invades, seduces, and infects all that's abhorrent to him by transforming the subject into the empirical self, a text among texts, a self that becomes a sign in its attempt to find meaning and value. All that is left is sex alone and naked value' (*My Mother: Demonology*, p. 52).
26. Juan Goytisolo, *Juan the Landless*, trans. Helen R. Lane. New York: Serpent's Tail [1975], 1977, p. 72. Acker was an advisory editor for the Serpent's Tail edition of the work in 1990.

27. Luis Buñuel, '*Découpage*, or Cinematic Segmentation', in *An Unspeakable Betrayal: Selected Writings of Luis Buñuel*. Berkeley: University of California Press, 2002, p. 133.

28. Ibid. p. 132.

29. Acker, 'Notebooks for *My Mother: Demonology*'.

30. Ibid.

31. John Cage, *Silence: Lectures and Writings*. London: Marion Boyars, 1995, p. 260.

32. Laure (Collette Peignot), *Laure: The Collected Writings*, trans. Jeanine Herman. San Francisco: City Lights, 1995.

33. Deren, 'Creative Cutting', in *Essential Deren*, p. 143.

34. Charles Baudelaire, 'Invitation to the Voyage', in *The Flowers of Evil*, trans. James McGowan. Oxford: Oxford University Press, 2008, pp. 109–11.

35. Maya Deren, 'Cinema as an Independent Art Form' (1945), in *Essential Deren*, p. 247.

36. Deren, 'Creative Cutting', in *Essential Deren*, p. 143.

37. Ibid. p. 148.

38. Ibid. p. 146.

39. Acker, 'The Language of Sex the Sex of Language'.

40. Eisenstein, 'Laocoön', in *Selected Works Volume II: Towards a Theory of Montage*, p. 197.

41. Ibid. p. 201.

42. Acker, *Empire of the Senseless*, p. 65.

43. Hugh J. Silverman, 'Preface', in *Philosophy and Desire*. New York: Routledge, 2000, p. 5.

44. Sigmund Freud, *The Complete Psychological Works of Sigmund Freud, Volume Four, Part 1, The Interpretation of Dreams*, trans. James Strachey. London: Vintage, 2001, p. 233.

45. Jacques Lacan, *Four Fundamental Concepts of Psycho-Analysis*, trans. Alain Sheridan. New York: Norton, 1978, p. 103.

46. Acker, 'Sexual Censorship', in 'More Short Pieces'. Undated, p. 2, Kathy Acker Papers, Box 4.

47. Ibid. p. 3.

48. Ibid. p. 4.

49. Ibid. p. 1.

50. Linda Williams, *Figures of Desire: A Theory and Analysis of Surrealist Film*. Berkeley: University of California Press, 1981, p. 109.

51. Ibid. p. 14.

52. Ibid. p. 109.

53. See Buñuel and Dalí, *L'Age d'Or*, Chapter 3.

54. There is a comparison to be drawn here with Buñuel's and Dalí's intertitles in *L'Age d'Or* that are listed as: 'Instruments of Aggression'; 'The Majorcans are Here'; 'Landing'; 'Imperial Rome'; 'Planning'; 'Goodwill'; 'Shooting'; 'Spill'; 'Garden'; 'Filthy Ruffian'; 'Falling'; 'Feathers'.

55. Severo Sarduy, 'Góngora: Squaring Metaphor', in *Written on the Body*, trans. Carol Maier. New York: Lumen Books, 1989, p. 45. Acker does not provide the reference in her essay.

56. Acker, 'The Language of Sex the Sex of Language', p. 2.

57. Ibid.

58. Metzger, *Terese and Isabelle*.

59. Acker, 'The Language of Sex the Sex of Language', p. 3.

60. Robert Scholes, *Paradoxy of Modernism*. London and New Haven: Yale University Press, 2006, p. 107.

61. Rebecca Beasley, *Ezra Pound and the Visual Culture of Modernism*. Cambridge: Cambridge University Press, 2007, p. 103. Beasley is citing Ezra Pound, 'Vorticism', *Fortnightly Review*, vol. 96, 1914, pp. 465–6.

62. Ibid.

63. Sitney, *Modernist Montage*, p. 2.

64. Ibid.

65. Maya Deren, in an interview first published in 1963 in the journal *Film Culture*, 'Poetry and the Film: a Symposium: with Maya Deren, Arthur Miller, Dylan Thomas, Parker Tyler. Chairman Willard Maas. Organized by Amos Vogel', collected later in Sitney, *Film Culture Reader* and cited by Sitney in *The Cinema of Poetry*. Oxford: Oxford University Press, 2015, p. 108.

66. Eisenstein, *Selected Works Volume II*, p. 53.

67. Ibid. p. 156.

68. Maya Deren, 'Interview with Maya Deren', in Kudláček's film, *In the Mirror of Maya Deren*.

69. Acker, 'My Mother' Reading Version, Kathy Acker Papers Box 4. The first page is marked page 4. There are twenty-two notes in total signifying a colour change.

70. Wittgenstein, *Philosophical Investigations*, p. 94.

71. Acker, 'Rejects from *Don Quixote*'.

72. Ludwig Wittgenstein, *Remarks on Colour*, trans. Linda L. McAlister and Margarete Schättle. London: Blackwell [1977], 2007.

73. Acker, 'Rejects from *Don Quixote*'.

74. Sitney, *The Cinema of Poetry*, p. 108.

75. Maya Deren in Sitney, *Film Culture Reader*, p. 174, cited by Sitney in *The Cinema of Poetry*, p. 108.

76. Paul Celan, 'Snow-Bed', in *Paul Celan: Selected Poems*, trans. Michael Hamburger. London: Penguin Books, 1995, p. 123. 'Snow-Bed' ('Schnee-bett') is part of Celan's 1959 collection of poems entitled *Sprachgitter*.

77. Paul Celan, 'The Meridian', Speech on the Occasion of Receiving the Georg Büchner Prize, Darmstadt, 22 October, 1960, in Celan, *Collected Prose*, trans. Rosemarie Waldrop. New York: Routledge, 2003, p. 51.

78. Pierre Joris, 'Introduction', in Paul Celan, *Breathturn into Timestead: The Collected Later Poetry*, trans. Pierre Joris. New York: Farrar, Straus and Giroux, 2014, p. xlv.

79. Ibid. p. xlvii.

80. Ibid. p. li.

81. Ludwig Wittgenstein, *Tractatus Logico-Philosophicus*, trans. D. F. Pears and B. F. McGuinness. London and New York: Routledge, 2001, p. 89.

82. Mark Anderson, 'Poet on the Border', Introduction in Ingeborg Bachmann, *In the Storm of Roses: Selected Poems by Ingeborg Bachmann*. Princeton: Princeton University Press, 1986, p. 6.

83. Ibid. p. 7.

84. Ibid. p. 6.

85. Ingeborg Bachmann, 'Songs in Flight', in *In the Storm of Roses*, p. 143.

86. Ibid.

87. Ibid. p. 145.

88. Georg Büchner, 'Woyzeck', in *Danton's Death, Leonce and Lena, and Woyzeck*. Oxford: Oxford University Press, 2008, p. 111.

89. Ibid. p. 151.

90. Acker, 'My Mother Demonology Typescript', p. 303, Kathy Acker Papers, Box 3.

91. Deren, 'Cinema as an Independent Art Form', in *Essential Deren*, p. 246.

Chapter 6

1. Murray Krieger, *Ekphrasis: The Illusion of the Natural Sign*. Baltimore and London: The Johns Hopkins University Press, 1992, p. 9.

2. Ibid. p. 11.

3. Ibid.

4. Ibid.

5. Acker, 'Outlines for Kiki'. Unpaginated, Kathy Acker Papers, Box 7.

6. Ibid.

7. Smith in interview with Acker, cited by Acker in 'Outlines for Kiki'.

8. Cindy Nemser, 'A Conversation with Eva Hesse', in *Eva Hesse*, ed. Mignon Nixon. London: MIT Press, 2002, p. 7.

9. Ibid.

10. Ibid.

11. Meyer, 'Non, Nothing, Everything', p. 60.

12. Ibid. p. 61.

13. Acker, 'Persephone Grown Up' (notebook), Kathy Acker Papers, Box 7.

14. Acker, draft of 'Running through the World: On the Art of Kiki Smith', Kathy Acker Papers, Box 7.

15. De Monchaux, 'Fax sent to Kathy Acker', p. 1. The non-annotated fax is also included in Cathy de Monchaux, *Cathy de Monchaux*. London: Whitechapel Gallery, 1997, pp. 64–5.

16. Kathy Acker, 'From Psyche's Journal', in de Monchaux, *Cathy de Monchaux*, pp. 24-31.

17. De Monchaux, 'Floor plan of gallery with sitings of pieces subject to change', in de Monchaux, 'Fax sent to Kathy Acker', p. 8.

18. De Monchaux, 'Fax sent to Kathy Acker,' p. 5.

19. Acker, 'From Psyche's Journal', in de Monchaux, *Cathy de Monchaux*, p. 1.

20. See Acker, *My Mother: Demonology*, p. 59. I have discussed the aesthetics of eversion in Acker's *My Mother: Demonology* in detail an earlier article. See Colby, 'Radical Interiors'.

21. Acker, 'From Psyche's Journal', in de Monchaux, *Cathy de Monchaux*, p. 13.

22. Acker, Untitled loose-leaf notes on Cathy de Monchaux. Unpaginated, Kathy Acker Papers, Box 1.

23. De Monchaux, 'Fax sent to Kathy Acker,' p. 5.

24. Ibid. p. 6.

25. Ibid.

26. Louisa Buck, 'Cathy de Monchaux', in de Monchaux, *Cathy de Monchaux*, p. 10. Buck is citing Primo Levi, *The Periodic Table*, trans. Raymond Rosenthal. London: Michael Joseph, 1985, p. 92.

27. Acker, 'From Psyche's Journal', in de Monchaux, *Cathy de Monchaux*.

28. McCaffery, 'From the Notebooks', p. 29.

29. Andrews, 'Writing Social Work & Political Practice', p. 3.

30. McCaffery, 'From the Notebooks', p. 29.

31. Acker, Untitled loose-leaf notes on Cathy de Monchaux. Unpaginated.

32. Charles Bernstein, 'Disfiguring Abstraction', *Critical Inquiry*, vol. 39, no. 3, Spring 2013, p. 497.

33. Acker, Untitled loose-leaf notes on Cathy de Monchaux. Unpaginated.

34. Acker, 'From Psyche's Journal', in de Monchaux, *Cathy de Monchaux*, p. 2.

35. Acker, Untitled loose-leaf notes on Cathy de Monchaux. Unpaginated.

36. Ibid.

37. Acker, 'From Psyche's Journal', in de Monchaux, *Cathy de Monchaux*, p. 1.
38. Bernstein, 'Disfiguring Abstraction', p. 488.
39. Gotthold Ephraim Lessing, *Laocoön: An Essay on the Limits of Painting and Poetry*, trans. Ellen Frothingham. New York: Dover Books [1766], 2005, p. 13.
40. Ibid.
41. Ibid. p. 20.
42. Ibid. p. 15.
43. Acker, 'From Psyche's Journal', in de Monchaux, *Cathy de Monchaux*, p. 6.
44. De Monchaux, 'Fax sent to Kathy Acker,' p. 1.
45. Acker, 'From Psyche's Journal', in de Monchaux, *Cathy de Monchaux*, p. 6.
46. Ibid. pp. 7–8.
47. Bernstein, 'Disfiguring Abstraction', p. 487.
48. Statement by Eva Hesse, cited by Lucy Lippard in *Eva Hesse*. New York: Da Capo Press, 1992, p. 131. In her note to the quotation, Lippard adds: 'The next line was to read: "In its simplistic stand, it achieves its own identity,"' but the line was omitted in the final version. See Lippard, *Eva Hesse*, p. 216, note 21.
49. Bernstein, 'Disfiguring Abstraction', p. 494.
50. Ibid. p. 495.
51. Acker, 'From Psyche's Journal', in de Monchaux, *Cathy de Monchaux*, p. 9.
52. Acker, 'Against Ordinary Language', in *Bodies of Work: Essays*, p. 147.
53. Elaine Scarry, *The Body in Pain: The Making and Unmaking of the World*. Oxford: Oxford University Press [1985], 1987, p. 12.
54. David Antin, 'Looking Back at *Talking*', in *Talking*. Champaign, IL: Dalkey Archive Press, 200, pp. 188–9.
55. Acker, 'Bodies of Work', in *Bodies of Work: Essays*, p. 145.
56. Ibid.
57. Ibid. p. 146.
58. Ibid. p. 143.
59. Ibid.
60. Acker, 'Against Ordinary Language', in *Bodies of Work: Essays*, p. 145.
61. Ibid. p. 146.
62. Kathy Acker, 'Opera: The Actual Working of Terror and Ecstasy', in Jan Fabre and Robert Mapplethorpe, *The Power of Theatrical Madness*. London: Institute of Contemporary Arts, 1986, pp. v–vii.

63. Acker, *Pussy, King of the Pirates*, p. 265.
64. Ovid, *Metamorphoses*, trans. Mary M. Innes. London: Penguin, 1955, p. 231.
65. Ibid.
66. Acker, 'Bodies of Work', in *Bodies of Work: Essays*, p. 146.
67. Ibid. p. 145.
68. Ibid. p. 148.
69. Ibid. pp. 148–9.
70. Scarry, *The Body in Pain*, p. 3.
71. Ibid.
72. Ibid. p. 161.
73. Ibid. p. 164.
74. Ibid.
75. Nicole Cooley, 'Painful Bodies: Kathy Acker's Last Texts', in *We Who Love to Be Astonished: Experimental Women's Writing and Performance Poetics*, ed. Laura Hinton and Cynthia Hogue. Tuscaloosa and London: University of Alabama Press, 2002, p. 193.
76. Kathy Acker, 'The Gift of Disease', in *The Guardian Weekend Magazine*, 18 January 1997.
77. Ibid.
78. Kathy Acker, 'Requiem', in *Eurydice in the Underworld*. New York: Arcadia Books, 1997, p. 181.
79. Acker, *Eurydice in the Underworld*, p. 12.
80. Acker, 'Bodies of Work', in *Bodies of Work: Essays*, p. 146.
81. Acker, 'Critical Languages', in *Bodies of Work: Essays*, p. 92.
82. Acker, *Eurydice in the Underworld*, p. 14.
83. Acker, 'Against Ordinary Language', in *Bodies of Work: Essays*, p. 150.
84. Acker, *Eurydice in the Underworld*, p. 16.
85. Derek Jarman, *Blue: Text of a Film by Derek Jarman*. Littlehampton: Littlehampton Printers [1993], 2007, p. 7.
86. Ibid. p. 14.
87. Ibid. p. 15.
88. Scarry, *The Body in Pain*, p. 161.
89. Acker, *Eurydice in the Underworld*, p. 16.
90. Acker, 'Against Ordinary Language', in *Bodies of Work: Essays*, p. 147.
91. Ibid.
92. Peter Osborne and Lynne Segal, 'Gender as Performance: An Interview with Judith Butler', *Radical Philosophy*, vol. 67, Summer 1994, p. 32.
93. Acker, 'Requiem', in *Eurydice in the Underworld*, p. 182.
94. Ibid. p. 183.

95. Ibid. p. 188.
96. Ibid., 188.
97. Rainer Maria Rilke, 'The Tenth Elegy', in *Duino Elegies and The Sonnets to Orpheus*, ed. and trans. Stephen Mitchell. New York: Vintage, 2009, pp. 61–7.
98. Harryman, 'Acker Un-formed', p. 37.
99. Acker, *Eurydice in the Underworld*, p. 188.
100. Georges Bataille, *Inner Experience*, trans. Leslie Anne Boldt. New York: SUNY Press, 1984, p. 16.
101. Ibid.
102. Bernstein, *A Poetics*, p. 38.
103. Acker, 'Kathy Acker: Top Ten'.
104. Olson, 'Projective Verse', in *Collected Prose*, p. 242. Peter Wollen has also remarked on Acker's debt to Olson in this respect. He remarks: 'She adapted his concern with writing as language-driven, with a certain kind of incantatory text, based on the bodily cadence of the breath, while introducing these preoccupations into the writing of prose rather than poetry.' See Wollen, 'Kathy Acker', p. 6. Regarding her experiments with bodybuilding and her quest for the languages of the body, Acker stated in interview with Rickels: 'I realised that the language I was trying to access was a meditative language, about breathing.' See Rickels, 'Body Bildung', p. 61.
105. Olson, 'Projective Verse', in *Collected Prose*, p. 249.
106. Scarry, *The Body in Pain,* p. 31.

Conclusion

1. Acker, 'Critical Languages', in *Bodies of Work: Essays*, p. 83.
2. Acker, 'NOTES ON WRITING – from THE LIFE OF BAUDELAIRE'.
3. Theodor Adorno, *Aesthetic Theory*, trans. C. Lenhardt. London: Routledge and Kegan Paul, 1984, p. 321.
4. Wollen, 'Kathy Acker', p. 6.
5. Gertrude Stein, *Picasso*, in *Gertrude Stein: Writings 1932–1946*. New York: The Library of America, 1998, p. 533. Here Stein is writing of Picasso, and perhaps herself.
6. Forrest-Thompson, *Poetic Artifice*, p. 16, cited by Bernstein in *A Poetics*, p. 12.
7. Acker, 'Critical Languages', in *Bodies of Work: Essays*, p. 83.

Bibliography

Works by Kathy Acker

Published works

Blood and Guts in High School. New York: Grove Press, 1984.

Blood and Guts in High School Plus Two. London: Pan Books, 1984.

Bodies of Work: Essays by Kathy Acker. London: Serpent's Tail, 1997.

Don Quixote: Which Was a Dream. New York: Grove Press, 1986.

Empire of the Senseless. New York: Grove Press, 1988.

Eurydice in the Underworld. New York: Arcadia Books, 1997.

Great Expectations. New York: Grove Press, 1982.

Hannibal Lecter, My Father. New York: Semiotext(e), 1991.

Homage to LeRoi Jones and Other Early Works, ed. Gabrielle Kappes. Lost and Found: The CUNY Poetics Document Initiative, Series 5, Number 1. New York: CUNY Poetics Document Initiative, Spring 2015.

'I Dreamt I Was a Nymphomaniac: Imagining', in *Portrait of an Eye: Three Novels*. New York: Grove Press, 1980.

In Memoriam to Identity. London: Pandora Press, 1990.

'Kathy Acker: Top Ten', *Women's Review Number Three*, January 1986, 13–14.

Literal Madness: 3 Novels, Kathy goes to Haiti, My Death My Life by Pier Paolo Pasolini, Florida. New York: Grove Press, 1988.

My Mother: Demonology. New York: Grove Press, 1993.

'Opera: The Actual Working of Terror and Ecstasy', in Jan Fabre and Robert Mapplethorpe, *The Power of Theatrical Madness*. London: Institute of Contemporary Arts, 1986.

Portrait of an Eye: Three Novels. New York: Grove Press, 1992.

Pussy, King of the Pirates. New York: Grove Press, 1996.

'Requiem' (1997), in *Eurydice in the Underworld*. New York: Arcadia Books, 1997, 151–88.

Rip-Off Red, Girl Detective [1973] and *The Burning Bombing of America: The Destruction of the U.S.* [1972]. New York: Grove Press, 2002.

The Adult Life of Toulouse Lautrec by Henri Toulouse Lautrec. New York: TVRT Press [1975], 1978.

The Childlike Life of the Black Tarantula by the Black Tarantula. New York: TVRT Press [1974], 1978.

'The Gift of Disease', in *The Guardian Weekend Magazine*, 18 January 1997.

'The Path of Abjection: An Interview with Kathy Acker', in Larry McCaffery, *Some Other Frequency: Interviews with Innovative American Authors.* Pennsylvania Studies in American Fiction, Philadelphia: University of Pennsylvania Press, 1996.

Works housed in the Kathy Acker Papers, David M. Rubenstein Rare Book & Manuscript Library, Duke University

'Annotations of Virgil's Bucolics and Georgics', Unprocessed Box 7.

'Artwork for *In Memoriam to Identity*', Box 9.

'Blood and Guts Book Banning Documents', Box 7.

'*Blood and Guts in High School* Original Manuscript', Box 1.

'Blood and Guts Original Artwork', Box 9.

'Bodybuilding'. Fax to Karen Marta, Box 4.

'Bruce Willis and Me', Box 1.

'Burroughs 2', Box 1.

'By Cesar Vallejo', Unprocessed Box 4.

'Commonsensical / Philosophical Use of Words', Box 3.

'Entrance into Dwelling in Paradise', Unprocessed Box 4.

'Exercises Writing Asymmetrically', Box 4.

Fax sent to Kathy Acker from Cathy de Monchaux dated 10 March 1997, Box 5.

'From Psyche's Journal: For Cathy de Monchaux', Box 1.

'Gender in Art', Box 7.

'Homage to LeRoi Jones', Box 4.

'Journal Black Cats Black Jewels', Box 4.

'Lecture on *Unworking*', Box 2.

Letter from James Grauerholz to Fred Jordan, Box 3.

'More Short Pieces', Box 4.

'MURDERERS-CRIMINALS JOIN SUNLIGHT', Box 4.

'*My Mother Demonology* Typescript', Box 3.

'My Mother' Reading Version, Box 4.

'Nonpatriarchal Language: The Body', in 'Writings 1990–1991', Box 4.

'Notebooks for *My Mother: Demonology*', Box 3.

'NOTES ON WRITING – from THE LIFE OF BAUDELAIRE', *L=A=N=G=U=A=G=E*, no. 9/10, October 1979, pp. 1–3, Box 4.

'On Burroughs', Box 4.

'Original Manuscript (Vols 1 & 2) for *Don Quixote*', Box 1.

'Outlines for Kiki', Box 7.

'Persephone Grown Up' (notebook), Box 7.

'Reading the Lack of the Body: The Writing of the Marquis de Sade', Box 4.

'Rejects from *Don Quixote*', Unprocessed Box 4.

'Running through the World: On the Art of Kiki Smith', Box 7.

'Sexual Censorship', in 'More Short Pieces', Undated, Box 4.

The Black Tarantula, 'Conversations', Box 4.

'The Destruction of the U.S. The Burning Bombing of America', Box 3.

'The Language of Sex the Sex of Language', in 'Writings 1990–1991', Unprocessed Box 4.

'The Malady of Death' (notes), Box 6.

'Ulysses Backwards', Unprocessed Box 6.

'Untitled loose-leaf notes on Cathy de Monchaux', Box 1.

'Working Set', Unprocessed Box 4.

'Writing Asystematicaaly', Box 4.

'Xerox of *Blood and Guts* for Sol Le Witt', Box 9.

'Xerox of Present for Sol LeWitt from *Blood and Guts in High School*', Box 9.

Works cited

Addis, Laird, 'Time, Substance, and Analysis', in M. S. Gram and E. D. Klemke, *The Ontological Turn: Studies in the Philosophy of Gustav Bergmann*. Iowa City: University of Iowa Press, 1974.

Adorno, Theodor, *Aesthetic Theory*, trans. C. Lenhardt. London: Routledge and Kegan Paul, 1984.

Adorno, Theodor, *Aesthetic Theory*, trans. Robert Hullot-Kentor. London: Bloomsbury [1970], 2013.

Alexandrov, Vladimir E., *Andrei Bely: The Major Symbolist Fiction*. Cambridge, MA: Harvard University Press, 1985.

Allen, Donald, *New American Poetry, 1945–1960*. Berkeley: University of California Press, 1999.

Althusser, Louis, 'Ideology and Ideological State Apparatuses', in *On Ideology*. London: Verso, 2008, 1–140.

Anderson, Mark, 'Poet on the Border', in Ingeborg Bachmann, *In the Storm of Roses: Selected Poems by Ingeborg Bachmann*. Princeton: Princeton University Press, 1986.

Andrews, Bruce, 'Writing Social Work & Political Practice', L=A=N=G=U=A=G=E, no. 9/10, October 1979, 3–5.

Antin, David, 'A Few Words', in *Selected Poems: 1963–1973*. Los Angeles: Sun and Moon Press, 1991.

Antin, David, *Talking*. Champaign, IL: Dalkey Archive Press, 2001.

Antin, David and Charles Bernstein, *A Conversation with David Antin*. New York: Granary Books, 2002.

Bachmann, Ingeborg, *In the Storm of Roses: Selected Poems by Ingeborg Bachmann*. Princeton: Princeton University Press, 1986.

Baker, Houston A., Jr., *Blues, Ideology and Afro-American Literature*. Chicago: University of Chicago Press, 1984.

Baron, Scarlett, 'Joyce, Genealogy, Intertextuality', *Dublin James Joyce Journal*, no. 4, 2011, 55–71.

Bataille, Georges, *Inner Experience*, trans. Leslie Anne Boldt. New York: SUNY Press, 1984.

Baudelaire, Charles, *The Flowers of Evil*, trans. James McGowan. Oxford: Oxford University Press, 2008.

Bauman, Zygmunt, *Life in Fragments: Essays in Postmodern Modernity*. Oxford: Blackwell, 1995.

Beasley, Rebecca, *Ezra Pound and the Visual Culture of Modernism*. Cambridge: Cambridge University Press, 2007.

Beckett, Samuel, *Complete Dramatic Works*. London: Faber and Faber, 1986.

Bely, Andrei, *St Petersburg*, trans. John Cournos. New York: Grove Press, 1994.

Benjamin, Walter, *Selected Writings, Volume 4: 1938–1940*, ed. and trans. Michael W. Jennings and Howard Eiland. Cambridge, MA: Harvard University Press, 2003.

Benjamin, Walter, *The Work of Art in the Age of Its Technological Reproducibility and Other Writings on Media*, trans. Edmund Jephcott et al. Cambridge, MA: Harvard University Press, 2008.

Bergvall, Caroline, Laynie Browne, Teresa Carmody and Vanessa Place (eds), *I'll Drown My Book: Conceptual Writing by Women*. Los Angeles: Les Figues Press, 2012.

Bernstein, Charles, 'The Dollar Value of Poetry', L=A=N=G=U=A=G=E, no. 9/10, October 1979, 7–9.

Bernstein, Charles, *A Poetics*. Cambridge, MA: Harvard University Press, 1992.

Bernstein, Charles, *Contents Dream: Essays 1975–1984*. Evanston: North-western University Press, 2001.

Bernstein, Charles, 'Jackson at Home', in *Contents Dream: Essays 1975-1984*. Evanston: Northwestern University Press, 2001, 252–70.

Bernstein, Charles, 'Disfiguring Abstraction', *Critical Inquiry*, vol. 39, no. 3, Spring 2013, 486–97.

Bernstein, Charles, 'Introduction', in *Louis Zukofsky: Selected Poems*, ed. Charles Bernstein. New York: Library of America, 2014.

Bernstein, Charles, 'The Expanded Field of L=A=N=G=U=A=G=E', in *The Routledge Companion to Experimental Literature*, ed. Joe Bray, Alison Gibbons and Brian McHale. London and New York: Routledge, 2015, 281–97.

Bernstein, Charles and Bruce Andrews (eds), *L=A=N=G=U=A=G=E*, no. 9/10, October 1979.

Blake, Nayland, 'Because I Want to Live Forever in Wonder', in *Lust for Life: On the Writings of Kathy Acker*, ed. Amy Scholder, Carla Harryman and Avital Ronell. London: Verso, 2006, 99–110.

Blanchot, Maurice. *The Infinite Conversation*, trans. Susan Hanson. Minneapolis: University of Minnesota Press [1969], 1993.

Blanchot, Maurice, *The Book to Come*, trans. Charlotte Mandell. Stanford: Stanford University Press [1959], 2003.

Boon, Marcus, *In Praise of Copying*. Harvard: Harvard University Press, 2010.

Bowie, Malcolm, *Mallarmé and the Art of Being Difficult*. Cambridge: Cambridge University Press, 1978.

Bowring, John, 'Introduction', in Murasaki Shikibu, *Murasaki Shikibu: Her Diary and Poetic Memoirs*, trans. John Bowring. Princeton: Princeton University Press, 1982.

Büchner, Georg, *Danton's Death, Leonce and Lena, and Woyzeck*. Oxford: Oxford University Press, 2008.

Buck, Louisa, 'Cathy de Monchaux', in *Cathy de Monchaux*. London: Whitechapel Gallery, 1997.

Buñuel, Luis, *An Unspeakable Betrayal: Selected Writings of Luis Buñuel*. Berkeley: University of California Press, 2002.

Bürger, Peter, *Theory of the Avant-Garde*, trans. Michael Shaw. Minneapolis: University of Minnesota Press [1974], 2009.

Bürger, Peter, 'Avant-Garde and Neo-Avant-Garde: An Attempt to Answer Certain Critics of *Theory of the Avant-Garde*', *New Literary History*, vol. 41, no. 4, 2010, 695–715.

Burroughs, William, *The Wild Boys: A Book of the Dead*. New York: Grove Press [1969], 1992.

Butler, Judith, 'Bodies That Matter', in *Engaging With Irigaray*, ed. Carolyn Burke, Naomi Schor and Margaret Whitford. New York: Columbia University Press, 1994.

Butler, Judith, '"Conscience Doth Make Subjects of Us All": Louis Althusser's Subjection', in *The Psychic Life of Power: Theories in Subjection*. Stanford: Stanford University Press, 1997.

Butler, Judith, *Gender Trouble: Feminism and the Subversion of Identity*. London: Routledge, 2006.

Cage, John, *Silence: Lectures and Writings*. London: Marion Boyars, 1995.

Canetti, Elias, *The Conscience of Words and Earwitness*. London: Picador, 1987.

Catullus, *Catullus (Gai Valeri Catulli Veronensis Liber)*, trans. Celia and Louis Zukofsky. London: Cape Goliard Press, 1969.

Catullus, *The Complete Poems*, trans. Guy Lee. Oxford: Oxford University Press, 2008.

Celan, Paul, *Paul Celan: Selected Poems*, trans. Michael Hamburger. London: Penguin Books, 1995.

Celan, Paul, *Paul Celan: Collected Poems*, trans. Rosemarie Waldrop. New York: Routledge, 2003.

Celan, Paul, *Breathturn into Timestead: The Collected Later Poetry*, trans. Pierre Joris. New York: Farrar, Straus and Giroux, 2014.

Cheek, Cris, Kirby Malone and Marshall Reese, 'TV TRIO Present CAREER WRIST', *L=A=N=G=U=A=G=E*, no. 9/10, October 1979, 14–16.

Ciprut, Jose V., *Indeterminacy: The Mapped, the Navigable, the Unchartered*. London and Cambridge, MA: MIT Press, 2008.

Cixous, Hélène, 'The Laugh of the Medusa', in *New French Feminisms*, ed. Elaine Marks and Isabelle de Courtivron. Cambridge, MA: University of Massachusetts Press [1975], 1981, 245–64.

Cixous, Hélène, 'Sorties', in Hélène Cixous and Catherine Clément, *The Newly Born Woman*, trans. Betsy Wing. London and Minneapolis: University of Minnesota Press [1975], 1986.

Cixous, Hélène and Catherine Clément, *The Newly Born Woman*, trans. Betsy Wing. London and Minneapolis: University of Minnesota Press [1975], 1986.

Clayton, Michelle, *Poetry in Pieces: César Vallejo and Lyric Modernity*. Berkeley: University of California Press, 2011.

Colby, Georgina, 'Radical Interiors: Cindy Sherman's "Sex Pictures" and Kathy Acker's *My Mother: Demonology*', *Women: A Cultural Review*, vol. 23, no. 2, 2012, 182–200.

Colby, Georgina, 'The Reappropriation of Classical Mythology to Represent Pain: Falling Silent in the Work of Kathy Acker and Robert Mapplethorpe', *Comparative Critical Studies*, vol. 9, no. 1, 2012, 7–35.

Conte, Joseph M., *Design and Debris: A Chaotics of Postmodern American Fiction*. Tuscaloosa and London: University of Alabama Press, 2002.

Cooley, Nicole, 'Painful Bodies: Kathy Acker's Last Texts', in *We Who Love to Be Astonished: Experimental Women's Writing and Performance Poetics*, ed. Laura Hinton and Cynthia Hogue. Tuscaloosa and London: University of Alabama Press, 2002.

Corbett, Jan, 'Words Hurt! Acker's Appropriation of Myth in *Don Quixote*', in *Devouring Institutions: The Life Work of Kathy Acker*, ed. Michael Hardin. Calexico, CA: San Diego State University Press, 2005, 167–88.

Cournos, John, 'Introduction', in Andrei Bely, *St Petersburg*, trans. John Cournos. New York: Grove Press, 1994.

DeKoven, Marianne, *A Different Language: Gertrude Stein's Experimental Writing*. Madison: University of Wisconsin Press, 1983.

Deleuze, Gilles, *Foucault*, trans. Seán Hand. London: Continuum, 1999.

de Monchaux, Cathy, *Cathy de Monchaux*. London: Whitechapel Gallery, 1997.

de Monchaux, Cathy, 'Fax sent to Kathy Acker', dated 10 March 1997, Box 5. Kathy Acker Papers, David M. Rubenstein Rare Books & Manuscript Library, Duke University.

de Monchaux, Cathy, *Cathy de Monchaux*. London: Whitechapel Gallery, 1997.

Deren, Maya, *Essential Deren: Collected Writings on Film by Maya Deren*, ed. Bruce R. Macpherson. New York: McPherson, 2005.

Dew, Spencer, *Learning for Revolution: The Work of Kathy Acker*. San Diego: San Diego State University Press, 2011.

Dostoyevsky, Fyodor, *Crime and Punishment*, trans. David McDuff. Harmondsworth: Penguin Classics, 2003.

Drucker, Johanna, *The Visible World: Experimental Typography and Modern Art, 1909–1923*. Chicago: University of Chicago Press, 1994.

Dworkin, Craig. *Reading the Illegible*. Evanston: Northwestern University Press, 2003.

Dworkin, Craig and Kenneth Goldsmith, *Against Expression: An Anthology of Conceptual Writing*. Evanston: Northwestern University Press, 2011.

Ebbesen, Jeffrey, 'Combative Textualities: Kathy Acker's *The Adult Life of Toulouse Lautrec by Henri Toulouse Lautrec*', in *Postmodernism and Its Others*. London: Routledge, 2010, 62–132.

Eisenstein, Sergei, *Selected Works Volume II: Towards a Theory of Montage*, ed. Michael Glenny and Richard Taylor, trans. Michael Glenny. New York: I. B. Tauris, 2010.

Elam, Keir, 'Not I: Beckett's Mouth and the Ars(e) Rhetorica', in *Beckett at 80 in Context*, ed. Enoch Brater. New York and Oxford: Oxford University Press, 1986, 124–48.

Engbretson, Terry, 'Re-educating the Body: Kathy Acker, Georges Bataille, and the Postmodern Body in *My Mother: Demonology*', in *Devouring Institutions: The Life Work of Kathy Acker*, ed. Michael Hardin. San Diego: San Diego State University Press, 2005, 69–84.

Evans, David (ed.) *Appropriation*. London: Whitechapel Gallery and MIT Press, 2009.

Forrest-Thomson, Veronica, *Poetic Artifice: A Theory of Twentieth Century Poetry*. New York: St. Martin's Press, 1978.

Foster, Hal, *The Return of the Real: The Avant-Garde at the End of the Century*. Cambridge, MA: MIT Press, 1996.

Foucault, Michel, *The History of Madness*, trans. Jonathan Murphy and Jean Khalfa. London: Routledge [1961], 2009.

ffrench, Patrick and Roland-François Lack (eds), *The Tel Quel Reader*. London: Routledge, 1998.

Freud, Sigmund, *The Complete Psychological Works of Sigmund Freud, Volume Four, Part 1, The Interpretation of Dreams*, trans. James Strachey. London: Vintage, 2001.

Friedman, Ellen G., 'A Conversation with Kathy Acker', *The Review of Contemporary Fiction*, vol. 9.3, Fall 1989, 12–22.

Friedman, Ellen G. 'Where Are the Missing Contents? (Post)Modernism, Gender, and the Canon', *PMLA*, vol. 108, no. 2, 1993, 240–52.

Friedman, Ellen G. and Miriam Fuchs (eds), *Breaking the Sequence: Women's Experimental Fiction*. Princeton: Princeton University Press, 2006.

Galef, David and Ellen G. Friedman, 'From Plagiarism to Appropriation', *PMLA*, vol. 108, no. 5, October 1993, 1174–5.

Ginsberg, Allen, 'Howl', in *Howl*, ed. Barry Miles. New York: Harper Perennial [1956], 2006.

Goodman, Michael B., 'The Customs' Censorship of William Burroughs' *Naked Lunch*', *Critique: Studies in Contemporary Fiction*, vol. 22, no. 1, 1980, 92–104.

Goytisolo, Juan, *Juan the Landless*, trans. Helen R. Lane. New York: Serpent's Tail [1975], 1977.

Gray, Jeremy, *Plato's Ghost: The Modernist Transformation of Mathematics*. Princeton: Princeton University Press, 2008.

Guyotat, Pierre, *Eden, Eden, Eden*, trans. Graham Fox. London: Creation Books, 1995.

Hardin, Michael (ed.), *Devouring Institutions: The Life Work of Kathy Acker*. Calexico, CA: San Diego State University Press, 2011.

Harryman, Carla, 'Roles and Restraints in Women's Experimental Writing', in *We Who Loved to Be Astonished: Experimental Women's Writing and Performance Poetics*, ed. Cynthia Hogue and Laura Hinton. Tuscaloosa: University of Alabama Press, 2001, 116–24.

Harryman, Carla, 'Acker Un-formed', in *Lust for Life: On the Writings of Kathy Acker*, ed. Amy Scholder, Carla Harryman and Avital Ronell. New York: Verso, 2006, 35–45.

Hartmann, Sadakichi, *Japanese Art*. Boston: L. C. Page, 1903.

Hawkins, Susan E., 'All in the Family: Kathy Acker's *Blood and Guts in High School*', *Contemporary Literature*, vol. 45, no. 4, Winter 2004, 637–58.

Heffernan, James A., *Museum of Words: The Poetics of Ekphrasis from Homer to Ashbery*. Chicago: University of Chicago Press, 1993.

Hejinian, Lyn, *The Language of Inquiry*. Los Angeles: University of California Press, 2001.

Henke, Suzette, 'Oedipus Meets Sacher-Masoch: Kathy Acker's Pornographic (Anti)Ethical Aesthetic', *Contemporary Women's Writing*, vol. 2, no. 2, December 2008, 91–110.

Hesse, Eva, *Eva Hesse*, ed. Elisabeth Sussman. New Haven and London: Yale University Press, 2002.

Hinton, Laura and Cynthia Hogue (eds), *We Who Love to Be Astonished: Experimental Women's Writing and Performance Poetics*. Tuscaloosa and London: University of Alabama Press, 2002.

Houen, Alex, 'Sovereignty, Biopolitics, and the Use of Literature: Michel Foucault and Kathy Acker', in *Foucault in an Age of Terror: Essays on Biopolitics and the Defence of Society*, ed. Stephen Morton and Stephen Bygrave. London: Palgrave, 2008, 63–87.

Houen, Alex, *Powers of Possibility: Experimental American Writing since the 1960s*. Oxford: Oxford University Press, 2012.

House, Richard, 'Informational Inheritance in Kathy Acker's *Empire of the Senseless*', *Contemporary Literature*, vol. 46, no. 3, Autumn 2005, 450-82.

Howe, Susan, 'Scattering as Behaviour towards Risk', in *Singularities*. Middletown, CT: Wesleyan University Press, 1990, 61–70.

Hubert, Renée Riese, *Surrealism and the Book*. Berkeley: University of California Press, 1988.

Irigaray, Luce, *Speculum of the Other Woman*, trans. Gillian G. Gill. New York: Cornell University Press [1974], 1985.

Irr, Caren, 'Beyond Appropriation: *Pussy, King of the Pirates* and a Feminist Critique of Intellectual Property', in *Devouring Institutions: The Life Work of Kathy Acker*, ed. Michael Hardin. Calexico, CA: San Diego State University Press, 2005, 211–35.

Irwin, Robert and Malcolm Lyons (eds), *The Arabian Nights: Tales of 1,001 Nights*, trans. Malcolm Lyons. London: Penguin Classics, 2010.

Jacobs, Naomi, 'Kathy Acker and the Plagiarized Self', *The Review of Contemporary Literature*, vol. 9, no. 3, Fall 1989, 50–5.

Jakobson, Roman, *On Language*, ed. R. Waugh and Monique Manville Burston. Cambridge, MA: Harvard University Press, 1990.

Jakobson, Roman, 'Two Aspects of Language and Two Types of Aphasic Disturbances', in *On Language*, ed. R. Waugh and Monique Manville Burston. Cambridge, MA: Harvard University Press [1956], 1990, 115–33.

James, David, *Modernist Futures: Innovation and Inheritance in the Contemporary Novel*. Cambridge: Cambridge University Press, 2012.

James, William, *The Principles of Psychology Vol. I*. London: Dover Publications, 2000.

Jarman, Derek, *Blue: Text of a Film by Derek Jarman*. Littlehampton: Littlehampton Printers [1993], 2007.

Jones, LeRoi, *The System of Dante's Hell*, First Evergreen Black Cat Edition. New York: Grove Press, 1966.

Jones, LeRoi, 'The Alternative', in *Tales by LeRoi Jones*. New York: Grove Press, 1967.

Joris, Pierre, 'Introduction', in Paul Celan, *Breathturn into Timestead: The Collected Later Poetry*, trans. Pierre Joris. New York: Farrar, Straus and Giroux, 2014, xxix–lxxix.

Just, Daniel, 'The Politics of the Novel and Maurice Blanchot's Theory of the Récit, 1954-1964', *French Forum*, vol. 33, no. 1–2, Winter/Spring 2008, 121–39.

Just, Daniel, *Literature, Ethics, and Decolonization in Postwar France: The Politics of Disengagement*. Cambridge: Cambridge University Press, 2015.

Keats, John, 'Ode on a Grecian Urn', in *Keats: The Complete Poems*, ed. Miriam Allott. London and New York: Longman, 1995.

Kocela, Christopher, 'A Myth beyond the Phallus: Female Fetishism in Kathy Acker's Late Novels', *Genders*, no. 34, 2001, <http://www.iiav.nl/ezines/IAV_606661/IAV_606661_2010_52/g34_kocela.html> (last accessed 24 February 2016).

Kocela, Christopher, 'Resighting Gender Theory: Butler's Lesbian Phallus in Acker's *Pussy*', *LIT*, vol. 17, no. 1, 2006, 77–104.

Krieger, Murray, *Ekphrasis: The Illusion of the Natural Sign*. Baltimore and London: The Johns Hopkins University Press, 1992.

Kristeva, Julia, 'The Father, Love and Banishment', in *Desire in Language: A Semiotic Approach to Literature and Art*, trans. Leon S. Roudiez. Oxford: Columbia University Press, 1980.

Kristeva, Julia, 'La femme ce n'est pas jamais ça', in *New French Feminisms*, ed. Elaine Marks and Isabelle de Courtivron. Cambridge, MA: University of Massachusetts Press, 1981.

Kristeva, Julia, 'Women's Time', trans. Alice Jardine, *Signs*, vol. 7, no. 1, Autumn 1981, 13–35.

Kristeva, Julia, *Revolution in Poetic Language*, trans. Leon S. Roudiez. Columbia: Columbia University Press [1974], 1984.

Kristeva, Julia, 'Towards a Semiology of Paragrams', in *The Tel Quel Reader*, ed. Patrick Ffrench and Roland-François Lack. London: Routledge [1967], 1998, 25–50.

Kuehl, John, *Alternate Worlds: A Study of Postmodern Antirealist American Fiction*. New York: New York University Press, 1991.

Kuleshov, Lev, 'The Principles of Montage', in *Critical Visions in Film and Theory: Classic and Contemporary Readings*, ed. Timothy Corrigan and Patricia White. New York: St. Martin's Press, 2011, 137–44.

Lacan, Jacques, *Four Fundamental Concepts of Psycho-Analysis*, trans. Alain Sheridan. New York: Norton, 1978.

Lacan, Jacques, *The Seminar of Jacques Lacan, Book XX: On Feminine Sexuality, the Limits of Love and Knowledge*, trans. Bruce Fink. London: Norton, 1998.

Laure (Collette Peignot), *Laure: The Collected Writings*, trans. Jeanine Herman. San Francisco: City Lights, 1995.

Lavin, Maud, *Cut with the Kitchen Knife: The Weimar Photomontages of Hannah Höch*. New Haven and London: Yale University Press, 1993.

Lawler, James, *Rimbaud's Theatre of the Self*. Cambridge, MA: Harvard University Press, 1992.

Lecercle, Jean-Jacques, *Philosophy through the Looking-Glass*. La Salle, IL: Open Court, 1985.

Lecercle, Jean-Jacques, *The Violence of Language*. London: Routledge, 1990.

Lecercle, Jean-Jacques and Denise Riley, *The Force of Language: Language, Discourse, Society*. New York: Palgrave Macmillan, 2005.

Lessing, Gotthold Ephraim, *Laocoön: An Essay on the Limits of Painting and Poetry*, trans. Ellen Frothingham. New York: Dover Books [1766], 2005.

Levenson, Michael, *Modernism*, trans. Raymond Rosenthal. New Haven: Yale University Press, 2011.

Levi, Primo, *The Periodic Table*, trans. Raymond Rosenthal. London: Michael Joseph, 1985.

Levine, Sherrie, 'Statement', in *Appropriation*, ed. David Evans. London: Whitechapel Gallery and MIT Press, 2009.

Lippard, Lucy, *Eva Hesse*. New York: Da Capo Press, 1992.

Lippard, Lucy R., *Six Years: The Dematerialization of the Art Object from 1966–1972*. Berkeley: University of California Press, 1997.

Llosa, Mario Vargas, 'Foreword', in César Vallejo, *The Complete Poetry: A Bilingual Edition*, ed. and trans. Clayton Eshelman. Berkeley: University of California Press, 2007.

Mac Low, Jackson, *Stanzas for Iris Lezak*. Barton, VT: Something Else Press [1971], 1981.

Mac Low, Jackson. 'H U N G E R- ST r i kE', in *Revolution of the Word: A New Gathering of American Avant-Garde Poetry 1914–1945*, ed. Jerome Rothenberg. Boston: Exact Change Books, 2004, 172–6.

Mac Low, Jackson, 'Poetry and Pleasure', in *Thing of Beauty: New and Selected Works*, ed. Anne Tardos. Berkeley and London: University of California Press [1999], 2008.

McCaffery, Larry, *Some Other Frequency: Interviews with Innovative American Authors*. Pennsylvania Studies in American Fiction, Philadelphia: University of Pennsylvania Press, 1996.

McCaffery, Steve, 'From the Notebooks', *L=A=N=G=U=A=G=E*, no. 9/10, October 1979, 29–31.

McCaffery, Steve, *North of Intention: Critical Writings, 1972–1986*. New York: Roof Books, 1986.

McCaffery, Steve, *Prior to Meaning: The Protosemantic and Poetics*. Evanston: Northwestern University Press, 2001.

Malabou, Catherine, *Changing Difference*, trans. Carolyn Shread. Cambridge: Polity Press, 1988.

Marx-Scouras, Danielle, *The Cultural Politics of Tel Quel: Literature and the Left in the Wake of Engagement*. University Park: Pennsylvania State University Press, 1996.

Mayer, Bernadette, *The Formal Field of Kissing*. New York: Catchwood Papers, 1990.

Melville, Herman, *Moby Dick*. Oxford: Oxford University Press [1851], 2008.

Meyer, James, 'Non, Nothing, Everything: Hesse's "Abstraction"', in Eva Hesse, *Eva Hesse*, ed. Elisabeth Sussman. New Haven and London: Yale University Press, 2002.

Miller, Tyrus, *Singular Examples: Artistic Politics and the Neo-Avant-Garde*. Evanston: Northwestern University Press, 2009.

Mintcheva, Svetlana, 'The Paralyzing Tensions of Radical Art in a Postmodern World: Kathy Acker's Last Novels as Exploratory Fictions', in *Devouring Institutions: The Life Work of Kathy Acker*, ed. Michael Hardin. Calexico, CA: San Diego State University Press, 2005, 47–69.

Mitchell, Kaye, 'The Gender Politics of the Experiment', *Contemporary Women's Writing*, special issue 'Experimental Writing', vol. 9, no. 1, March 2015, 1–16.

Moszynska, Anna, *Abstract Art*. London: Thames and Hudson, 1990.

Mukherjee, Ankhi, 'Missed Encounters: Repetition, Rewriting, and Contemporary Returns to Charles Dickens's *Great Expectations*', *Contemporary Literature*, vol. 46, no. 1, Spring 2005, 108–33.

Mulford, Wendy, 'Afterword', in *Out of Everywhere: Linguistically Innovative Poetry by Women in North America & the UK*, ed. Maggie O'Sullivan. London: Reality Street Editions, 1996.

Murphy, Richard, *Theorizing the Avant-Garde: Modernism, Expressionism, and the Problem of Postmodernity*. Cambridge: Cambridge University Press, 1998.

Muth, Katy R., 'Postmodern Fiction as Poststructuralist Theory: Kathy Acker's *Blood and Guts in High School*', *Narrative*, vol. 19, January 2011, 86-110.

Nemser, Cindy, 'A Conversation with Eva Hesse', in *Eva Hesse*, ed. Mignon Nixon. London: MIT Press, 2002, 1–24.

Olson, Charles, *Collected Prose*. Berkeley and Los Angeles: University of California Press, 1997.

Olson, Charles and Ezra Pound, *Charles Olson and Ezra Pound: An Encounter at St Elizabeth's*. New York: Grossman Viking, 1975.

Osborne, Peter and Lynne Segal, 'Gender as Performance: An Interview with Judith Butler', *Radical Philosophy*, vol. 67, Summer 1994, 32-9.

O'Sullivan, Maggie (ed.), *Out of Everywhere: Linguistically Innovative Poetry by Women in North America & the UK*. London: Reality Street Editions, 1996.

Ovid, *Metamorphoses*, trans. Mary M. Innes. London: Penguin, 1955.

Picabia, Francis, *Poèmes et dessins de la fille née sans mère*. Lausanne, 1918.

Pitchford, Nicole, *Tactical Readings: Feminist Postmodernism in the Novels of Kathy Acker and Angela Carter*. Bucknell, PA: Bucknell University Press, 2002.

Place, Vanessa, *Dies: A Sentence*. Los Angeles: Les Figues Press, 2005.

Pound, Ezra, 'Vorticism', *Fortnightly Review*, vol. 96, 1914, 461–71.

Quartermain, Peter, *Disjunctive Poetics: From Gertrude Stein and Louis Zukofsky to Susan Howe*. Cambridge: Cambridge University Press, 1992.

Quartermain, Peter, *Stubborn Poetries: Poetic Facticity and the Avant-Garde*. Tuscaloosa: University of Alabama Press, 2013.

Randall, Marilyn, *Pragmatic Plagiarism: Authorship, Profit, and Power*. Toronto: University of Toronto Press, 2001.

Reich, Wilhelm, *The Function of the Orgasm: Sex-Economic Problems of Biological Energy*, trans. Theodore P. Wolfe. London: Panther Books, 1968.

Reich, Wilhelm, *The Mass Psychology of Fascism*, trans. Vincent R. Carfagno. Harmondsworth: Penguin [1933], 1983.

Reynolds, Margaret (ed.), *The Penguin Book of Lesbian Short Stories*. London: Penguin, 1994.

Rhees, R. R., 'Introduction' (March 1958), in Ludwig Wittgenstein, *The Blue and the Brown Books: Preliminary Studies for the 'Philosophical Investigations'*. Oxford: Blackwell, 2008, v–xiv.

Rickels, Lawrence A., 'Body Bildung – Lawrence A. Rickels Talks with Kathy Acker', *Artforum*, 1 February 1994, 60–3, 103–4.

Riley, Denise, 'Does Sex Have a History? "Women" and Feminism', *New Formations: A Journal of Culture, Theory and Politics*, no. 1, Spring 1987, 35–46.

Riley, Denise, *Am I That Name? Feminism and the Category of 'Women' in History*. London: Macmillan, 1988.

Riley, Denise, *The Words of Selves: Identification, Solidarity, Irony*. Stanford: Stanford University Press, 2000.

Riley, Denise, *Impersonal Passion: Language as Affect*. Durham, NC and London: Duke University Press, 2005.

Rilke, Rainer Maria, *Duino Elegies and The Sonnets to Orpheus*, ed. and trans. Stephen Mitchell. New York: Vintage, 2009.

Rimbaud, Arthur, *Arthur Rimbaud: Selected Poems and Letters*, trans. Jeremy Harding and John Sturrock. London: Penguin Books, 2004.

Rolph, C. H., *The Trial of Lady Chatterley: Regina v. Penguin Books Limited*. London: Penguin, 1961.

Rose, Jacqueline, 'Psychoanalysis, Politics and the Future of Feminism: A Conversation, Juliet Mitchell and Jacqueline Rose with Jean Radford', *Feminist Futures, Women: A Cultural Review*, vol. 21, no. 1, 75–103.

Rothenberg, Jerome (ed.), *Revolution of the Word: A New Gathering of American Avant-Garde Poetry 1914–1945*. Boston: Exact Change Books, 2004.

Ryan, Judith, *The Novel after Theory*. New York: Columbia University Press, 2012.

Sarduy, Severo, *Written on the Body*, trans. Carol Maier. New York: Lumen Books, 1989.

Scarry, Elaine, *The Body in Pain: The Making and Unmaking of the World*. Oxford: Oxford University Press [1985], 1987.

Scarry, Elaine, *Resisting Representation*. Oxford: Oxford University Press, 1994.

Schiller, Friedrich, *On the Aesthetic Education of Man, in a Series of Letters*, trans. Elizabeth M. Wilkinson and L. A. Willoughby. Oxford: Clarendon Press, 1967.

Scholes, Robert, *Paradoxy of Modernism*. London and New Haven: Yale University Press, 2006.

Shikibu, Murasaki, *Her Diary and Poetic Memoirs*, trans. Richard Bowring. Princeton: Princeton University Press, 1982.

Shikibu, Murasaki, *The Tale of Genji*, trans. Royall Tyler. London: Penguin [1008], 2003.

Shklovsky, Viktor. *Theory of Prose*, trans. Lee T. Lemon and Marion J. Reis. Lincoln, NE: University of Nebraska Press, 1965.

Siegel, Carol, 'The Madness outside Gender: Travels with Don Quixote and Saint Foucault', in *Devouring Institutions: The Life Work of Kathy Acker*, ed. Michael Hardin. Calexico, CA: San Diego State University Press, 2005, 3–27.

Siegle, Robert, 'Postmodernism', *Modern Fiction Studies*, vol. 41, no. 1, Spring 1995, 165–94.

Silliman, Ron, *The New Sentence*. New York: Roof Books [1977], 2003.

Silverman, Hugh J. (ed.), *Philosophy and Desire*. New York: Routledge, 2000.

Sitney, P. Adams, *Modernist Montage: The Obscurity of Vision in Cinema and Literature*. New York: Columbia University Press, 1990.

Sitney, P. Adams (ed.), *Film Culture Reader: The Essential Companion for Filmmakers and Festival Goers*. New York: Cooper Square Press [1970], 2000.

Sitney, P. Adams, *The Cinema of Poetry*. Oxford: Oxford University Press, 2015.

Sorrell, Martin, 'Introduction', in Arthur Rimbaud, *Collected Poems*, trans. Martin Sorrell. Oxford: Oxford World's Classics, 2009.

Stein, Gertrude, *Three Lives*. London: Penguin, 1990.

Stein, Gertrude, *Gertrude Stein: Writings 1932–1946*. New York: The Library of America, 1998.

Stein, Gertrude, *Look at Me Now and Here I Am: Selected Works 1911–1945*. London: Peter Owen, 2004.

Stivale, Charles J., 'Acker/Rimbaud "I"-dentity Games', *Anglelaki: Journal of the Theoretical Humanities*, vol. 3, no. 3, 1998, 137–42.

Sullivan, Hannah, *The Work of Revision*. Cambridge, MA: Harvard University Press, 2013.

Tschumi, Bernard, *Cinégramme folie: le Parc de La Villette, Paris nineteenth arrondissement*. Sevenoaks: Butterworth Architecture, 1987.

Vallejo, César, *The Complete Poetry: A Bilingual Edition*, ed. and trans. Clayton Eshelman. Berkeley: University of California Press, 2007.

Vergili Maronis, Publius, *Bucolica et Georgica*. London: Macmillan, 1922.

Walsh, Richard, *Novel Arguments: Reading Innovative American Fiction*. Cambridge: Cambridge University Press, 1995.

Watten, Barrett, 'Writing and Capitalism', *L=A=N=G=U=A=G=E*, no. 9/10, October 1979, 46.

Watten, Barrett, 'Foucault Reads Acker and Rewrites the History of the Novel', in *Lust for Life: On the Writings of Kathy Acker*, ed. Amy Scholder, Carla Harryman and Avital Ronell. New York: Verso, 2006, 58–77.

Weil, Simone, *Oppression and Liberty*, trans. Arthur Willis and John Petrie. London: Routledge and Paul, 1958.

Williams, Linda, *Figures of Desire: A Theory and Analysis of Surrealist Film*. Berkeley: University of California Press, 1981.

Wittgenstein, Ludwig, *The Blue and the Brown Books: Preliminary Studies for the 'Philosophical Investigations'*, trans. R. R. Rhees. Oxford: Blackwell [1958], 1969.

Wittgenstein, Ludwig, *On Certainty*, trans. Denis Paul and G. E. M. Anscombe. London: Blackwell, 1975.

Wittgenstein, Ludwig, *Tractatus Logico-Philosophicus*, trans. D. F. Pears and B. F. McGuinness. London and New York: Routledge, 2001.

Wittgenstein, Ludwig, *Remarks on Colour*, trans. Linda L. McAlister and Margarete Schättle. London: Blackwell [1977], 2007.

Wittgenstein, Ludwig. *Philosophical Investigations*, trans. G. E. M Anscombe, P. M. S. Hacker and Joachim Schulte. London: Blackwell, 2009.

Wollen, Peter, 'Death (and Life) of the Author', *London Review of Books*, vol. 20, no. 3, 5 February 1998, 8–10.

Wollen, Peter, 'Kathy Acker', in *Lust for Life: On the Writings of Kathy Acker*, ed. Amy Scholder, Carla Harryman and Avital Ronell. London: Verso, 2006, 1–12.

Yuknavitch, Lidia, *Allegories of Violence: Tracing the Writing of War in Late Twentieth Century Fiction*. London: Routledge, 2001.

Films cited

Argento, Dario, *Suspiria*. Nouveax Films [1977], 2012.

Buñuel, Luis, *L'Age d'Or* (directed with Salvador Dalí) and *Un Chien Andalou*. British Film Institute [1930], 2011.

Deren, Maya, *Experimental Films*. Re: Voir, 2000.

Goldwyn, Samuel and William Wyler, *Wuthering Heights*. HBO Home Video [1939], 1997.

Jarman, Derek, *Blue*. Artificial Eye, 2007.

Kudláček, Martina, *In the Mirror of Maya Deren*. Zeitgeist Video, 2004.

Metzger, Radley, *Terese and Isabelle*. First Run Features, NTSC, Letterboxed, Dolby, 1968.

Index

Printed and bound by CPI Group (UK) Ltd, Croydon, CR0 4YY

18/03/2025

01834110-0002